The Multinational Subsidiary

Also by Neil Hood

Chrysler UK: A Corporation in Transition (with S. Young)

European Development Strategies of US Multinationals Located in Scotland (with S. Young)

Foreign Multinationals and the British Economy: Impact and Policy (with S. Young and J. Hamill)

Industrial Marketing: A Study of Textiles (with R. T. Hart)

Industry, Policy and the Scottish Economy (eds N. Hood and S. Young)

Marketing in Evolution (with S. Shaw as co-editor)

Multinational Corporate Evolution and Subsidiary Development (with J. Birkinshaw as co-editor)

Multinational Investment Strategies in the British Isles (with S. Young)

Multinationals in Retreat: The Scottish Experience (with S. Young)

Scotland in a Global Economy: The 2020 Vision (with S. Young, E. Peters and J. Peat as co-editors)

Scottish Financial Sector (with P. Draper, I. Smith and W. Stewart)

Strategies in Global Competition (with J.-E. Vahlne as co-editor)

The Economics of Multinational Enterprise (with S. Young)

The Globalization of Multinational Enterprise Activity and Economic Development (with S. Young as co-editor)

Transition in the Baltic States: Microlevel Studies (with R. Kilis and J.-E. Vahlne as co-editors)

Transnational Corporations in the Man-Made Fibre, Textile and Clothing Industries (with S. Young)

The Multinational Subsidiary

Management, Economic Development and Public Policy

Neil Hood

First published 2003 by
PALGRAVE MACMILLAN
Houndmills, Basingstoke, Hampshire RG21 6XS and
175 Fifth Avenue, New York, N.Y. 10010
Companies and representatives throughout the world

PALGRAVE MACMILLAN is the global academic imprint of the Palgrave
Macmillan division of St. Martin's Press, LLC and of Palgrave Macmillan Ltd.
Macmillan® is a registered trademark in the United States, United Kingdom
and other countries. Palgrave is a registered trademark in the European
Union and other countries.

ISBN 1–4039–1490–7

This book is printed on paper suitable for recycling and made from fully
managed and sustained forest sources.

A catalogue record for this book is available from the British Library.

Library of Congress Cataloging-in-Publication Data
Hood, Neil.
    The multinational subsidiary : management, economic development and
    public policy / Neil Hood.
        p. cm.
    "The main body of the present volume presents a selection of his [i.e. the
    author's] articles, published in diverse journals"—Intord.
    Includes bibliographical references and index.
    ISBN 1–4039–1490–7 (cloth)
    1. Subsidiary corporations.   2. Subsidiary corporations—Management.
    3. International business enterprises—Management.   4. Investments,
    Foreign.   5. Economic development.   I. Title.
    HD62.3.H66 2003
    338.8'8—dc21   2003053275

10   9   8   7   6   5   4   3   2   1
12   11   10   09   08   07   06   05   04   03

Printed and bound in Great Britain by
Antony Rowe Ltd, Chippenham and Eastbourne

Contents

Foreword

It is my very great pleasure to introduce this volume, which colleagues and I have initiated and edited as a tribute to Professor Neil Hood. The core of the book presents a selection of Professor Hood's academic papers. Neil is an outstanding academic researcher in the area of international business and MNE subsidiaries, who, throughout his career, has also continued to work at top level in both business and government service. The academic, business and public policy dimensions of Neil's work have been highly synergistic, providing enrichment, reinforcement and balance. Thus his involvement as an adviser and director of MNE subsidiaries and other internationalising companies, plus his work as director of an inward investment agency and other government service, provides a breadth and depth of experience which is perhaps unrivalled around the world. These experiences and insights have informed academic research, and Neil's work on the multinational subsidiary is characterised by its conceptual and empirical strength allied to and conditioned by business and policy realism.

The articles presented here are united by Neil's deep and genuine interest in enquiry and knowledge and especially in its application in terms of scholarship, management practice and policy-making. They are also united by his concern for the Scottish economy – its people and its economic performance.

Neil and I have been friends and academic colleagues for many years, and it is therefore an especial pleasure for me to write this Foreword. This volume represents only a small part of the output of a very prolific author. Neil's writings, moreover, encompass much more than his academic work: in 2002 he published *Whose Life is it Anyway?* (Authentic Lifestyle), and in 2003 *God's Payroll – Whose Work is it Anyway?* (Authentic Lifestyle), one of a planned series on practical Christian living. They reflect Neil's strong commitment to the Christian faith, which is evidenced in a busy preaching and teaching schedule, his involvement with Christian ministries and in his chairmanship of Send the Light Ltd.

Despite his seemingly boundless energy, Neil would be the first to admit that he could not have achieved all that he has done without considerable support. In particular, I am sure Neil would like me to thank two people who in very different ways have been critical to his success in handling a huge portfolio of activities. First is his wife, Anna, who has been enormously supportive, encouraging and loving and patient (and who has shown great kindness to me and other colleagues over the years). Second, is his Personal Assistant, Irene Hood, who provides the organisational skills, commitment to quality, calmness and determination to enable Neil to juggle his competing demands and busy schedule.

And from me, a very personal, sincere and warm thanks.

We commend this volume to you.

STEPHEN YOUNG

List of Contributors*

Julian Birkinshaw,[†] Stockholm School of Economics, Sweden/London Business School, UK.

Stewart Dunlop, University of Strathclyde, UK.

Peter Haug, University of Washington, USA.

Neil Hood,[†] University of Strathclyde, UK.

Stefan Jonsson, Stockholm School of Economics, Sweden.

David Lal, University of Strathclyde, UK.

Ewen Peters,[†] Scottish Enterprise National/University of Strathclyde, UK.

Thorsten Truijens, Hochschule St Gallen, Switzerland.

Stephen Young,[†] University of Strathclyde, UK.

---

* With affiliation(s) at time of original publication of article(s).
[†] These authors have, in addition, written new contributions for this volume. Their affiliations remain unchanged, except for: **Julian Birkinshaw**, London Business School, UK; and **Ewen Peters**, private consultant/University of Strathclyde, UK.

Acknowledgements

The author and publishers are grateful to the following for permission to reproduce copyright material:

Academy of Management Review for J. Birkinshaw and N. Hood, 'Multinational Subsidiary Evolution: Capability and Charter Change in Foreign-Owned Subsidiary Companies', 23(4) (1998), 773–95.

Harvard Business Review for J. Birkinshaw and N. Hood, 'Unleash Innovation in Foreign Subsidiaries', in March (2001), 131–7. Copyright © 2001 by Harvard Business School Publishing Corporation. All rights reserved.

International Business Review for N. Hood and T. Truijens, 'European Locational Decisions of Japanese Manufacturers: Survey Evidence on the Case of the UK', 2(1) (1993), 39–63; N. Hood, S. Young and D. Lal, 'Strategic Evolution within Japanese Manufacturing Plants in Europe: UK Evidence', 3(2) (1994), 97–122. © 1994 Elsevier Science Ltd. All rights reserved.

Journal of Common Market Studies for N. Hood and S. Young, 'Inward Investment and the EC: UK Evidence on Corporate Integration Strategies', 26(2) (1987), 193–206. The views expressed in the paper are personal and are not to be construed as reflecting government policy.

Journal of International Business Studies for J. Birkinshaw and N. Hood, 'Characteristics of Foreign Subsidiaries in Industry Clusters', 31–1 (2000), 141–54. This paper benefited greatly from seminars given at the Institute of International Business and the Invest in Sweden Agency, and a presentation at the Academy of International Business annual meeting, Monterey, Mexico, October 1997. Thanks to Örjan Sölvell, Rod White, Alan Rugman and Don Lessard for their comments and advice.

Management International Review for J. Birkinshaw and N. Hood, 'An Empirical Study of Development Processes in Foreign-Owned Subsidiaries in Canada and Scotland', 37(4) (1997), 339–64. © Gabler Verlag 1997.

Regional Studies for P. Haug, N. Hood and S. Young, 'R&D Intensity in the Affiliates of US-Owned Electronics Companies Manufacturing in Scotland', 17(6) (1983), 383–92; S. Young, N. Hood and S. Dunlop, 'Global Strategies, Multinational Subsidiary Roles and Economic Impact in Scotland', 22(6) (1998), 487–97. The views expressed in this paper are personal and should not be construed as reflecting UK government policy; S. Young, N. Hood and E. Peters, 'Multinational Enterprises and Regional Economic Development', 28(7) (1994), 657–77. See the Website of *Regional Studies* at http://www.tandf.co.uk.

Scottish Journal of Political Economy for N. Hood and S. Young, 'US Investment in Scotland – Aspects of the Branch Factory Syndrome', 23(3) (1976), 279–94. The authors would like to thank the editors for their comments on an earlier draft of this paper. Thanks are also due to R. Mowbray.

Strategic Management Journal for J. Birkinshaw, N. Hood and S. Jonsson, 'Building Firm-Specific Advantages in Multinational Corporations: The Role of Subsidiary Initiative', 19(1998), 221–41. © John Wiley & Sons, Ltd. The authors are grateful for comments from Gunnar Hedlund, Jonas Ridderstråle, Örjan Sölvell, Udo Zander, Jan Johanson and other members of the Institute of International Business and University of Uppsala. Earlier versions of this paper were presented at the Academy of Management and Academy of International Business meetings in 1996 and a conference at the Australian Graduate School of Management, 1997.

1
Introduction and Overview*

Ewen Peters and Stephen Young

One of the most stimulating and productive areas of research in international business over the years has been that concerning the multinational (MNE) subsidiary. In the recent past much of this research effort has been directed at the theme of managing the MNE subsidiary, exploring the entrepreneurial potential of and ways of unleashing innovation in foreign subsidiaries. However, the economic development dimension of foreign direct investment (FDI) and MNE subsidiaries' operations has also been a significant research area for academics, especially those in regional economics and economic geography (recognising that more research is required – see Paterson and Brock, 2002). Host country governments have drawn on this research to devise policies to attract, sustain and develop inward investment activities.

These areas of multinational subsidiary research, relating to management, economic development and public policy, have largely developed separately (and tend to be published in different journals). However, Neil Hood has made a major and enduring contribution to all of these research streams, and the main body of the present volume presents a selection of his articles, published in diverse journals. The selected contributions represent articles only, although much of the author's work has been published in reports and edited volumes. The selection of articles also excludes the more specifically policy-oriented papers; many of these are, however, referred to in the concluding chapter (Chapter 15) in this volume.

The objectives of this volume are thus to highlight the evolution of inquiry into the multinational subsidiary, as seen through the lens of one its most pre-eminent scholars; and to look to the future in MNE subsidiary research.

---

* Written for this volume.

In seeking to develop research and inform policy into the future, there is much to be learned from a historical perspective, and the articles included span a period of nearly thirty years. Despite their longevity, the issues developed in the early papers still have major relevance, especially, for example, for developing and emerging nations which are in the early stages of attracting inward FDI. The recent articles, by comparison, develop new and emerging themes and concepts concerning, for instance, innovation and entrepreneurship in MNE subsidiaries, and point the way forward to new research.

Following the selection of Neil Hood's contributions in Chapters 2–13, Julian Birkinshaw provides stimulating and insightful perspectives on a future research agenda in Chapter 14. Finally, Neil Hood concludes the volume with an overview of his work entitled 'Living at the Academic–Practitioner Interface' (Chapter 15). This not only illustrates his enormous talent and energy, but also helps the reader to understand the genesis and evolution of his work and to place it in context.

The evolution of the multinational and its subsidiaries

To contextualise Neil Hood's research on subsidiaries, the present section provides a short overview of the evolution of multinational management research and practice (Young, 2000). A good starting point is the early work of Perlmutter (1969; see also Chakravarthy and Perlmutter, 1985) which was a classic in its predictions regarding the evolution of the MNE. Management culture and mentality was considered to evolve from ethnocentrism or polycentrism to geocentrism, with a regiocentric mentality as an intermediate state. In a prophetic observation, Perlmutter (1969: 13) observes that in a geocentric corporation, 'the firm's subsidiaries are neither satellites nor independent city states, but parts of a whole . . . each part making its unique contribution with a unique competence'.

The evolution of MNE strategy from the 1950s mirrors this perspective of Perlmutter (1969). Early multinationals were required to develop local operations in national markets across the world in order to circumvent barriers to trade and investment, and to meet the specific customer requirements of these markets. This led to the dominant type of polycentric multi-domestic MNE, mainly of US origin, as the principal player at the time. This stage of evolution was characterised by a duplication of the value chain across countries and stand-alone subsidiaries. Subsequently researchers observed the emergence of regionally or globally integrated MNE strategies (Porter, 1986; Bartlett and Ghoshal, 1989; Rugman, 2000; Tallman and Yip, 2001). Harzing (1999, following

Bartlett and Ghoshal, 1989) labelled these eras as the 'International era' and the 'Global era'. A third epoch was, however, also proposed, namely, the so-called 'Transnational era'. Here the MNE is perceived as an enterprise comprising a network of diverse and differentiated relationships, in which subsidiaries have distinct strategic roles and scope (Harzing, 1999; O'Donnell, 2000).

Some researchers reached a somewhat similar endpoint from an MNE structure perspective. Thus beginning with Stopford and Wells (1972), authors highlighted the evolution of MNEs' hierarchical structures. Based on Swedish experience, however, Hedlund (1986) introduced the contrary notion of heterarchy and the loosely structured heterarchical MNE. This provided an important stimulus to research in subsequent years, and represented a bridge to the work of other Nordic scholars concerning networks and centres of excellence within the MNE. The essence of the argument is that MNE structures are evolving towards network-based systems, within which a subsidiary's position can give it influence over the strategic orientation of the MNE.

A paper by Canadian authors White and Poynter (1984) provided a significant stimulus to academic research on the subject of MNE subsidiary roles and evolution. Of particular importance was the distinction between Miniature Replicas (subsidiaries which produce and market some of the parent's product lines in the host country); Rationalised Manufacturers (subsidiaries which produce a particular set of component parts or products for a multi-country or global market); and Product Specialists (the subsidiary develops, produces and markets a limited product line for global markets). A review by Paterson and Brock (2002) revealed a substantial body of subsequent research on typologies of subsidiary roles/strategies (for example, Bartlett and Ghoshal, 1989; Jarillo and Martinez, 1990; Taggart, 1997) and on the factors influencing subsidiary evolution (including Birkinshaw and Hood, 1998, Chapter 11 in this volume; Birkinshaw, Hood and Jonsson, 1998, Chapter 12 in this volume; and Rugman and Verbeke, 2001).

Particular interest has centred on subsidiaries which possess specialised resources which are valuable for the MNE as a whole (Birkinshaw, Hood and Jonsson, 1998). Terms applied include the specialised contributor, strategic leader and active subsidiary types, as well as world product mandate (WPM) and centre-of-excellence designations. The WPM term has a particularly long tradition, having been widely used by Canadian researchers to refer to subsidiaries which have the autonomy and authority to develop, manufacture and market a product-line worldwide (Crookell, 1987); this subsidiary category is closely linked to White and Poynter's (1984) Product Specialists. Such 'high contributory role subsidiaries' (Birkinshaw, Hood and Jonsson 1998) are contrasted with the implementer and rationalised subsidiary types, which lack the autonomy and authority – and, indeed, the capabilities – to generate independent competences. Recent work has had stronger conceptual underpinnings, and has made major contributions to issues such as the nature of subsidiary development (Birkinshaw and Hood, 1997, Chapter 10 in this volume); processes of subsidiary evolution (Birkinshaw and Hood, 1998, Chapter 11 in this volume); and subsidiary innovation and entrepreneurship (Birkinshaw and Hood, 2001, Chapter 13 in this volume).

Interestingly, while the literature on subsidiary roles and evolution has chiefly had a managerial emphasis in recent years, the early work in Canada was primarily focused upon the impact of particular subsidiary types on Canadian economic development. For example, strong criticism was directed at the truncated Miniature Replica category, which produced at low volume and high cost in Canada behind protective tariff barriers. Conversely there was considerable research and policy interest in Canada in identifying and promoting the innovative WPM subsidiaries (without too much success, it has to be said). The early thrust of the work of Neil Hood had a similar economic development emphasis, albeit mainly UK-oriented. Aside from the papers in this volume, perspectives on the relationships between subsidiary strategies and impact are presented in Young, Hood and Hamill (1988). Later, Young, Hood and Peters (1994, Chapter 8 in this volume) proposed a distinction between 'branch plant production' and innovative 'developmental' subsidiaries in respect of their relative economic impacts. The work of a number of scholars associated with the University of Reading has followed a similar tradition (for example, Pearce and Papanastassiou, 1997; Pearce, 1999; Tavares, 2001).

Within a European context, the issue of economic integration introduced an important additional dimension to research on corporate strategy, subsidiary roles and economic impact. Authors such as Dunning and Robson (1988); Blomström and Kokko (1997); Clegg and Scott-Green (2000); and Dunning (2000) have studied the effects of EU integration on FDI. The emphasis in empirical work has been on the impact of economic integration on FDI flows into the regional bloc. Major issues concerning the impact of economic integration on intra-regional FDI, linked to corporate integration and restructuring, have been subject to less investigation. However, there is evidence that MNEs evolve from country-centred to regional (EU) strategies as economic integration proceeds. Horizontally organized subsidiaries within the region may be replaced by centralised, specialised and integrated networks (Pelkmans, 1984). The outcome is likely to be more rationalised subsidiaries and greater intra-firm and intra-regional trade flows. This is a continuing process.

From the early years of its formation, US MNEs treated the six original members of the European Economic Community (EEC) (as it then was) as one market, and commenced production specialisation and vertical production integration following the expansion of the bloc to include the UK and other members in 1973. Further expansions (actual and pending) plus the Single Market Programme and the single currency have provided further stimuli to both economic and corporate integration. A number of the chapters in this volume provide important evidence on the responses of US and also Japanese firms to these processes of integration. Although initial motivations were often related to overcoming trade friction, the evidence indicates advantages for 'latecomer' MNEs such as the Japanese which were able to take a pan-European approach from the outset. By comparison, European companies were disadvantaged by their national market orientation.

Multinationals, subsidiary roles and strategies and economic impact in host nations

The early work of Neil Hood has its roots in the studies of Dunning (1958), Forsyth (1972) and Steuer *et al.* (1973) relating to US investment in the UK and Scotland; and that of Firn (1975), who made the important distinction between long-term, innovative, entrepreneurial decision-making and short-term routine management supervision activities in MNE subsidiaries. The latter was deemed to be a feature of multinational branch plants, and Chapter 2 in this volume investigates 'aspects of the branch factory syndrome' by examining the extent of research and development and marketing operations in US subsidiaries in Scotland. The importance of value-adding activities and decision-making responsibilities in manufacturing branch plants in order to maximise economic benefit for a host economy was thus recognised in this 1976 paper. This became an important policy focus in the UK and other host countries in subsequent years.

Similar themes underlie a number of the other early empirical contributions in this volume. For example, Chapter 3 probes more deeply into foreign affiliate R&D, building on some of the work of Ronstadt (1977) relating to classifications of research and development units in MNEs. The findings suggest a variety of benefits associated with subsidiary

R&D including high-level employment. The R&D units acted as a conduit for technology transfers, and commercialisation of research results was deemed to be high and based at affiliate level.

Neil Hood's inquiry into MNE subsidiaries widened to consider the characteristics and behaviour of non-US multinationals, reflecting the changing patterns of country of origin of FDI. For example, a 1981 paper (Hood, Reeves and Young, 1981) assesses the impact of continental European plants, where the economic development debate focused primarily upon mode of entry issues. In particular, acquisition entry was common for continental European-based MNEs in UK/Scotland, introducing new elements into the benefit/cost equation. Subsequent studies investigated Japanese FDI, and the two empirical studies presented in Chapters 4 and 5 in this volume concern locational decision-making and strategic evolution. The structure of the locational decision process (Chapter 4, Figure 4.3, p. 63), distinguishing initial impulse, discussion and decision phases, is important and has been widely cited. The long-term nature of the process is indicated, even if the final decision was taken quickly, often driven by the threat of EU trade sanctions. Similarly the thoroughness of the search process, involving multiple countries and sometimes multiple feasibility studies by independent teams, is demonstrated.

These country studies have made a major contribution to our understanding of MNE activity in host countries, by tracking the successive waves of US, European and Japanese investment into the UK. As Neil Hood observes in Chapter 15 in this volume, much of this early work emerged from studies sponsored by UK government departments, where a particular area of interest concerned the dynamics of multinational strategy in Europe and the implications for the UK. Around this same period, the idea of formally identifying and classifying subsidiary roles and strategies and linking these to economic impact also began to emerge.

The link between economic integration and corporate integration is important for the study of the evolution of multinational subsidiaries in Europe. An influential group of papers on the subject appeared in the *Journal of Common Market Studies*, later edited in book form by Dunning and Robson (1988). The contribution in Chapter 6 in this volume derives from this source, and develops two streams of thinking, namely that relating to the evolution of the EU and its effects on corporate integration, and that concerning MNE subsidiary roles and strategies. Interestingly, despite the fact that the UK had then been a member of the EU for some ten years, multinational corporate integration was not strongly in evidence among the sample of MNE subsidiaries in the UK. Country-centred strategies were still common, with significant numbers of relatively free-standing affiliates. The paper by Cantwell (1988) in the same volume similarly found that the process of the reorganisation of European industry to European integration was far from complete. One suggestion as to the explanation was that this concerned the failure to create a single market which abolished discrimination in terms of nationality (Dunning and Robson, 1988).

In a significant 1988 contribution (Chapter 7 in this volume), the subsidiary typology developed by White and Poynter (1984) was again utilised to help understand the roles and characteristics of MNE subsidiaries in Scotland, and to assist the interpretation of the empirical results. The data revealed 'a large group of conventional branch plants (rationalised manufacturers), even if these are high-tech versions of the branch-plant syndrome' as identified previously. They were characterised by small size, substantial output and input linkages with other group plants and low levels of decision-making authority. More optimistically, there were also suggestions from the cluster analysis of a significant group of product specialist subsidiaries, including some of the largest employers in the foreign-owned sector.

The linkage of subsidiary roles and economic impact was pursued further in a number of studies. For example, Chapter 5 in this volume applied the White and Poynter (1984) model to the evolution of Japanese manufacturing plants in the UK. The conclusion was that while the net economic outcome seemed positive, it was too early in the evolutionary process to ascertain whether plants would develop into well-developed and integrated product specialist units. A more recent paper which pursued a somewhat similar approach was that by Hood and Taggart (1999), which investigated subsidiary development in German and Japanese manufacturing subsidiaries in the British Isles. The results for the Japanese subsidiaries indicate greater scale, growth, market area mandates, and potentially higher levels of local sourcing and R&D. But while they possessed greater development potential, they also had less managerial discretion than their German counterparts to exploit this potential.

The 1994 paper on 'Multinationals and Regional Economic Development' (Chapter 8 in this volume) represented an effort to synthesise and consolidate what was known about the subject area to that point in time. It attempted to integrate the literature on economic development (emphasising the regional dimensions) with that on multinationals and their subsidiaries. A linkage was proposed between subsidiary strategies and notions of virtual and vicious cycles of technological development; and it highlighted the potential contribution of MNE subsidiaries to dynamic benefits and dynamic comparative advantage at the country and regional level. The paper introduced the concept of the 'developmental subsidiary', linked to changing organisational forms and the heterarchical MNE; and to subsidiary roles such as the world product mandate category, Bartlett and Ghoshal's (1989) 'strategic leader' and Gupta and Govindarajan's (1991) 'global innovator'. For a review of other terms applied to this notion of the developmental subsidiary, see Crone and Roper (1999).

Recognising that one or a small number of sectorally or technologically diverse developmental subsidiaries would have little impact, Chapter 8 in this volume discusses the integration of multinationals and cluster strategies (which following Porter, 1990, were beginning to become fashionable in regional economic circles around the world). Two routes to cluster formation are proposed, namely, local sourcing and technological innovation, within which developmental subsidiaries may play a key role alongside a concentrated package of innovative policy measures at the micro level, and effective management of the macro-economy and investment in the infrastructure.

Interest in the potential differential economic development implications of production and developmental subsidiaries led to the commissioning of a study of the subject in Scotland (Firn Crichton Roberts Limited and University of Strathclyde, 2001). This questioned the significance of the difference between developmental and production subsidiaries in manufacturing industry in economic impact terms, as well as proposing the requirement for an integrated approach to regional development in which inward investment is not the sole or major driver. In essence by the start of the millennium, there were signs that with the commoditisation of manufacturing industry in, for example, electronics, developed countries were no longer competitive.

The 1994 conceptual paper was not fully explored in subsequent empirical work, although there were and continue to be a wide range of contributions on aspects of cluster development strategies. Chapter 9, in this volume examines the characteristics of foreign subsidiaries in industry clusters based on a three-country sample (Canada, Scotland and Sweden). It finds that subsidiaries in leading-edge clusters tend to be more autonomous, more embedded in the local cluster and have greater international market scope than their counterparts in other industry sectors. However, there was also tentative evidence that those clusters with high levels of foreign ownership have subsidiaries that are less autonomous and have weaker capabilities. These results are capable of various interpretations and further research is required. A very useful contribution on the implementation of the cluster approach, which dovetails with the general approach of the present volume is contained in Hood and Peters (2000b).

Subsidiary roles and strategies, evolution and innovation

While the studies referred to above mostly emphasise economic development and public policy, the later chapters in this volume have a strong managerial focus and solid conceptual underpinnings. The theoretical models applied include, in particular, 'competence-based' perspectives such as the resource-based view (Barney, 1991), dynamic capabilities (Teece, Pisano and Shuen, 1997) and evolutionary theories (Cantwell, 2001); as well as network perspectives (Andersson, 1997; Gupta and Govindarajan, 2000). These indicate how the subsidiary may acquire or develop distinctive competences or control critical resources, and hence contribute to an understanding of subsidiary evolution and development.

In Chapter 10 in this volume, Julian Birkinshaw and Neil Hood make a very significant contribution in their conceptual model of subsidiary development and supporting empirical research. Their organising framework identifies three drivers of subsidiary development: parent development, internal development, and host country development. Trajectories of development are also identified in the research, with a distinction being made between establishing viability and building sustainability (mandate development process and specialist development process).

Chapter 10 represents a significant step forward in our understanding of subsidiary development and evolution. It is taken further in Chapter 11 in this volume in the continuation of Neil Hood's highly creative and productive cooperation with Julian Birkinshaw. This is a conceptual contribution, mainly drawing upon the dynamic capabilities' perspective. The notion of subsidiary evolution was formally defined, and a series of generic subsidiary evolution processes identified. The five evolutionary processes, derived from combinations of capability and charter change, were: parent-driven investment, subsidiary-driven charter extension, subsidiary-driven charter reinforcement, parent-driven divestment and atrophy through subsidiary neglect. A number of factors impacting the generic processes were proposed: from the corporate level, these were competitive internal resource allocation mechanisms, the autonomy granted to subsidiaries and parent management ethnocentrism; subsidiary-level factors were represented by the track record of the operation, the quality of parent–subsidiary relationships and subsidiary entrepreneurship; and host country factors by the dynamism of the local business environment, the relative cost of factor inputs, host government support and the strategic importance of the host country. The primary message is that attention should be directed at the capabilities of the subsidiary.

The related theme of Chapter 12 in this volume concerns how subsidiary enterprises are able to contribute to the firm-specific advantages of the multinational. Key findings from the empirical evidence were, first, that subsidiary leadership and an entrepreneurial culture seem to influence the development of specialised resources; and these resources, in turn, are strongly associated with subsidiary initiative. Second, parent–subsidiary relationships, and, particularly, subsidiary autonomy, had an important influence on both initiative and contributory role. The significant overall conclusion was that it was not possible to choose between head office assignment, subsidiary choice and environmental determinism in respect of impact on the subsidiary's contributory role.

The *Harvard Business Review* paper in Chapter 13 ('Unleash Innovation in Foreign Subsidiaries') is a fitting end to the selection of Neil Hood's articles. It is a significant contribution for two reasons. First, it highlights and strengthens the emerging theme of innovation and entrepreneurship in the MNE subsidiary (see Birkinshaw, 2000). Second, it suggests managerial actions for promoting innovation, namely giving seed money to subsidiaries; using formal requests for proposals; encouraging subsidiaries to be incubators; and building international networks.

Subsidiary roles, resources and evolution: retrospect and prospect

At the time of writing, the international scene has rarely been as uncertain and volatile following a series of unprecedented shocks to the global economy and cyclical downturns in Japan and the Asia-Pacific region, in the USA and in Europe. The continued growth and internationalisation of services and the emergence of the knowledge economy, moreover, are manifestations of an on-going process of structural adjustment that is especially active in the continental triad. The purpose of this final section, therefore, is to re-consider some of the key findings from Neil Hood's research on subsidiary roles, resources and evolution in the light of such change and the drivers which underpin it.[1]

Subsidiary roles and autonomy in a changing Europe

In the context of European integration and enlargement, the findings on subsidiary roles (see Chapter 8 in this volume), based largely on the UK and Scottish experience, help to explain the recent rapid contraction of manufacturing activity in sectors such as electronics where overseas ownership is a pronounced feature. The high incidence of rationalised manufacturers, low incidence of product specialists and virtual absence of any developmental subsidiaries clearly highlighted the generally low level of autonomy enjoyed by many manufacturing subsidiaries with US, Japanese and German parents in the late 1980s and early to mid-1990s. Although there is some evidence of foreign-owned subsidiaries enjoying a greater degree of autonomy (Pearce and Papanastassiou, 1997; Pearce, 1999), it is apparent that substantially little has altered since then. Thus at a time of rapid change and uncertainty, the low level of autonomy that has been such an enduring feature of the overseas-owned manufacturing sector in the UK represents a major constraint on subsidiary development as local management (alone or in partnership) do not have the legitimacy to explore alternative viable futures and to initiate, develop and deploy strategies that allow these futures to be pursued and realised.

It is also clear from this work that product specialists are the type of subsidiary that is most likely to survive the current re-structuring, perhaps as part of extended European networks that exhibit both greater specialisation and sophistication (of function) and centralisation (of coordination and control). In the case of IBM's large subsidiary located in Scotland, for example, adapting to change has involved outsourcing a previous core competence (that is, PC and laptop manufacture) and diversifying into complementary specialist services (European customer support), rather than upgrading to some higher-order function. Indeed, the rise of service-oriented specialists within the subsidiary networks of industrial MNEs during the 1990s was a significant phenomenon and an aspect of the internationalisation of services that has largely remained under-researched (see, for example, Hood and Peters, 2000a).

The low incidence of product specialist also suggests that the contraction of the installed base of overseas-owned manufactures is a trend that will continue as many existing MNEs pursue least-cost strategies in Europe and re-configure their manufacturing and logistics operations to exploit more attractive locations that have emerged in Eastern and Central Europe and elsewhere. This experience is by no means atypical of the manufacturing belts of the more advanced economies where manufacturing MNEs are tending to think regional (rather than global) and act local (Rugman, 2000).

Subsidiary resources, local linkages and sustainable competitive advantage

In Chapter 9 in this volume, the conclusion that greater autonomy and international market scope are associated with foreign subsidiaries in leading-edge clusters is of special interest from the perspective of the resource-based theory of the multinational enterprise. By entering a leading-edge cluster and building strategic linkages, MNEs are able to tap and exploit new complementary assets that are advanced, specialised, well embedded and otherwise difficult to access. From the parent's perspective, such strategies may be described as asset-augmenting rather than efficiency-seeking (Dunning, 1997). However, it is clear from the evidence to hand that there is little sign that emerging or developing clusters have an inherent propensity to evolve rapidly towards higher-order clusters that are well formed and fully functioning and which serve as a natural home base for dominant MNEs – as classically described by Porter (1990). Accordingly, the incidence of such subsidiary types remains low – even on a global basis.

Moreover, since the 1990s or so the accelerated pace of market liberalisation combined with the so called 'death of distance' (Cairncross, 1997), has enhanced the attraction of direct investment as a means of accessing locally embedded assets that are complementary and strategically important. The appeal of this growing opportunity is reflected in the apparent greater willingness of MNEs to decouple and re-locate their activities, including higher-order functions. Indeed, the ability to strategically manage the more or less continuous process of mixing and matching MNE activities/functions with locally embedded resources and knowledge is an increasingly vital core competence. Moreover, quickly developing best practice and then leveraging advantage in an efficient, far-sighted and innovative manner could become a key success factor that helps differentiate MNE winners from losers. The ARK (Activities, Resources and Knowledge) theory developed by Enright (2001) captures the essence of this process. This illustrates how localisation will continue to matter to MNE competitiveness in the deconstructed and highly networked global economy of the twenty first century where many traditional industry boundaries may have all but dissolved. Local subsidiaries and partners have a key role to play in this scheme. Thus, an important task for future research will be to define the nature of the competence more formally and how this competence can be developed and deployed – whether this should be done, for example, on a network-wide basis, at multiple centres of excellence or only at the centre.

Enright's (2001) framework introduces the important issue of knowledge. With the emergence of the knowledge economy, it has been argued (Solvell and Birkinshaw, 2000) that *the* core competence that will matter most to the diversified, innovation-driven MNEs of the twenty-first century will be the ability to access and exploit various kinds of knowledge that is widely dispersed, highly specialised and commercially valuable. The relevant literature (Aydalot, 1985; Malliat, 1995; Malmberg, Sölvell and Zander, 1996) shows that such knowledge is often tacit in nature and deeply embedded in local milieux (local business networks, institutions and learning communities) whose unique social capital facilitates rapid generation and diffusion on a local basis. Such milieux can provide local learning opportunities for MNEs around which 'best practice' may be developed and subsequently levered. However, unlike activities and functions which can only be discretely transferred (that is, moved from *A* to *B* with loss at *A*), usually at high cost, best practice may be transferred to many nodes of a network without loss and at relatively low cost and then incrementally exploited. This is felt to be most feasible where an appropriately strong and supportive corporate culture exists. A five-year study by Doz, Santos and Williamson (2001) of around twenty new and established MNEs well illustrates this emerging phenomenon. These businesses gained new advantages by 'connecting and leveraging dispersed pockets of knowledge' from 'non-traditional sources' over and above the knowledge residing in their headquarters and subsidiaries. This new competence has been called '*metanational advantage*' and provides some evidence that the geocentric attitude forecast by Perlmutter (1969) may finally be emerging into the MNE mainstream.

As noted previously, the five evolutionary processes identified in Chapter 11 in this volume are primarily derived from combinations of subsidiary capability and subsidiary charter change. Moreover, the above discussion identifies the strategic management of network configuration and knowledge accumulation as key competences and capabilities on which future competitive advantage can be built by innovation-driven MNEs. Further research is now needed to establish the implications of this for subsidiary roles, resources and evolution. The work that Neil Hood has undertaken with Julian Birkinshaw, suitably modified to take account of these developments, clearly provides an excellent framework for this important and challenging task.

Note

1. The main drivers underpinning some of the more fundamental change we are witnessing include *inter alia*: the de-regulation of markets, trade and investment; new governance structures above and below the national level; the creation of the Euro Zone and EU enlargement; continued rapid techno-logical advance; the intensification of international competition between added-value systems rather than between individual firms; the continued rise and spread of the MNE – with parent strategies largely mediated through an increasingly complex network of subsidiaries and strategic partners; the emergence of India and China as world-class hubs, respectively, for IT services and manufacturing; and the widening gap between rich and poor, etc.

2
US Investment in Scotland: Aspects of the Branch Factory Syndrome (1976)*

Neil Hood and Stephen Young

I

Introduction

The costs and benefits of increased direct foreign investment for recipient developed and less developed countries have been discussed widely in the literature in recent years. The impact of inward foreign investment has also been the subject of government investigations in a number of countries, reflecting fears of the potential loss of sovereignty implicit in a branch-factory type economy, and aimed at devising legislation to maximise the net benefits derived from the presence of international corporations.[1] While some such studies have referred to the implications of inward investment for regions within host countries, many important regional growth and regional policy aspects have been explored only superficially. The present paper, based on an empirical study of US investment in Scotland, attempts to make a small contribution in this latter context by examining certain characteristics of the functional development of US branch plants. Since plant functions give at least some indication of the authority and decision-making potential delegated to local management, the results to be presented have implications for any assessment of the gains and losses of increasing external control in Scotland, and through this for UK regional policy.

* *Scottish Journal of Political Economy*, 23 (3) (1976), 279–94. The authors would like to thank the editors for their comments on an earlier draft of this paper. Thanks are also due to R. Mowbray.

The branch factory syndrome

A definition of branch plants

For the purpose of this article 'branch plants' are taken to include all manufacturing branches and subsidiaries where the locus of ultimate control lies with the parent company in the USA.[2] This definition thus includes plants which are not separate legal entities but part of an enterprise whose headquarters are in a separate location (usually England), and subsidiaries with operational headquarters in Scotland. The latter are included under the definition of branch-plants since the major distinction between branches and subsidiaries, namely that of local headquarters designation may be more a reflection of intra-company strategy than of local delegation of ultimate decision-making.

The Scottish case

For some time now attention has been directed to the implications of the emerging control pattern in the Scottish economy.[3] It has been shown that while over 70 per cent of manufacturing plants were domestically owned in 1973, such plants provided only 41 per cent of employment, leaving the remaining 59 per cent as the branch factory sector (as defined above). External control, moreover, was greatest in the fastest growing industrial sectors and was concentrated in the largest enterprises. External control in this regional context means non-Scottish control and inevitably most branch plants are controlled by companies located elsewhere in Great Britain. However, North American plants also occupy a highly significant position in the Scottish economy: the number of such plants almost doubled in the ten years up to 1973, and by the latter date accounted for 15 per cent of total manufacturing employment. A principal consequence of the time span of this investment is the concentration in the highly scientific and technologically based industries. Thus North American plants accounted for nearly one third of employment in the mechanical and electrical engineering sectors and 60 per cent of employment in instrument engineering. As a result the areas of major growth potential are placed under a very significant degree of American control.

The gains and losses of US investment in Scotland

In assessing the consequences of this degree of US ownership and control, the central issue, but the one most difficult to identify, concerns the assumption as to what would have happened in the absence of US foreign investment. In particular, whether, and to what extent, foreign and indigenous investments are substitutive or supplementary, makes an enormous difference to the analysis of the effects of foreign investment. This is particularly a problem when one tries to assess the effects in relation to the Scottish economy *in isolation*. In practice it is unlikely that unemployment rates would have been permitted to reach the kind of levels implied by a complete absence of US investment, although some of the investment has probably used resources that would otherwise have been unemployed. Regional policy instruments would almost certainly have been operated to provide some replacement investment. However, the important point is that if the resources used by US firms had been employed elsewhere, the control of such resources may still have resided outside Scotland, given the ownership pattern mentioned earlier. Thus one form of external control may have been replaced by another, assuming one regards the Scottish economy as an autonomous sector for the purpose of the analysis. The following discussion of the gains and losses emanating from Scotland's increasing dependence on American investment has, therefore, to be viewed in this context.

The potential benefits accruing from the establishment of US manufacturing operations are well-known. The capital contributions of incoming firms may assist in filling the resource gap and have a favourable effect on the balance of payments. Inward foreign investment may also contribute to filling the management and skill gap by providing foreign management and training local managers and workers. In addition, the contribution of US firms to the Scottish economy may include: firstly, the transfer of technology, providing access to cheap or free research and development (R&D) inputs. Secondly, indigenous entrepreneurs may be encouraged through subcontract work to ancillary industries and component suppliers etc., and through the foreign firm's relationships with its customers. The limited evidence confirms that the presence of American firms in Scotland has had some positive effects on the level of activity in the indigenous sector, at least in certain industries. Access to finance may also be improved and market outlets widened, and finally, benefits may accrue from additional employment and improved job security, both factors of particular relevance in a Scottish context given the massive decay loss which has occurred; from improvements in market structure and performance; and through improvements in Scotland's income terms of trade arising from a reduced dependence on foreign products, or from cost reductions in excess of those of export prices (Streeten, 1974.)

Many of these potential gains, of course, have possible counterparts on the cost side:

1. Instead of improving general industrial performance, US firms in Scotland could exploit any technological and managerial advantages by eliminating indigenous competition.
2. On the balance of payments side, dividend repatriation, transfer pricing and claimed higher import propensities may substantially affect any gains on capital account, and the capital inflow itself could be reduced by raising funds locally. For the Scottish economy, however, Forsyth (1972: 252) suggested that the net balance of payments effect was favourable by a wide margin in 1969.
3. Labour relations problems are also frequently mentioned as a cost to host countries resulting from different industrial relations practices and work methods, and the employment of foreign personnel. The Forsyth study (1972: 205) concluded that the strike performance of US-owned firms in Scotland in the years 1960–9 was markedly worse than that of indigenous firms.
4. The low ratio of employment creation of highly skilled and managerial jobs could be a cause for concern in a Scottish context, and the female bias in employment creation, while raising female participation rates, has not offset the decline in male employment opportunities.

Perhaps most emphasis, however, has tended to be placed on the sovereignty and autonomy loss associated with direct foreign investment from the USA. Positive economics take political ends as given, but the costs and benefits of attaining such ends have economic consequences.[4] Such problems arise essentially from the international nature of US firms, so that policy towards any one branch plant may presumably be constrained by, and be subordinate to, the pursuit of some global objective.

The balance between centralisation and autonomy in decision-making at the branch plant level may depend on a large number of factors, e.g. the size of the plant, and the number of countries in which branch factories are located; the size, age and profitability of any individual branch plant; the organisation structure chosen for international operations; the product strategy of the firm (horizontal versus vertical specialisation, etc.); overall objectives, and so on. For some of these factors, furthermore, there is no *a priori* reason to expect a particular impact in terms of either greater or less autonomy for a branch operation.

Loss of autonomy for a regional economy, such as that of Scotland, could take a number of forms. The issue that has been most widely debated relates to the possibility of technological dependence of branch factory operations, and of branch factory economies, on externally controlled enterprises, resulting from the centralisation of R&D at the parent plant. Another area where the sovereignty costs could arise is in sales and marketing, due to the centralisation of product policy, market development and, possibly also, pricing policy decisions. Finally, one might hypothesise that decisions on investment and general financial policy, purchasing and employment policy would all typically be made externally and imposed upon the branch plant.

Some of these sovereignty/autonomy factors are not readily distinguishable from the other costs of external control, but the feature general to them is that all lie within what may be broadly called long-term, strategic and planning decision-areas. Such 'entrepreneurial-type decision-making' (Firn, 1975: 164) may be contrasted with short-run, operational decisions which encompass production-scheduling, costing and budgeting, labour relations, maintenance and repair, etc. On the basis of his study of autonomy among US plants in Scotland, Forsyth (1972: 249) concluded that firms had not been prevented from raising output and employment *in the short run*, but strategic decision-making is much more relevant when considering external control since it is this which determines whether or not a regional economy, such as that of Scotland, is to become as 'a hewer of wood and a drawer of water'. The distinction between strategic and operational decision-making is clearly arbitrary at the margin. In general, nevertheless, whereas the latter will normally be a branch-plant function, the former exists only at the discretion of the parent, and within this 'discretionary decision area' inevitably some elements will be missing at the branch factory level. In so far as the Scottish economy can be shown to be dominated by externally controlled enterprises, with management concerned essentially with operational decision-making, this may be presumed to influence markedly the economy's growth potential.

II

Survey background and results

The survey of US investment in Scotland, upon which this article is based, attempts to establish the extent to which discretionary decision-making is permitted within such externally-controlled enterprises, by examining the functional responsibilities delegated to the plants in two areas, viz. Research and Development (R&D) and Marketing. The presence or absence of such functions, and the decision-making flexibility permitted within these functions, does not indicate the loss of autonomy which might have occurred in Scotland had US direct investment been replaced by another form of control (external or otherwise). However, it does at least shed some additional light on the regional economic problems associated with greater external control, and may point the way forward to further research.

Research and development

In discussing R&D activities in the context of the international firm, writers have been fairly divided as to the desirability of encouraging the decentralisation of R&D to the branch plant level. This is so even when foreign direct investment is being considered from the host country viewpoint: the Steuer Report (Steuer *et al.*, 1973: 46) for the UK perhaps went furthest in 'debunking' the claimed advantages of indigenous R&D, suggesting that 'research comparative advantage should be pursued like any other comparative advantage'. A somewhat similar view has been taken by Dunning (1972: 394) who stated that host country R&D should not be encouraged if the economy was likely to grow faster or more efficiently by borrowing technology and using the freed resources in other ways.

From a Scottish viewpoint, however, the economy has long suffered from the outflow of skilled personnel such as those employed in R&D labs; and, the existence of such labs within the region might also produce various externalities that would be important. In addition, developmental personnel on the spot are more closely in touch with market requirements, and provide branch operations with at least autonomous growth potential, so that they are not completely tied to the innovative progress of the parent company. Moreover, the argument for centralising R&D because of the cost of undertaking science-based technological developments has been disputed by the work of Arrow (1962) and Hollander (1965) who stressed the importance of minor changes and of learning by doing.

Statistics on the R&D activities of US affiliates are very scanty. Forsyth (1972: 130) estimated that expenditure (in-house and purchased) by US-owned firms in Scotland in 1969 amounted to 1.4 per cent of sales. Mansfield (1974: 166) quotes an R&D/sales ratio for US firms in the UK in 1966 of 1.9 per cent; the equivalent figure for domestic US R&D was 2.0 per cent, whereas average US foreign affiliate R&D was 1.1 per cent. Not too much emphasis can be placed on the comparative ratios for the UK and Scotland; in particular, the great expansion in US direct investment in Scotland between 1966 and 1969 may have had the effect of diluting the R&D component in the short run while the newly established plants were concentrating on operational matters. Unfortunately figures were not available for indigenous manufacturing firms in Scotland.

In undertaking the present survey of R&D in Scotland, major definitional problems were encountered. Some companies might include only fundamental scientific research within R&D, whereas others would consider every minor product or process modification. The former is both unsuitable and unlikely to be widely delegated to branch factories, the latter too trivial to be taken as a reflection of plant status. Back-up interviews tended to confirm that R&D is, on the whole, closely related to product development and not to fundamental research, and it is on this basis that the categorisation given in Table 2.1 has been employed.

As indicated, more than half of the plants in the sample undertook no R&D in Scotland; conversely, one-quarter of all plants appeared to engage in fairly fundamental product and process R&D. These figures compare with those produced by the American Chamber of Commerce (1971), which showed that 180 of 270 (67 per cent) leading US industrial subsidiaries had R&D activities in the UK in 1970. The implication of the results for Scotland seems to be that the Scottish plants have been viewed in a majority of cases as bases for extending distribution rather than modifying or enlarging product lines. The presence of R&D at plant level is not, furthermore, to be taken as a proxy for product autonomy within the plants. Indeed in interviews several examples were found of considerable product exclusively at plants, derived from successful intra-group tendering for product responsibility rather than from local R&D activity.[5]

Table 2.1 Research and development categories

Category	%	No. of plants
1 Fundamental product and process development	25.0	22
2 Product adaptation and modification	11.4	10
3 R&D on specific materials and techniques	2.3	2
4 R&D for sales/service back-up only	3.4	3
No R&D	54.5	48
Unspecified	3.4	3
	100.0	88

Mention was made earlier in the paper of some of the factors that might be deemed to influence the functional responsibilities of externally-controlled plants. In order to test the influence of these, Table 2.2 relates R&D in US plants to four variables:

1. The period of establishment/takeover of the plant in Scotland.
2. Employment in the Scottish plant.
3. SIC order.
4. The number of other European affiliates owned by the parent company.

Table 2.2 Research and development in US plants in Scotland[2]

	R&D category 1 & 2[1]	R&D category 3 & 4	No R&D	All plants	
	% of plants			%	No.
Period of establishment in Scotland (to 1974)					
Under 5 years	33.3	8.4	58.3	100.0	12
5–10 years	35.3	5.9	58.8	100.0	34
11–20 years	24.0	4.0	64.0	100.0	25
Over 20 years	58.8	6.9	29.4	100.0	17
Employment range					
Under 100	25.0	8.3	66.7	100.0	24
101–400	42.9	3.6	53.6	100.0	28
401–1000	35.3	5.9	47.1	100.0	17
Over 1000	47.1	5.9	41.1	100.0	17
SIC order					
V	23.1	7.7	69.2	100.0	13
VII	33.3	9.6	57.1	100.0	21
VIII and IX	44.0	4.0	40.0	100.0	25
Other	37.9	3.5	58.6	100.0	29
No. of other European affiliates[3]					
No others	40.6	6.3	53.1	100.0	32
1	33.3	14.3	47.6	100.0	21
2	41.2	—	58.8	100.0	17
3 and over	27.8	—	61.1	100.0	18
All plants[4]	**36.4**	**5.7**	**54.5**	**100.0**	**88**

Notes: [1] For R&D categories see Table 2.1.

[2] Two firms did not provide size classifications.

[3] 'Number of other European affiliates', excludes plants in the UK.

[4] Totals include 'Unspecified' category.

Interpretation of Table 2.2 is hindered by the small size of sample, but a number of points can be made. There seems to be a tendency for fewer long-established and large plants to have no R&D, indicating that as production facilities grow in maturity, R&D, as a production related activity, is required *in situ*. The results give limited support to the hypothesis that plants in the more scientifically based industries have more developed functions for fundamental or product-based research (R&D categories 1 and 2). SIC orders VIII and IX (Instrument and Electrical Engineering) are in this position and both have been major growth areas, but plants in the Mechanical Engineering and Chemical Industries (SIC orders VII and V), also high growth sectors, do not show a greater than average concentration of R&D.

Previous work (Steuer *et al.*, 1973: 119) has shown that the size of the parent's network of affiliates was a significant factor in influencing the autonomy of individual branch plants. Table 2.2, however, does not support this with respect to R&D in Scotland. Rather the figures suggest, again, that much of the US multinational activity in Europe is based at least as much on the diffusion of technology as on R&D at market level.

Apart from the types of R&D being undertaken and the character of US subsidiaries with R&D, one presumably important question in a branch factory is the degree of flexibility and autonomy which firms appear to have in setting up R&D projects. In an attempt to identify the criteria by which the suitability of Scottish-based R&D projects was determined, companies with R&D functions were invited to indicate any defined constraints. Among the 31 respondents to this question, a wide variety of specifications was found. Most firms claimed that the suitability was defined in terms of financial ceilings and overall market objectives set by the parent. Others expanded on this, incorporating remarks which shed more light on branch plant R&D in Scotland. Comments included: 'European market potential for products based on the company's technology'; 'any product within our normal market and agreed budget'; 'financial ceilings, effect on product costs, improvements in quality'; 'projects for R&D required to meet laid down economic objectives before approval is given'. From an analysis of the replies, it was clear that the constraints were tighter in cases where the local plant had more sophisticated R&D activity. Even among the firms which appeared to be less tightly constrained, however, budgetary controls seemed likely to produce a very limited result.

Marketing

There is in many ways a close relationship between R&D and Marketing. Lack of marketing orientation, for example, may be inferred from the fact that over half of the sample of branch plants undertook no locally based R&D. Even if marketing functions are decentralised to the level of the Scottish operation in these circumstances, the personnel involved face the unenviable task of finding markets for products developed and already sold elsewhere. On the other hand, the fact that fundamental product and process development was being undertaken at a number of plants at least suggested that some firms were becoming more market-centred in their operations.

In examining the role of marketing within US plants in Scotland, the survey tried to ascertain, as with R&D, the extent and significance of the marketing activities delegated by the parent company. These are clearly important issues in trying to assess the innovative and developmental potential existing at the plant and within the Scottish economy. In the case of R&D, from the limited information available, it seemed that the advantages accruing from the presence of an R&D function could be ameliorated by restrictive parent company controls over the actual research undertaken. Such controls are perhaps even more important with marketing, and the extent to which export controls are placed on branch plants has been warranted important enough to have been considered by numerous authors on the multinational enterprise. Because of this, both the functional development of marketing at plant level and the constraints placed on area of export from the plant are considered in the following paragraphs.

Marketing functions.   In examining marketing functions a distinction has been made between the development and the implementation of policy towards the market, the former including activities such as market research and product planning, the latter being a purely selling operation. Within these limits there exist a wide range of different combinations of marketing functions posing serious definitional problems. While these are acknowledged, the basic hypothesis is that the presence, even on a limited scale, of marketing functions of varying types reflects, *inter alia*, the status of the branch factory and may be assumed to be fairly closely related to the developmental potential of the plant (Table 2.3).

The defined categories of marketing functions are presented in Table 2.3. With nearly two-thirds of the sample claiming that some functions were located at the Scottish plant, this activity was more widely represented than R&D. This is not unexpected, as even the most rudimentary plants often have a selling function and the presence of marketing functions is consistent with distribution-based strategies towards

Table 2.3   Marketing functions

Category	%	No. of plants
1 All marketing functions	19.3	17
2 Selected functions in product planning, market research, advertising and sales areas	25.0	22
3 Sales function only	20.5	18
No marketing functions	31.8	28
Unspecified	3.4	3
	100.0	88

Europe. Further, marketing is a more limited and controlled overhead cost than R&D. This is not to say that the delegation of marketing may not be relatively superficial; while the functional areas noted may be present, they may operate at a secondary rather than at a primary level. In any event, only 17 firms in the sample claimed to have a fully developed marketing operation in Scotland, with a further 22 indicating that some, at least, of the more sophisticated marketing functions were present at the Scottish plant (Table 2.4).

As in the previous section, the analysis of functional categories has been extended to cover some possible influencing factors in Table 2.4. The proportion of companies with no marketing functions present appears to increase as size increases: a pattern exactly opposite from that in R&D activity. This may in part be a reflection of the question posed but, it can be explained in other terms, related in part to the peripheral location of Scotland. As suggested earlier, as companies develop their European operation, R&D would tend to increase as an essentially production-related activity located at plant level, whether to develop new products or as a service back-up facility. In contrast, the larger the production unit, the stronger perhaps the argument for locating the marketing function nearer the market centre.

The data presented in Table 2.4 does not indicate that either the existence of marketing functions or the category varies with the period of establishment in Scotland. With respect to industrial classification, however, it does seem that plants in the expanding SIC orders VII, VIII and IX are more likely to have marketing functions delegated to them, although the smallness of the numbers makes this a very tentative conclusion. The table also indicates that the presence and distribution of functions is markedly different where the Scottish plant is the sole, or one of only two, European manufacturing units. In particular a much higher proportion of plants within these categories had some marketing

Table 2.4   Marketing functions in US plants in Scotland[3]

	Marketing functions[1] – % of plants				All plants	
	Category 1	Category 2	Category 3	No marketing functions	%	No.
Period of Establishment in Scotland (to 1974)						
Under 5 years	16.7	25.0	16.7	41.6	100.0	12
5–10 years	28.1	25.0	21.9	25.0	100.0	32
11–20 years	12.5	29.2	25.0	33.3	100.0	24
Over 20 years	17.6	23.5	17.7	41.2	100.0	17
Employment range						
Under 100	26.1	26.1	26.1	21.7	100.0	23
101–400	28.5	28.5	14.3	28.5	100.0	28
401–1000	6.2	25.0	31.3	37.5	100.0	16
Over 1000	12.5	25.0	12.5	50.0	100.0	16
SIC order						
V	23.1	7.7	38.5	30.7	100.0	13
VII	23.8	23.8	33.5	19.1	100.0	21
VIII and IX	16.0	44.0	12.0	28.0	100.0	25
Other	19.2	23.1	7.7	50.0	100.0	26
No. of other European affiliates						
No others	19.4	29.0	22.6	29.0	100.0	31
1	23.8	33.3	28.6	14.3	100.0	21
2	29.4	17.6	5.9	47.1	100.0	17
3 and over	6.3	18.7	25.0	50.0	100.0	16
All plants[2]	**19.3**	**25.0**	**20.5**	**31.8**	**100.0**	**88**

Notes: [1] For marketing function categories, see Table 2.3.

[2] Totals include three firms which did not make returns on marketing functions.

[3] Two firms did not provide size classifications.

activities delegated to the Scottish operation, reflecting, presumably, the greater necessity in these cases. Conversely, the off-central location of Scotland is likely to be significant in explaining why the number of plants with more developed marketing functions decreases as the size of the parent firm's network increases. Although the data are not shown in the table, it is revealing that whether or not plants had their UK headquarters in Scotland did not lead to a different level of functional activity.

Controlled markets.   There is little doubt that the existence of market controls could be an important influence on the growth and development of Scottish plants. This is particularly so when there is related evidence

Table 2.5   Controlled markets

Category	%	No. of plants
1 UK only	3.4	3
2 Europe or selected parts of Europe	12.5	11
3 Europe and selected parts of the world (e.g. Europe and Middle East; Europe and India)	14.8	13
4 Selected parts of Europe and other specified parts of the world (e.g. nominated European countries and Japan)	10.2	9
5 Worldwide with specific limited restrictions (e.g. excluding Comecon countries)	18.2	16
6 US only	1.1	1
Uncontrolled markets	39.8	35
	100.0	88

that such plants are undergoing a process of long term adjustment to the market strategy of the parent and to the structure of the European market. If market and product allocations between plants become more restricted, it becomes progressively more important for Scottish operations to have allocations with growth potential.

As Table 2.5 shows, 53 firms, 60 per cent of the sample, indicated that the geographical area within which output from the Scottish plant was to be marketed was specified by the parent company. This was one of the areas where Steuer *et al.* (1973: 148), by contrast, found high degrees of autonomy at plant level, but such a lack of constraint on market development would be rather surprising in view of the importance of market potential to the European strategy of multinationals.[7] Steuer *et al.* found that only 22 per cent of foreign affiliates in the UK were geographically restricted by their parent company in marketing and expressed the view that even this proportion was unexpected. There are several possible reasons to account for the difference in these findings, not least of which may be the higher response rate in the present study, the concentration on US investment only, the Scottish population (as distinct from total UK) and finally, but perhaps most importantly, the question asked, which was more straightforward, and distinctly geographical in its orientation.[8] The conclusion, therefore, is that there is evidence of a significant amount of geographical restriction of sales and exports from US plants in Scotland.

Table 2.6   Controlled markets for Scottish subsidiaries[1]

	Controlled markets – % of plants[2]				All plants	
	Category 1 & 2	Category 3 & 4	Category 5 & 6	Uncontrolled markets	%	No.
Period of establishment in Scotland (to 1974)						
Under 5 years	16.7	16.7	16.6	50.0	100.0	12
5–10 years	23.5	29.4	8.8	38.3	100.0	34
11–20 years	12.0	12.0	20.0	56.0	100.0	25
Over 20 years	5.9	41.2	41.2	11.7	100.0	17
Employment range						
Under 100	20.8	29.2	4.1	45.9	100.0	24
101–400	17.9	17.8	25.0	39.3	100.0	28
401–1000	11.8	23.5	11.8	52.9	100.0	17
Over 1000	11.8	35.3	41.1	11.8	100.0	17
SIC order						
V	23.1	15.4	–	61.5	100.0	13
VII	14.3	23.8	28.6	33.3	100.0	21
VIII and IX	20.0	36.0	20.0	24.0	100.0	25
Other	10.3	20.7	20.7	48.3	100.0	29
No. of other European affiliates						
No others	15.6	21.9	18.8	43.9	100.0	32
1	23.8	33.3	23.8	19.1	100.0	21
2	11.8	11.8	23.5	52.9	100.0	17
3 and over	11.1	27.8	11.1	50.0	100.0	18
All plants	15.9	25.0	19.3	39.8	100.0	88

Notes: [1] Two firms did not provide size classifications.
[2] For controlled market categories, see Table 2.5.

The essentially European market orientation of US investment in Scotland is reflected in Table 2.5, the majority of firms with markets specified by their US parents, citing Europe or a part of Europe as the basic geographical market for their products. Among the plants which claimed to be free from parent company controls, most still indicated the countries in which their products were presently marketed: over two thirds of these were in the first four categories, that is, were again essentially European in their market base.

Extending the analysis to Table 2.6, the data suggest that the longest established and the largest plants are most likely to be subject to external controls over their geographical markets, although these plants are also likely to have the widest remits. The former conclusion is not entirely consistent with the findings of Steuer *et al.* (1973: 148), where no support was found for the hypothesis that larger plants are more likely to be controlled (geographically) in their export policy. Similarly the data on the number of other European plants and size of markets cannot be interpreted in a way which accords with the Steuer *et al.* (1973: 150) findings. Steuer *et al.* found that geographical restrictions tended to increase as the size of the parent company's international network (expressed in number of subsidiaries) increased. As a final comment on Table 2.6 the industry in which plants operate does not appear to be related to external control over geographical markets.

III

Conclusions

In the context of fears of increasing external control in the Scottish economy, this article has sought to examine two functional areas of activity where the potential effects of autonomy loss are greatest. The fears associated with loss of autonomy are primarily two-fold. Firstly, that in the absence of such functions an imbalance could occur in the employment structure of the population, with adverse effects on the supply of indigenous managerial talent. Secondly, through this and other factors, the Scottish economy's potential for future self-generating growth is weakened.

The data presented do seem to lend some support for such fears, since a majority of US firms in Scotland either undertake no marketing or R&D in Scotland, or the functions delegated are not particularly meaningful. Moreover, parent company controls over marketing and R&D activities seem, in general, fairly tight.

One important reason for the results obtained seems to derive from the fact that US industrialists view Scotland in a European rather than a UK context. The branch factories studied were generally located in Scotland for initial development in the European market. It is clear that Scotland's off-central position does not necessarily make it an optimum location either for copying with developing European markets or for such functions as may be delegated to a true European headquarters. This is particularly true of the marketing function, where 'market centre', in terms of concentration of income and population, attracts functional location. As the survey results suggest, the greater the parent company's involvement in Europe, the lower the likelihood of marketing activities being directed from Scotland. By the same line of argument, the larger the size of the Scottish operation, the wider its remit and the greater the probability of marketing being based near the market centre. It would appear thus that marketing is increasingly unlikely to be located in Scotland. However, work is undoubtedly required to assess the benefits and costs of separating the marketing and production functions: the marketing services (advertising and market research agencies, for example) are not generally located in Scotland and there must be advantages in ease of liaison with customers, but against this must be set the costs of communicating with production, and the sense of frustration that may be engendered in production units. Where marketing and production functions are spatially separated, furthermore, the possibility of the branch plant successfully arguing a case for broader or less rigidly defined export markets is much reduced. This is particularly a problem for branch factories of international firms, where the carve-up of products and markets becomes crucial to the growth potential of any individual operation. The impact on the Scottish economy of a single decision, such as that to manufacture the new Chrysler model in France, can, in these circumstances, be very large. On the other hand, it is worth noting that the enlargement of the EEC could be to the advantage of Scottish plants in a number of cases particularly where the geographical market had been constrained to EFTA or non-EEC countries previously.

The low prevalence of R&D in US plants in Scotland is also disturbing, although the rather greater propensity for local R&D among firms in the scientific industries moderates this conclusion. If the results of such R&D are applied elsewhere, of course, the impact will be substantially reduced: it has already been noted that with a number of firms new products are allocated on the basis of intra-Europe tenders, irrespective of the location of R&D; another firm stated that while fundamental research might be undertaken in Scotland, the development phase could be pursued on the Continent. Even so, the very presence of R&D in Scotland has economic implications derived from the employment of high quality personnel and from any 'spin-off' effects.

In judging the significance of the results obtained one is necessarily handicapped by the absence of data relating to indigenous firms and other branch plants in Scotland. However, given the situation as it stands, the objective for the US-owned branch factory sector must be to max-imise its contribution to the Scottish economy. Given that there is no way in which branch factories will be permitted to function as fully autonomous units, what is required at a minimum is an increase in the presence of significant decision-making functions in branch plants and maximum participation in such functions. The limited evidence of this article is that with regard to R&D and marketing, a much higher level of functional delegation and autonomy is required. Unless and until this occurs the cost of loss of control has to be built into any equation of the gain and losses from increasing US direct investment in Scotland.

Notes

1. See, for example, the Gray Report (1972) on foreign investment in Canada and the report by Steuer *et al.* (1973) for the Department of Trade and Industry.
2. Control is inferred if:
    (i) 50 per cent or more of the voting stock was owned by residents of the USA, or
    (ii) 25 per cent or more of the voting stock was concentrated in the hands of a single holder or organised group of holders in the USA, or
    (iii) the Scottish firms were foreign branches of US companies, or
    (iv) the Scottish firms were proprietorships or partnerships owned by Americans.
3. The information in this paragraph summarises work by Firn (1975).
4. For a further discussion of this point see Dunning (1974: 28).
5. Overall just under half of all plants manufactured products which were also made elsewhere in Europe (Young and Hood, 1976a).
6. This is an issue the present authors have developed elsewhere (Young and Hood, 1976b).
7. The question asked was:
    (a) Is the area (e.g. EEC, EFTA, UK only, etc.) within which output from the Scottish plant(s) is to be marketed specified by your USA parent company? Yes/No.
    (b) If yes, please indicate the countries/areas concerned.

Appendix   Sample and Survey Details

This study deals with US-owned firms engaged in manufacturing industry in Scotland in 1973, the population of which was obtained from lists provided by the Scottish Council for Development and Industry. The survey was begun in the Spring of 1974 when a number of lengthy and very helpful discussions were held with the executives of various US firms. From these discussions and the information collected in a pilot questionnaire, a revised and very much briefer questionnaire emerged, to be sent to firms in the late Autumn of 1974. The bulk of the information was therefore obtained from a postal survey, although subsequently clarification was obtained in a number of instances by telephone.

In total 123 US-owned manufacturing firms were identified (excluding firms which established operations during 1974), from whom 88 usable questionnaires were obtained, a response rate of 72 per cent. A further three questionnaires were returned, but one was unusable and two were from fabricators who were excluded, admittedly somewhat arbitrarily, from the population.

Data on the SIC order of US firms in Scotland was inferred from product details provided in the Scottish Council lists and employment details were obtained from the same source.

Numerous US firms had more than a single plant in Scotland, but information obtained related to the entire Scottish operation in each case.

With regard to the European operations of US firms, the questionnaire related only to activities within the same broad product area as that of the Scottish operation, thus excluding conglomerate operations.

In interpreting the results it should be noted that data were obtained on the other European countries in which manufacturing operations existed during the survey period, but firms were not required to specify closures or the abandonment of operations in particular areas.

3
R&D Intensity in the Affiliates of US-Owned Electronics Companies Manufacturing in Scotland (1983)*

Peter Haug, Neil Hood and Stephen Young

Introduction

Relatively little is known about the research and development activity of US or other foreign-owned companies in the UK. This is in part due to the disclosure difficulties surrounding research effort, but is also a function of serious definitional problems as to what constitutes R&D, especially where cross-company and cross-industry comparisons are concerned. These are discussed here and some now conventional solutions are adopted. The main purpose of this paper is, however, to summarise a number of interesting and potentially important propositions which have emerged over recent years on the nature of R&D activities in US multinational enterprises (MNEs) and thereafter to apply them to an empirical study recently conducted among a sample of US-owned electronics affiliates in Scotland. It might be expected that this sample will prove to be a rather special case within the spectrum of US MNEs, given the R&D orientation. On the other hand, there is a particular Scottish interest in the sector given that it accounts for some 25 per cent of employment in US-owned affiliates, and is also the most expansive sector in recent years, especially when set against a backcloth of substantial decline in many MNE affiliates in Scotland (Hood and Young, 1982). Arguably, too little attention has been given to the nature of activity within electronics affiliates in Scotland until a recent SDA sector study (Scottish Development Agency, 1979). The piece of

* *Regional Studies*, 17 (6) (1983), 383–92.

research reported here is designed to complement that work by looking specifically at the origins, nature and broad determinants of R&D activity in electronics. For the purposes of this paper R&D is taken to include basic research, applied research and development but to exclude quality control, routine product testing and technical services.

R&D in US MNEs: some propositions from the literature

In order to provide a frame of reference for the empirical section and at the same time summarise some rather diffuse and partial data, this section is grouped into a number of headings under which related topics can be considered.

Growth and characteristics of US multinational R&D

Bearing in mind the limitations of data availability, several studies (National Science Foundation, 1979, 1982) confirm that foreign affiliate R&D expenditures have grown more rapidly than domestic R&D over the period since the mid-1960s. The foreign proportion of the total company-funded R&D in the US was estimated to have grown from 7.4 per cent in 1966 to 10.7 per cent in 1980.[1] However, it should be noted that only an estimated 15 per cent of the major US industrial companies maintain foreign R&D operations (Creamer, 1976), so that among these firms the overseas proportion of R&D spending is clearly a good deal higher than this.

In terms of sectoral distribution, there is a general association between the stock of US foreign direct investment in manufacturing in developed countries and the level of R&D in US foreign affiliates, except in low-technology industries such as food and metals and in sectors such as drugs. The latter was strongly influenced by new US Food and Drug Administration (FDA) requirements which were adopted in 1975 and liberalised the policy regarding foreign testing, thereby encouraging some drug companies to increase resources devoted to foreign R&D. Recent changes by the FDA may reduce this incentive for the future. Foreign affiliate R&D in the electronics industry has also been rising rapidly: between 1974 and 1980, US spending abroad in the electronic components sector grew from $4 million to $29 million, increasing from 0.3 per cent to 0.9 per cent of total US foreign affiliate R&D spending (National Science Foundation, 1982). No data are available on overseas as a proportion of total US company-funded R&D spending in electronic components (SIC Code 367), but taking electrical equipment as a whole (SIC Code 36), the figure was 8.9 per cent in 1980.

While there are problems with the statistics in this area, all studies point to a marked geographic concentration of US R&D abroad. The EC(9) plus Canada accounted for over four-fifths of R&D abroad in both 1966 and 1975, but important shifts have taken place in the relative importance of the leading R&D locations (the UK, France, Germany and Canada). Estimates (Creamer, 1976) indicate that the gains in Germany were principally at the expense of the UK and Canada, the UK falling from some 24.4 per cent of the dollar value of R&D abroad by US MNEs in 1966 to 18.8 per cent in 1975. In recent years, there is some evidence that particular growth has occurred in France (US Department of Commerce, 1981).

Looking in more detail at the UK position, in 1966 the UK accounted for 45.8 per cent of US foreign direct investment (FDI) in the EC, while the 1975 figure was 34.2 per cent. On the other hand, the UK's share of US affiliate R&D in the EC fell from 38.5 per cent to 27.1 per cent between these same two years (Hood and Young, 1981). While there is, therefore, a reasonably close relationship between the declining shares of foreign direct investment and of R&D, the UK was apparently less attractive as an R&D location than as a manufacturing base even in the mid-1960s. The West German position stands out in marked contrast, with under 25 per cent of the US FDI but over 40 per cent of the R&D expenditure in 1975.

As regards the type of activity undertaken under affiliate R&D, most research has shown that this is largely development work. Under 1.5 per cent of US foreign affiliate R&D expenditure was used for basic research in 1972, compared to 1.9 per cent being devoted to basic research among the parent MNEs. This pattern for US parent companies is much affected by US Federal Government funding of R&D, which is directed more to development than to either applied or basic research. For company-funded R&D only, 7.3 per cent of total spending was used for basic research by parent MNEs compared with 1.1 per cent by foreign affiliates (Hood and Young, 1981).

As might be expected, while the US Federal Government is important in the financing of US MNE R&D at parent company level, host country government involvement in financing affiliate R&D is much less important. One of the few sources (Creamer, 1976: 75–9) estimates that 70 per cent of affiliate R&D expenditures were financed by the subsidiaries themselves, and host government funding was only significant in Japan and Canada. In the former, nearly half of US MNE affiliate R&D funds came from the Japanese government, while in Canada 13 per cent of finance came from the host government. Elsewhere host government funding was zero or negligible.

Explanations for the growth of foreign affiliate R&D

The theoretical work on the MNE, although not generally applied to R&D locational decisions, tends to predict centralised research and development. It has been speculated that given the widespread expansion of the global networks of firms, there is a greater likelihood of R&D being decentralised at affiliate level (Vernon, 1979). Again, there is a possibility that rivalistic and oligopolistic reactions might lead to a decentralisation of R&D.[2] Other authors have indicated that changes in the organisation of the firm internationally could influence R&D decisions, but the predictions are ambiguous (Hewitt, 1980; Malecki, 1980). While there are clearly industry, technology and strategy dimensions to the question of R&D activity within the MNE, none of these provides compelling reasons why R&D (especially basic research) should be decentralised.

Although the case for centralisation remains strong there is, as noted, a growing tendency for some R&D work to be undertaken outside the home country. Empirical research directed towards explaining this tendency has drawn attention to the importance of a number of matters which have a bearing on the centralisation/decentralisation of R&D. The first of these concerns the critical mass or minimum efficient scale (MES) for R&D. While this is widely recognised as important, its relevance varies substantially between industries and is linked to the nature of the R&D and the product range. Several fairly recent studies have examined these aspects in detail (Mansfield, Teece and Romeo, 1979; Behrman and Fischer, 1980), concluding that consumer-oriented industries and process-oriented R&D require the lowest MES, and that the critical mass for minor product changes is lower than that for research activity. Secondly, it has been argued that the relative costs and productivity of inputs in different locations is important. In fact, the relative cost differences for R&D personnel between US and Europe largely disappeared during the 1970s and the slender evidence which exists (Mansfield, 1978) does not suggest that relative productivity levels affect the real cost of undertaking R&D outside the US. A third dimension lies in the influence of host developed countries through policies of 'negative inducements' to compel the location of R&D centres in their country. Evidence is again scant in this area, but it does point to 'negative inducements' having had a greater influence than government subsidies and other positive inducements (Behrman and Fischer, 1980: 109–10). Finally, both the empirical and theoretical work confirm that the principal reasons for undertaking R&D abroad are the requirements of foreign markets. A number of these issues have been explored in recent econometric studies (Mansfield, 1978; Lall, 1979; Hewitt, 1980). Data limitations and lack of contemporary material would lead to cautious interpretation of these results. But they do indicate that the level of foreign subsidiary sales had a positive impact on affiliate R&D and that the average age of foreign subsidiaries is positively correlated to R&D abroad.

The nature of R&D units in foreign affiliates

In an effort to order this type of discussion, various authors (Cordell, 1971; Ronstadt, 1978) have attempted to classify R&D units on the basis of their primary purpose. At least three distinct types of affiliate R&D operation can be identified. Support laboratories/technology transfer units are concerned with product adaptation and the translation of foreign manufacturing technology. Secondly, there are locally integrated R&D laboratories/indigenous technology units where the prime concern is the development of new and improved products specifically for foreign markets. In laboratories of this type the products developed are not the direct result of new technology supplied by the parent corporation. The third group are international interdependent laboratories/global technology units where the activity is closely integrated into the parent's international research programme. It has already been noted that the determinants of overseas R&D are complex, but that the market orientation of the firms is clearly associated with the type of R&D unit established. Thus, 'host market' firms (Behrman and Fischer, 1980: 15–22), where the operations are oriented to the national market which they serve, will require support laboratories. In contrast 'world market' firms, serving a standardised international market, may tend to centralise research at the parent's base (with some support laboratories abroad) or, less likely, may organise R&D on a worldwide basis.

Of the categories outlined, the world market firm and the international interdependent laboratory are perhaps of special interest. From the host governments' perspective these are large employers of highly qualified manpower; involve substantial capital investment and are almost exclusively in developed countries. Having suggested the desirability of such investments, it should be noted that they are frequently not closely integrated with local production facilities and are invariably decentralised only in location and not in the determination of work undertaken.

Entry methods and the evolution of foreign R&D activities

Comment in the previous sections on the motivation for and types of R&D units overseas has implied that MNEs set up completely new R&D

facilities. The possibility of affiliate R&D units emerging from a variety of modes of entry must, however, be allowed for. Research indicates that between 25–30 per cent of the overseas R&D laboratories of US MNEs came into being as a result of acquisitions (Creamer, 1976: 84; Behrman and Fischer, 1980: 25; Ronstadt, 1977: 61). In the first of these studies, acquisitions accounted for 29.7 per cent of US R&D units abroad but only 9.5 per cent of foreign affiliate R&D spending; and they seemed to be frequently omitted from corporate R&D planning after takeover, performing work in support of the existing business only. Other work (Ronstadt, 1977: 95) indicates that some of the characteristics of acquired R&D units include a tendency to experience very low growth rates in the annual increase of R&D professionals; to maintain the same geographic level of national R&D responsibility over time; and to be comprised entirely of host country nationals.

On the matter of evolution, many US affiliate R&D departments seem to have evolved from technical service operations. In some cases the process of evolution is relatively slow, with some 5–10 years of quality control/technical service work being common before any progression to more sophisticated activity. Some of the evidence (Behrman and Fischer, 1980: 26–9) points to evolution to higher functions being most common among host market companies while, for world market MNEs, R&D groups tend to be created by direct placement. Other work goes further in distinguishing between the evolutionary patterns of different types of foreign R&D units, especially that from technology transfer to indigenous technology units (Ronstadt, 1977). Among the reasons for this is the need to provide challenging work to attract and retain staff, together with the requirement for new products. Such progression usually results in at least a doubling of the number of R&D professionals employed.

US multinational R&D: UK and Scottish evidence

Compared with some other countries, such as Canada, the knowledge available on multinational R&D in the UK is very limited indeed. Data are, for example, rather scant on reliable international comparisons. One other important area is the comparison between the R&D intensities of foreign affiliates and indigenous firms in the UK. Here the publication in recent years of *Business Monitor* figures have shed some light. These data do not show much difference between the two R&D/sales ratios when the figures for both indigenous and foreign enterprises are adjusted to include company-funded R&D only. The R&D intensity in foreign-controlled industry is, nevertheless, not only higher for all manufacturing, but also for each of the sectors for which data are available – although this gap in R&D intensities between foreign and indigenous companies would appear to have narrowed substantially over time.

Foreign affiliate R&D expenditure in the UK has stabilised at a level of 18 per cent of all R&D spending. In sectoral terms, electrical engineering (including electronics) as a whole has experienced a decline, with overseas-controlled enterprises' share of gross R&D in the industry declining from 18 per cent to 16 per cent between 1972 and 1978 (*Business Monitor*, MO14, 1975, 1978); at the same time employment in foreign-owned electrical engineering firms was continuing to rise as a share of total employment in this sector (*Business Monitor*, PA1002, various issues). The relative position of electronics within this is likely to be different but there are no data to confirm or deny this point. To date there has been little research work aimed at explaining the underlying causes of these changes in foreign affiliates. Indeed the whole question of the relationship between inward investment and UK technology has not been fully explored. A number of authors have taken a fairly relaxed view about the nature of US affiliate R&D in Britain (Steuer *et al.*, 1973; Dunning, 1976), suggesting that the trend may be towards less subsidiary dependency. Given the state of knowledge in this area and the general evidence reviewed in the last few paragraphs it is difficult to regard these perspectives as anything other than complacent.

Turning specifically to the Scottish case, the evidence points to most R&D in the foreign-owned affiliates being a production-related activity, with relatively little fundamental product or process development. There is some limited evidence of more sophisticated functions evolving, but this rarely involves the coexistence of R&D and marketing functions of a high order (Hood and Young, 1980). Recent information on the electronics sector (McDermott, 1979) has shown that R&D personnel are not well represented in either indigenous or externally owned companies; although other work has shown that R&D and design engineering staff comprised about one-third of the technical manpower of US firms in Scotland (Scottish Development Agency, 1979). The limited evidence which has been considered in this section illustrates that there is ample scope for a study such as that undertaken in this paper, since there are many gaps in knowledge concerning R&D in the MNE sector in Scotland.

Survey evidence

The empirical material summarised in this section is based on a study undertaken during 1981 of fifteen US-owned electronics affiliates in Scotland, accounting for over 70 per cent of US-owned employment in the sector. At the time of sample selection the population of such companies was 24. Comparing the sample with the population in terms of affiliate size, age and product category, and thereafter applying chi-square tests, showed the sample to be representative. The 15 companies manufacture a wide spectrum of electronic components: four major in data processing – these generally being the largest and oldest affiliates; five in industrial and commercial products (such as potentiometers, metering and instrumentation systems); the remaining six concentrate on the production of support components. The size of the Scottish affiliates relative to their parent companies is again wide-ranging, with six of the affiliates employing between 7 per cent–17 per cent of total corporate employment, while the remaining nine accounted for less than 2 per cent of the total. For reasons of confidentiality the companies are not named in this paper.

Interviews were conducted with senior management at each of the sample affiliates using a structured questionnaire, full details of which are available from the authors. In addition to identifying the characteristics of R&D activity within the sample, the questionnaire was designed to examine the evolution of this activity and provide a basis for distinguishing between R&D-and non-R&D-intensive affiliates.

The determination of the affiliate R&D intensity required the use of both quantitative and qualitative measures. In the former category, two measures have been widely used in the literature. The first, and perhaps most common, is the ratio of R&D expenditures to sales (Malecki, 1980; Hirschey and Caves, 1981); the second is the number of scientists and engineers in R&D as a percentage of total employment. In many cases individual firms differ on what they would identify as 'R&D', hence the role of qualitative considerations in evaluating intensity. It is with all these difficulties in mind that Table 3.1 should be interpreted. Four separate measures are employed in that table, although data on R&D expenditure relative to sales were not always given by the companies. As the division within the table suggests, it was necessary to interpret the quantitative data fairly carefully since the number of scientists and engineers employed at the plant did not always relate to the duration of longer-term projects and hence to more fundamental R&D activity. In the light of discussions with senior technical staff in the affiliates a weighting system was applied to categorise the technical activity undertaken. This resulted in some reclassification: thus, for example, although company 13 has the largest single technical group, its operations are solely process engineering and not R&D as such. The R&D-intensive group are distinguished from the others by the nature of the activity remit and the duration of the projects, rather than by expenditure

Table 3.1 Determination of R&D intensity

	R&D activity rankings[1]						R&D expenditure by duration of project (%)					1980 R&D (% affiliate sales)	Technical unit	
	Basic research	Applied research[2]	Major development	Minor development	R&D materials	R&D costs	1-6 months	7-12 months	13-18 months	19-24 months	Over 24 months		Size (no. of employees)	1980 employment at plant (%)
R&D-intensive group[2]														
1	–	–	2	2	1	1	–	–	10	10	80	n.a.	250	20.8
2	–	2	2	1	–	1	–	1	5	90	5	n.a.	31	6.9
3	–	2	2	1	2	1	–	–	–	60	40	8.2	99	12.5
4	–	–	2	2	–	1	5	20	70	5	–	n.a.	120	7.7
5	–	–	2	2	–	–	–	–	–	100	–	n.a.	80	8.4
6	–	1	1	1	–	2	50	–	–	50	–	2.7	2	2.5
7	–	1	2	1	1	–	–	–	50	50	–	2.9	54	5.4
													Mean 91	12.6
Non-R&D-intensive group[2]														
8	–	1	1	1	2	2	–	50	50	–	–	n.a.	8	4.0
9	–	–	2	2	–	2	75	20	5	–	–	0.5	2	2.7
10	–	–	–	–	2	–	20	80	–	–	–	2.7	40	8.0
11	–	–	–	1	1	1	95	5	–	–	–	n.a.	15	2.5
12	–	–	–	–	2	2	5	75	10	5	5	4.2	4	2.7
13	–	–	1	1	1	1	–	50	50	–	–	n.a.	300+	23.0
14	–	–	1	1	–	1	80	20	–	–	–	6.5	3	6.0
15	–	1	2	1	1	–	50	–	50	–	–	6.6	5	4.2
													Mean 48	12.7

Notes: [1] The categories were defined as follows: Basic research, to discover new knowledge in electronics; Applied research, to discover new commercially viable knowledge for new product innovations; Major development work, to produce, adapt or modify new products or processes; Minor development work, to produce, adapt or modify existing products or processes; R&D on specific materials and/or techniques; R&D for customer service support. Company respondents' rankings shown as 2 (very important), 1 (important), (–) not important or not applicable.
[2] The numbers refer to the sample firms.

relative to sales. On the whole, the 'technical unit' size is higher in the R&D-intensive group, although not all of these staff numbers are directly involved in R&D work.

An examination of the nature of these R&D units, confirmed the broad Behrman and Fischer (1980) findings regarding host market category, seven of whom were in the low R&D-intensity affiliates. As in other studies (Cordell, 1971, 1973), there was a suggestion in the Scottish sample that wider market remits for an affiliate might be associated with higher levels of R&D. In terms of the evolution of R&D in the Scottish sample, all affiliates started as technology transfer units (TTUs) in the Rondstadt (1977) classification. All the non-R&D affiliates have remained in that group, while two of the R&D-intensive affiliates now display characteristics of indigenous technology units (ITUs) and two have become global technology units (GTUs). As yet none of the sample electronics companies was in the final stage of evolution where they operated as corporate technology units (CTUs).

Reviewing the background to the establishment of these R&D units in Scotland, the dominant motivation emerging from the company studies in both R&D intensity groups was the competitive pressure to develop new products. Thereafter, the R&D-intensive affiliates rated the availability and cost of R&D labour as a major factor underlying the establishment of their unit; other reasons included the European market franchise of the affiliate, corporate strategy towards the decentralisation of R&D and the market requirement for local R&D. In contrast, and reflecting their engineering orientation, the non-R&D-intensive affiliates stated that their units were conditioned by the need for a local technical support function due to the nature of the product range. In both sets of affiliates, marketing and cost factors were seen to be of considerable importance in shaping the R&D requirement.

Some further consideration of this issue is possible from the data in Table 3.2. It has been suggested in the literature that the existence of more extensive product mandates may well lead to higher-order R&D in foreign affiliates. Table 3.2 outlines the sourcing roles played by the Scottish sample affiliates within their respective corporate networks and the 1980 sales distribution by market area. While simple interrelationships are not to be expected in this area and generalisations are to be made with caution given the sample size, there is some hint that the R&D-intensive group have slightly more extensive primary and secondary sourcing roles outside Europe. These may account for only a small percentage of sales volume, although it is still true that the R&D-intensive group are more export-oriented. It would have to be noted that this

Table 3.2 Affiliate marketing characteristics

Type of affiliate		Number of firms operating as supply source[2] for market area				
		Scotland	UK	Europe	USA	Other
R&D-intensive[1]:	Primary source	6	6	6	3	2
	Secondary source	1	1	2	4	–
Non-R&D-intensive:	Primary source	7	8	7	1	3
	Secondary source	1	–	1	1	–

Type of affiliate	1980 sales distribution by value (%)					
	Scotland	UK	Europe	USA	Other	Total
R&D-intensive[1]	3.5	28.2	50.8	7.2	10.3	100.0
Non-R&D-intensive	6.0	42.4	46.3	1.0	4.3	100.0

Notes: [1] One company did not respond.
[2] The number of firms acting as primary and secondary supply sources may be greater than the sample size. In some cases a company operated as a primary source for one product line but a secondary source for another.

group is generally part of smaller European networks than the non-R&D-intensive category of firms and this could exert an equally, if not more important, influence on the role of the Scottish R&D units.

When considering the contribution of affiliate R&D, one issue which is often discussed concerns the employment of highly qualified technical staff. The sample data revealed that over 85 per cent of scientists and technicians in the R&D-intensive affiliates were graduates, while the equivalent figure for the non-R&D-intensive group was 57 per cent. Table 3.3 permits a further aspect of this variation to be explored: the R&D-intensive affiliates have a much higher proportion of technical staff recruited externally and a lower proportion being internally recruited. In itself this is probably a fairly clear indication of the relative levels of activity. Perhaps somewhat disappointing from the regional perspective, are the related findings of the nationality of these staff.

Table 3.3   Technical staff composition

Type of affiliate	Recruitment source (%)			Nationality (%)				
	Affiliate	Corporation	External	Scotland	UK	US	Continental European	Other
R&D-intensive	18.6	1.0	79.3	56.6	41.0	1.0	1.0	1.0
Non-R&D-intensive	31.2	5.6	63.1	79.1	19.6	1.0	1.0	–

Table 3.4 suggests that there is some relationship between affiliate size and R&D intensity. R&D-intensive affiliates were found to be generally older and larger than the non-R&D-intensive group. This finding is open to various interpretations, all of which have perhaps some validity. The maturity of the affiliate and the strength of its position within a corporate network does contribute to the level of work designated to it. It would not be reasonable to imply from this small sample that higher-order R&D functions will come to Scotland given time, as there are clearly many other influences. It is interesting to note the time lag between plant and technical unit establishment in both levels of research intensity, although some mechanisms for receiving transferred technology obviously pre-dated both of these types of unit. While it is not easy to identify these mechanisms in detail, Table 3.5 indicates the current channels for the sample companies. Technology transfer through licensing was not employed by any of the affiliates. On the other hand, all of the sample used intra-network visits and many depended on

Table 3.4   R&D, affiliate age and size

	R&D-intensive	**Non-R&D-intensive**
Average age of affiliate (number of years)	24.1	14.3
Average age of technical unit (number of years)	12.1	9.1
Average employment in affiliate (number of employees)	810	518
Average employment in technical unit (number of employees)	79	47

Table 3.5 Channels for technology transfers from the parent

Channels	R&D intensive	Non-R&D intensive	Total number of affiliates
Technical licensing agreements	–	–	–
Transfer of R&D/production personnel	5	1	6
Corporate technical conferences	4	4	8
Capital transfers	2	1	3
Visits from the parent	7	8	15
Visits to the parent	7	8	15
Corporate R&D literature	5	6	11
Published literature	4	1	5
External professional contacts	5	3	8

allied corporate R&D literature. As expected, the channels point to the strength of the internal market for proprietary information within the corporation, although this only seems to have extended to personnel transfers in a limited number of cases. For many of the companies, progression along the path of greater research intensity was, at least in part, motivated by a desire to make technology transfers more effective and thereby reinforce the processes outlined in Table 3.5.

The organisation of R&D and its functional relationship to other parts of the affiliate's operation is obviously of some importance in determining the impact of technical output. The evidence of this study was that R&D-intensive units were generally more integrated (at both affiliate and corporate level) with other technical and managerial functions such as marketing and quality control. It was also claimed that in many cases the existence of an R&D-intensive unit did accelerate the speed with which 'learning curve' benefits occurred from production.

Table 3.6 extends the analysis to a consideration of project success and time lags in innovation. The percentage of affiliate R&D projects resulting in commercial applications was very high. The indication is, therefore, that affiliates showed a propensity to work only on technically safe products at affiliate level. The fact that this is so perhaps emphasises the view that most of what is pursued, even in the R&D-intensive firms, is closer to development than research. Time lags between concept/design and first commercial application were, however, longer in the R&D-intensive group, which does suggest that R&D in this group is more fundamental, even if it would still be characterised as 'major development' work.

Table 3.6   Project success and time lags

(a) Affiliate technical projects developed into commercial applications (% of projects)

	Under 50	51–70	71–80	81–90	91–100	Total number of affiliates
R&D-intensive	–	2	1	2	2	7
Non-R&D-intensive	1	2	2	1	2	8

(b) Average technical lag time[1]

	1–6 months	7–12 months	13–18 months	19–24 months	Over 24 months	Total number of affiliates
R&D-intensive	1	–	2	2	2	7
Non-R&D-intensive	3	2	2	1	–	8

(c) Average lag time between corporate innovation and affiliate production

	No transfer	1–12 months	13–24 months	35–36 months	Over 36 months	Total number of affiliates
R&D-intensive	2	–	3	1	–	7
Non-R&D-intensive	2	1	3	–	2	8

Note: [1] Time period between concept/design and first commercial delivery.

From the point of view of a host economy, the process of the evolution of technical units is of some considerable interest. Taking the seven R&D-intensive cases in this sample, only two emerged from an engineering function being upgraded into an R&D lab. The remaining units were created by direct placement due to corporate decentralisation policies, the availability and cost of R&D or the need for closer linkage between production and technical activities. The evidence in Table 3.7 confirms that it is not only the establishment but also the development of R&D which is conditioned primarily by market/product requirements. The availability of R&D labour was considered as of significance by only a small number of the MNE affiliates; it is perhaps surprising that this did not rank more highly given the high education level of R&D professionals. Interestingly, no companies considered government incentives as of any importance in influencing the progression of R&D[3]; this supports other evidence, where as indicated previously, 'negative inducements' (where governments insist on companies setting up an R&D lab as a condition of market access) have been successfully employed

Table 3.7 Ranking of reasons underlying changes in technical units

Reasons	R&D-intensive			Non-R&D-intensive			Number of affiliates
	Very important	Important	Not important	Very Important	Important	Not important	
Market/product requirements	6	–	1	5	–	3	15
Customer service support	2	1	4	–	3	5	15
Parent allocation of R&D	3	1	3	n.a.	n.a.	n.a.	n.a.
Availability of R&D labour	2	1	4	–	1	7	15
Production capacity	–	3	4	–	1	7	15
Competitive activities	2	1	4	3	1	4	15
Rate of product innovation	2	3	2	3	1	4	15

Table 3.8 Affiliate technical unit development 1981–6

	R&D employ- ment	Laboratory space	Expenditure levels	Number of projects	Number of products	Market sales area
	(Number of affiliates)[1]					
Significant increase	3 (2)	5 (3)	8 (4)	3 (2)	2 (1)	1 (–)
Slight increase	8 (3)	6 (1)	5 (1)	6 (1)	8 (2)	5 (3)
No change or decrease	4 (2)	4 (3)	2 (2)	6 (4)	5 (4)	9 (4)
	15 (7)	15 (7)	15 (7)	15 (7)	15 (7)	15 (7)

Note: [1] R&D-intensive units in parentheses.

by some countries, but 'positive inducements' (government subsidies) have been unimportant (Behrman and Fischer, 1980: 109–10).

Within the non-R&D-intensive group, some trend toward expansion can be detected, although three of this group predicted that no higher-status R&D function would emerge, while one other was about to lose its existing status. In short, some upgrading was predicted but relatively few were expected to cross the definitional threshold during the period up to 1986.

Conclusions

The sample survey based on US-owned companies in the Scottish electronics sector has produced evidence which largely supports the propositions examined from the literature where it was possible to address these directly. The emergence and growth of the R&D activity was seen to be largely induced by the need for response to market signals, and related to the age of affiliates, rather than subject to the direct influence of either cost or incentive considerations (Table 3.8). On the specific nature of R&D units in foreign affiliates, the Scottish sample could readily be viewed in terms of established classification systems, although there was little sign of fully integrated global R&D responsibilities yet emerging in this sector. In spite of the relative size of the foreign-owned electronics sector in Scotland, the full benefits of world market firms and international independent laboratories are not yet on the horizon. As regards allied research on entry methods and evolution processes, the Scottish data confirm the propensity to establish both R&D and engineering functions *de novo*.[4] Various forms of progression were also identified in this study, and again the pace was seen to be relatively slow.

What do these results mean for the regional economy in Scotland? The foreign-owned electronics industry is of major importance at present and is likely to become even more significant in future: for the years 1980–2, 61 per cent of offers of selective financial assistance (the best indicator of short-term trends) made to foreign-owned companies were to electrical engineering enterprises, almost certainly nearly all in electronics.[5] There is undoubtedly considerable optimism but also trepidation about the contribution of this sector to the Scottish economy, and this paper has tried to shed some light on one dimension of this, at least in respect of the existing stock of companies.

The data indicate that the fifteen sample US MNE affiliates employed over 1,000 people in their R&D labs, with about three-quarters of these being graduates. These are not insignificant direct employment benefits. The R&D units seemed to provide a mechanism for facilitating technology transfers from the parent multinationals, and the proportion of commercial applications from the research results was high and tended to be based in the affiliates themselves. Future prospects for the units also seemed reasonably optimistic. The results thus reveal that affiliate R&D is to be encouraged as a means of improving the status and contribution of multinationals in regional economies such as Scotland. As the paper showed, nevertheless, even within R&D units the contribution differs, with greater research intensity bringing more and higher-level employment, more responsibility in terms of the work undertaken and an association with wider market areas for plant output.

The evidence from this research is that technical units are not established until the affiliate has been operating for *a* period of years. With respect to the future for R&D in the electronics industry in Scotland, this suggests, therefore, that the recent surge of electronics investment will involve fairly low-status test and assembly activity for a number of years. Whether the behaviour of these firms subsequently follows that of the present sample remains to be seen.

Notes

1. These estimates are obtained by relating the figures of company R&D performed by foreign affiliates of the top 200 US R&D-performing domestic companies to total company-funded R&D (National Science Foundation, 1982).

2. There has been some contention over this issue. For different sides of this debate see for example Graham (1978); Grabowski and Baxter (1973).
3. At time of establishment, there was no indication that regional and industrial assistance played an important role either. Moreover, the effect of incentives on affiliate technology was also shown to be minor, having almost no effect on the product or process technology, the timing of the introduction of new technology or the capital intensity of new projects.
4. The Scottish position differs slightly from the UK in this regard, namely there is a lower propensity to enter by acquisition among US MNEs in Scotland.
5. Data obtained in private correspondence from the Scottish Economic Planning Department.

4

European Locational Decisions of Japanese Manufacturers: Survey Evidence on the Case of the UK (1993)*

Neil Hood and Thorsten Truijens

Introduction

Japanese foreign direct investment (FDI) in Europe has attracted much attention from competitors, consumers, academics and governments, especially over the past decade. This attention has been particularly focused on manufacturing investment, not only because of its relationship to competition and trade policy, but also due to the intense efforts which have been directed towards the attraction of that investment to relatively disadvantaged regions within the EC with a view to employment creation and industrial regeneration. Moreover, the distribution of this investment has been concentrated in a limited number of countries, the UK and Germany playing dominant roles in terms of project numbers and investment, with the UK being substantially ahead as regards employment. For a variety of reasons related to both competitive and anti-competitive issues and economic nationalism, almost every one of the major investment decisions has been the subject of some controversy.

This study considers only one aspect of this phenomenon, namely the locational decision-making processes employed by Japanese companies when they are planning to commence manufacturing in the European market. Based on survey evidence from the UK, these corporate processes are examined from both the company's viewpoint and from the perspective of an economic development agency, endeavoring to track and understand the particularly considered Japanese approach to the taking

* *International Business Review*, 2 (1) (1993), 39–63.

of sensitive, strategic decisions in order to attract the investment to a particular location. The role of regional economic development agencies is important in this context. In the UK these are normally based in 'development areas', so designated because of high unemployment levels. They are wholly or partly government funded, but involve private sector executives on their boards, and in some cases there is a funding contribution from that source. There is no common structure across the UK and hence they range from powerful, multi-functional development bodies, such as Scottish Enterprise or the Welsh Development Agency, to smaller, less well-resourced regional agencies whose activities are mainly related to business development. All of these bodies have some responsibility for attracting overseas investment, and many have overseas representation in the main home countries. They operate under the umbrella of the Invest in Britain Bureau (IBB) which has a loose co-ordinating role for the UK as a whole. Both IBB and the regional agencies have been very active in Japan since the early 1980s.

There were three principal aims underlying the study, the realisation of which determines the contribution which it makes to the existing stock of knowledge in this field:

1. To dissect and illuminate this strategic process in Japanese companies with respect to their manufacturing investment in a major market.
2. To identify pivotal decision areas within what was already known to be a lengthy and complex process.
3. To determine some of the most important relationships between the various location-determining variables.

Since Japanese manufacturing investment in Europe is a relatively recent phenomenon, there has been very little research into the detail of the process within the European context. The context itself is somewhat distinctive in view of the Japanese perceptions of uncertainty associated with EC integration, and the intense inter-country competition for direct investment. By linking the process and the context, the paper thus offers a rather distinctive perspective. Much of this process is closely observed from within economic development agencies whose responsibility it is to follow potential investment projects within the Japanese corporations. However, it is rarely able to be considered in depth in the academic literature due to restrictions on data access, company and government sensitivities.

The paper itself is in three main parts. The first briefly examines the context of Japanese direct investment in Europe over recent years and some of the conceptual considerations underlying it. The second reviews the survey evidence based on locational decisions made by 22 Japanese companies who commenced manufacturing in the European market through establishing a plant in the UK, tying in the economic development agency perspective. The third section considers the findings with a view to drawing conclusions and highlighting some policy implications.

Japanese direct investment in Europe

Strategic environment

Although still relatively small, Japanese manufacturing direct investment in the EC has been growing very rapidly [since 1980] (Trevor, 1983; Dunning and Cantwell, 1991). However, the 1991 data shows that only 22.5 per cent of all Japanese FDI is currently in Europe, as against 48.4 per cent of all US direct investment. These relative positions are important for a number of reasons. Japanese investment is much more recent and it has generally been oriented towards Europe as a whole, not to any particular national market. Moreover, it is largely import substituting investment where many major Japanese companies already have substantial European market shares before they commence manufacturing. For both these reasons it is geared towards gaining the benefits of, and avoiding the potential barriers associated with, European integration. In contrast, since it commenced in volume in the 1950s, US direct investment was initially oriented towards serving a national market and it has been progressively (and often painfully) adjusted and expanded to become fitted for the integrated market. In effect therefore, Europe has emerged as one of the major contested markets for direct investment from these two sources, at a time of dramatic internal economic restructuring and transition.

While there is little doubt that market access and protectionist measures have been a major factor underlying much of Japanese manufacturing investment in Europe, nowhere has this been in sharper relief than in the consumer and industrial electronics fields as the three illustrations in Figure 4.1 demonstrate. The bunching of printer investment decisions in 1987 is particularly striking. Evidence from government investment attraction agencies would confirm that most of these projects had been under consideration for several years before these events triggered off the investment decision. Thereafter many of these companies would plan to be in production in Europe within three to six months. One of the

VCRs

(Potential) European trade restriction		□	⊠				
Decision of Japanese company to start production in Europe		Hitachi/D JVC/UK/D Matsushita/D	Mitsubishi/UK	Alps El/UK Sanyo/D Sharp/UK	Akai El/F Sanyo/UK Toshiba/UK	NEC/UK Orion/UK	Funai/UK Matsushita/F
Year	1981	1982	1983	1984	1985	1986	1987

□   Initiative of the French government ('Poitiers Incident') leads in October 1982 to the effective stopping of all Japanese VCR imports into France.

⊠   The 'Poitiers Incident' is followed by an import limit for Japanese VCR imports into the EC

MATRIX PRINTERS

(Potential) European trade restriction					⊠	▨	
Decision of Tapanese company to start production in Europe			Kyushu Matsushita /UK		Brother/UK Canon/F Citizen/UK Epson/UK NEC/UK Oki/UK Star/UK	NEC/UK Orion/UK	Fujitsu/UK
Year	1983	1984	1985	1986	1987	1988	1989

⊠   Start of anti-dumping proceedings against Japanese manufacturers

▨   Imposition of anti-dumping duties of between 5% and 47%

PHOTOCOPIERS

(Potential) European trade restriction					⊠	▨	
Decision of Japanese company to start production in Europe	Canon/D	Ricoh/UK Canon/F			Matsushita/D Konica/D Toshiba/F	Canon/I Ricoh/F Minolta/D	
Year	1972	1983	1984	1985	1986	1987	1988

⊠   Imposition of anti-dumping duty of 20% against Ricoh in August 1986
Start of further anti-dumping proceedings against Japanese manufacturers
▨   Imposition of anti-dumping duties of between 7.2% and 20%

Figure 4.1 Time comparison of European trade restrictions and decisions of Japanese companies to start production in Europe

earliest examples of protectionist pressure stimulating Japanese production was in the colour TV industry in the 1970s and these became the first products to be manufactured on a large scale by Japanese companies in Europe, with all the leading producers setting up in the UK (Burton and Saelens, 1987).

Manufacturing investment

At 22.2 per cent in 1991, manufacturing is only a relatively small proportion of all Japanese outward investment stock in Europe. 74.4 per cent of the total is in services, with banking and insurance accounting for 39.6 per cent of the total in 1991. Although the asset value of the manufacturing investment is spread over a range of industrial sectors, electronics, electrical equipment and transport equipment dominate. This is even more the case when employment is taken into account and helps to explain why this investment has attracted attention beyond its present size. Of course, this rapidly growing investment, from some 130 manufacturing subsidiaries in the EC in early 1980 to an estimated 676 by 1991, has been most evident in sectors within which Japan has for a long period had competitive and innovation advantages. These advantages had, as noted, been readily exploited by exports. Both the restrictions placed on European imports from Japan and the dramatic yen appreciation have served to accelerate this flow [since 1980]. The currency appreciation weakened Japan's trade competitiveness in low-value-added manufacturing activities, but as Ozawa (1989) notes it had the effect of a major subsidy which resulted both in the transplanting of such industrial activities overseas and in the investing of excess financial capital in foreign securities, real estate and other assets. He regards this as in effect a 'recycling of surplus industries' and one which has inevitably posed major competitive threats to European business.

Geographical distribution

By way of setting the context of this particular study, the geographical distribution of the Japanese FDI stock in Europe is of some importance. The UK has historically dominated and displays a pattern which is reminiscent of that of US direct investment in Europe from the 1960s. Thus, for example, in 1970, 85.1 per cent of Japan's outward FDI stock in Europe was in the UK, a figure which progressively diminished in relative scale to 44.9 per cent by 1980, and 31.3 per cent by 1987, as the investment was diffused throughout Europe.[1] These figures are, of course, dominated by investment in the financial sector and, while the manufacturing relative positions have never been quite as extreme and were much later to develop, the UK has remained a preferred entry point, with Germany a close second. By the early 1990s probably no more than 15 per cent of total Japanese assets in the UK were in the manufacturing sector and probably accounted directly and indirectly for under 3 per cent of the UK manufacturing labour force.

There are two other interesting aspects of Japanese manufacturing in the UK (Dunning, 1986; Oliver and Wilkinson, 1988). Firstly, over 80 per cent of Japanese manufacturing affiliates in the UK are wholly-owned subsidiaries, compared, say, to Italy where the figure is around 40 per cent and France where it is about 60 per cent. One explanation of this lies in the Japanese showing a higher propensity to enter manufacturing by acquisition in some other European countries thus buying in to market share and technology, and being willing, or required, to do so with indigenous partners. This is partly related to industry and partly to country differences. In sectors where Japanese companies are less competitive many prefer to enter Europe through alliances and joint ventures. But there are also country-specific influences at work. Spain is a good illustration of this, where over half of Japanese manufacturing employment is in three large investments by Nisshin Steel (Acinerox), Suzuki (Land Rover Santana) and Nissan (Motor Iberia). In large measure this pattern reflects the peculiarities of Spanish industrialisation, where Spanish companies looked for ventures to import technology and Japanese companies responded, regarding these as the only way in which the restrictive import quotas and high tariff levels could be offset. Equally in France, Japanese investment in the transportation equipment sector has been acquisition led as in the cases of Yamaha's acquisition of MBK Industrie and Honda's taking of a 25 per cent stake in Peugeot Motorcycles. There is every reason to believe that the Japanese preference would be for 100 per cent ownership from both an empirical and theoretical viewpoint (Kujawa, 1986; Buckley and Casson, 1988). Indeed in Europe there is evidence of a progressive movement of Japanese investment in that direction. While Japanese acquisitions and joint ventures have occurred in the UK, for reasons which will be considered later, the major thrust has been wholly-owned new plants. However different this aspect appears, it should be emphasised that only part of the underlying strategy is reflected in ownership patterns and that the main issue is the organisation of contractual networks of all kinds on an EC-wide basis with the objective of supplying the entire unified market from these locations (Yannopoulos, 1990).

Secondly, there is the underlying question as to why the UK was both the first choice for early investments and remains the primary choice for first European manufacturing ventures on the part of many major Japanese companies (Figure 4.2). This is again an issue which has been scrutinised in the literature (Dunning, 1986; Morris, 1988) and upon which some further light is hopefully shed by this paper. All studies report the dominance of protectionist measures in their requirement to

FIRST FULLY-OWNED MANUFACTURING AFFILIATE IN EC[a]				PRODUCTION START, PRODUCT AND COUNTRY OF OTHER FULLY-OWNED MANUFACTURING AFFILIATE
COMPANY	YEAR OF PRODUCTION START	PRODUCT	HOST COUNTRY	
CONSUMER ELECTRONICS				
Matsushita	1974	Colour TVs	UK	numerous affiliates in D, E, B and F
Mitsubishi	1979	Colour TVs	UK	1989 car telephone sets in F; 1991 semiconductors in D
Sanyo	1982	Colour TVs	UK	1984 video recorders in D; 1988 microwaves in UK
Sharp	1985	VCRs	UK	1988 components in UK; 1990 copying machines in F
Sony	1974	Colour TVs	UK	numerous affiliates in D, F, I and A
Toshiba	1981[b]	Colour TVs	UK	1984 semiconductors in D; 1987 VCRs in D; 1990 computers in D
INDUSTRIAL ELECTRONICS				
Brother	1985	Typewriters	UK	1989 components in IRL
Canon	1972	Copiers	D	1983 copying machines in F
Seiko Epson	1988	Printers	UK	1988 printers in F
ELECTRONIC COMPONENTS				
Alps Electric	1985	Components	UK	1988 components in D; 1988 components in IRL
Fujitsu	1981	Semiconductors	IRL	1989 printers in IRL; 1991 semiconductor manufacturing in UK
Hitachi	1981	Semiconductors	D	1982 video recorders in d; 1984 colour TV in UK[c]
NEC	1976	Semiconductors	IRL	1982: semiconductors in UK; 1988 VCRs and printers in UK
ENGINEERING				
Citizen	1974	Watches	D	1988 printers in UK; 1989 NC lathes in D
Komatsu	1985	Construction Equipment	UK	1989 construction equipment in D (acquisition of Hanomag)
TRANSPORTATION EQUIPMENT				
Honda	1988	Engines	UK	1992 cars in UK
Nissan	1984	Cars	UK	various other car parts in the UK
Toyota	1992	Cars and Engines	UK	

Notes: (*a*) Includes only fully-owned affiliates. Host country has to be EC member country at time of location decision.
(*b*) From 1978–80 joint venture with Rank Organisation, in 1980 fully taken over by Toshiba.
(*c*) From 1978–84 joint venture General Electric Corp., in 1984 fully taken over by Hitachi.

A = Austria; B = Belgium; D = Germany; F = France; I = Italy; IRL = Ireland; N = Netherlands; UK = United Kingdom

Figure 4.2   Location of fully owned manufacturing affiliates of most important Japanese employers in the EC

manufacture in Europe, with large domestic markets, lower labour costs, language and consistent Government encouragement in general, aided by specific regional incentive programmes, all being positive features of the UK environment. The nature of the UK market, together with the lack of competitiveness of UK manufacturers of consumer goods may well have been among additional factors to lead to the UK being an effective European springboard. In some cases, however, there has been evidence of buyer pressure leading to decisions on UK manufacturing locations in the television industry (Burton and Saelens, 1987). There is as yet no material evidence to suggest that as the relative position of the UK changes and investment disperses, that it will gain in terms of advanced and high value adding functions through this early role.

This is an issue which is particularly important from an economic development point of view, but about which little is known. Figure 4.2 illustrates the progression of plant development and product diversification within the wholly-owned manufacturing affiliates of some of the largest employing Japanese companies in the EC. The dominant role of the UK as a point of entry emerges in these five industrial sectors, but it is evident that many subsequent manufacturing locations within these companies are in the major markets of Continental Europe, especially France and Germany. From the Japanese company perspective the UK provides both a useful production testing ground and a locus for gaining international operational experience – a commodity in short supply within many of these businesses at the time of entry.

Theoretical context

Since the focus of this paper is exclusively on the processes behind locational decision-making within certain Japanese companies, there is no single theoretical framework within which the study readily fits. Moreover, it is acknowledged that there is a wealth of literature in allied disciplines, such as regional and development economics which is more concerned with the underlying economics of locational decisions. It is, of course, recognised that the location decision is the net outcome of a large number of factors, including the behavioural and evaluative patterns within the organisations concerned. This study is process-oriented, but takes many of these related dimensions into account. There are a number of specific strands in the literature on business decision making to which this survey evidence relates and two groups of these are briefly considered in this section.

Internationalisation

The first concerns the various developments within the theory of internationalisation which have a bearing on these processes. The Uppsala internationalisation model (Johanson and Vahlne, 1977, 1990) which has its theoretical base in both the behavioural theory of the firm and in theory of the growth of the firm, is seen as a process in which the enterprise gradually increases its international involvement. This process evolves in an interplay between the development of knowledge about foreign markets and operations on one hand and an increasing commitment of resources to foreign markets on the other. A distinction is made between state and change aspects of internationalisation, where the former are market commitment and knowledge, and the latter are current business activities and commitment decisions. The presumption of causal cycles linking these two aspects is particularly relevant in this study. Market signals, especially those associated with potential trade restrictions, might be deemed in the short term to alter the state aspects, while change aspects are only impacted in the medium term after a lengthy information collection and evaluation process. This model implies that additional market commitments are made in small steps, with a few exceptions. The proponents of this theory do not foresee a context where the company is in all material respects capable of making larger steps, but does not do so due to both internal and external uncertainty. What they do see, however, is that the firm is a loosely coupled system in which different actors have different interests and ideas concerning its international development. In spite of the distinctiveness of Japanese corporations in many regards, this latter dimension might well underlie aspects of this study, especially in the differential levels of knowledge which exist in overseas sales and corporate offices.

One related theoretical issue is relevant to the processes discussed here. At its root, the strategic challenge for Japanese companies under threat of trade restriction is that of the optimal timing of a foreign direct investment decision. Among the previous considerations of this aspect is the work of Buckley and Casson (1981) who attempt to specify the timing of a switch in the mode of market servicing in terms of the costs of servicing the foreign market, the demand conditions in that market and the growth in the host market. This present study suggests a lengthy contingency planning approach to evaluating the weight which is to be given to these variables such that when the episodic (but predictable) event occurs, the company is able to move quickly to implement a manufacturing solution. Moreover, the trade restriction effect ultimately acts as an overrider which leads to a recalibration of the costs of not servicing the European market, within which existing export sales are already substantial.

Before leaving the perspectives associated with the theory of international business, some brief reference is necessary to the debate as to whether Japanese foreign investment can be explained within conventional theory. The origins of this lie in the premise that early Japanese

FDI displayed different patterns from that of other countries, related to its later take-off, focus on developing countries, on extractive industries, greater propensity to engage in joint ventures and so on. This led to Kojima (1982) and others contesting, *inter alia*, that Japanese-type FDI did not substitute for international trade but complemented it, not least because of his basic theorem that it should originate in the investing country's comparatively disadvantaged (or marginal) industry, which is in turn potentially advantaged in the host country. Some comment will be made later on the 'industry shift' outcome of the processes examined in this study. But at another level Kojima argued that most direct investments between advanced countries were designed to overcome trade barriers and should not be encouraged since (viewed from the perspective of static 'trade effects') they did not generate substantial economic gains to the host country. Of course, the development agency perspective, which is part of the approach in this study, lays greater stress on the dynamic benefits such as employment creation, increased technological capacity and so on which flow from such investments.

Conventional eclectic theory (Dunning, 1988) would reject the Kojima type of approach, and perhaps see the phenomenon underlying the locational decision processes as representing the search for location-specific advantages, expressed in terms of a stable and supportive environment, low labour and transport costs and so on, which could complement the specialist ownership skills developed within Japanese corporations.

Decision-making

The second group of considerations relates to Japanese management practice and especially to the processes of decision-making. This is clearly a vast subject and beyond the scope of this paper. Yet it does underlie any consideration of locational decisions and deserves selective comment from related literature. Kagona, Sakamoto and Johansson (1985) provide an interesting empirical perspective on this. Their work on the strategy formulation processes in Japanese business emphasises continuous in-house resource accumulation and development with a view towards ensuring survival under any type of environmental change; the tendency to distribute risk factors through inter- and intra-organisational networks; and the stress on establishing competitive superiority through inductive, incremental reasoning, seeking superiority in production (rather than in product) strategy. All of these aspects could well proffer explanations for the observations in the next section of this paper.

Closely linked to this is the question about the perceived portability of Japanese competitive advantage. Several studies have noted the particular tension in the matter of localisation and integrated control within Japanese companies. Abo (1989) expresses this as an 'application–adaptation dilemma' whereby the more the company adapts the more difficult it might become to apply their human-related comparative advantages to their subsidiaries. This type of dilemma probably does underlie the cautious, iterative and confirmatory approach to investment decisions such as are implicit within Figure 4.3 (p. 63). Moreover it is important to note that the Japanese investor's globalisation process is different in several regards from that of western multinational companies. It is typically that of the global supplier, based on export-centred global expansion with all systems such as R&D, procurement, sales and marketing, distribution and organisational structure designed to enhance exports of products manufactured in the home country. Nonaka (1990) highlights the massive challenge of changing this as more direct investment is required and views the key concept being one of moving to world-wide organisational information creation as a self-renewing process. It may well be that parts of the evidence picked up in this study represent some of the corporate birth pangs, as they respond to the challenge of a new type of globalisation.

Survey evidence

Methodology

The intention of this study was to trace each of the decision processes from its initiation to the final conclusion, thus attempting to capture all the determinants of the locational decisions. Structured interviews were conducted with senior executives, principally at managing director level, at 22 manufacturing plants, geographically distributed throughout the UK, four in North East England, five in Telford, four in Scotland and nine in Wales; 18 of the companies were in consumer or industrial electronics or related supplier investments, the other four being in engineering. All of the operations were established in the 1980s. In the light of undertakings given to the companies regarding data disclosure, they are not named in this paper. Discussions were also held in Japan with corporate representatives of six of the 18 key electronics investments within the sample, with officials from government and European country investment attraction agencies.

The company interviews were conducted in the second half of 1990 and early in 1991. They were supplemented by a series of discussions with the senior individuals within the four regional development agencies in the UK which were responsible for attracting the investments. All of these decisions involved establishing wholly-owned manufacturing affiliates, but not all constituted truly greenfield investments, although all were start-ups. A characteristic of many Japanese companies who decide to enter UK rapidly in the wake of trade sanctions is that they have often been prepared to convert existing empty factories at minimum cost for first stage assembly operations. The interviews focused primarily on the major household brand name companies, all of whom already had considerable European exports before the commencement of manufacture. Only three of the companies were outside this category and are reflective of the second stage of market development in electronics companies where the original equipment manufacturer prefers, or requires, to encourage a Japanese sub-contractor to set up generally in close proximity to the main plant. As such, this group have a rather constrained set of consequential locational decisions to make. Two of the companies were geared to serving the national market, either because their products had to be delivered to their customers very rapidly in view of market demands, or because, in the case of certain types of photographic material, it was perishable. Apart from these limited cases, all the companies surveyed could in principle have chosen from a very wide range of options to establish production to offset trade sanctions, whether existing or potential. It is these companies which are the primary theme of this section.

Structure of the locational decision process

The evidence from this study points to a process such as that illustrated in a stylised form in Figure 4.3, with three main phases lasting over a period of up to five years, with the time generally being heavily biased towards the first two phases which typically took up to three to four years. In general terms these three phases cover the 'why', 'when' and 'where' of the investment decision, with the 'when' being a major corporate and industry-wide issue. Each of these phases is now examined.

Initial impulse

In any such process it is difficult, if not impossible, to be clear as to precisely who initiates a foreign investment project. This is particularly so in this sample where up to five years may have elapsed before the final decision (Figure 4.3). As Aharoni observed 'the decision results from a

Initial impulse | Discussion phase | Decision phase (Country selection, Country evaluation, Region selection, Regional evaluation)

	Initial Impulse	Discussion phase	Decision phase CS	Decision phase CE / RS / RE
Timescale:	3–5 years from final decision to manufacture.	Lasting up to 3 years.		May last between 1–2 years
Activity focus.	European trade restriction signals interpreted; establishing strategic intentions.	Building corporate consensus; establishing relationships with European governments and their agencies; determination of timing of investment decisions.	Feasibility studies; systematic confirmation and reconfirmation at each of the four parts of this phase.	
Data needs:	Corporate sales impact; trade-related issues, protectionist activity, EC and European country policies.	All trade-related data. Preliminary material to inform country choice collected informally.	Determined by form and content of the company's country evaluation framework – hard and soft data.	Micro-level detail determined by the project(s) under consideration, to cover all operational variables.
Key influence groups:	Corporate–European sales offices; corporate planning and International depts. EC Commission	Corporate–ditto, plus product divisions. Japanese government (MITI). European governments, and in particular the preferred host country's policy-makers.	Corporate – as in discussion phase; plus European project team, including executives with overseas experience. Host government attitudes, professionalism and flexibility of their development agencies. Confirmation on timing from Japanese government (MIT). Japanese reference plants already in Europe.	
Principal outcomes:	Agreement in principle to manufacture overseas	Timing of investment decision; choice of host country in most cases.	Confirmation of preferred host country having reviewed the options from a project-specific perspective.	Choice of particular region and site within which to locate the manufacturing plant. Production start date established, local content programme set out in principle. Response to trade restrictions completed.

Figure 4.3 Main phases of the locational decision process

chain of events, incomplete information, activities of different persons (not necessarily in connection with the particular project), and a combination of several motivating forces, some of them working in favour of such a decision, some against it' (Aharoni, 1966: 55). While this is undoubtedly accurate, it would appear that in the Japanese cases considered, it is at least possible to trace the source of the primary impulse to the European sales offices of the companies, as is suggested in Figure 4.3. Most of these were long established in Europe, regarded as influential and well able to interpret primary and secondary signals which would put pressure on the parent company to consider a European manufacturing project. For example, the 'Poitiers Incident' in 1983, where action by the French government on the port of entry for Japanese electronics products led to a dramatic decline in Japanese VCR imports for several months, proved to be a highly influential event in Japan, simply because it demonstrated just how easy it was to close a major European market to Japanese exporters. On another front, the EC started a survey to investigate anti-dumping charges on VCRs in 1982, and by 1984 10 Japanese VCR plants had been announced for Europe. Similarly, for example, when in 1987 a survey was started on printers, five Japanese plants were initiated that year. It became very clear in the company interviews that only trade sanctions had the force to overcome the strong resistance of the Japanese production engineers to transfer production abroad, although others at a more strategic level were often more open-minded. Discussions with the development agencies in the UK confirmed the intense interest which these companies showed in matters such as the detailed nature, timing and impact of trade sanctions; the detailed capability of the local supply base to operate to Japanese standards, and so on. Such scrutiny from the earliest project development phase reflects the need for thorough investigation as to how domestic competitive advantage could be transferred to Europe, when required (Ishikawa, 1991).

Before leaving this phase, it is interesting to compare the findings of this project with a recent similar study on Japanese investment decision-making processes directed towards investment in the US (Yoshida, 1987). Although facing less pressing trade pressures in view of both the mix and timing of the investments, the marketing and information-gathering role again emerged strongly in providing initial impetus to consider manufacturing. In this case, however, both the data and the range of constituent influence groups appeared to be much wider. This perhaps points to the peculiarity of the nature and time of the European cases under consideration, with EC integration being a powerful, overarching and compelling interest.

Discussion phase

Depending on the reporting structure in the company, the initial impulse from the sales office reaches the corporate level either through the corporate planning or the international department. It is frequently the latter, however, that has the specific responsibility of preparing the corporation for possible trade sanctions, hence it is from this source that initial information is gathered about locational alternatives in Europe. It would appear in the companies studied that the internal dialogue thereafter is usually three-way, involving the European sales office, the international department product division and middle management. In most cases this also involves consultation with Japanese banks, national and regional development agencies in different European countries. The survey evidence suggests that from the outset, even at this early stage, the discussion concentrates only on a few countries. However, there is ample evidence from within development agencies that these early enquiries can readily be misinterpreted in several ways, including failing to recognise that the project is probably not defined in any detail, is perhaps not at all likely to go to several of the countries to whom enquiry is directed for presentational reasons, and is in any event probably three to four years from actually taking place.

Major issues.   From the evidence in this study there are three dominant issues in this lengthy, and often informal, information-collecting phase. Firstly, and at the root of the whole matter, is the question of market size. The presence of sales offices in the large country markets, namely France, Germany and the UK, invariably means that they are part of the consideration. They do not, however, have equal weight in that France is usually developed later and these offices often report through German or UK routes to Japan. Among other factors, this places France at a disadvantage in locational competition as regards manufacturing sites. Secondly, there is the question of the number of Japanese manufacturing affiliates in a country. All the evidence points to Japanese companies having or having had, considerable uncertainties about setting up production facilities in Europe. It came over very powerfully in this project. Equally, experience within development agencies highlights the important part played by role models of companies with manufacturing plants already in a country. The potential investor will normally wish to examine these from every possible aspect, both at home and in the prospective manufacturing location. It is not unusual for this to happen, even where the Japanese companies are direct competitors in the same product market, plan to use a common supplier base and perhaps even recruit in the same labour pool. From an investment attraction agency perspective, this is not without its problems, not least because it is difficult to put into practice where there are few existing investments. In short it is one of the forces which contributes to the agglomeration of Japanese investment in Europe, and which in this sample ensured that the UK was under consideration as an option from the earliest stage in all cases.

The third issue which emerged in this study is that of country visibility through vigorous marketing efforts directed to major Japanese companies. A number of countries emerge as being included in the preliminary data collection phase for that reason even where they have neither a large home market or a significant number of manufacturing affiliates. Holland and Ireland were among the examples given, not least perhaps because active promotional efforts are perceived to indicate governmental support for investors.

The process by which these three influences interact during the discussion phase is clearly complex. The push of the trade sanctions, and pull of market size and growth are reinforced in a variety of ways. Important among these appears to be the determination and consistency shown by European governments and their agencies in keeping close to the company, providing all the information required with both speed and accuracy. More intangible, but nonetheless real, is the confidence that is built up by this process which amounts to a political interest in, and identity with, a project which may be regarded by the corporate management as being of higher risk than normal. In effect therefore both sets of interests coincide, the one inherently interested in European job generation, the other in securing explicit economic and implicit political assistance to implement its strategy towards Europe. Both fully realise that they are engaged in two different types of competitive process, but with a common interest. For these reasons in the majority of the locational decisions reviewed in this study, the companies had already developed a consensus about national and regional preferences during the discussion phase.

Home government involvement.   There is, however, another powerful set of players operating throughout this process, namely the Japanese government and its agencies, although some companies are evidently more open to such influences than others. The encouragement of outward foreign direct investment has continued to serve as an outlet for pressures building up in both the domestic Japanese economy (through rising wage rates, maturing industries and a rising cost base for exporters) and overseas through trade friction. In effect, Japanese policy towards outward investment has long been closely linked with its strategic goals for domestic industrial restructuring. Not only does the government (via MITI) play a critical role in the interpretation of the nature and timing of trade pressures which will trigger off direct investment decisions, it has also at times acted to regulate the flow and sequence of investment decisions made in Europe. Most UK development agencies cite examples of this. In one case a lesser known consumer electronics company, which specialised in producing branded products for European distributors and large US retailers, had gone through all the search processes for a European location, made an announcement to that effect, but finally rescinded its decision to enter Europe under 'advice' from Japanese government agencies. It had apparently failed to consult adequately and it was felt that their European investment decision was premature and would put undesirable pressure on other major companies to act before they were ready. More frequently reported by investment agencies are instances where trade and investment policy dialogue with government delays announcements until it is considered the project has appropriate domestic support, especially in the case of strategically significant projects in sectors such as automobiles and semiconductors.

Such action has, of course, to be seen in the context of the extensive experience which the Japanese government has had of major political contention over trade matters from the 1960s onward in industries such as textiles, automobiles, telecommunications equipment and semiconductors (Destler and Sato, 1982). While many of these were trade related and in the USA, the cumulative experience has undoubtedly led to successive Japanese governments making substantial inputs into European market decisions involving foreign direct investment. These inputs range from publishing strategic industry studies, drawing together consultative groups, informal briefing, to more direct advice on market conditions.

It is, of course, difficult to trace the exact nature of political pressures on the emergence of a corporate consensus on locational decisions. What did emerge from the interviews was that there was a link between the strength of the influence which the Japanese government and its agencies had on decisions and the degree of centralised decision-making within the corporation. For example, in some of the largest and oldest *Keiretsu*, the corporate level has a particularly strong influence over product divisions. Moreover such companies often employ former government officials in high executive office, and thereby have particularly strong links with government thinking and processes. Conversely, in more decentralised models, the interests of the product division, specifically with reference to production, appeared to dominate the locational decision. In some of the cases, the production priorities had apparently been over-ruled on occasion in order to make a contribution to better EC-Japanese trade relations.

Decision phase

Under the pressure of trade sanctions of one form or another, the company subsequently enters the decision phase which stretches over one or two years (Figure 4.3), less if the pressure is greater or if other compelling factors intervene. At this stage a project team of between three and 10 people is established to conduct feasibility studies. Most of these last 6–12 months. The teams would frequently consist of members drawn from the corporate planning and international departments, together with representatives of the product division concerned. It is quite common for several product divisions within the same company to be undertaking feasibility studies simultaneously without any apparent linkage or contact between them. These teams would normally contain a member with international operating experience. In the case of European decisions, this would often be an executive with production experience in the USA (or more rarely in Europe) and this individual would not only play a key role in the balance of judgment on location, but frequently would be sent to establish the new European manufacturing plant. Equally, when a second European production plant is planned, usually in another country as Figure 4.1 shows, the managing director of the first plant invariably plays a key role in this locational decision.

Country selection and evaluation.   In terms of these two related activities, most of the companies in this sample declared that they had already developed a preference for the UK by the time they entered this phase. However, one of the explicit responsibilities of the feasibility team is to contribute to the process of confirming that preference through a range of actions. Firstly, there is the detailed examination of all the options. In none of the 22 cases did a company include more than five European countries in this part of the analysis. In addition to the UK, Germany was selected in almost all instances, while France, Holland and Ireland were the most regular alternatives. Spain and Portugal were included in only one case where a very labour intensive product was involved. Otherwise no other European country appeared to have been considered, an issue of some importance given that a number of others have ambitions to attract more Japanese investment.

Secondly, in order to evaluate the selected countries, the team defines the most important locational determinants, initially based on the information accumulated during the discussion phase. At this level, it emerged that there is generally no specific consideration of sites or other detailed locational matters. The methodology adopted clearly varies from company to company.

Figure 4.4 presents a typical evaluation from one of the sample companies where four countries were under review and nine critical aspects were highlighted. Inevitably this type of approach is open to all kinds of interpretation and different weightings are given according to company preferences. Part of the skill of the investment attraction agency is to understand these during the discussion phase and make sure that at the very least they are based on solid information and correctly interpreted. This study suggested that the country evaluations were both simple and subjective, but that they were regarded as a basic tool to force the feasibility team to evaluate the different countries with regard to the factors which had, by consensus, been established as critical.[3] It was interesting to note that at this stage none of the companies attempted to compare different locations by setting up financial projections, this type of exercise being only regarded as meaningful at the project-specific level.[4]

The principal reasons for investing in the UK in this set of companies emerged as had been previously reported in other studies (Dunning, 1986; Morris, 1988). At the country selection level, English language,

ASPECT	UK	GERMANY	FRANCE	NETHERLANDS
Labour availability	8	7	7	7
Wage level	9	6	8	6
Labour unions	8	8	8	8
Supporting industries	9	8	6	7
Support of Development Agency	10	7	4	7
Investment incentives	6	9	8	8
Language	10	7	4	8
Feelings against Japanese	8	7	3	7
Presence of other Japanese manufacturers	8	7	4	4
Total score	**76**	**66**	**52**	**62**

Figure 4.4   Country evaluation

labour supply and costs, together with a welcoming and supportive attitude by government and its agencies emerged as the three dominant issues. Since most of the companies had production facilities in the USA, the presence of production engineers with international experience and English language ability was regarded as critical. A major practical outcome of this was seen to be in the importance of process technology and on-going technology transfer from Japan, which placed a premium on the ability to communicate at shop floor level. On the labour side, the supply and cost profile led the UK to score well compared to Germany and the Netherlands in these cases, while in terms of UK regions, the skill base, unemployment levels and lower wage rates in northern parts of the country were an element in the overall review. The relevance of supportive attitudes on the part of all government authorities was emphasised in the previous section.

The strength of these factors and the overall balance of advantage which a UK location was deemed to hold, apparently made it relatively easy to reach a decision in its favour within most of the companies in this study. In the majority of cases the country selection and evaluation phases led to the choice of UK without considering specific sites in other European countries. This is somewhat surprising from the position of investment attraction agencies where there is often a perception (which may be fostered) that the company maintains specific alternatives in other European countries in order to strengthen their bargaining power when seeking government financial assistance. Only in some of the larger investments did the companies appear to keep the country issues open until the final parts of the decision phase, comparing specific sites in different countries.

Before leaving the country-level considerations, some comment is necessary on the German dimension. A further component of this overall project consisted of an examination of locational processes leading to the choice of entering Europe through production in Germany, since the two countries are in close competition. These results will be reported separately but the two major factors which were shown to have had a bearing on the German choice are important. The first relates to the fact that in many of the German cases the international experience of the company was almost exclusively centred around their sales organisations, with relatively little on either the production side or at corporate level. In such circumstances the role of the European sales offices in the decision phase is much more critical, the largest and most influential of which are often located in Germany. In short, a different set of circumstances points to the requirement to set up production close to the international experience which resides within the sales offices. Moreover, in some of the cases the manufacturing facilities were not established as separate legal entities, but as parts of the sales company with the head of sales being in effect head of the production unit, assisted by production engineers from Japan. The second factor points to political considerations underlying the discussion about alternative European locations. In some of the German cases the objective of seeking to influence EC trade policy by locating centrally in one of the most important EC member countries had become a dominant consideration. For such companies, which were characterised by strong corporate control of their product divisions, France and Germany emerged as the preferred European countries.

Regional selection and evaluation. Following the country choice, the next stage of Figure 4.3 is at the regional level. In terms of selecting regions, none of the companies interviewed included more than five, and once again the visibility of the region in the Japanese market determined its chances of being selected. The two factors which seemed to determine this were, not surprisingly, the number of Japanese manufacturing affiliates (hence Northern England, Scotland and Wales were included in almost every case) and the existence of determined marketing efforts over a long period of time. The extent and complexity of the discussion phase gives investment attraction agencies many opportunities to build long term relationships. It was evident from the interviews that this existed in the case of the three regions noted, and in the new towns of Telford and Milton Keynes, all of which have clusters of Japanese manufacturing plants. While, of course, the UK government has national representation in the form of the Invest in Britain Bureau (IBB), such was the strength of established regional links that only two of the interviewed companies used this route to get in touch with suitable regions. Even in these instances, the search was limited to areas in which Japanese investors were already present.

The final stage of this process involves the micro-level examination of each of the selected regions to determine which of these will provide the optimum production base. In this study the companies were all located in development areas, as is the case for the majority of Japanese manufacturing plants in the UK. They were therefore dealing with agencies with considerable experience of both corporate decision-making processes and their locational preferences. At one level, as regards desired sites or factory space, levels of government financial assistance associated with development areas, proximity to reference plants of other Japanese manufacturers and so on, the locational options have many things in common. They are therefore frequently differentiated from the company's viewpoint by the professionalism of the development agency in terms of the total package of service which they can bring to a particular project or by some special circumstance which points to one region or another. Evidence elsewhere confirms this (Haigh, 1989). Among the latter is the often unspoken agenda as to whether the UK government has any preference as to where they locate their plant; or whether there will be any particular difficulties of their being welcomed by local business in general.

In approaching this phase, the feasibility team normally has an elaborate catalogue of criteria which are applied to the evaluation of proposed sites. Evidence from both companies and development agencies confirm the diversity of data needs and the thoroughness with which its collection is pursued. The range frequently stretches from the probability of earthquakes to the local bus schedules on Sundays, and into many other areas of life. In this sample, three areas of dominant interest emerged, with the first of them being labour. This is an area which is consistently evaluated by most Japanese feasibility teams in considerable detail. Many are interested in recruiting young people with low salary demands, this being one of the reasons why the age structure of new towns is attractive. Of particular concern to Japanese feasibility teams is the question of high labour turnover rates which they understandably regard as posing serious problems for the continuous improvement of manufacturing efficiency and thus impairing their ability to transfer products and technology into new plants. For all these reasons areas of high unemployment, within which there is a demonstrable high level of skill and trainable labour available, are attractive. Moreover, these characteristics are seen as associated with low levels of mobility and as providing a base for building a high degree of employee loyalty.[5]

The second area of consistent interest with the companies interviewed was the availability of quality suppliers. Here the context of trade pressures and very significant levels of exports to Europe have to be particularly borne in mind. This expresses itself in various ways when the final locational choices are being made. For example, there is often a premium on moving into production as rapidly as possible. But there is also strong pressure to begin to address European local content requirements from an early date, and hence to identify and qualify as many sub-contract suppliers as possible. Although cast at an EC level, the early intensity in this search in many consumer and industrial electronics products is in the regional economy.

Figure 4.5 provides an illustration of the build up of a Japanese VCR plant in the UK over a seven-year period from its inception. Several aspects are worth noting in the three stage transition from an assembly plant to one where the highly specialised and sophisticated engineering and production skills existed for the in-house manufacture of drum cylinders. The transition was gradual and cautious, but it was combined with rapid product and process technology change at all times. Of particular importance in this context is the major effort in years two to four to accelerate local sourcing in order to raise local content. The final push in years four to seven in this type of project invariably has to be in-plant, but the importance of the surrounding suppliers to the first and second phases cannot be over-emphasised. In this regard the development agencies play a particularly active role, including the conducting of extensive component sourcing studies for the planned product range in some cases. The suppliers are not only evaluated with regard to their current products, but specifically with their regard to their willingness to co-operate with the Japanese company in manufacturing parts to Japanese standards. It is commonly reported by development agencies and suppliers that the rigours of this process are often far beyond those faced when sub-contractors are accustomed to complying with non-Japanese standards. Equally these agencies report the Japanese companies

	Year	Local plant activity	Component/source
Stage 1	1	VCR assembly	PCBs, drivers, decks imported from Japan. European content (inc. labour) 30–35%[1]
Stage 2	2	Deck assembly-pilot	Main source Japan
	2–4	Local sourcing of components	European content to 50% in Year 4
	3	PCB assembly introduced	
	5	Full deck assembly	
	6	Automatic PCB assembly	
Stage 3	7	Drum cylinder production	European content 60–65% depending on product

Note: [1] There is considerable controversy about the measurement of European content. Japanese industry tends, for example, to include assembly labour costs of imported parts and components, local transportation costs, etc. and thus overstate 'real' local content.
Source: Company data.

Figure 4.5 Japanese VCR plant development

as seeking political support for a gradual approach towards meeting local content requirements.

The intense interest in quality suppliers has to be viewed in a wider context. This company sample reflects the stage of Japanese multinationalism involving high income-oriented assembly industries, specifically electronics goods. In such industries the export advantages of Japanese companies are highly dependent on a multi-layered system of subcontracting from which final assemblers and their parts suppliers mutually gain in productivity growth and technological improvement. As Ozawa expresses it, how to transplant this vertical industrial system is therefore the most critical strategic consideration for Japanese industry (Ozawa, 1991). The issue is therefore not only one of making an individual investment successful, but rather how a whole industry can be effectively multinationalised. Some of the sensitivities in this set of interviews reflect the fact that these were still early-stage investments, many of them pre-dating the subsequent investments of lead suppliers.

The final issue to emerge at regional level is the availability of support, whether financial or non-financial. Since the companies in this sample chose to locate in development areas and were generally making comparisons as between such areas the governmental financial assistance is only one part of the equation. In any event, the rules governing such assistance are such as to preclude one UK development area out-bidding another in direct financial assistance in order to attract an investor from whatever source. Japanese companies do, however, drive a hard bargain at the regional level as development agencies confirm, and seek as much financial assistance as possible to offset the start up costs and perceived production risks. It was interesting to note, however, that the emphasis from the company interviews was placed much more on differences in non-financial support, the area of differentiation upon which development agencies are able to concentrate by flexible use of their powers, close public and private sector collaboration in encouraging a project, and by drawing on political support at regional level. This support can range over many areas such as recruitment, housing, infrastructure, suppliers, and so on. Characteristically the interviews highlighted the strength of personal relations at a regional level which were deemed by many of the companies to have been a material, and ultimately a decisive, influence on the final choice of location (Vogel, 1979; Clark, 1987).

Earlier mention was made of the ways in which all the processes in Figure 4.3 are designed in the Japanese company context to confirm and reconfirm perspectives and decisions in order to build a consensus.

In some cases the whole of the feasibility study within the decision phase is designed to confirm a decision which has already been made in principle. In others the regional dimension is more open. It is not uncommon for the feasibility work to be undertaken by a team which divides into two or three with each of these sub-teams conducting their visits to the region separately as they pursue quite different agendas. There may, for example, be a marketing, sales and logistics group whose dominant interests concern supplying Europe as a whole from any given production base; a production team whose interests are confined to all aspects of efficient manufacturing; and a finance team who handle detailed costs and negotiate the framework for government financial assistance. These groups frequently appear to start from very little prior detailed knowledge of the region and on occasion frustrate development agencies by apparently not sharing information. All such processes have to be regarded as part of the development of consensus which ultimately emerges, perhaps up to three or four months after feasibility work is completed. The Japanese system of intensive discussion (*Newamashi*) and the circulation of decisions throughout the company (*Ringi*) are clearly part of the final determination of locational decisions. In the case of direct investment decisions the evidence here and elsewhere points to much of this being centralised at headquarters' level, but as was observed earlier there are distinct variations within this model.

Conclusion and policy implications

In the pursuit of the three objectives set out in the Introduction, this paper has concentrated on the processes of locational decision-making within Japanese companies in a distinctive sector and at a particularly critical time. The 22 investments concerned, with one exception, are characteristic of the third phase of Japanese manufacturing expansion, involving assembly-based, sub-contracting dependent, mass production. The FDI decisions examined were on the whole made reluctantly and as a second best, defensive solution to maintain market shares. The lengthy and complex processes underlying the decision to manufacture can probably be attributed to several variables. The first is the normal procedure of building consensus within Japanese hierarchies. The second may be specifically connected to the sources of competitive advantage for Japanese industry in the sectors concerned which were in the past largely home-based and linked to both local markets and local industries. Sub-contract relationships, quality and inventory control systems, rapid and demanding consumer response to product changes, vigorous commercialisation of new technologies and so on, all fall into these categories. Acting together these factors probably account for much of the preparatory diligence and for the investment clustering within specific assisted regions of the UK. Equally they explain the consequent pressures on lead suppliers to move in tandem with their principal customers. The third variable is the nature and timing of protective measures against Japanese exports to Europe, and the desire on the part of companies and the Japanese government for collective action in response. The final issue is that of the shortage of international production experience within the major corporations concerned, which adds to the risk aversion.

Many of the aspects of the decision process which have emerged in this study are consistent with the principles outlined in the theory section. For example, much of the evidence underlying Figure 4.3 is reflective of the iterative approach set out in the Uppsala model and it has much to do with the balance of judgement which is exercised by a Japanese corporate entity about the optimal timing of a foreign investment decision. While the study was not designed to address the Kojima-eclectic theory debate, it proffers more evidence to support the latter than the former with the emphasis on the long term search for location-specific advantages within the European market.

Any study of this type of process has to be undertaken with humility in view of the many different forces at work, and in the light of the difficulties of corporate access and disclosure. The perspective of the development agencies assists in providing a counter balance to the company evidence, and a further interpretation of a process which it is their business to attempt to understand. The importance of their role clearly emerges in the study, with some lessons for governments in Europe who aim to gain a greater share of this investment. A long term and patient commitment of resource is required, combined with a close knowledge of the potential customer's strategic interests and operational needs. But this study should not be interpreted out of context, in that it is not easy to distinguish the role of such bodies in promoting the UK as a whole as distinct from their regional interests during the lengthy discussion phase. Clearly most companies had chosen the UK from among a number of European options before the final decision phase, within which the competitive arena for investment attraction became intra-UK. In any event, any European country wishing to benefit from this wave of investment as part of their own industrial restructuring would have to take a long term view of the opportunity in the light of this evidence. Moreover, they would probably have to carefully define the level of 'customer care' which they are willing to offer to Japanese investors, given that the UK experience has witnessed further developments in the co-ordination of existing and the provision of new services, such as those related sub-contracting, with others, such as advanced factory space, being fostered to meet the requirements of this particular type of investor. They would also, of course, have to form a view about the long term impact of investment attraction strategy directed towards Japan, an issue outside the scope of this particular study (Eltis, 1992; Strange, 1993).

The policy implications of this study can be examined at four different levels. Firstly, there is the EC dimension where it could be deemed that the signals associated with market access were interpreted as intended, and the desired outcome ensued. Compliance was reluctant, and at a slow pace if the total time frame within Figure 4.3 is borne in mind. Moreover, given the role of regional financial incentives, some of the compliance costs were borne by EC members. There is little doubt that stronger or different signals would have been accommodated within the processes outlined and the end result could have been achieved earlier. Secondly, there is the question of the relevance of this study for European governments. It adds fuel to the debate about the preference for the UK which greenfield Japanese investment has tended to show within Europe. But it should be recalled that it is based on the evidence of companies who actually chose a UK location. At the very least, however, it emphasises that for this type of investment there is not a 'level playing field' within Europe, for reasons which were noted and which seem to have more to do with attitudes and environment than with other variables, such as financial incentives. This leads to the third level, namely that of economic development agencies. From this evidence countries should brief their investment attraction agencies to pay considerable care to the market segments which they target within the Japanese economy, since some waves of investment have a very restricted horizon in terms of country-specific locational choices. In short, significant resources can readily be devoted to attracting investment to a country where the probabilities for success are almost negligible. The final set of policy conclusions concerns the Japanese companies themselves. They are already well aware of the considerable competition to attract their projects, and of the fact that they are being wooed from many quarters. Equally, they are sensitive to the criticism of investments being clustered, and of the bias of certain major manufacturing investments to the UK. It is inevitable that this focus will change, as Japanese investment is distributed more evenly across the major EC markets and as more international production experience is accumulated. In that context, the lessons for them would be to be proactive in that direction, and at an early date.

Notes

1. This is well illustrated in the case of Sony who, having established their first European greenfield operation at Bridgend, Wales, in 1974, now have plants in France, Spain, Germany, Austria and Italy. It should be noted, however, that the aggregate data quoted here have to be interpreted with considerable care. For example, some Japanese investments in the Middle East have been undertaken through UK contractors and thus the data may overstate the true UK position. For a more detailed consideration of this issue see Burton and Saelens (1986).
2. It should be recalled that these are usually large departments by Western standards and often play a distinctive role in major developments, see for example, Campbell N, Goold M and Kase K (1990).
3. The attempt to quantify issues which are essentially qualitative is frequently encountered at this stage of foreign investment decision-making, irrespective of the country of origin. On this issue see, for example, Kelly and Philippatos (1982). For a consideration of how such qualitative measures apply in general to planning in Japanese companies see Rehfeld (1990).
4. This is consistent with the findings of Yoshida (1987: 68–9), on the nature of decision rules.
5. It is interesting to note that labour-related issues dominated the feasibility study phase in the US work of Yoshida (1987: 52).

5
Strategic Evolution within Japanese Manufacturing Plants in Europe: UK Evidence (1994)*

Neil Hood, Stephen Young and David Lal

Introduction

Although still relatively small, Japanese manufacturing investment in the EC has been growing very rapidly [since the mid-1980s]. It has been largely import-substituting investment, oriented towards Europe as a whole rather than to any particular national market. For both these sets of reasons it has been geared towards gaining the benefits of, and avoiding the potential barriers associated with, European economic integration. In terms of geographical location, the UK has historically dominated as a preferred entry point for Japanese foreign direct investment (FDI) in manufacturing, with Germany a close second. The background to this has been extensively examined in the literature (Dunning, 1986; Oliver and Wilkinson, 1988; Hood and Truijens, 1993).

The particular purpose of this paper is to explore the relationship between the strategic intentions behind the establishment of manufacturing plants in Europe and the directions in which these plants have evolved. It is evident that the timing of much of this investment activity reflects the threat of EC protectionist measures against selected Japanese imports, and that in most cases it is designed to protect existing market shares already held prior to the commitment to a manufacturing presence. As such, the investments are invariably strategic and long term,

* *International Business Review*, 3 (2) (1994), 97–122. © 1994 Elsevier Science Ltd. All rights reserved.

yet are often undertaken in the uncertainty as to how manufacturing competitive advantage can be transferred into Europe (Hood and Truijens, 1993; Burton and Saelens, 1987). The UK government and its regional development organisations have consistently pursued supportive policies to assist this transition for all foreign investors, and there is little doubt that these have been material in establishing the high UK market share of Japanese FDI. Since the early 1980s several UK regions have benefited from this inflow, and the empirical component of this paper is based on one of these, namely on data collected from Japanese manufacturing plants operating in Scotland.

While there is a growing body of academic literature on Japanese investment in Europe, the link between the underlying strategies of the parent companies, plant characteristics, plant performance and the evolution of the manufacturing operation as a whole has not been widely examined. In part this is because of the recent date of entry of the companies, but it is also because this issue is difficult to study without considerable assistance from them. In the case of this project, it was possible to bring two perspectives to most of the cases, namely that of the company at plant level and that of the development agency which had been closely involved in attracting the investors and which had therefore had extensive discussions at the company headquarters level in Japan regarding European strategy. The survey which forms the core of this paper was thus undertaken with the following objectives in mind:

1. To determine the characteristics of a recently established sample of Japanese manufacturing subsidiaries.
2. To relate these to the strategic intentions of the parent, as revealed at both corporate and plant level.
3. To identify the development path along which each plant has pro-gressed, especially in the light of the performance criteria which had been set for it.

In pursuit of these issues, this paper is in four main parts. The first briefly considers some contextual characteristics of Japanese FDI in Europe. The second reviews a selection of the relevant academic literature which has a bearing on this issue, and in particular that related to subsid-iary strategies, subsidiary development, and performance evaluation. The following section sets out the methodology and findings of the company survey; thereafter conclusions and policy implications are drawn out in the final section.

Japanese direct investment in Europe

At one level, Japanese manufacturing investment in Europe is both recent and reluctant (Trevor, 1983; Dunning and Cantwell, 1991). It has lagged behind that in the USA to a considerable degree (Yoshida, 1987). Its timing, distribution and scale can be attributed to the three interdependent motivating factors of globalisation, countering trade friction and the comparative advantage of local production (Kume and Totsuka, 1991). While the asset value of manufacturing is spread over a range of industrial sectors, electronics, electrical equipment and transport equipment dominate on both an asset and employment basis.

Much of the context in which this investment has occurred would lead to the expectation of Japanese investors having little to fear as they plan to commence manufacturing in Europe. Yet it is evident that the locational decision making process is a lengthy and deliberate one, within which the parent companies record uncertainties of many kinds (Hood and Truijens, 1993). Evidence from investment attraction agencies in Europe would emphasise this in several ways. For example, relatively few of the Japanese corporations commencing manufacturing in Europe have experience of production of any kind within that environment. Indeed several would claim to lack international production experience in western economies as a whole, although most have some executives who have set up plants in the USA. For these, and associated cultural reasons, Japanese companies are among the most rigorous when it comes to the evaluation of an investment environment for manufacturing, paying meticulous attention to each detail which could affect plant performance; and conscious of the corporate responsibility to supply their own marketing systems with quality products. Two of the most common elements of this which are both consistently reported concern the quality and adaptability of the labour force and the capabilities of sub-contractors. In short, there is consistent evidence from attraction agency sources that the fulfilment of the strategic intention of local manufacturing has the highest priority once decisions have been made; and specifically that the achievement of local content requirements to ensure recognition as being technically a European product, together with market acceptance on grounds of quality, are the early twin peaks of achievement.

Multinational enterprise strategy and subsidiary development

The strategies underlying the successes of Japan's world-class firms, her *Kaisha*, have of course been the subject of much study and have generated many different theoretical approaches. Smothers (1990), for example, identifies three components of a meta-pattern of Japanese strategies. These are knowledge-based strategies within which there is a constant drive to make better products and, thereby, to create value; alliance-based strategies formed with both external and internal stakeholders, but not with competitors, in order to create mutual gains and to decrease overhead control costs; and productivity-based strategies, where productivity gains are a top-priority goal at all times. For some time it has become clear to observers of Japanese business that one of its distinctive features lies in its ability to consistently combine and implement groupings of strategies, described for example by Kotler, Fahey and Jatusripitak (1985) as 'sequence market development'; and by Abegglen and Stalk (1986) as a 'winner's competitive cycle'. Smothers (1990) and others see this as a sequenced and combined framework, expressed in terms such as 'deploy, improve, redeploy' in a manner which suggests systematic patterns of behaviour. In these terms the strategies considered in this paper reveal elements of all three of the basic strategic components considered above, within a timeframe where the companies involved have been redeploying resources overseas.

This study has therefore to be viewed in this context, as providing an insight into a continually developing strategic process within which the (largely) new decision to redeploy resources into European manufacturing has been recently initiated and is in its formative years. The rather narrower aim of this particular section is, however, to establish an empirical base of related academic work in order to allow the proper interpretation of the findings of this study. As a starting point, the evidence on the types of subsidiary roles which MNEs specify for their operations is critical, since these provide tangible evidence of the implementation of grand strategies towards the European market. Thereafter some comment is made on the trajectories of subsidiary development, especially in the light of what is known about Japanese subsidiaries. The final part of this section briefly considers the measurement of subsidiary performance since this is one of the fundamental determinants of the strategic evolution of units within any multinational enterprise (MNE) network.

Subsidiary strategies

As regards the classification of subsidiary strategies, a model developed in Canada by White and Poynter (1984) has been shown to be of relevance in the setting of MNE strategies within the UK and directed towards European market penetration (Young, Hood and Dunlop, 1988). The model (see Appendix 1, p. 105) identifies five basic subsidiary groupings ranging (in terms of product and market franchise, and plant managerial maturity) from the marketing satellite to the strategic independent. The details of the alternative strategies will be considered at a later stage. It is sufficient in this section to suggest that the global strategic intentions of companies will to some considerable degree be reflected in the subsidiary strategies of their manufacturing units. Clearly this relationship may not always be a direct one. It is however more likely to be the case in recent Japanese affiliates given the trade environment in which they have been established and recalling the existing European market shares of many of the Japanese brands concerned. This working assumption was thus made in the design of the company survey and the White and Poynter (1984) framework was utilised.

There is much evidence to suggest that whatever the subsidiary strategy chosen at point of entry to Europe, the progression towards higher value added and more integrated plant structures in Japanese manufacturing investments in Europe will be much dependent on local sourcing. In the terminology used above, this points to an extension of alliance-based strategies. Thus initial assembly operations are transferred, followed by component part suppliers (Dunning and Cantwell, 1991), while quality, availability and continuity of supply will be critical determinants of localisation programmes and key success factors for the operations as a whole (Oliver and Wilkinson, 1988; Ozawa, 1991). It is evident, however, that the pressure for local sourcing within Europe, principally for local content and supply chain efficiency reasons, has to be balanced against an opposite force pulling towards global sourcing. In effect this is part of the tension of implementing productivity-based strategies on a global scale.

There has been considerable academic debate about the global–local sourcing balance, most of which is outwith the scope of this paper. For the purposes of this study on the strategic evolution of manufacturing plants, there are however two aspects which are of importance. The first concerns the strategic linkages between product policy and manufacturing which is acknowledged to lie at the heart of much of Japanese manufacturing competitiveness and would be expected to feature considerably in the planning of subsidiary development. Some of the work which has been undertaken on strategic linkages has emerged out of studying Japanese FDI. For example, Kotabe (1990), examining European and Japanese MNEs in the USA showed that, although they were not yet engaging in outsourcing as extensively as US firms, a negative relationship was suggested between outsourceability and the magnitude of process innovations by the foreign multinationals. This is a tentative, but interesting finding, and of importance for this study. At one level it poses a series of questions as to whether the Japanese FDI focus on outsourcing at new locations is only a relatively short-term one, or whether their capacity to manage these processes and maintain product innovation far exceeds that of their competitors, irrespective of the mix of global production and sourcing locations.

The second aspect of global–local sourcing balance concerns the ability of any production location (in this case, the UK) selected by a Japanese MNE to support the local component of its chosen strategy. In view of the fact that Japanese FDI in the UK mainly dates from the mid 1980s and that Japanese manufacturers have effectively passed on their EC local content pressures to their supply base, this appears to have been a critical locational determinant (Hood and Truijens, 1993). The nature of Japanese buyer–supplier relations has, of course, been widely studied, including ways in which these have been adapted to western contexts (Morris and Imrie, 1991). The process of adjustment within the UK to the rigorous standards set by Japanese companies has not always been easy. There is now consistent evidence that this has improved considerably in the UK through extensive collaboration programmes of supplier development supported by corporate and public interests (Trevor and Christie, 1988; Morris and Imrie, 1991). As will be observed in the empirical section, much attention has been given to this by the sample companies and it is regarded as a central factor in determining market share retention, volume growth, product transfer to Europe, and so on.

Subsidiary development

The discussion in the last few paragraphs has explored only one set of variables which might exert an influence on the development path of a particular manufacturing facility. There are clearly many others and it is evident that plants progress through different roles within categorisations such as that of White and Poynter (1984), and others. This issue is considered in greater detail in the empirical section, since it is central to the subject matter of this paper. At this stage two related matters are examined, namely an illustration of plant progression as provided by Sony and a broader consideration of the early characteristics of Japanese manufacturing plants in the UK. Both will aid the interpretation of the survey data.

Table 5.1 sets out the Sony model for its European manufacturing in broad terms as declared by the company. It is important not to infer a causal relationship between these stages, since it is evident that many factors will influence the direction and timing of such progressions.

Table 5.1 Sequence of Sony manufacturing in Europe

---

1. Export of knock-down kits for local assembly
2. Moves to local manufacture with some procurement of electrical and mechanical components
3. Certain design facilities localised, so that local components can be designed into products
4. Total design in Europe and manufacturing moves to a just-in-time (JIT) philosophy. As a result a R&D centre is required
5. Specialisation by plant within Europe, controlled by Sony Europe HQ

Source: MD, Sony UK Ltd (1988).

Moreover, it may not always be possible to infer a common pattern even within any one company, or in any location. For example, trade restriction and local content issues have strongly influenced many companies, including Sony, in the way they have developed their European plants. Nor is it possible to infer that any given plant facility will be given the opportunity to progress along the route to full integration. Much more will be said on this issue in the survey section, with reference to the White and Poynter (1984) framework.

Relatively little work has been undertaken in the UK by way of longer-term comparisons of strategic development and plant evolution. One such (Dunning, 1985) provides some relevant context for this study. Dunning examined the similarities and contrasts between US manufacturing affiliates in the UK in the early 1950s and those from Japan in the early 1980s. Among the points to emerge was that the Japanese affiliates exercised closer influence and control over general managerial philosophy and style than did their US counterparts in the 1950s, this being partly a function of type of activity, pattern of ownership and age of affiliate. Dunning expressed the view that it was perhaps largely due to the more holistic approach adopted by the Japanese to decision making. For example, the US subsidiaries had more freedom to introduce new products or adapt existing ones; however, there was less insistence in the meeting of the quality standards in the US case. The lack of any willingness to compromise on such matters, together with rigid standards and inspection procedures at all levels in the value added chain were marked features of the Japanese plants. By way of an overview, Dunning concluded that, while both waves of investment were mainly import substituting, the perceived asset advantages of the two groups were different and strongly reflected in the contemporary comparative advantage of the resource endowments of the home country.

He drew attention to the fact that the Japanese investment in the UK was part of a consciously planned regional strategy.

These findings are an important backdrop to this study. They highlight many features which emerged in the survey work and stress the strategic regional role of early Japanese manufacturing operations within the UK. They also suggest that there would be an expectation of rapid evolution of key subsidiaries wherever the conditions were found to sustain such development. This in turn points towards the centrality of performance, hence the following section.

Subsidiary performance

Several studies have reported that many US-based MNEs evaluate foreign subsidiaries on virtually the same basis as domestic subsidiaries (Robbins and Stobaugh, 1973) and that they do so by processes which are shared with many other corporate contexts (Schoenfeld, 1986). It is, of course, evident that in certain basic areas of evaluation, considerable differences in approach would be expected. Thus, for example, financial evaluations of initial foreign investments using traditional cash flow techniques are not relied upon as heavily as in domestic investments because of greater perceived business, political and foreign exchange risks (Eiteman, Stonehill and Moffett, 1992).

The academic literature has frequently commented on the conceptual and practical problems associated with the evaluation of foreign subsidiary operations. For example, studies on the interaction of financial statement translation and performance evaluation have highlighted the paucity of adequate performance evaluation systems for appraising subsidiaries and their managers (Morsicato and Radebaugh, 1979). Other studies (such as Choi and Czechowicz, 1983) have found strong evidence pointing towards the importance of non-financial criteria in the evaluation process, stressing the role of increasing market share as the single most important non-financial variable for US MNEs, while other MNEs ranked productivity improvement as equally important. It is interesting to note that Japanese investors are rather distinctively regarded as having a long-term approach to both subsidiary strategy and evaluation, and thus perhaps being capable of taking a more rounded view of performance (Dunning, 1986; Yoshida, 1987). At the same time attention has been drawn to the fact that research on these aspects of MNE strategy has tended to neglect routines in spite of their importance in the process of co-ordination and control, being allegedly too concentrated on formal mechanisms such as departmentalisation and centralisation (Martinez and Jarillo, 1989; Kilduff, 1992). Such work emphasises the peculiar difficulties faced by many MNEs in co-ordination through the transmission of system-wide standard routines. Yet it is in this area where much of the efficiency gain of Japanese FDI networks resides, not least through their commitment to transferring their own unique production technology. Thus, for example, foreign production data on Honda, Sony, Matsushita and other Japanese pioneers of internationalisation show little difference in productivity among employees in their plants in Japan, Europe and North America (Ohmae, 1987).

There is little doubt that the criteria set for subsidiary performance will at any point in time be derived from the priorities which the parent sets for it. Thus the competitive priorities of Japanese MNEs will determine both the subsidiary priorities and performance measures. Over the recent past, there have been many studies on the different types of competitive priorities which emerge from MNEs in similar environmental conditions. For example, De Meyer *et al.* (1987) identified certain priorities as characterising Japanese, European and US companies in a major manufacturing study. Thus it is evident in this particular context that low cost, rapid design and volume changes were ranked higher by Japanese firms, which the authors suggested might reflect the importance which Japanese companies attach to set-up time reduction, small batch quantities and flexibility. Although undertaken in a quite different context, and not a comparative study, this project generates evidence of similar interests in recently established Japanese manufacturing units where a high priority was placed on establishing a flexible, quality European production base for the first time and, invariably, at considerable speed. Stated another way, many of the sample companies in this project were established in a situation where early manufacturing success was of a strategic importance for the parent which far exceeded the scale of the initial investment. This being the case, the relationship between subsidiary strategy, competitive priorities and performance criteria would be expected to be critical in determining the medium-term future of the local operation. As indicated earlier, there is little work on these relationships as they apply to recently established Japanese manufacturing plants in Europe, hence the motivation for this study.

Survey evidence

Methodology

When this project was undertaken in summer 1992 there were 24 Japanese companies listed by government sources as manufacturing in

Scotland, all of whom were contacted to seek their participation. In fact, two recent entrants had not yet commenced manufacture since their plants were under construction, and six of them declined to co-operate. Interviews were subsequently held during May and June 1992 with the senior plant management in the remaining sixteen, representing 72.7 per cent of the Japanese companies manufacturing in Scotland at that time. Over the past decade Scotland, along with Northern England, Wales, Telford and Milton Keynes, has emerged as one of a number of locations within which Japanese manufacturing FDI in the UK has clustered. In all cases the regional development authorities have been very active in promoting these areas for inward investment as part of government regional development policy. Being thus based on a high response rate from within one of these clusters, this study gives some important insights into certain operational aspects of Japanese manufacturing in the UK as a whole. To preserve undertakings which were given on confidentiality, the companies are not named.

Sample characteristics

Eleven of the 16 plants (68.8 per cent) were established in the period 1987–93 and the remainder between 1977 and 1986. As regards sector, eleven were in electronics products or components. This concentration is interesting, since UK estimates show that some 40 per cent of projects are electronics or related, while the JETRO estimates for Europe are about 25 per cent. This may be partially explained in the Scottish case by the fact that Japanese investment was attracted to Scotland as a result of the existence of a long-established, diversified electronic industry which already had substantial US and European MNE involvement within it.

In terms of employment, the plants were initially set up on a small scale, but several have built up rapidly over a short period. Thus the total number of employees in the sample companies after one year of establishment was 701, with a mean figure of 44: the mid-1992 figure was 4,337, and the mean 271. Most of the sample expected this growth to be maintained over the next few years as the facilities were expanded through the addition of further product ranges.

Findings

Subsidiary mission and strategy

Since this study is primarily concerned about the early results associated with strategic manufacturing investments, it is essential to examine the ways in which this was translated into operational activity. As communicated to, or perceived by, senior local management there were three groupings of subsidiaries. Nine (56.3 per cent) cited the support of the European market which already existed for the parent's products as being their primary mission. In that sense their view was a defensive one. Six (37.5 per cent) regarded themselves as representing a more aggressive strategy reflecting the parent company's drive for world leadership in their product/technology; while the remaining one was located in Scotland at the request of a major adjacent Japanese customer which had specialist requirements for plastic injection moulding.

In order to begin to address the importance of the subsidiary mission, Table 5.2 relates it to a range of characteristics which might be expected to be indicative of plant standing. The early development stage of these facilities must be borne in mind, in that the average plant age was 5.3 years. The first issue in Table 5.2 concerns subsidiary strategy, based on the White and Poynter (1984) model. This classification system has two polar positions, namely the marketing satellite at the stage before the miniature replica, and the strategic independent as the development beyond the product specialist. Neither of these two are represented in the sample, the former because it is located elsewhere in the (invariably) well-developed European sales and marketing facilities of the parent; the latter for a number of reasons including plant and managerial maturity, judgements on risk, policy on R&D allocation, and so on. The survey showed that eight (50 per cent) of the plants were set up as rationalised manufacturers; and by 1992 only one had progressed into the product specialist role. In reality all of the rationalised manufacturers could more accurately be described as rationalised assemblers when they were established, consistent with the first stage of the Sony model (Table 5.1). One of the initial miniature replica plants had progressed to a product specialist, effectively doubling the number from two to four by 1992.

Before leaving this introduction to subsidiary strategies, it is worth noting that the miniature replicas were the smallest and youngest plants with a mean employment of 90 and period of establishment ranging from 2 to 6 years. The equivalent rationalised manufacturer figures were 420, and 2 to 13 years; and for product specialists 236, over 1 to 15 years.

The data in Table 5.2 on subsidiary strategies are for 1992. It is notable that the most advanced subsidiary role is only represented in the plants where world leadership missions were quoted. The interpretation of this issue is important and can be illustrated from one of the sample companies. In this case, the corporate strategy underlying its establishment of manufacturing in Scotland was related to its plan to build a three

Table 5.2 Subsidiary mission, strategy and operating characteristics

Subsidiary	Mission (no. of companies)	Subsidiary strategy[a] (no. of companies)	No. of products		Location of	
			At est	1992	European HQ[b] (no. of companies)	R&D[b]
European market support	9	(RM: 6) (MR: 3)	41	202	S:3 OUK: 5 E: 1	J: 9
World leadership	6	(PS: 4) (RM: 1) (MR: 1)	11	268	S: 4 OUK: 1 E: 1	S: 4 J: 2
Local Japanese customer support	1	(MR: 1)	6	30	S: 1	J: 1
	16	16	28[c]	216	16	16

Notes: [a] Subsidiary strategies: RM, rationalised manufacturer; MR, miniature replica; PS, product specialist.
[b] Locations: S, Scotland; OUK, other parts of UK; E, continental Europe; J, Japan.
[c] Overall averages.

Source: Survey data.

centred global network with Japanese plants supplying Asia; US plants, the Americas; and the Scottish facility, which started production in 1988, as the centre for Europe. The intention is that each of these three nodes will have three core activities, namely R&D, sales/distribution and manufacturing. Outside Japan, the USA was established as a model from the early 1980s, with both west and east coast operations in each of the core activities. That model is now being extended to cover each of the three main product groupings which in this case are telecommunications equipment, data products and semiconductors. Although under consideration for some time, this model has been applied to Europe only [since 1990]. It was effectively launched through the sample plant being set up as a corporate facility, namely not as a unit for any one of the product divisions. It is therefore in that sense that its role is strategic in manufacturing terms and designed to represent a major step forward towards what the parent regards as world leadership in its products and technologies. By the time of this survey this plant had revenues of some £140 million; was selling 25 per cent to UK, 35 per cent to Germany and 15 per cent to Scandinavia; and had moved from a position where all material inputs were imported to one where 55 per cent by value came from European sources. This case is that of a product specialist, growing and absorbing products from Japan, and set up to begin to be the focus for the third leg of its parent's global strategy.

Turning back to Table 5.2, it is difficult to imagine that the pursuit of global missions could be associated with plants remaining in either the miniature replica or rationalised manufacturer categories. Examining the other variables associated with this group, it is clear that as a whole the growth in the number of products being manufactured is much more rapid than in either of the others, and equally that the Scottish operations have more substantial roles as both European headquarters and R&D centres. In situations such as those illustrated in the earlier example, this is not entirely surprising, but should be interpreted with care. The manufacturing strategies of these companies towards Europe are not mature and while in some instances they were conceived over a long period, they were often implemented at short notice. Initial manufacturing investments in a market might well be allocated product and market franchises (and occasionally development responsibilities) as a holding operation and much change in the distribution of such functions is to be expected over time if past precedents are considered (Hood and Young, 1980, 1983).

The other major subsidiary mission grouping in Table 5.2 is associated with European market support. It is evident that many Japanese electronics companies have well-established brand names and substantial market shares in Europe before they commenced local manufacturing. However, there are also examples of relatively long established plants in this group where a more gradual and iterative growth trajectory has been pursued, with various experiments in marketing, distribution and production over several years. One such example is in sporting goods. It was set up as a joint venture in Scotland in 1977 as a substitute for Japanese and Taiwanese production. The joint venture with a UK business whose interests included sporting goods lasted only three years for manufacture, but 12 years for distribution. Over that period it closed a French plant in 1987 and bought equipment and production to Scotland as part of a rationalised manufacturing strategy. From a small R&D base in 1982, the plant is now home to European R&D for a key product group, which has a 35 per cent market share in the UK. Its product range was 40 strong in 1978, but had developed to 450 by mid 1992; recording productivity levels at 90 per cent of the Japanese parent and on a par with a sister Taiwanese plant. In the terminology used in this paper it had moved from a miniature replica to a rationalised manufacturer.

As Table 5.2 suggest, the predominant subsidiary strategy under this mission is the rationalised manufacturer, with the miniature replicas generally being younger plants. Again the product range growth is striking, but lower than that of the world leadership group. Probably because these groups had powerful marketing operations in Europe long before manufacturing commenced, a relatively small proportion have European headquarters in Scotland. The London area and South East England region account for most of the locations in the 'Other parts of the UK' category. Perhaps most noteworthy is that this group all record the source of R&D as Japan, even though, as in the example cited, some plants might have a measure of responsibility for European R&D.

Subsidiary strategy and local sourcing

The significance of the quality and availability of local sourcing for Japanese manufacturers entering Europe in the last decade has already been emphasised and analysed in detail elsewhere (Hood and Truijens, 1993). According to the company claims the existence of local sourcing was not in itself at the top of their selection criteria in the Scottish case. However, there is little doubt that component sourcing capability is closely related to the transfer of Japanese competitiveness to Europe in industries such as electronics, a sector strongly represented in this study.

Table 5.3 sets out some of the more important survey findings on strategy and sourcing. The first item to stress is that seven (44 per cent) of the

Table 5.3 Local sourcing and subsidiary strategy

Local % range	Sourcing[a] no. of companies	Subsidiary strategies[b]			Average no. of years since establishment
81–100	3	PS: 1	RM: 1	MR: 1	4.0
61–80	5	PS: 2	RM: 3		6.6
41–60	0				–
21–40	1	PS: 1			[c]
0–20	7		RM: 3	MR: 4	2.7
–	16	4	7	5	–

Notes: [a] Local sourcing percentages are on a cost basis and cover purchases from within the EC as a whole. There is considerable controversy about such measurements and they can only be regarded as indicative. Japanese industry tends, for example, to include assembly labour costs of imported parts and components, local transportation costs, etc. and thus overstate 'real' local content.

[b] Categorisation as in note to Table 5.2.

[c] Number not disclosed since only one company is involved.

Source: Survey data.

companies were under the 20 per cent local sourcing figure, although this group had been established for an average of 2.7 years in Scotland. This figure needs to be interpreted with care for several reasons. All of these are electronics companies which, as part of their locational search processes, undertook detailed studies of local sub-contracting capability throughout UK. The locational choices made were thus informed ones. Further, although established for 2.7 years, several of these companies have been in production for a much shorter period and when they did commence, it was largely on the basis of assembling pre-packed kits for components and material from other plants in South East Asia. Thus, although firms were under 20 per cent local content in Table 5.3 and this may appear to be a high figure, the investments were at an early stage and the data in the table suggests that age of plant is a factor related to increased levels of local sourcing. Further inspection of the data confirms this. For the firms established between 1977 and 1984, three quarters have over 60 per cent local sourcing.

The second issue arising from Table 5.3 is that the product specialist group was generally found to have higher levels of local sourcing. It will be recalled from Table 5.2 that these plants are associated with local R&D and offensive plant missions. Rather more surprising is the diversity of local sourcing patterns displayed by the rationalised manufacturers, and especially the fact that three (43 per cent) of them are in the category of under 20 per cent. Once again, this might well be a function of time and plant immaturity. However, Table 5.2 did emphasise the speed of product expansion within most of the plants and this in itself might well have contributed to the inability of sourcing policies to keep up with this process, in spite of the extensive evidence of the high level of executive resource devoted to it. Overall, the position of most of the miniature replicas in Table 5.3 is perhaps to be expected, not least because these are on the first rung of the plant development ladder and are of recent origin, with one exception which has the highest level of local sourcing.

In common with similar UK surveys, several companies within this sample expressed a level of frustration about the inability to increase local sourcing as rapidly as they would have liked to. The predominant reason for lack of local sourcing lay in the non-availability of material, with high cost of locally sourced goods and concerns over quality as secondary issues but some way behind the supply availability. Experience in dealing with Japanese manufacturers suggests that, while the concept of 'local sourcing' is technically that from within the EC, the desire to develop quality suppliers at a much more regional level, for all the well known reasons associated with Japanese manufacturing practices, means that experience at that level tends to dominate responses. At the same time it will be remembered from earlier comments that the local (Scottish) supply base was not cited high among the reasons for plant establishment. It is interesting to note in this survey that even when providing reasons for a slower build up of local sourcing than was strategically desirable, some of the companies with the lowest levels pointed out that, due to the low levels of duty on imported kits coming into the UK, it would not be prudent to source more locally in the short term. Further, in these instances it was claimed that further local sourcing in such a situation would require additional overheads in inspection and supplier development. Clearly such judgements have to be made against the necessity for increased local content to meet the requirements for a European product, and such hesitancy for these reasons might be short-lived and company-specific. Outwith this context, it was evident in the survey that considerable effort was being directed at supplier development, frequently with the direct involvement of Scottish Enterprise and other economic development agencies.

Performance evaluation

Criteria.   In the light of the strategic intentions behind the establishment of these manufacturing plants, the survey examined the performance criteria by which the parent company was measuring their performance. Based on a review of criteria employed in similar contexts Japanese MNEs, the executives were provided with a listing of 28 measures in seven distinct groupings as set out in Appendix 2 (p. 106). They were invited to rank the criteria within each group which were deemed to be of primary importance as part of the internal performance assessment of the plant. The overall response is in itself interesting, in that there were on average seven criteria selected for each of the 16 respondents, with a range from three to nine. The findings are summarised in Table 5.4.

While all of the companies responded, not all featured in the four predominant groupings of quality, financial, productivity and market/product development criteria. For example, there were two sample companies where quality measures did not explicitly feature, and the primary evaluation criteria were in the financial and productivity categories. Overall, however, the weight of emphasis in Table 5.4 reflects the characteristics of these plants which have been previously outlined. They are still largely production units in the process of rapidly absorbing products from other group operations in the Far East. Although criteria related to market development feature in 12 of the sample, it is generally a responsibility shared with marketing teams located in other parts of Europe as part of the corporate measurement of overall regional performance. The latter aspect is evident in the low level of comments on customer criteria, in that the plant priority is quality product, implicitly satisfying customers. Most Japanese MNEs would regard the requirement for explicit customer satisfaction criteria as an admission of failure. The same could be said for the personnel measures. The relevance of labour

Table 5.4 Performance criteria at plant level

Criteria groupings[a]	Sample no.	Companies %	No. of measures
Quality	14	87.5	28
Financial	13	81.2	25
Productivity	14	87.5	27
Market/product development	12	75.0	19
Process	3	18.7	5
Personnel	2	12.5	4
Customer	3	18.7	4

Note: [a] As detailed in Appendix 2.
Source: Survey data.

related variables in the locational choice was noted earlier and quality performances would be expected to flow from a combination of effective locational choice and good management. The fact thus that neither personnel not customer criteria emerge in Table 5.4 should not be misinterpreted. As regards the process criteria, again the plant age and responsibilities have to be remembered, as a result of which most are recipients of technology and process engineering. It is interesting to note, for example, that two of the larger rationalised manufacturer plants which have respectively moved from 150 to 830 and 30 to 530 products since establishment have process improvements as one of their primary criteria, thus reflecting the greater maturity and sophistication of these operations.

Relating the performance criteria to subsidiary missions, Table 5.5 shows the first ranked criteria for the four main groupings in Table 5.4. There would be no immediate expectation for these to be substantially different since performance by the standard criteria are essential ingredients of fulfilling any of these missions. The only issues to emerge, upon which commentary must be tentative, is that there is a tendency for the world leadership group to have rather different and broader criteria on both markets and productivity. Thus they have evidently more accountability for market share, cost leadership (on both productivity and finance criteria) and output measures associated with their more offensive role, than does the European market support group.

In order to obtain a closer appreciation of the manner in which the competitive priorities for the plant were translated into operational priorities, respondents in the companies were invited to rank these according to a schematic employed for similar purposes by De Meyer *et al.* (1987). The results of this exercise, categorised by subsidiary strategy, are shown in Table 5.6, based on a ranking of the arithmetic means of the respective responses from each grouping of subsidiaries. The consistent theme once again emerges as quality for a whole variety of reasons. Among these is the strategic issue related to the need for effective import substitution from high performing source plants, the desire to defend and develop European market share through quality indigenous production, and so on. Some of the relative priorities in Table 5.6 are consistent with previous findings in this survey. Thus, for example, high performance products would be expected to be a priority in the product specialists; as would dependable deliveries for both this group and the rationalised manufacturers. It is also consistent with the product specialist that rapid volume changes are not high on the list. Quality, price, performance and speed of deliveries are of greater importance to

Table 5.5 Subsidiary mission and first ranked performance criteria

Subsidiary mission	No. of companies	Quality			Finance			Productivity				Markets	
		%			%			%				%	
		1	2	5	1	2	3	1	2	3	4	1	2
European market support	9	21.5	7.1	–	23.1	15.4	7.7	28.5	7.1	7.1	–	41.6	–
World leadership	6	50.0	7.1	–	38.5	–	15.4	7.1	21.4	14.3	7.1	33.3	25.0
Local Japanese customer supplier	1	–	–	7.1	7.7	–	–	7.1	–	–	–	–	–
No. of cos.		14 (100%)			13 (100%)			14 (100%)				12 (100%)	

Note: [a] Categories as detailed in Appendix 2, with the components within each of the four main headings as coded in the Appendix. The % figures are related to the numbers in each category. Because of rounding, they may not add up to 100%.

Source: Survey data.

Table 5.6 Competitive priority ranking by subsidiary strategy

Competitive priorities	Subsidiary strategies				De Meyer *et al.* results
	Miniature replica (5 companies)	Product specialist (4 companies)	Rationalised manufacturer (7 companies)	Total sample (16 companies)	
Low prices	2	4	8	5	1
Rapid design change	8	6	6	6	2
Consistent quality	1	1	1	1	3
Dependable deliveries	5	3	2	3	4
Rapid volume changes	7	8	4	6	5
High performance products	3	2	3	2	6
Fast delivery	4	7	7	6	7
After sales service	6	5	5	4	8

Source: Survey data, based on the categorisations employed in De Meyer *et al.* (1987).

the miniature replica group. This would be expected, given the role which they play. Equally for them, and others to a lesser degree, rapid design changes are much less important.

Table 5.6 also provides the aggregate priorities for this survey as a whole to allow these to be compared with the Japanese companies in the study by De Meyer *et al.* (1987). From this it is evident that the priorities of the two sample groups are rather different. This may be a reflection of the recent foundation of many of the Scottish based plants where quality, high-performance products and dependable deliveries are dominant issues, in what are largely manufacturing units rather than strategic business units. Thus the timing and context of trade-restriction motivated investment would be expected to rank both low prices and rapid design changes as less important in the short term. If the Scottish sample is considered to have the characteristics of a 'bridge-head' type of manufacturing investment for the EC, then it is likely that the operational priorities might be less directed to areas where high performance will be regarded as axiomatic in the medium term. Into this category might fall the three lowest ranking issues of design and volume change, and after sales service.

Outcomes. The evaluation of performance against the established criteria is clearly no easy matter for a number of reasons. Companies, even under a guarantee of confidentiality, are understandably reluctant to reveal too much detail on this issue. Equally, it is inevitable that shorter term issues such as the effects of recession in Europe on financial performance become intertwined with the longer term, more strategic measures. Bearing these issues in mind, Appendix 3 (p. 107) sets out a summary of the individual company responses. They are presented in this way in order to give an impression of the overall flavour of the way in which the various criteria were regarded in practice, rather than in concept as previously discussed. Of all the other plant characteristics considered in this study, the one deemed most likely to be material to the development of performance is the length of time the plant has been established, and the sample is grouped to reflect this.

A number of dominant themes emerge from the data in Appendix 3. Firstly, quality and productivity measures are usually equal to or better than those in Japan, though not always so when compared to other parts of S.E. Asia. The relatively favourable position across these and other variables is seen to hold for all of the 1977–83 plants. It is notable that in this group of plants, there was little short-term, recession-related comment on financial performance or capacity utilisation. As such, these examples probably reflect the long-term nature of both the parent and local executive perspective. For the purposes of this exercise, they are styled as 'consolidators'. The second group, the 'builders', established over the 1984–9 period, record a greater variety of operational experience. While invariably performing in line with expectations, several are below benchmarks adopted elsewhere, against which they are ultimately measured. This is the case with quality and productivity measures; and to a lesser degree as regards market share and development. However, the overall impression in these seven cases was of consistent progress being made in the plants and no fundamental performance concerns emerged in the interviews. In that sense they are still within the first five to ten years of establishment, building up operations and playing an increasing role in the parent companies' EC market strategies.

The third group of 'developers' are at an even earlier stage, generally experiencing rapid growth in physical space, employment and product range. In particular there are positive signs on quality, rather less so on productivity to date, and encouraging evidence on market shares. It should be stressed that while this initial experience gives critical feedback to the parent, it is based on a rather short time scale. Having said that, this group is not materially different from the performance mix recorded for the builders.

The classification system used has its foundation in another set of considerations. It is reasonable to assume from the other evidence that the plans which these plants will be allowed to bring forward for future investment and further development of their role, will be much influenced by the performance record established at local level as compared to other group and industry benchmarks. The companies were thus invited to comment on the major elements in the next stage of their development as this was being considered within the corporation. It goes without saying that there are some risks in such a line of enquiry since it may reflect local managerial aspirations rather than corporate intentions. At the same time, it is probable that the responses are reflective of the discussion agendas between parent and subsidiary, and give some insight into the strategy of the former. It also points to some tentative evidence as to how the plant team as a whole is regarded.

The four oldest plants listed in the 'consolidators' category cited the expansion of product families within the Scottish operation (in two cases); the bringing in of R&D; and the expansion of production facilities. The first two of these are reflective of a more mature plant where new products and processes are sought rather than further transfer from within the partial range which they handle for Europe. Equally, R&D is unlikely to flow at earlier stages and the evidence within development agencies suggests that such transfers are particularly difficult for Japanese manufacturers at the early stages of their European strategy. In terms of subsidiary strategy three of these are rationalised manufacturers and one is a product specialist plant.

The 'builders' show some rather different planning concerns. Two of the plants indicated the setting up of a satellite plant in Eastern Europe and another UK (or Continental European) production plant as forthcoming corporate events in which they would be expected to play a role. All of the others were still at the stage of expressing their plans in terms of adding new products from existing families, establishing a wider range of the parents' products in the market, raising capacity utilisation, and so on. Again this is consistent with the earlier observations made about this group in terms of solid progress with many of the functional aspects of a fully fledged plant yet to be internalised. However, it is interesting to note the diversity of subsidiary strategy characterising this group in that it contains product specialists (two); rationalised manufacturers (three); and miniature replicas (two). The later two are younger plants, and list further UK/European plants and the addition of tool making capacity as their planning priorities.

It would be expected that the 'developers' group would have more immediate concerns about adding people and premises. The survey evidence confirms this. They are small, and in some ways embryonic operations, all of whom were dealing with short-term capacity, recruitment and training plans. The longer term considerations of market development and R&D only featured at the margins. This is largely a miniature replica group (three), but has a rationalised manufacturer and a product specialist within it where it might be anticipated that these more strategic considerations would emerge in the next few years.

Before concluding this discussion of subsidiary performance criteria and outcomes, it is useful to relate back to some of the earlier comments in the literature. This survey confirms the expectation of common measures across emerging subsidiary networks and the active use of forms of benchmarking to chart progress against subsidiary missions. Equally the importance of nonfinancial criteria emerges quite strongly, with the Japanese parent companies evidently evaluating performance in a rounded manner and with longer term intentions in view. In the context of this particular study, the evidence points to the majority of the operations conforming to their subsidiary missions at this early stage in their life. Few as yet have sister European plants and little intra-EC competition for investment funds or development projects. There is some limited evidence that this is in the pipeline. However, several of the sample companies are some considerable distance from the stage where they might be expected to have an integrated network of development, manufacturing and marketing in Europe in each of the Triad areas (Ohmae, 1985).

Conclusions and policy implications

This paper has been concerned with the early stages in the strategic evolution of a sample of Japanese manufacturing affiliates established in a region of the UK, largely within a time frame associated with trade friction between the EC and Japan. For many of the sample companies these were the first European manufacturing plants to be established. It is evident, both in terms of the overall motivating forces behind Japanese manufacturing within Europe and in the light of the relatively low asset base which Japan has in Europe when compared to that in both the US and Asia, that the significance of Europe will increase considerably over the 1990s. However, it is possible to argue that trade friction is likely to decline in importance as a driving force behind Japanese FDI in Europe and that anti-dumping has passed its peak. In reality in one of its most vigorous phases between 1980 and 1988 only about 8 per cent of the anti-dumping measures initiated were against Japanese firms, compared to 41 per cent against products from state trading nations. While this Japanese figure roughly conformed to the country's share of EC imports, it has been highly visible and has had a profound influence on FDI trends. It is, however, likely that Japanese companies will move to less defensive strategies towards Europe and into more positive EC market oriented strategies, both in terms of locations and products – linking both of these into a global management framework.

It has been suggested that major Japanese electronics corporations are moving towards a situation in Europe where they will progressively add more value, not least by the transfer of more engineering and R&D to draw on foreign expertise in areas such as software, and to increase the international opportunities for indigenous management (McKinsey & Co., 1988). For example, Hitachi and Fujitsu are among the companies to set up UK software centres in recent years. Equally, the persistent effort directed towards the development of multiple, high responsive medium- and small-sized component suppliers is part of the same process. In the short term, as evidenced, this may be driven by local content requirements, but in the more strategic sense it is an intrinsic part of Japanese competitive style. Many electronics companies rely more on frequent new product introduction and rapid production build-up, than they do on long-term plans based on exhaustive market research. This study has merely picked up the beginnings of these processes for recent entrants, not all of whom are of a scale where major strategic development on a pan-European scale can be expected.

However, it is not unreasonable to suggest that the locus of early manufacturing entry might continue to play an important role as such strategies evolve. This study confirms the findings for other parts of the UK, namely that the environment has proved to be one within which the most stringent performance measures set by the parent can be achieved or bettered through time. But experience elsewhere has led Japanese companies to expect that this would be the case, thus reinforcing the value of the diligence which goes into their choice of plant locations. In effect, given conformity to a series of carefully researched external variables, the corporations are confident of their own managerial and technical capabilities. The evidence in this sample points in this direction. In some instances, the plants have conformed to desired standards over a short time period, recognising that these are being progressively recalibrated. Equally, others have proved to be capable of absorbing new products while growing rapidly and have done so without detriment to performance measures. All of this was no more than was expected of them.

From the perspective of the Japanese companies entering the UK with considerable government encouragement and invariably with its financial support, the net outcome to date would appear to be positive on most counts. In most cases it is too early in the evolutionary process to determine whether this will lead to well-developed and integrated product specialist units, with wide market and product franchises for Europe and beyond. While it has been observed that early plant performance is a necessary condition for such transitions to begin to occur, it may not be a sufficient condition. More positive EC strategies, such as was suggested above, might well combine with the logistics of market servicing and with political pressures to add value within the major markets, thus leading to a much lesser role being played by UK manufacturing than at present. This may happen even within a Single European Market environment. However, there is little doubt that the sample plants examined were largely European in both concept and reality, which gives at least the basis of a platform for wider development centred in the UK.

Viewed from the angle of those promoting Scotland in an increasingly competitive European environment for foreign investment, there is much which is positive in this detailed look at performance and strategy. There would have to be some caution exercised about assuming all signs are equally favourable, in that in a multi-variable performance setting, there will always be some leading and lagging variables. Not all of these are controllable at plant level in that these are both external and internal (group) environmental factors which can obscure the fundamentals of how a plant is regarded by its parent. However, the very dynamic situation in these relatively young plants is evident and the actual trajectories for development are not easy to predict. Some tentative planning priorities did emerge, but the existence of a range of options open to Japanese parents on European recovery from recession is such that close attention should be paid both to aftercare for this group of plants and to the emergence of group strategy towards Europe.

As a final comment, it would, of course, be naive to suggest that the process of market entry and the transference of competitive skills in the context considered in this study has been universally smooth and problem free. There is consistent evidence to the contrary in many different environments as issues of managerial culture, organisation forms and production methods are addressed (Kidd, 1991; Tackiki, 1991; Dirks, 1992). While these were not matters which were within the objectives set for detailed examination in this study, such evidence as did emerge pointed to high levels of workforce and managerial flexibility being reported, and effective consultative mechanisms operating. In many cases this was perhaps assisted by the relative youth of the labour forces, the high emphasis placed on training both in the UK and in Japan, and the demand for employment in the region as a whole.

Appendix 1 Subsidiary strategy

Subsidiary strategy	Features
– Marketing satellite	Marketing a standard product whether at regional, UK or wider level. No development role.
– Miniature replica	Produces some of the parent's products/services in the local plant. Activity ranges from adopting, adapting or involving some innovation to the product/service offering.
– Rationalised manufacturer	Designated set of products produced locally for a European or global market. Development generally still with the parent company, but some local and growing. Marketing usually with the parent.
– Product specialist	Develops, produces and markets a limited product line for multi-country or global markets. Much more self-sufficient in most areas.
– Strategic independent	Plant has both the freedom and resources to develop lines of business, normally for a multi-country or global market.

Source: White and Poynter (1984).

Appendix 2   Performance criteria

Description	Code
Quality criteria	
Quality output level	1
Parts per million	2
On-time delivery ratio	3
Yield	4
% defect ratio	5
Reliability	6
Average quality level	7
Financial criteria	
Profit	1
Orders/sales/turnover	2
Cost reduction	3
Budget	4
Return on investment	5
Productivity criteria	
Standard time per unit	1
Cost/unit	2
Output	3
Efficiency	4
Market/product criteria	
Market development	1
Market share	2
Product development	3
Process criteria	
Improvements in process	1
Cycle-time	2
Noise reduction	3
Local material content	4
Personnel criteria	
Labour turnover	1
Attendance	2
Overall employment relationships	3
Customer satisfaction criteria	
Customer complaints	1
Enquiries-to-orders ratio	2

Appendix 3   Performance evaluation

Period of establishment	No. of companies	Outcomes, by company
'Consolidators': 1977–83	4	– Quality higher and cost per unit lower than Japan. Taiwan subsidiary ahead of Scotland. Turnover and profit ahead of forecast. Market share increasing and on target. – Quality levels rising but still lower than both Japan and targets. Productivity considerably above Japan; market share and market development on target. – Quality levels equal to Japan; productivity levels close to Japan, and both ahead of target. Cost reductions on schedule, market development behind target. – Quality levels ahead of Japan; financial performance marginally ahead of forecast.
'Builders': 1984–9	7	– Quality better than Japan and US plants, but productivity lower. Market share and development growing, but behind target. – Both quality and productivity lower than Japan and below target. Profitability ahead of plans. – Productivity and financial criteria showing improvements, but marginally under plan. Market share and product development ahead of target. – All quality, market and product performances below target. – All productivity and market development measures ahead. All measures, except cost per unit, ahead of Japan. – Quality levels under Japan and Taiwan, but on target; productivity level equal to Japan, but lower than Taiwan. Financial side under budgets. – Quality levels on target, but lower than Japan; productivity below Japan and target. Financial criteria improving, but under target.
'Developers': 1990–2	5	– All criteria better than all other subsidiaries, and ahead of targets. – Quality/yield comparable to Japan and ahead of plan. Efficiency lower than Japan, but improving.

Period of establishment	No. of companies	Outcomes, by company
		All productivity measures higher than expected in first year of trading. Finance, behind budget but return on investment (ROI) as expected.
		– Quality levels slightly lower than SE Asia; productivity also lower, but both improving on target. Profit and revenues both ahead of plan, as is market share.
		– Quality levels better than Japan, but productivity less than expected. Market development and share ahead of target.
		– Quality, finance and productivity measures all ahead of target; the productivity and quality better than Japan. Market share ahead.

Source: Survey data.

6

Inward Investment and the EC: UK Evidence on Corporate Integration Strategies (1987)*

Neil Hood and Stephen Young

Introduction

This contribution explores some aspects of the strategic integration of inward investing companies within the EC as these organisations have adjusted to the competitive environment of the last decade and as they have progressively come to terms with an integrated market. Attention is drawn to some of the propositions which have emerged about the processes of adjustment which might be expected to occur within multinational firm networks and to the limited empirical evidence which exists to allow these to be tested. Subsequent concentration is on the analysis of a set of UK data based on an empirical study of MNE affiliates from the USA and Continental Europe which was undertaken by the authors on behalf of the Department of Trade and Industry (Hood and Young, 1983). In the final section some conclusions are drawn and policy implications suggested.

As is observed by Cantwell (1987), the literature on the effects of integration on the activities of MNEs in European industries is sparse. It is, therefore, not reviewed further in this paper and attention is focused largely on employing a corporate strategy framework as the basis for analysing the development paths pursued by MNEs in Europe [since the late 1960s]. This approach allows a linkage to be established between

* *Journal of Common Market Studies*, 26 (2) (1987), 193–206. The views expressed in the paper are personal and are not to be construed as reflecting government policy.

international strategies, foreign subsidiary roles and host country impact – the last being in this case the UK. It has become increasingly clear to both academics and policy makers that such an holistic approach is essential to the understanding of the nature and direction of integration. Some of the approaches to this are explained in the next section.

Internationalisation and integration

Perspectives

Over the past few years, various attempts have been made to develop international strategy models at the company level which would effectively analyse the issues associated with globalisation and global competitiveness. These have invariably made implicit reference to integration effects within the emerging corporate systems, such effects being driven by environmental change, technology, product convergence and so on. At an empirical level, however, the evidence remains principally that of corporate or sectoral case studies. At a more aggregate level, extensive integration of manufacturing and sourcing among MNEs is suggested by evidence showing, for example, that around half of MNE exports took the form of intra-MNE transactions in the early 1980s (Dunning and Pearce, 1981).

Although the motivations for growing levels of integration to reduce manufacturing costs have been both defensive and offensive, other factors have played a major part as more mature MNEs have sought to reshape their competitive advantage. Thus, effective integration can raise barriers to entry, maximise advantages accruing from different fiscal and incentive regimes, and provide a flexible level of response to host government negotiating demands. On the other hand, there are risks associated with these developments. For instance, system performance is placed at a premium, the network as a whole being more open to problems associated with individual subsidiaries, exchange rate fluctuations, and the excessive use of host nation bargaining power. Moreover, there are, on occasion, costs arising from the inflexibility of some integrated systems where the focus on overall optimum performance can reduce levels of market responsiveness. Doz (1986) suggests that integration strategies have been implemented most extensively in Western Europe, where free trade and free investment conditions prevail (as a result of the creation of the EC), and where high manufacturing labour costs combine with a large market over a small geographic expanse to maximise the benefits of integration strategies. He goes on to suggest, however, that it is in the European arena that the tensions between national responsiveness and global integration within MNEs are particularly prevalent, not least because of the partial nature of integration in some market segments. Looked at more widely, while there is some evidence that global strategies are on the increase, it is still more common for MNE strategies to be regional in character with the integration within the region far exceeding that within the system as a whole.

A classification of international and subsidiary strategies

In the context of this paper, the focus of interest is on one set of regional strategies (namely towards Europe) and the perspective on these is principally from one country, namely the UK. For the purposes of positioning that interest in its global setting, and providing a framework within which strategies towards subsidiaries can be considered, Figure 6.1 provides a useful illustration based on the work of White and Poynter (1984) and Porter (1986).

Relatively few attempts have been made to relate these two dimensions in any detail and Figure 6.1 should be regarded as indicative of the likely subsidiary outcomes emerging from a series of typical international strategies. Of course, the subsidiary groupings suggested were developed from Canadian data and are not immediately transferable to the UK/European context. Moreover, US MNEs have, for example, tended to regard Europe as a single market area and one of greater opportunity and complexity than Canada. In that sense, subsidiaries in the UK, or in any other EC Member State, are invariably not designed for a national market alone. Bearing all these qualifications in mind, the subsidiary strategies model is suggestive of a number of relationships. Thus, for example, an export-based strategy with decentralised marketing will probably result in a Marketing Satellite as a subsidiary; similarly, a strategy involving extensive co-ordination among manufacturing operations (on a global or regional basis) would tend to produce a Rationalised Manufacturer at subsidiary level. Less predictable, however, are some of the other outcomes from the two extremes of country-centred or global strategies. Arising from the former, a Miniature Replica may emerge, as Figure 6.1 suggests. But subsidiaries do not necessarily develop along predictable paths and, in a European setting, a number which started as Miniature Replicas have progressed to be 'strategically independent' by being permitted to develop new product lines for a local, regional or, occasionally, global market. Equally, the parent company pursuing a purely global strategy could have many specialist subsidiaries in its portfolio.

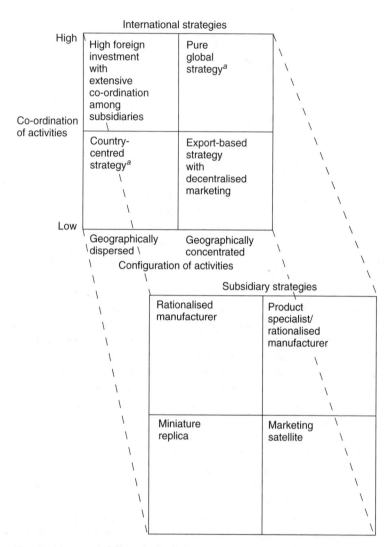

Figure 6.1 International and subsidiary strategies

Note: [a] Strategic independent subsidiaries could emerge from either of these two international strategies.

Sources: White and Poynter (1984); Porter (1986).

Subsidiary strategy at UK/EC level

The varieties of option emerging from Figure 6.1 are best illustrated against a set of data. From earlier work of the present authors it is possible to apply these principles to subsidiary strategies at the British and Continental European level as a prelude to the more formal consideration of the empirical evidence later in this paper. One earlier study (Hood and Young, 1980) which examined a sample of US MNEs operating in Scotland provides interesting evidence of the general role played by the UK. Its findings are summarised in Figure 6.2. For each development phase, market, corporate and subsidiary level characteristics are highlighted; so too are the overriding strategic issues faced by the parent. Stage 1 for these companies invariably involved the formation of a Marketing Satellite, although a number were direct exporters with no local support, and a few had little or no former connection with the market. By Stage 2 the companies often used the UK as their first production base in Europe, and generally this was their first overseas manufacturing plant. These were principally green-field operations, and in most ways Miniature Replicas of the parent. In early examples, some were literally copies of US plants in almost every respect – these home-based plants being used as 'controls' for managerial purposes. At that stage market roles were often defined to include Europe and beyond; on occasion Canada was included due to Commonwealth Preference rules.

Stage 3 was initially characterised by the extension of Miniature Replicas into Continental Europe, with West Germany, France and Belgium being the most common locations. One sample study indicated that among a group of 1950s and 1960s US entrants to Britain, the firms had a further one or two manufacturing affiliates on the continent by 1973 (Young and Hood, 1976). Plants were thus built to serve dominant markets and ensure market access. The fact that the EC and EFTA did not come into being until the late 1950s had a major influence on this strategy. Subsequently, the fact that the two economic blocs were separate meant that UK and Continental European subsidiaries often supplied different markets. For many US corporations, however, Stage 3 was short-lived.

The enlargement of the Community (including UK membership), the first oil price shock, growing competition from indigenous European producers and from Japan, together with the dramatic technology changes in electronics, all combined to induce a different type of Europeanisation. Thus corporate strategy was concentrated on a movement towards the Rationalised Manufacturer stage, as manufacturing and marketing systems were brought together and as decisions were made on product and component allocation. Many of these decisions were made under extreme competitive and cost pressures, and hence were under tight time constraints. As a result, few displayed really integrated operations until Stage 4. At corporate level, manufacturing integration and rationalisation were twin priorities, while subsidiaries began to be in more

Development phase	Subsidiary type	Market	Corporation	Subsidiary	Key issues
Stage 1: Export-led	Marketing satellite	UK	US market focus	Sales/service function	Timing of manufacturing overseas: international management skills
Stage 2: International production (1950s–1960s)	Miniature replicas	UK or entry route to Europe	Low international experience: high technological advantage	Parent product range: high import content: wide market role: control as profit centre	Implementing international plans
Stage 3: Europeanisation (1960s–early 1970s)	Miniature replicas → Rationalised manufacturers	Plant by market expansion	Product reallocation between subsidiaries: centralisation/ decentralisation decisions: diminishing technological advantage	Emerging interplant linkages: selective product development: control through regional profit centres	Centralisation/ decentralisation: penetrating high growth markets; positioning for integration
Stage 4: Integration (mid-1970s–early 1980s)	Rationalised manufacturer/ Product specialist	Europe by product or function	Manufacturing integration: rationalisation	Part of integrated production system: in competition for products and markets: control as cost centres in a system	Integration and control systems: rationalisation/ disinvestment, R&D location; product allocation methods

Figure 6.2 Strategic evolution: a model based on US MNEs in Scotland
Source: Derived from data presented in Hood and Young (1980).

active competition for product sourcing roles and market franchises. In turn, subsidiaries were found to be tightly constrained to perform within the system rules as part of an integrated whole. Among the prizes to be won at such a stage were R&D responsibilities, product specialist status and, in a limited number of cases, progression towards strategic independence with mainline hemispheric or global product charters.

The outcome of the integration phase in Figure 6.2 is not readily predictable. Much depends on the general level of competitiveness of corporations and their plant configuration as they emerged from Stage 3. The integration phase implies that fundamental choices will be made. At one extreme, UK manufacturing could cease and a residual Marketing Satellite re-emerge; for most, the plant role emerges as that of Rationalised Manufacturers within a European system.

There are reasonable grounds for believing that the general pattern of these trends is similar for US MNEs of that generation throughout the UK, although there has been little comparable empirical work. The early use of a Scottish production base and the heavier concentration on mechanical and electrical engineering companies compared to Britain as a whole, has perhaps some localised effect, but probably not sufficient to invalidate the broad thrust of Figure 6.2. What is much less clear is how more recent MNE entrants to Europe have behaved, entering as they have into an integrated market.

[Since the late 1970s] inward investment to Europe has, as is reflected in the UK, been more varied in terms of home country and method of entry, although the USA is still the dominant source for new investments. Some of the diversity of entry method is in itself a response to the demands of integration and market responsiveness. For instance, the higher propensity to acquisition shown by US firms in recent years is often a way of short-circuiting the iterative process implied in Figure 6.2. Equally, the more extensive use of non-equity agreements has the potential spin-off of establishing a variety of European links to serve a number of competitive purposes. However, the past decade has witnessed large volumes of electronics investment flow into Europe in the standard form of establishing greenfield manufacturing bases, but with non-standard constraints associated with rapid growth rates, short product cycles, high initial investment levels and global products. Although usually committed to high levels of manufacturing, a number of these companies have set up a range of European plants in very rapid succession, but by-passing the plant-by-market phase. Thus, from the early stages Product Specialists and even Strategic Independents start to emerge. A notable feature of this wave of investment is sensitivity to local infrastructure and sourcing capability, as well as to a measure of trade balance between the plants and the countries in which they operate. The ensuing input and output pressures mitigate against using any one country as a single supply point.

The relatively recent date of most Japanese manufacturing in Europe again makes prediction difficult. In general, European facilities are designed for European markets, rather than as points for global markets. This may of course only be a phase, given the massive scope for import substitution which exists in Europe for Japanese MNEs. Equally, the Japanese have set up few genuine networks of manufacturing units in Europe as yet. As Dunning (1986) has observed, it is possible that among the Japanese industrial electronics companies such networks may never develop, given the strength of factors which favour the centralisation of production. Again, this may simply be a phase of development, since the same principles could be applied to numbers of US MNEs who have felt the need for networks. The current political and market pressures on Japan are first order, namely to manufacture in Europe; the second-order pressures for higher levels of local sourcing, trade balance and employment distribution are following on with increasing speed. What can be claimed with some confidence is that at present the Japanese MNEs in the UK are at the Miniature Replica stage, albeit with market franchises encompassing Europe as a whole (for a useful review of these issues, see Dunning, 1985).

Empirical evidence

The preceding sections have been concerned with the development and illustration of a general model which identifies some of the integrative processes which are associated with MNE systems in Europe. It remains difficult to obtain data to allow micro-level testing of such models, although it is clear from the foregoing discussion that there are various implicit hypotheses which are amenable to statistical testing. The data considered in this section were not initially collected to facilitate the testing of hypotheses on integration as such. However, a series of variables were identified as part of the study mentioned which are directly linked to the characteristics identified in the model outlined.

The present authors undertook a study on behalf of the Department of Trade and Industry on the subject of 'Multinational Investment Strategies in the British Isles', with data being collected on the basis of personal interviews from 140 MNE subsidiaries. This work, published in 1983, was based on a sample of US and Continental European chemical, mechanical engineering and electrical engineering enterprises; the sample of companies was drawn from each of the assisted areas in the UK, the South East of England and the Republic of Ireland. The sample was deliberately selected in this way because the aim was to identify and contrast the nature of multinational manufacturing activity in these various regions and to consider the effects of regional incentives on investment decision-making. The results showed a reasonable similarity among the MNE subsidiaries in the British assisted areas, but the Irish operations (both Northern Ireland and the Republic of Ireland) and the South East England facilities appeared to be quite different in terms of activity and role. This may have implications for the analysis undertaken for the present article.

Data collected as part of this study related to many of the issues discussed earlier, including, for example, market and product roles, sourcing of inputs, plant activities in the areas of research and development, finance, etc. and subsidiary relationships within the multinational group. On the other hand, as noted, data collection was not specifically orientated towards the hypotheses developed in the previous section, which is an obvious disadvantage. However, given the paucity of this type of evidence and the difficulty of exploring some of the integration hypotheses, it is worthy of re-examination.

The statistical technique selected for use was that of cluster analysis, a technique for identifying structures and patterns in data sets. Clusters are formed of groups (in this case MNE subsidiaries) which are similar in terms of the classification data employed. There is no statistical test for determining the optimal number of clusters present, and in this case a fairly arbitrary cut-off was made at the four-cluster level; although the cubic clustering criterion did in fact indicate reasonably tight clusters at this level. A description of the statistical technique employed is given in Appendix 1 (p. 122), and Appendix 2 (p. 123) lists the variables incorporated into the analysis.

The results are shown in Tables 6.1 and 6.2 and the interpretation in terms of subsidiary strategies is presented in Figure 6.3. As is suggested, 21 per cent of sample subsidiaries seem to fit the category of Strategic Independents, with a further 26 per cent as Product Specialists. The largest group – Cluster 2 – comprising 45 per cent of the sample, is the most difficult to interpret, although allocated to the Miniature Replica category in Figure 6.3. It is surprising that such firms, especially since they are well-established in general, still have strong purchasing linkages with other group plants; local sourcing would have been presumed to develop to a larger extent over time. At the same time the market area served is apparently wider than for other subsidiaries, although cautious

Table 6.1   Average scores for cluster variables – four-cluster solution

Variable[a]	Cluster 1	Cluster 2	Cluster 3	Cluster 4
1. Employment range	3.72	3.44	2.44	3.92
2. Establishment	3.24	2.71	3.22	2.58
3. Network	1.10	2.79	1.25	10.91
4. Corporate integration	3.03	2.84	3.36	2.58
5. Output value	1.97	2.25	1.56	2.67
6. Input value	2.52	3.37	2.28	2.75
7. Cost/Profit centre	2.00	1.78	1.86	1.58
8. R&D activity	2.28	2.30	1.83	1.67
9. Market area	2.24	2.41	1.94	2.00
10. US sales	1.52	1.13	1.53	1.08
11. Regional sales	1.45	1.71	1.50	1.75
12. Product range	1.31	1.83	1.08	1.50
13. Mindex	1.76	1.44	1.44	1.42
Sample size	29	63	36	12
Per cent of total	21	45	26	9

Note: [a] For details of variables, see Appendix 2.

interpretation is required since differences between the groups are not statistically significant. What should be remembered, of course, is that there may be several different types of Miniature Replica subsidiaries, even though they are sufficiently cohesive as a group to form a single cluster. Cluster 4, comprising 9 per cent of the sample, can be allocated more straightforwardly to the Rationalised Manufacturer category: within very extensive plant networks (on average eleven Continental European facilities), the UK plants tend to be relatively large and well-established cost centre operations with substantial intra-group linkages. Inspection of the data indicates that these were the firms most subject to employment rundown in the face of the changing environmental conditions of the 1970s. Among a variety of explanations for this is the existence of different investment options when the network is large; the excess capacity which emerges from differential productivity growth; and the pressure which an integrated corporate network faces for the elimination of poor performing plants.

In general, then, there is some evidence that the subsidiaries studied can be allocated to hypothetical groups, although the 'fit' is clearly far

Table 6.2 F ratios and significance tests[a]

Variable	F-ratios	Significance
1. Employment range	4.94	0.0027
2. Establishment	2.32	0.0076
3. Network	85.90	0.0000
4. Corporate integration	6.36	0.0005
5. Output value	42.10	0.0006
6. Input value	3.02	0.0319
7. Cost/Profit centre	4.32	0.0060
8. R&D activity	1.46	0.2282
9. Market area	3.01	0.0320
10. US Sales	1.84	0.1412
11. Regional sales	6.25	0.0005
12. Product range	19.16	0.0000
13. Mindex	1.99	0.1172

Note: [a] The table indicates that some variables (e.g. Network, Product range) are good group separators, while others (e.g. Input value, Market area) are more questionable. They have been reported in the table because the cluster results, despite low significance, seem to accord with the hypotheses.

Cluster 1	Strategic independent (*n* = 29)	Above-average employment, most recently established, few other European plants; above-average R&D index; profit centres; narrow product range, European/global markets.
Cluster 2	Miniature replica (*n* = 63)	Longer established; significant linkages especially on the input side; wide product range, substantial local sales but fairly wide market area overall.
Cluster 3	Product specialist (*n* = 36)	Smaller, recently established, few other European plants; low linkages with other group plants; low R&D score; very narrow product range, UK/European markets in general but fairly high sales to USA.
Cluster 4	Rationalised manufacturer (*n* = 12)	Large employment, longer established, large European plant network; substantial linkages with other group plants; cost centres; low R&D score; UK/European sales.

Figure 6.3 Characteristics of clusters

from perfect. This is probably for several reasons. First, there is the issue of the questionnaire itself which was not explicitly designed to test the subsidiary strategy model outlined earlier in the paper. Second, and linked to the first point, the categorisation of some variables was insufficiently refined to be able to separate the groups, or, in some instances, findings were swamped by a particular result such as the absence of R&D at plant level, which was apparent in nearly three-fifths of the entire sample.

Some of the similarities between groups are, nevertheless, worthy of note. The broad market areas served by the different groups did not differ as much as might have been anticipated (although when considering particular markets, such as the USA, there were differences). The conclusion is that multinational subsidiaries in the UK tend to have European market briefs, irrespective of differences in other roles such as integration and intra-firm linkages; this may have been one of the major impacts of European integration. It should be added that while US and European firms were not significantly different in terms of strategic choice, the American MNEs were more European-orientated in their markets than their European counterparts.

Equally interestingly, there appeared to be few discernible differences by industry. This is perhaps explained by the nature of the variables employed and their low representation of industry-specific parameters, such as value-added, capital intensity, value to weight ratios and so on. On the other hand, they emphasise market-related variables to a larger extent. Based on the analysis of this data set at least, the strategy clusters are not apparently a consequence of industry-specific, economic or political imperatives – although such differences could exist at the sub-sectoral level.

Is it possible to draw any conclusions, however tentative, on the basis of the empirical results presented above? In the first place, multinational integration was not strongly in evidence among the sample firms. This is evidenced both from the limited inter-plant product and component flows, and from subsidiary responses to the question on the perceived degree of corporate integration. Second, emphasising a point made above, strategy is largely European-focused. It is still true, nevertheless, that this is not incompatible with a global strategy by multinationals: in essence what is being picked up in the results is the strategic response to meet the market supply and competitive conditions of the European region. On the other hand, the large group of well-established Miniature Replica subsidiaries is suggestive of country-centred or at least region-centred strategies.

Conclusions

This contribution has examined two types of evidence on corporate integration on the part of inward-investing companies within the EC over recent years. Although their limitations are recognised, they both point to modest but growing levels of integration on a number of counts. The empirical work presented at the end of the paper does, however, suggest that there is a long way to go before MNE corporate structures can be said to be truly reflective of an integrated market at EC level or be said to be driven by globalisation pressures. And this for companies who might be expected to be strongly motivated towards integrated systems.

From a policy dimension, these findings pose some interesting questions. Large numbers of MNE affiliates are still relatively free-standing and therefore perhaps more open to alternative locations than might first be suggested by centralisation hypotheses. Moreover, the data suggest that there are significant adjustments yet to come in many MNE systems within the EC, if the broad progression of development outlined in the paper is accepted. Meanwhile, EC Member States, including the UK, have shown increasing levels of sensitivity to the relationship between corporate strategy and public policy and hence are likely to be aware of the need to apply some such categorisations to their stock of foreign investment in order to predict the shape and timing of emerging policy issues. It is, therefore, against such settings that the economic pressures towards integration, even though they may be slower in their effect than anticipated, have to be balanced against the political imperatives stemming from host country markets.

Appendix 1

Cluster analysis

The central idea behind the technique of cluster analysis used in this paper, is that clusters or groups are formed of affiliates 'near' to one another or similar to one another in p-dimensional space. A wide variety of measures of nearness are available but the one used in this paper is the simple Euclidean distance function, $d_p{}^2$. For any p-dimensional vector x, this is defined as

$$d_p^2 = (x_1 - c_1)^2 + (x_2 - c_2)^2 + , \ldots, + (x_p - c_p)^2$$

where $x' = (x_1, x_2, \ldots x_p)$ and $c' = (c_1, c_2, \ldots c_p)$ is the centre of the group or cluster. Details of the procedure are presented in Beale (1969) and an algorithm written in FORTRAN is provided by Sparks (1973). Initially the trial cluster centres are supplied and each profile in the sample is assigned to its nearest centre. New centres are calculated and an iterative procedure is applied to reassign profiles to clusters in order to minimise the overall, within-cluster, sum of squares. In particular, if an observation is in the kth cluster it is worthwhile transferring it to the lth cluster if

$$\frac{n_l}{n_l + 1} \cdot d_l{}^2 < \frac{n_k}{n_k - 1} \cdot d_k{}^2$$

when n_k, n_l are the current numbers of observations in clusters k and l, respectively. A problem with the Euclidean distance function is that it gives particularly high weight to extreme values, but this problem is minimised in the present work by standardisation of the variables.

Appendix 2

Definition of variables reported in the cluster analysis

1. Employment range

Score:	1	2	3	4	5	6	7
	Up to 50	51–99	100–199	200–499	500–749	750–999	1,000 and over

2. Period of establishment in UK

Score:	1	2	3	4	5
	1950 or earlier	1950–9	1960–9	1970–9	1980s

3. Number of other group plants in Europe ... actual numbers

4. Degree of corporate integration

Score:	1	5
	Highly integrated global production system	System of non-integrated subsidiaries

5. Proportion of plant output (by value) to other group plants for further processing

Score:	1	2	3	4	5	6
	None	1–5%	6–10%	11–25%	26–50%	Over 50%

6. Proportion of British subsidiary inputs received from other group plants

Score:	1	2	3	4	5	6
	None	1–5%	6–10%	11–25%	26–50%	Over 50%

7. Operation of UK plant as cost/profit centre

Score:	1	2
	Cost centre	Profit centre

Definition of variables reported in the cluster analysis (*Continued*)

8. R&D activity at UK plant level

Score:	1	2	3	4
	None	Customer Technical Services	Product Adaptation	Product & Process Development; R&D in Materials & Techniques

9. Market area served by UK plant

Score:	1	2	3	4	5
	UK	Europe	Global	Some European, some Global (depending on product)	Other

10. Percentage of final sales destined for USA (US sales)

Score:	1	2	3	4	5
	0–10%	11–25%	26–50%	51–75%	76–100%

11. Percentage of final sales within region (Regional sales)

Score:	1	2	3	4	5
	0–10%	11–25%	26–50%	51–75%	76–100%

12. Product range supplied out of UK plant (in relation to product range of parent)

Score:	1	2
	Narrow	Broad

13. Presence/absence of a marketing department at UK plant level (Mindex)

Score:	1	2
	Yes	No

7
Global Strategies, Multinational Subsidiary Roles and Economic Impact in Scotland (1988)*

Stephen Young, Neil Hood and Stewart Dunlop

Introduction

Reflecting the changing nature of industries and competition worldwide, there has been an explosion of writings on the themes of global strategies and the globalisation of business, including authors such as; Doz and Prahalad (1987); Porter (1987); Hood and Vahlne (1988). A multinational company (MNE) pursuing a global strategy conceives its manufacturing, marketing, technology and other policies on a worldwide basis, and co-ordinates its resources worldwide in pursuit of global objectives, such as worldwide market share.[1] It is not yet clear how many companies and industries can be categorised as global; but the view is that there is a strong trend towards globalization with developments in the world economy, including the emergence of new industries like informatics and biotechnology, the revolution in information and communication systems, the need to amortise investment in world-scale plants and R&D programmes, and a growing standardisation of tastes (Leontiades, 1986).

What is very unclear is how MNE global strategies will impact upon the foreign subsidiaries of these multinationals and the national and regional host economies in which the latter are located. There is an extensive literature on the impact of MNEs in the UK, much of which at regional level has focused upon the characteristics and impact of

* *Regional Studies*, 22 (6) (1988), 487–97.

foreign-owned branch plants. The evidence is summarized most recently in Young, Hood and Hamill (1988). In the main, this has not taken a corporate strategy approach to the issue of economic impact. With globalisation, however, this will become an increasingly important topic in years to come: the roles of foreign subsidiaries (ranging from production-only branch plants through to quasi-autonomous operations with world-wide innovation, manufacturing and marketing rights), how stable they are and how they evolve over time will have a major influence upon regional economies in the UK. The purpose of this paper is to provide some preliminary evidence on the topic from the subsidiary perspective, based on a postal questionnaire survey of MNE affliliates in Scotland undertaken during 1986. An attempt is thus made to classify the roles of foreign subsidiaries of MNEs in Scotland, and to consider possible impacts on the economy; to provide some guidelines for further work; and to draw out the policy implications of the results obtained.

Multinational and subsidiary strategies

Over the past few years, there have been various attempts to develop international strategy models at the company level which would ana-lyse the issues associated with globalisation and global competitiveness (Fayerweather, 1978; Stobaugh and Telesio, 1983; Doz, 1986). The most systematic of such approaches is that of Porter (1986), who distinguishes between a number of different types of global strategies, and contrasts the latter with country-centred or multi-domestic strategies, where MNEs treat markets on an individual basis with manufacturing operations in those countries where local demand will justify this.

From the present perspective, the interest is in the outcome of MNE strategies *at subsidiary level* in the UK. A good deal of conceptual and empirical study has been undertaken on the subject of subsidiary level strategies in Canada reflecting long-standing concerns over the branch plant nature of the economy. One such piece of work has suggested a distinction between the following groups of affiliates (White and Poynter, 1984):

- *Marketing satellite*: marketing subsidiaries which sell products which are manufactured centrally into the local trading area
- *Miniature replica*: a subsidiary which produces and markets some of the parent's product lines or related product lines in the local country
- *Rationalised manufacturer*: where the subsidiary produces a particular set of component parts or products for a multi-country or global market

- *Product specialist*: where the subsidiary develops, produces and markets a limited product line for global markets
- *Strategic independent*: where the subsidiary is permitted independence to develop lines of business for either a local, multi-country or global market.

Viewed from a microeconomic perspective, the impact of MNEs derives from performance in a number of areas, including: technology transfer; innovation and entrepreneurial capacity; market structure; trade and the balance of payments; and linkage and spillover effects. Some of the economic effects of the different types of subsidiary operations on the Canadian economy have been evaluated in an *ad hoc* way. The marketing satellite affiliates are simply importers, whose impact is restricted to the balance of payments. Among the production operations, the miniature replica group have been the subject of a great deal of criticism. The latter are viewed as 'truncated manufacturing operations that do no R&D, export only to the United States and import components on a scale that contributes to a huge balance of payments deficit' (Science Council of Canada, 1980). The true branch plants – rationalised manufacturers – are production-only units which are integrated within other parts of the multinational system; this may mean substantial component exports but, equally, high levels of imports and the operations are dependent for their growth and innovation on parent-level decision-making. By comparison, the product specialist and strategic independent subsidiaries were viewed as being beneficial from a host country perspective. In a Canadian context, considerable attention has been paid to the former, especially in connection with the concept of World Product Mandates (WPMs), where the subsidiary is given total responsibility for all aspects of R&D, manufacturing and international marketing. The implication is, therefore, of positive employment, technology and balance of payments impacts, and possibly improved linkage effects given that decision-making is decentralised to subsidiary level. In reality, however, no attempt has been made to formally link subsidiary roles to economic impact in Canada (although Table 7.1 represents a preliminary attempt to do this for foreign affiliates in Scotland).

The model of subsidiary roles, developed in a Canadian context, is not necessarily directly transferable to the UK or UK regional economies. Certainly the British market is not so insular as that of Canada, and foreign multinationals (particularly American and Japanese) have tended to treat Europe as a single market area. Therefore, even miniature replica subsidiaries may have a significant export business within Europe. The

Table 7.1 Subsidiary strategies and impact in Scotland

Type of multinational	Impact area			
	Employment	Balance of trade	Technology transfer	Entrepreneurial capacity
1. *Miniature replica*: new/recent entrant to Europe e.g. Japanese companies	Growing rapidly	Substantially negative – will be exacerbated if subsidiary acts as marketing agent for parent corporation	Substantial	Very limited
2a. *Rationalised manufacturer*: multi-site manufacturer (expansion) e.g. computer and semiconductor firms	Growing – albeit in discrete steps dependent upon new product introduction, facility extension etc. High-quality employment	Negative or positive	Substantial	Limited
2b. *Product specialist/strategic independent*: multi-site manufacturer (autonomy)	Growing. High-quality employment	Negative or positive	Limited – depending on balance between own and parent induced developments	Significant – local R&D, international marketing responsibilities, etc.

2c. *Rationalised manufacturer*: multi-site manufacturer (rationalisation) e.g. mechanical engineering and electro-mechanical producers	Declining or stabilized at much lower level than peak	Possibly positive	Mainly process	Limited – but successful rationalisation will mean efficiency of existing operations
3a. *Miniature replica*: host-market oriented e.g. food companies	Stable or declining with technological innovation	Limited exports and imports – possibly positive in net terms	Limited	Some possibility of developments for UK market
3b. *Miniature replica*: host-market oriented e.g. European company, acquisition entrant	Stable or declining with technological innovation	Possibly negative – limited exports; imports from parent	Limited	Limited

Source: Young, Hood and Hamill (1988: 170–1).

large European market may increase the likelihood of some R&D activity, at least to adapt products to market requirements; and the science and technology base in Scotland could provide an additional stimulus to local R&D. Many Scottish subsidiaries, too, are likely to be integrated within European production networks, meaning more rationalized manufacturers and substantial intra-group trade (both imports and exports). Nevertheless this subsidiary strategies model appears to be sufficiently robust to be used as the basis for the discussion of strategies in the UK (and Scotland) which follows. The marketing satellite category of affiliates is, however, largely excluded from further comments, since the empirical research undertaken related to manufacturing operations only.

MNE subsidiary roles and economic impact in Scotland: previous work

Earlier work has highlighted the entry strategies and changing roles of US MNEs with subsidiaries in Scotland (Young and Hood, 1976, 1980). The country-by-country approach to European markets by US MNEs in the 1950s and 1960s was associated with the establishment of miniature replica subsidiaries. The economic shocks of the 1970s and the loss of competitiveness of some major American companies led to substantial rationalisation and reorganisation, mainly in the direction of greater integration on a Europe-wide basis – the rationalised manufacturer stage. Since then, US subsidiary strategies have depended upon the success or otherwise of the changes introduced during the 1970s (Young, Hood and Hamill, 1988: 159–63). Among more recent entrants, especially Japanese firms (Dunning, 1986), there is some evidence of a more integrated approach in subsidiary strategies from the outset in Europe; this is at least in part due to the high market shares which some of these companies already have in Europe at point of entry – in marked contrast to many of the recent US electronics investments. Among Continental European companies, investment has often been *ad hoc*, designed to serve the British market, with acquisition entry as a means of easing start-up problems and accelerating market penetration. Evidence of such country-centred strategies among Continental European entrants is apparent from the work of Buckley, Berkova and Newbould (1983).

As at the late 1980s, therefore, a cross-sectional view of the population of MNE subsidiaries in Britain and Scotland would reveal a variety of strategy types, relating to period of entry, life cycle phase, sector, nationality and so forth. Some indication of this variety, together with suggestions as to the economic impacts are shown in Table 7.1. The table draws on the accumulated evidence derived from research on MNEs in Scotland, but the association with different subsidiary roles is hypothetical at this stage. The purpose of the empirical work undertaken for this paper was to establish whether foreign subsidiaries in Scotland could be classified according to the Poynter and White (1984) model, what proportions of MNE affiliates were located in the different categories and what impacts could be inferred on the Scottish economy.

Empirical evidence

The data and general findings

A postal questionnaire survey was undertaken among MNE subsidiaries in manufacturing industry in Scotland by the present authors in 1986; details are provided in Appendix 1 (p. 143), together with basic classification data for the 129 responding firms (the actual questionnaire used is available on request from the authors). Information was collected for a series of variables which were considered to be important in a strategy context, including subsidiary R&D, market areas supplied from the Scottish factories, the nature of production operations, intra-MNE import and export trade, width of the product ranges, and locus of decision-making for market areas and product ranges as well as data on employment, period of establishment and nationality of ownership.[2]

The sample firms represented over 40 per cent of the total population of overseas-owned companies in Scotland. Summarizing the characteristics of the sample: about two thirds had been set up in Scotland from 1960 onwards; 57 per cent had under 200 employees, but almost a quarter had over 500 employees; and three-fifths of the companies were American-owned. The market orientation of foreign companies in Scotland appears to have widened over the years, since 28 per cent of MNEs claimed to be supplying world-wide markets. Intra-company trade was significant, especially on the input side, with one quarter of firms obtaining in excess of 25 per cent of material inputs from other group plants outside the UK.

Perhaps the most interesting responses related to research and development. Earlier work on this subject, summarised in Haug, Hood and Young (1983), showed a limited but perhaps growing incidence of R&D in MNE plants in Scotland. R&D performers were, however, more export-oriented and had more extensive primary and secondary sourcing roles outside Europe; R&D units seemed to provide a mechanism for facilitating technology transfers from the parent MNEs; and the proportion of commercial applications from the research results was high and tended to be based in the affiliates themselves.

The results of the present survey suggest a marked increase in the incidence of R&D since earlier studies had been undertaken, with 53 per cent of foreign affiliates claiming to undertake some significant research and development work and only 15 per cent recording no R&D. Given that the definitions of R&D were fairly similar in the different surveys, what appears to have occurred is a significant increase in the number of companies with relatively low level research and development units. Explanations for the apparent growth in R&D are inevitably speculative. Scotland may now be viewed by investors as a more mature manufacturing location; companies may be keen to exploit the supply of low cost R&D talent readily available from the Scottish universities; and a greater awareness may exist concerning European market differences. Where research and development is cross-tabulated with other variables even more interesting results emerge. Thus wider market areas and product ranges are associated with the presence of R&D; decision-making authority and plant status is associated with the existence of R&D; and proportions of material inputs imported from group plants outside the UK were lower in the R&D-performing subsidiaries. There are at least suggestions, therefore, of a key role for R&D in the operations of MNEs in Scotland, which accords with the strategy model presented earlier, given that both product specialist and strategic independent firms were likely to have development responsibilities for their own product lines (see Table 7.1).

Statistical analysis

To test the subsidiary strategies model, the approach which was followed was to use the technique of cluster analysis to identify groups of firms: the hypothesis would be that the groups or clusters emerging would accord with the typology of strategies discussed earlier. Thereafter some supplementary analytical results, derived from the technique of discriminant analysis using R&D categories as the dependent variable, are presented.

Cluster analysis and the subsidiary strategies model

The statistical technique of cluster analysis is explained more fully in Appendix 2 (p. 145), but essentially the purpose of the technique is to group together firms which are similar with respect to certain strategic and/or definitional variables. Categories or groups are, therefore, formed, with all group members showing common features. The technique can be applied to unordered data and indeed its main purpose is to sort unordered data into a manageable form by the formation of cognate groups. Any desired number of groups can be formed, and the inclusion or exclusion of variables is at the discretion of the investigator. These are important points: essentially the technique is primarily used for sifting and sorting, and the results obtained are more useful for hypothesis formulation than hypothesis testing. It is accepted, therefore, that the results presented here must be viewed as very preliminary and that further investigation will be required.

Initially all the variables for which data were collected in the postal survey were incorporated into the analysis. The resulting output was then sifted and the final results reported include variables which were either considered important *a priori* (e.g. because of their link with the subsidiary strategies model of White and Poynter) or were statistically significant in terms of *F*-ratios. As noted above any desired number of groups can be formed and, once again because of the link with the subsidiary strategies model, only the four-cluster solution is presented here.[3] Although techniques are available to test the 'goodness-of-fit' of sets of clusters generated, and therefore to select a 'best' cluster, these were not accessible in the SPSS package used in the present research.

The results for the four-cluster solution are presented in Table 7.2. The variables included show respectable *F*-ratios, with the factors relating to material inputs, subsidiary roles, R&D and decision-making authority for markets showing up especially strongly. Most of the sample firms are included in Group 1 (45 companies) and Group 2 (50 companies), and these are also the largest subsidiaries on average in employment terms.

The statistical results are interpreted in Table 7.3. The Group 1 subsidiaries appear to contain some of the features expected of the more autonomous strategy types, and the fact that 35 per cent of the sample fall into this category is encouraging from a Scottish impact perspective. These firms are characterised by wide market areas (and therefore substantial exports), significant R&D activities, high value added and, apparently, a fair degree of decision-making autonomy for subsidiary managers. From the White and Poynter (1984) model, it is not too easy to distinguish between the product specialist and strategic independent subsidiary strategies, especially if the latter sells into worldwide markets when effectiveness would probably necessitate a fairly narrow and specialised product range. But certainly the Scottish subsidiaries in Cluster 1 meet the criteria for one of these strategy groups.

Table 7.2   Cluster results for four groups[a]

Variable	Group 1	Group 2	Group 3	Group 4	F-ratio
Market area supplied	3.96	3.52	2.06	2.88	6.45
Product range (compared to parent)	2.93	2.16	2.24	3.00	4.67
Nature of production operations	4.29	3.32	3.94	4.59	5.62
Outputs transferred to group plants abroad	1.49	2.12	1.71	1.59	2.31
Material inputs from group plants abroad	2.22	4.60	1.41	2.24	39.55
Category of R&D	4.38	2.78	2.53	3.59	15.97
Existence of marketing department in Scotland	1.47	1.70	1.94	1.65	4.83
Decision-making responsibility for markets	2.87	1.88	2.18	2.76	9.64
Decision-making responsibility for products	2.98	2.32	2.65	2.76	4.26
Subsidiary roles at present	3.64	2.06	2.23	2.76	4.26
Subsidiary roles in 1976 or at date of establishment	3.42	1.84	2.06	2.35	20.98
Employment range	4.02	3.02	2.17	2.94	5.26
Nationality of ownership	1.24	1.38	1.65	1.53	3.56
Number of firms	45	50	17	17	
Percentage of firms	35.0	38.6	13.2	13.2	

Note: [a] Scores relate to the codings set out in the questionnaire in Appendix 2. The only variable not shown there is nationality of ownership, which is coded 1 for US firms and 2 for others. Categories 5 and 6 of R&D activity, development of new products and processes for world markets and generation of new technology for corporate parent, have been merged.

Turning to the largest sample category – Group 2 – subsidiaries in Scotland are largely assembly operations, closely integrated into the manufacturing networks of the parent MNE, with little in the way of R&D and very limited decision-making responsibility. These are the true branch plant – rationalised manufacturer – operations, a fact indeed confirmed by the responses of subsidiary managers. The only consoling features of this group from an impact perspective are the wide market areas supplied out of the plants, together with the fact that there is some evidence of evolving role over time.

Table 7.3 Interpretation of cluster results for four groups

	Group 1	Group 2	Group 3	Group 4
Ownership, size and period of establishment	Second largest group of firms, mainly American, employing up to 500 people on average and relatively well-established in Scotland	Largest group of subsidiaries, again mainly American, employing under 200 people at plant level in Scotland	13% of sample firms in this group; average employment about 100; highest proportion of non-American MNEs	13% of sample companies; again quite small in employment terms and significant non-US representation
Behavioural characteristics	Widest market area (European and possibly world markets); fairly self-contained manufacturing operation; limited output and input linkages with other group plants; significant R&D operations undertaking product and/or process development for European/world markets	Wide market area; closest to assembly end of production spectrum; substantial output and input linkages with other group plants (over 25% of inputs imported from the MNE); low-level R&D	Market area limited to UK (and perhaps selected Continental European countries); narrow product range; little R&D	Market mainly Europe; wide product range; self-contained manufacturing; R&D mainly concerned with adaptation; limited output and input linkages with other group plants
Decision-making	Significant tendency for in-house marketing in Scotland; relatively high level of authority allowed to Scottish management on market and product decisions	Lowest levels of decision-making authority in Scotland	Marketing mostly outside Scotland. Moderate autonomy	Some marketing departments in Scotland; relatively high level of authority permitted to subsidiary management in Scotland
Interpretation	Results above indicate product specialist/strategic independent strategies, but difficult to distinguish between the two strategies	Rationalised manufacturer status	Results suggest miniature replica at present, but future development is uncertain	Clear indication of miniature replica status, albeit more well-developed than Group 3

For the Group 3 firms, there is a difference between executive perceptions of strategy (which seem to indicate rationalized manufacturer or product specialist) and the results as set out which point clearly to miniature replica status. This group, the smallest in employment terms in the sample, contains the highest proportion of Continental European MNEs. Evidence earlier suggested that many such companies were set up through acquisition (in order to ensure direct market servicing following British entry into the European Community). And, as confirmed in Table 7.3, these subsidiaries mostly sell into the UK market with little in the way of product development or marketing responsibilities at Scottish level.

The Group 4 subsidiaries are similar in some respects to Group 3, but the former are rather larger in employment terms; and, perhaps reflecting this, there are indications of greater autonomy, with some R&D and marketing responsibilities and wider market areas and product ranges.

In both Group 4 and Group 3 there are signs of role-evolution over time, and further changes would be expected in future. The companies are small and must be vulnerable to competitive pressures. White and Poynter (1984), observed the same point in a Canadian context (as shown in Figure 7.1), suggesting that divestment, leaving only a marketing

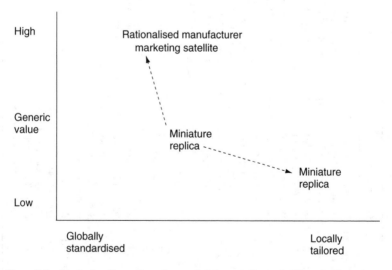

Figure 7.1   Strategic alternatives for a miniature replica subsidiary in Canada
Note: Miniature replica illustrates shift towards increased local tailoring.
Source: White and Poynter (1984).

satellite operation, or greater integration via a rationalised manufacturer strategy were possible; or that the subsidiary would become more local-market oriented focusing on unique preferences and niches within the domestic Canadian market. In any of these cases there were potential problems for the subsidiary; hence the argument for world product mandates. Marketing satellite subsidiaries were not studied in the 1986 survey in Scotland and, indeed, such operations are likely to be rare in Scotland. So the options include: complete divestment; greater integration or, the reverse, greater local tailoring; or enhanced product and market responsibilities through world (or regional) product mandates.

There is clearly still considerable room for developing this type of approach and using it to derive policy implications. For example, the results presented here do not assist the understanding of how particular strategic roles are formulated and allocated to subsidiaries. Is the process 'top-down', with the formulation of global corporate strategy being followed by the establishment of policies and roles for foreign subsidiaries? Or does the evolution and performance of the subsidiary, and the environment within which it operates (regarding, for instance, indigenous supplier capabilities) influence subsidiary roles? There is also the more general question of whether strategy is formulated in an aggregate way as the models and statistical analysis imply, or whether it is articulated in terms of a limited number of key variables only. It is perhaps relevant that two of the key variables in Table 7.2, as established by the F-ratios, were material inputs from group plants abroad and R&D. The cross-tabulations referred to previously also suggested an important role for R&D. In order to assess the possible inter-relationships between R&D strategy and subsidiary strategy overall, therefore, further statistical work was undertaken using the technique of discriminant analysis.

Discriminant analysis and R&D activity

The technique of discriminant analysis is again described more fully in Appendix 2, but in essence this statistical tool facilitates the identification of variables which are important in determining membership of *pre-determined* groups (as opposed to cluster analysis, where data are entered initially in an unordered fashion). Discriminant analysis can, therefore, be used to test an existing hypothesis, in this case that the R&D activity at plant level *per se* is an important determinant of the role of the subsidiary as regards markets supplied, decision-making authority, the nature of production operations and so on. It could be, for instance, that a corporate decision to award a product innovation and development mission to a particular subsidiary (and thus an R&D

facility) then influences subsequent production, marketing and general managerial activities.

The results in Table 7.4 show that for some variables there is a fairly close correlation between the 'status' of R&D work and plant status overall. For example, firms that undertake higher order R&D operations (e.g. product and process development for world markets and/or corporate technology generation) tend to serve wider markets and have greater decision-making autonomy; and there is some slight evidence that high-value R&D work is associated with a plant level marketing function. On the other hand, the 'hits and misses' tabulation shows that only two-thirds of cases were correctly classified. This result, together with the generally modest F-ratios, indicates that R&D alone is not sufficient to explain corporate strategy. Nevertheless, there would be merit in undertaking further work directed specifically to this theme, since it is possible that policy instruments could be devised to encourage subsidiary level R&D; whereas regional or national policy may not be able to impact upon corporate strategy as a whole.

Concluding remarks

By way of a general introductory observation, there is no doubt that the corporate strategy approach to analysing MNE activity is helpful in distinguishing between foreign manufacturing subsidiaries in Scotland. Previous work on branch plant activity in regional economies could be criticised for its static nature, whereas this approach offers a more dynamic basis for analysis. The conceptual work of both Porter (1986) and White and Poynter (1984) is useful in this regard, although there is still room for further development of the ideas. For instance, Scottish membership of the European Community free trade area puts it in a quite different position to that of Canada, and the work of Doz (1986) which was specifically concerned with strategies in Europe is probably worth further consideration. Additionally, the implications of Porter's (1986) 'value chain' concept have not been fully considered in a subsidiary strategy context. Downstream activities in Scotland were proxied by the presence or absence of a marketing department at factory level.

Further work, of a qualitative nature initially, among MNE subsidiaries in Scotland (and elsewhere) is thus called for. Qualitative research should be directed towards exploring the strategy formulation process, the key factors at both firm and environmental level which influence strategy and the major strategy components (markets, R&D, local sourcing etc.). Such work would preferably be matched by similar investigations at

Table 7.4 Discriminant results for 'R&D activity' of the Scottish operation[a]

Variable	R&D category					F-ratio
	None	Customer technical services	Adaptation of manufacturing technology	Development of new and improved products for UK/European markets	Development of new products/processes for world markets and generation of new technology for corporate parent	
Market area supplied	2.68	2.83	3.75	2.75	4.32	5.74
Product range (compared to parent)	2.00	2.50	2.08	2.90	2.77	3.18
Nature of production operations	3.42	3.50	3.96	4.06	4.12	1.14
Outputs transferred to group plants abroad	2.15	1.44	1.71	1.69	1.84	0.87
Material inputs from group plants abroad	3.53	3.55	2.92	2.75	2.77	1.09
Existence of marketing department in Scotland	1.89	1.67	1.67	1.56	1.58	1.73
Decision-making responsibility for markets	2.00	2.28	1.70	2.94	2.61	6.88
Decision-making responsibility for products	2.37	2.50	2.54	2.91	2.65	1.23
Subsidiary roles at present	2.00	2.17	2.33	3.06	3.35	7.54
Employment range	2.42	2.16	3.16	3.53	3.97	3.87

Table 7.4 (*Continued*)

Cases correctly classified ('hits and misses' result)		
R&D category	Actual number	Predicted number
None	19	14 (= 73.7%)
Customer and technical services	18	12 (= 66.7%)
Adaptation of manufacturing technology	24	15 (= 62.5%)
Development of new and improved products for UK/European markets	32	21 (= 65.6%)
Development of new products/processes for world markets etc.	36	25 (= 69.4%)
Overall, 67.7% of cases were correctly classified.		

Note: [a] Variable codings set out in questionnaire.

corporate level. Allied to this is the need for a much greater understanding of the processes of intra-corporate bidding for projects since this determines the trajectory of subsidiary development to a large extent. Equally, little is known about the transition from one subsidiary category to another and the critical variables in that transition. Globalisation, *inter alia*, entails a loss of structural autonomy and greater volatility as the economy becomes more vulnerable to international demand and supply conditions, shortening product life cycles and so on. The ultimate pay-off from such research, which lies in policy initiatives designed to anchor within Scotland (and the UK) substantive subsidiary level activity through, for example, product specialist and strategic independent strategies, may therefore be substantial. Finally, the present study did not identify differences in strategy as between sector; this is surprising since the strategic behaviour of electronic-based subsidiaries is likely to be very different from that of, say, engineering and chemical firms.

What do the preliminary results presented here say about economic gains and losses for the Scottish economy? The first point is to stress that not too much should be claimed from the statistical tests, especially cluster analysis which is a rather weak technique. Nevertheless, the substantial proportion of affiliates identified as product specialists/ strategic independents – around one third of firms in the sample were in this category – is a cause for some optimism. These are some of the largest employers in the foreign sector, and both direct and indirect benefits are suggested for the economy. This still leaves a very large group of conventional branch plants (rationalised manufacturers), even if these are high-tech versions of the 'branch-plant syndrome' as identified in 1976 (Hood and Young, 1976). There is, in addition, a further group of UK-centred miniature replicas whose present contribution to the economy must be limited and whose future is uncertain.

The automatic assumption would be to suggest that policy measures should be directed towards further increasing the proportion of product specialists and strategic independents in Scotland. But as has been pointed out in a Canadian context, the number of products for which worldwide responsibility could be allocated to a foreign subsidiary might be quite small. They may be niche businesses, where market size is quite small and the activity is outside the mainstream business of the MNE, as well as facing threats from the focused strategies of larger competitors. Globalisation, moreover, may point to centralized planning and operations to exploit economies of scale or economies of scope and to facilitate rapid and efficient response to changes in environmental and internal factors. So the debate on the way ahead is by no means clearcut.

As a final comment, it might be noted that this type of work, while based on the Scottish situation, has considerable applicability for other regions which also depend upon externally owned plants. Work in other UK regional economies would not only help to improve the conceptual and empirical foundations of the corporate strategy approach, but would also assist in distinguishing the nature of branch plant activity between regions, an area of enquiry which has not been pursued to this point.

Appendix 1

The views expressed in this paper are personal and should not be construed as reflecting UK government policy.

The postal survey, which formed the basis for this paper, was conducted among overseas-owned companies manufacturing in Scotland based on lists obtained from the Scottish Development Agency – *Overseas and European Companies Manufacturing in Scotland and North American Companies Manufacturing in Scotland, 1985* (Table 7A.1). This source was also used to obtain details of industry and nationality of ownership. The SDA lists identified 342 overseas-owned units in Scotland; this compares with Industry Department for Scotland estimates for 1984 of 375 overseas-owned manufacturing plants belonging to 280 firms.

The postal questionnaire was sent out on 11 June 1986 with a reminder on 30 June. The results discussed are based on the 129 completed questionnaires received. The information requested related to overall operations in Scotland rather than individual plants, although in a few cases more than one questionnaire was returned by the same firm (in industries where plants or business units in Scotland were manufacturing different products and/or performing different roles). Comparison of the sample and the population of foreign firms in Scotland (where data were available for the latter) shows substantial accord, except in regard to nationality of ownership where US firms are slightly under-represented in the sample.

Table 7A.1 Postal survey results: selected data

	Sample size[a]		Sample size
Period of establishment in Scotland		*Market area*	
		UK and selected Continental European countries	49
Pre-1950	29		
1950–9	14	Europe and selected other parts of the world	45
1960–9	23	Mainly world-wide	36
1970–9	34		
1980s	29		
		Outputs transferred to other group plants outside UK for further processing and/or final assembly	
Employment range			
Under 50	29	None	79
50–199	44	Under 5%	25
200–499	25	6–25%	19
500 and over	31	Over 25%	6
		Material inputs from group plants outside UK	
Industry			
Engineering	39	None	34
Electronics	31	under 5%	31
Other	59	6–25%	32
		Over 25 %	32
Nationality		*Category of R&D*	
US	79	None	19
Other	55	Customer technical services; adaptation of manufacturing technology	42
		Development of new and improved products for UK/ European markets	32
		Development of new products and processes for world markets	31
		Generation of new technology for corporate parent	5

Note: [a] sample size = 129 foreign subsidiaries located in Scotland.

Appendix 2

Cluster analysis

Given a sample of N entities measured on P variables, cluster analysis will sort these entities into g groups, with $g < N$. Its major use is, therefore, in suggesting a typology by sorting entities into groups, where all group members share common features, i.e. are similar with respect to the variables included in the analysis.

The technique proceeds by defining a similarity index, where the scores for all variables (which can be standardised) are indexed – any two cases which score similarly with respect to the variables included will, therefore, be more likely to be allotted to the same cluster. It proceeds in a case-by-case fashion, so that after the first step there is one cluster (consisting of the two most similar cases in one group) and N–Z unordered cases. At the next stage, either the next most similar case is added to the existing cluster, or another two-case cluster is formed. This continues until all cases are allotted, and the procedure can be stopped at any desired number of clusters. Various methods of clustering can be used, the differences largely being due to the methods used to calculate the similarity index and the procedure used to define group formation. In the analysis reported above, Ward's method was used; for details see Everitt (1980).

Discriminant analysis

If one is given: (1) a predetermined set of mutually exclusive categories; and (2) a set of variables measured on a number of cases (including measures for the above categories), discriminant analysis will indicate whether the variables are useful in separating the cases into the suggested categories, i.e. whether or not the categories suggested in (1) differ with respect to the variables in (2). The method proceeds by calculating a discriminant score for each category, using the measures for all variables. This score is calculated such that the ratio:

Between-group variance
Within-group variance

is at a maximum, the implication being that such a ratio will ensure a set of groups which are 'tight' (low variance) within themselves, but have a high variance relative to other groups.

Examination of the F-ratios then allows the researcher to determine the degree of differences between groups by variable, i.e. whether any particular variable differs widely between groups; and examination of mean scores for each variable enables the exact degree of difference by variable for each group to be determined. F-ratios in excess of 1 indicate that the between-group differences are unlikely to have resulted by chance. F-ratios are also used in the cluster analysis and should be interpreted in the same fashion.

Notes

1. To this point in time there is no unanimity of the meaning of terms such as 'globalisation', 'global strategy', 'global industry'. But implicit in the concepts are the notions of: viewing strategy in world-wide terms rather than on a national market basis; co-ordinating company resources behind global market share objectives in terms of worldwide R&D programmes, international manufacturing and marketing policies and so on; and having a competitive presence in the major world markets of Europe, North America and Japan.

2. It should be added that respondents were also given descriptions of international strategies from the Porter (1986) model (viz. 'country-centred' through to 'pure global'), and of subsidiary strategies from the White and Poynter (1984) work and asked to relate their own strategic systems to these. In general, executives' perception of strategy (at both parent and subsidiary level) must be regarded as very preliminary. Plant management frequently does not have access to information relating to the strategic thinking of the parent MNE. And, in relation to subsidiary roles, there may be some tendency for executives to overstate, consciously or unconsciously, the status of their plant operations. Misunderstanding was possible too given that the information was collected by means of a postal survey. Therefore an analytical approach which used international strategies or subsidiary strategies as the dependent variables in discriminant analysis was rejected.

3. In the White and Poynter (1984) model, the Miniature replica category was divided into three sub-strategies, namely adopter, adapter and innovator. Therefore a 6-Cluster analysis was also undertaken, but since the results do not add appreciably to the discussion, they have been omitted here.

8
Multinational Enterprises and Regional Economic Development (1994)*

Stephen Young, Neil Hood and Ewen Peters

Introduction

The objective of this paper is to provide an overview and synthesis of the different strands of literature relating to multinational enterprises (MNEs) and regional economic development, with especial reference to foreign MNEs in the European Community (EC). The international business subject area is of interest to researchers from several disciplines, whose contributions have developed partly in isolation and certainly with different foci of attention. By integrating them with the regional development interest at the forefront of attention, it is hoped to provide new insights for academics and policy makers. The timing is appropriate since early evidence and forecasts point to a difficult environment for the attraction of new greenfield manufacturing foreign direct investment (FDI) through the 1990s. This is a consequence of the growth of FDI in services and the changed modality of new investment activity, away from greenfield projects towards joint ventures, acquisitions and alliances involving different components of the value chain (United Nations, 1992). This pattern is occurring at the same time as the average project size, in terms of number of jobs, is falling, while the limited volume of new greenfield investment will be further restricted for part of the 1990s both by recession conditions in major home countries and by the after-effects of the pre-Single European Market-induced boom in foreign direct investment, especially from Japan. Maximising the regional contribution of the new and existing inward direct investment

* *Regional Studies*, 28 (7) (1994), 657–77.

is thus of paramount importance, yet at odds in many ways with the demands of global or European corporate integration. Within Europe, specifically, there are fears that the periphery may lose out from the process of integration (Nam and Reuter, 1991; Oughton, 1993) and that multinationals will concentrate higher value added activities in core regions (Young and Hood, 1993).

The impact of multinational activity: a regional perspective

There is reasonable agreement that multinational enterprises possess the potential for providing both static and dynamic benefits for the global economy, for individual host countries and for regions within countries. For countries and regions, static gains derive from inward direct investment augmenting comparative advantage, the equivalent of the trade theory models of Ricardo and Heckscher–Ohlin (after dropping various restrictive assumptions such as perfect competition and immobility of factors of production). Improved allocative efficiency will be observed in terms of production by MNEs in host nations in sectors of advanced technology and high productivity, and improved technical efficiency emanates from the ability to produce more efficiently than indigenous competitors. The outcome is likely to be short run benefits in capital formation, employment, trade and the balance of payments. Dunning (1993) adds to these conventional measures the comparative efficiency with which MNEs can fully exploit economies of scale and scope, and the efficiency with which resources are reallocated between uses to meet changing demand and supply needs (structural adjustment efficiency). In regard to the latter, because of their characteristics, MNEs might adjust more quickly to changes in technology and demand conditions than indigenous firms which could create adjustment problems for affected host countries and regions; such potential difficulties will be exacerbated in an era of global strategies and global competition. To be added to the direct effects are the indirect consequences of MNE activity which concern their impacts on suppliers or customers and on competitors or firms producing complementary goods, which generate linkage and spillover gains.

The interest in this paper is less on the impact of MNEs on regional economies within a comparative static framework than on the effects on dynamic comparative advantage. Structural upgrading clearly has dynamic consequences as do the spillover effects of MNE activity, but there is no multinational theory of economic development *per se* (Ozawa, 1992). Following a brief review of some of the evidence on the direct static effects of MNE activity, the remainder of this paper high-lights different strands of literature which have a contribution to make, mainly at a conceptual level, to the subject of multinationals and regional development, that is the dynamic consequences of multi-national operations.

Empirical studies are plagued by the problem of trying to assess the difference between the actual impact of MNEs and those which would have occurred in their absence, i.e. the counterfactual situation. Summarising the results of studies from 12 developed and developing countries (which resolved the counterfactual problem in different ways), Dunning (1985) concluded that MNEs had a beneficial effect on resource allocation at least in a static sense, although about half of the studies stressed that the beneficial effects might have been increased with different government policies. Regarding the spillover effects, in larger, advanced industrial economies it was concluded that MNE con-tributions had been positive and in some sectors substantial, whereas in the small developed and less developed countries, mixed results were reported.

Narrowing the focus to an individual country such as the United Kingdom and regions within that country, there is a reasonable degree of similarity in the results from a variety of recent studies (see, for example, Young, Hood and Peters, 1993, on Scotland; Northern Ireland Economic Development Council, 1992, on Northern Ireland; Welsh Affairs Committee, 1988 and Hill and Munday, 1991, on Wales; and The English Unit, 1991, on the English regions), namely that the direct effects have been positive whereas the spillover effects, especially with respect to local sourcing, have been very disappointing. With such results, the issue of generating dynamic gains from MNE activity is a very real one, the more so since many authors believe that there are other negative features associated with external control in regional economies. A recent review of the evidence, focusing especially on the UK, is in Ashcroft and Love (1993), who question whether the alleged benefits occur to any significant degree and argue that, 'on the contrary, there is evidence that the truncated nature of much MNE activity in peripheral regions can act to the regions' long run disadvantage by restricting their supply potential' (1993: 27). Dividing the hypothesised costs and benefits into four categories – organisation and autonomy, structure of production, performance and wider regional effects – what the authors present is a more sophisticated version of the 'branch-plant economy' argument which has been prevalent since the 1960s and 1970s, but is still relevant to the issue of the entrepreneurial potential of a region and therefore its potential for long-run development. Firn's (1975) distinction between 'innovative, entrepreneurial-type decision making' and 'routine, management-type supervision' is still very important, and runs through some of the discussions on the nature of the multinational subsidiary presented later in this paper. Current debates centre on whether or not best practice manufacturing techniques, associated with flexible specialization, will change the nature of branch plant activity and improve embeddedness within regional economies (Schoenberger, 1988b; UNCTC, 1990; Morris, 1992).

Ashcroft and Love's careful work on external control and the regional economy is primarily concerned with the effects of takeovers and mergers (for an analysis of Scottish takeovers 1965–89, see Ashcroft and Love, 1993 – it is worth pointing out that most of the acquiring companies were Rest of UK-owned as opposed to foreign-owned; an earlier study covering the period 1965–80 is in Ashcroft, Love and Scouller, 1987). Their conclusion was that the internal effects (improved availability of investment funds, improved financial techniques, and the supply of management, technical help and marketing skills) tended on balance to be favourable to the acquired companies. Conversely the external effects appeared to be unfavourable to the Scottish economy, particular importance in this regard attaching to some reduction in local linkages and organisational functions as the firms' demands shifted away from Scotland.

In the present paper the emphasis is on establishing the potential of the multinational to generate long run benefits for regional economies. As the above evidence shows, the conclusion at present is that foreign direct investment is not fulfilling this role. Most of the discussion which follows focuses upon new greenfield investment or the evolution/reorganisation of existing investments. It has to be recognised, therefore, that any beneficial impacts which might be assisted by policy initiatives directed towards these types of investment, could be undermined if takeovers and mergers were to increase in an unrestricted fashion.

Stages of growth and related paradigms

As indicated above, the crucial debate relates to the potential dynamic gains and the role of MNEs as 'engines of growth' (United Nations, 1992), where a number of interrelated approaches can be identified. Ozawa (1992) has presented 'a dynamic paradigm of FDI-facilitated development'. This stages approach has its origins in the work of Rostow (1959);

Chenery (1979); and Balassa (1980); and in a multinational context is an extension of Vernon's (1966) product life cycle theory of trade and investment. In the Ozawa model a typical developing country progresses through a series of development stages. In $t1$, the country adopts an outward-looking export-led development path, which leads in $t2$ to the attraction of inward investment (mainly through joint ventures) in standardised labour-intensive manufacturing activities (comparative advantage augmenting) with intra-firm exports by MNEs. The critical transformations occur in time periods $t3$ and $t4$: through the apprenticeship of local firms to foreign MNEs, 'localised learning and technological accumulation' (1966: 47) leads on to 'internationalised learning' (1966: 48) as local entrepreneurs, as well as inward investors, move upmarket domestically (into higher value added activities with greater capital intensity) and transfer existing operations to lower wage developing countries. By $t5$ the country is on the verge of the 'investment-driven stage' in which industry is primarily physical-capital and scale-intensive. Here the role of Government becomes crucial in providing infrastructure, education, public health, R&D support and other public goods to enhance dynamic comparative advantage.

Earlier ideas on a similar theme are contained in Dunning's (1981, 1986) investment development cycle concept, based on the proposition that the level of inward and outward investment of different nations and their net investment position depends upon their national stage of development. The investment development cycle has been extended by others (Tolentino, 1987, 1993; Cantwell and Tolentino, 1990) to show how the dynamic interaction between inward investment by foreign MNEs and the indigenous sector strengthened the competitive and technological position of local firms (see also Wong, 1992, on technological development through subcontracting linkages), and leads on to outward investment; the complexity of the form of outward investment itself is related to the stage of industrial development of the particular country.

Most of this work is derived from the experience of the high performing Asian economies (HPAEs), some of which have effectively utilized inward (and outward) FDI as catalysts of industrial development. In the Ozawa model these countries have progressed through the factor driven stage (based on natural and labour resources) and are in the midst of investment driven industrialization, with physical capital as the primary factor. The author recognises, however, that more conceptual work is needed to explore the third, innovation-driven (human capital) stage of MNE-facilitated growth, while commenting that demand-side factors would play a greater role at this point, with Japan as an obvious exemplor. Dunning (1993) pays some attention both to the innovation-driven Stage 3 and to an information-processing Stage 4, again pointing out the importance of government activity in ensuring that inward investment supports a virtuous as opposed to vicious cycle of economic activity.

While these stylised models of MNE-induced development tend to use the HPAEs as examples, in fact the common characteristic of the Asian economies concerned is that they were open to foreign technology in whatever form (World Bank, 1993). Japan, Korea and, to a lesser degree, Taiwan relied substantially on licensing, machinery imports and reverse engineering. It was Hong Kong, Singapore and the Southeast Asian HPAEs which, in addition, welcomed FDI.

The concepts of virtuous and vicious cycles of technological development are constituents of what Dunning (1993) terms the asset accumulation and restructuring paradigm, linked to the work of Cantwell (1989, 1993) (see also Dunning, 1988; Pavitt, 1988). Emphasis is on the accumulation and diffusion of technology, with the argument being presented that multinationals may play a part in a 'virtuous cycle' of increasing technological capability in host countries. By a process of cumulative causation, countries growing rapidly and devoting resources to encouraging indigenous technological development are likely to attract inward investment in research intensive activities and local research and development (R&D); the activities of the latter, in turn, stimulate local rivals to a higher rate of innovation and encourage agglomerative economies in technological centres of excellence in host economies. The benefits to the MNE accrue from its ability to tap into the technological specialisation of different country locations and hence configure its research related activity so as to improve its capabilities to generate new technology. The one note of caution, supported by other work (e.g. Galbraith and De Noble, 1988) concerns the diseconomies of technological agglomeration such as labour shortages and high rates of employee turnover. Cantwell's work places great importance on MNEs' activities in establishing internal and external networks to facilitate international production and technological development. One interesting issue not considered is the role of networking within the host country and whether network possibilities can help or hinder technology development, and indeed other aspects of international production such as local sourcing and personnel recruitment.

By contrast to these beneficial impacts, a 'vicious cycle' of declining technological capability may occur in weaker host country sectors (at the same time as another national industry is in a virtuous cycle). Inward investment may still take place, but primarily in assembly activities with higher value added intermediate products being imported. Because of their greater efficiency (derived from parent R&D, etc.) or deliberate strategy, MNE activities may lead to lower sales, profits and R&D expenditures by indigenous enterprises and hence a reduction in domestic technological capability.

Cantwell does allow for the possibility of MNEs in such circumstances helping to upgrade local skills, production engineering and incremental process improvement, but in the 'vicious cycle' approach the argument does link in some ways to radical industrial organisation, market power and dependency models of MNE impact from Hymer (1975); Bornschier and Chase-Dunn (1985) and Newfarmer (1985); to Cowling and Sugden (1987). Hierarchies of economies and central and peripheral locations are associated with the hierarchical organization structures of MNEs, with peripheral economies unable to break out from their role as providers of low grade activities (Schoenberger, 1988a). Some writers in the dependency school also use the core/periphery concept to discuss regional inequalities within countries (both core countries and peripheral countries – see Galtung, 1971). Thus MNEs may contribute to the development of foreign enclaves within host economies by importing a complete package of production techniques and utilising capital-intensive technologies, where linkages, either backwards or forwards, with local firms are limited or non-existent (Biersteker, 1981). Within regional economies in developed economies, far from acting as 'growth poles', it was alleged in the 1960s and 1970s that MNEs established capital intensive, low-skill 'cathedrals in the desert' (Morris, 1992). These arguments concerning the role of MNEs in forming enclave economies are still made strongly in the poorer developing countries of Latin America and Africa (Bornschier and Chase-Dunn, 1985); and as the earlier discussion on the branch plant economy showed, the fundamental concerns still remain in developed economies.

In his work on *The Competitive Advantage of Nations*, Porter (1990) distinguishes four stages of national competitive development, with the wealth-driven stage of drift and ultimate decline representing Stage 4. But Porter largely omits foreign direct investment from his analysis of the principal ways in which countries may improve their competitiveness through his 'diamond of competitive advantage' (the forces in the diamond are factor conditions; demand conditions; related and supporting industries; and firm strategy, structure and rivalry; with government and chance being added since their role can influence the entire diamond).

Porter's limited contribution is to observe that: 'A developmental strategy based solely on foreign multinationals may doom a nation to remaining a factor-driven economy' (1990: 679), although he does more interestingly suggest that inward investment may represent one component of a developmental strategy, especially if attempts are made to attract a cluster of MNEs in a single industry. Dunning (1992), however, has argued the case for including multinational activity as an additional exogenous variable affecting the Porter diamond, and illustrates the potential influence of MNEs on each component of the diamond. Particular interest attaches to the postulated links between MNEs and the development of related and supporting industries within the diamond, and to Dunning's observations on the potential interaction between MNEs, government and competitiveness. For a country seeking to upgrade its diamond, other work (Peters, 1993) has emphasised the role of technology (pick technologies, develop technologies, integrate technology into products, monitor product markets and technologies) and the development of advanced factor conditions.

Regional economic development

There is an extensive literature around the theme of regional economic development. Issues considered in detail concern the attraction of industry, especially high-tech, and the creation of clusters and development of linkages in pursuit of self-sustaining and innovative development. The conclusion increasingly reached is that a region's ability to innovate and develop is determined by many factors, with no single path to regional technological development (Aydalot and Keeble, 1988). Given the diversity, there are major policy difficulties in, say, selecting the most effective incentives to encourage indigenous entrepreneurs or to attract companies from elsewhere. Perhaps understandably, a wide range of public policies have, therefore, been adopted at national and local level, including: research parks; innovation centres; public venture funds; subsidies in the form of grants and tax incentives specifically directed at R&D, new or small firm development; government procurement; and 'picking winners', meaning targeting government assistance on those particular innovating small and medium-sized firms which contribute to indigenous regional growth (Christy and Ironside, 1987).

From the current perspective, however, rather limited attention has been paid to the multinational dimension in regional economic development. Aydalot (1988) has made a distinction between development efforts in Europe based on *attraction* as compared with *polarisation*. In the former case development reflects the actions of firms external to the regional environment, and since this approach is often pursued in areas with older, declining industries, there is no framework of local know-how on which to build or links with the former specialisation. The polarisation case involves firms creating, by their development and the links formed between each other, opportunities for new enterprises to appear. The emphasis is on development based on scientific knowledge and a reliance on small firms to take the major risks involved in radical innovation, even if the driving mechanism is large technology-based institutes or enterprises, e.g. government research centres, military demand historically, large aviation plants etc.

Since a variety of processes can be observed within the attraction/ polarisation distinction, a fuller typology of technologically innovative areas has been developed (see Table 8.1). The implicit assumption is that large, externally-owned firms (including multinationals) do not permit the formation of a true industrial complex facilitating cumulative development (see also Segal and Quince, 1985).[1] However, the difficulty in such generalizations is shown by Perrin (1988), who concludes from the Sophia Antipolis experience that: 'In mixing incubators with R&D and multinational high-technology production establishments, innovation

Table 8.1 Factors in development of technologically innovative areas

	Development mechanism	Illustrations
Local dynamism	Demand	Government demand: defence spending: concentration of innovation capacity; subcontracting demand for technologically advanced products.
	Supply	Spin-off from knowledge centres.
External dynamism	Large firms	Location of large firms (production plants), based on supply of location factors including government subsidies.
	Small firms	Location of innovative SMEs, attracted by supply of location and 'atmospheric' factors.

Source: Adapted from Aydalot (1988) (the author actually notes a further distinction between regions with and without an industrial tradition but this has been excluded).

capacities may be greatly enlarged' (1988: 141). In addition, Del Monte and De Luzenberger (1989) hint at the possibility of non-local enterprises bringing about the birth and further growth of local firms in Southern Italy. A distinction is also made among multinationals. Traditional corporate policies in older MNEs inherited from the growth period emphasise the establishment of research units, production activities and marketing services in different places; only when such firms develop regional sub-contracting policies is local know-how created which can have a cumulative developmental impact. The contrast is made with mainly younger MNEs in which decentralised teams are given freedom to develop synergistic relations with neighbouring academic laboratories and R&D intensive enterprises. Among the long-established MNEs too, the cost and risk of R&D investment is suggested as leading to co-operative agreements with other large and small firms and institutions, and to organizational changes in the direction of greater decentralization.

In revisiting the process of clustering and the generation of agglomeration economies, accepted as vital to cumulative innovation and development, considerable emphasis has been given to the theory of the 'industrial districts' (Harrison, 1992).[2] The view is that a new wave of regional economic growth is being driven by inter-linked networks of small and medium sized enterprises, exploiting the diffusion of flexible computer-controlled production technology. However, much of this work emanates from Piore and Sabel (1984), and the specific illustration of north-central and north-eastern Italy ('Third Italy'), and recent writings have been sceptical of the generality of this process (Amin and Dietrich, 1990; Amin and Malmberg, 1992).

Scott (1992) has proposed the extension of the definition of large industrial districts to include large production units (see also Sabel, 1989). The author suggests that the conventional distinction between production units into flexible specialists, e.g. printed circuit boards, ASIC semiconductors and mass producers (e.g. autos, petrochemicals), is inadequate and a three-fold categorisation including 'systems houses' (e.g. aerospace, military communications equipment) is suggested. The latter is defined as a production unit which has large internal economies of scope emanating from a design-intensive or R&D-intensive production process, manufactures complex outputs in small batches often over a lengthy production period, and has a complex internal structure employing large numbers of workers. Compared with the standardisation of inputs in mass production, systems houses require a wide range of diverse and variable inputs, and are connected with large numbers of flexibly specialised producers. For this reason, it is argued, they are commonly located in dense, flexible, production agglomerations, although the critical question of which comes first, the SME agglomerations or the systems houses, is still open. Concluding with a specific link to the MNE, Scott comments that 'The internationalization of the economy...is to a significant degree realized as the interlinkage of industrial districts across the globe, with the multinational corporation often playing a facilitating rather than a purely destructive role' (1992: 274). In evaluating this work, the fact that the evidence is so far restricted to Southern California is a limitation, and there is a need to identify other manufacturing and service sectors where the systems house concept may exist. Until then it must remain an open question whether they are or can be regional catalysts.

The literature on regional development thus suggests some possible routes through which MNEs may play a positive role, but only if regional incentive policies designed to attract internationally mobile investment are integrated closely with a package of other measures designed to stimulate clustering. The needed conceptual work is still underdeveloped, however, and within Europe there seem to be rather few examples of successful growth centres in which MNEs play a leading or active role. The study by the Netherlands Economic Institute (1992) identified several core areas where economic activity and technological activity were concentrated. Mostly these were within the core triangle bounded by Paris, London and Amsterdam and including the Ruhr Basin (work suggesting a concentration of activity within the central area of Europe goes back to Clark, Wilson and Bradley, 1969; Kaldor, 1971; Dunning, 1972; for more recent writings, see Panić, 1992; Shepley and Wilmot, 1992). Outside this arc were other centres like Hamburg, Copenhagen and the regions stretching from Southern France to Northern Spain. Additional 'islands of innovation' (Hilpert, 1991) were found in areas like Berlin, Toulouse and Bordeaux where specialisms in particular techno-industrial fields could be identified, but this was a very selective process involving 'spots' instead of 'belts'. The precise involvement of non-EC MNEs in their development is, however, not clear.

Local linkages and regional development

In the context of regional economic development again, an issue recognised as being of vital importance and one which bridges the static/dynamic distinction concerns the second order impacts relating to the linkage and spillover effects of inward investment (Hirschman, 1958). The focus has tended until fairly recently to be on the scale and value of supplies and jobs created among suppliers within a static framework, although spillover effects extend to technology spin-offs, new firm creation and demonstration effects on suppliers, customers and competitors. In the context of work on new forms of industrial organization such as flexible specialization (Piore and Sabel, 1984; UNCTC, 1990), greater stress has been placed on these dynamic linkages, although conceptual work is still lacking. Turok (1993) has distinguished two distinctive alternatives from the debates, namely 'developmental' and 'dependency'. In the former, vertical disintegration of production is linked to collaborative partnerships between MNEs, suppliers and distributors, encouraging geographical clustering to minimise transaction and transport costs and maximise networking benefits. The clusters, in turn, could form the basis of internally generated growth poles. In the dependency case, linkages with suppliers are hierarchical, governed by price considerations or other short-term objectives. Inward investors' ties to the locality are thus weakly embedded, in marked contrast to those in the developmental scenario.

Whether such a clearcut distinction exists is in fact dubious (but see Thoburn and Takashima, 1993), since a typical inward investor could have a range of relationships with suppliers depending on the importance and perhaps technological sophistication of the inputs. The concept of 'developmental linkages' may be too static and idealized for a high-tech, internationally-integrated economy. Furthermore, as Morris (1992), has pointed out, spatial agglomeration will not automatically occur and requires heavy investment *inter alia* in the education and training infrastructure. There are also many different types of inward investor, and nationality of ownership is a factor in Europe given 'local content' requirements on Japanese investors. Even if companies are committed to outsourcing and just-in-time (JIT) production, the likelihood of this encouraging customer–supplier clustering *within a region* in Europe may be limited. Requirements may be met from suppliers across Europe with, if necessary, supply companies establishing warehousing facilities to facilitate JIT without relocating production (Schoenberger, 1988b; Morris, 1989; Peck, 1990).

It is true that in an industry like electronics, there are key imperatives leading to increased contracting: these include the ability of supply specialists to offer quality and efficiency, speed and flexibility, the latter two factors being critical as product life cycles continue to shorten. In addition, with some capital intensive processes, the level of utilisation by original equipment manufactures (OEMs) could not justify in-house manufacture. From the OEM side, too, is a trend to a concentration on core competencies. However, the contracting companies which are exploiting these trends are themselves globalising and therefore their international investment decisions are likely to have, say, a pan-European rather than a regional focus (*Financial Times*, 1993).

If sectoral clustering, involving different components of the value chain, is problematic, MNE clustering by nationality of ownership in Europe has occurred to some extent, linked to regional incentive policies – witness the example of Japanese investment in South Wales. Such clusters do produce spin-off benefits such as purchasing of business services, joint training with local firms and standard setting, and collaboration with academic institutions (English Unit, 1991) but the benefits are hardly 'developmental' in the sense in which they are being discussed here.

Development through the multinational subsidiary

Contributions to development questions can also be inferred from work in the international management and organisational behaviour fields on multinational corporate and subsidiary strategy. The exclusive focus on factors driving globalisation in the late 1970s and early 1980s began to be replaced by a recognition of the existence of counterbalancing influences such as flexible automation which reduced the minimum efficient scale in many sectors and created the possibilities for product variation (Bartlett, 1986; Etemad and Séguin Dulude, 1986; Bartlett and Ghoshal, 1989); the latter was also linked to the growing importance of distribution, marketing and services (Young and Hood, 1992) to provide products more tailored to the local needs of consumers. From this emerged a debate on the balance between forces requiring global integration as opposed to national responsiveness in the MNE and on the appropriate organizational form, parent–subsidiary relationships and subsidiary roles in multinationals.

Organisational form

The origins of most work on the organization of the modern corporation derive from Chandler (1962) who fostered an approach, based on business history research, in which environmental factors determine strategy which, in turn, leads on to firm structure (the strategy–structure paradigm); and in which structures are hierarchical in nature. In international management the pioneering study within this framework was that of Stopford and Wells (1972) on American MNEs who developed a 'stages model' of international organisational structures. In the early stages of internationalisation, companies would typically operate a domestic functional structure allied to an international division; later reorganisation would be in the direction of global structures, based around product, area or functional divisions. In its updated form (Egelhoff, 1988), companies evolve towards worldwide product divisions and matrix structures as the extent of foreign product diversity and percentage of foreign manufacturing increases. Within European (especially continental European) companies, a different organizational tradition has been observed, with a high incidence in the past of the 'mother–daughter' form (Franko, 1976; Hedlund, 1984, Hedlund and Åman, 1984) with relatively strong and autonomous foreign subsidiaries, loosely co-ordinated through informal networks of personal management contacts across the groups. From research among Swedish companies, it has been observed that many companies subsequently introduced global product divisions as a response to global competition and environmental change, although performance results were disappointing (Håkanson, 1990).

In interpreting the implications for subsidiaries and regions it is useful to add to the structural classifications the concept of firm orientation, which is derived from Perlmutter (1969) (see also Chakravarthy and Perlmutter, 1985). A distinction has been made between ethnocentric (home country culture), polycentric (host country culture), regiocentric (regional culture) and geocentric (global culture) MNEs – this is the so-called 'EPRG profile'. And a link can be drawn broadly between orientations and structures, as shown in Table 8.2.

Table 8.2   MNE orientations and organisation structures

Prevailing orientation	Structural archetype	Network structure
Ethnocentric	International division	Centralised hub
Polycentric	(Mother–daughter)[a]	Decentralised federation
	Global structure (area, product, function)	Centralised division
Geocentric		
	Transnational	Integrated network
	Heterarchy	Heterarchy

Note: [a] Mother–daughter is bracketed, because some firms with either international divisions or even global structures could operate in a polycentric, decentralised manner.
Source: Extended from Håkanson (1990).

The centralisation/decentralisation debate is a long-standing one which, in many ways, is related to the ebb and flow of corporate fashion; but ethnocentric orientations and international divisions would tend to be associated with centralised control from parent headquarters and hence limited scope for entrepreneurial and innovative behaviour at subsidiary level. The mother–daughter form is one illustration of the polycentric/decentralised MNE model, where subsidiaries may have significant authority and autonomy, although this may be limited to the host country in which the subsidiary operates. As in Porter's (1986) multi-domestic/country-centred MNE, legislative, taste and cultural differences, and tariff and non-tariff barriers help explain polycentrism and decentralisation.

More recent work has tended to reject the rigid structural implications of the above models, accepting that great differences exist within the same multinational across the world in terms of environments and resources, suggesting in turn intra-MNE strategic diversification. Some authors have continued to stress the need for 'fit', nevertheless, between environment, strategy and structure, while recognizing that the internal structures of the MNE should be differentiated to match the circumstances of its different national subsidiaries (Ghoshal and Nohria, 1989, 1993). Bartlett and Ghoshal (1989) developed the concept of the 'transnational organization'. This was an alternative to the 'multinational' (worldwide operations viewed as a portfolio of national businesses), 'international' (resembling the multinational form but with subsidiaries more dependent on the headquarters for the transfer of knowledge and information and with formal systems and controls in HQ–subsidiary relationships) or 'global' (centralization of assets, resources and responsibilities, with subsidiaries assembling and selling products and implementing plans and policies developed at headquarters) organisation. The transnational is seen as an integrated network organization with some resources centralised in the home country, others distributed among national operations and all integrated through strong interdependencies (Bartlett and Ghoshal, 1989; see Leong and Tan, 1993, for an empirical test of the Bartlett and Ghoshal model); and is appropriate in highly variable environments among countries (Ghoshal and Nohria, 1993). The national subsidiary in the transnational organisation could thus perform very different roles, and the distinction was made by the authors between: the 'strategic leader', a highly competent subsidiary which serves as a partner of headquarters in developing and implementing strategy; the 'contributor', which has a distinct capability, while operating in a small or strategically unimportant market; and the 'implementer' which, as it implies, has the role of implementing overall corporate strategy.[3] The possibility of competitive innovative national subsidiaries (particularly in the strategic leader form) contributing positively to regional economic development could thus begin to be foreseen.

Other authors have rejected the strategy–structure paradigms and emphasised instead the roles of ambiguity and chaos within organisations (see Mintzberg's, 1973, anarchic organisation; Weick, 1987; Nonaka, 1988). For continuous evolution, it is regarded as necessary to allow freedom among the constituent units in an organisation and to encourage creative conflict between them. Yet other writers discuss the emergence of hybrid organisational arrangements, represented by strategic partnerships, networking and alliances, the influences of vertical disaggregation, the shift towards more flexible forms of production, research costs and shortened product life cycles, and a greater emphasis on innovation and more specialised, higher quality product lines (Powell, 1987; Borys and Jemison, 1989; Ohmae, 1990). Such changes are seen to require faster responsiveness and are best provided by small or flat, decentralised firms rather than by large companies with multiple hierarchical layers, and by co-operative arrangements. Although the link has not really been made in the literature, it is possible that MNEs may be more confident of loosening relations intra-firm when they themselves are involved in many hybrid arrangements. In this way more entrepreneurial behaviour at subsidiary level may be permitted or, indeed, encouraged.

The most formal approach to the development of an alternative model is contained in Hedlund's (1986) concept of the 'heterarchical MNE'. This has its roots in chaos theory and 'messy' structures (Hedlund and Rolander, 1990), and rejects the deterministic conclusions of the strategy–structure paradigm in favour of an approach which does not necessarily start with the environment but recognises multiple interactions. The view of structure is thus 'as a complex heterarchy of geographically diffused but globally coordinated core functions' (Hedlund and Rolander, 1990: 41). The heterarchical MNE may have many centres with notions such as 'headquarters', 'home country' and 'corporate level' disappearing. Some empirical work to support the heterarchical MNE concept (mostly based on Swedish evidence) is presented in Bartlett, Doz and Hedlund (1990), and in the work of Forsgren and colleagues (for example, Forsgren and Johanson, 1992; Forsgren and Pahlberg, 1992), in which multinationals are seen as 'loosely coupled political systems rather than tightly bonded, homogenous, hierarchically controlled systems' (Forsgren, Holm and Johanson, 1992: 247). It is possible to view the multi-centred MNE as the natural outcome of relatively unrestricted subsidiary growth in the mother-daughter structures of earlier days. In that sense it is a European (or perhaps simply Swedish) model, whereas the Bartlett and Ghoshal transnational has its roots firmly in the American organisational tradition.

Subsidiary roles

As the focus of attention in the literature has changed from the MNE as a whole to the whole plus its constituent parts, so increasing interest has been paid to the MNE subsidiary and its potential contribution to the group. This latter work is still firmly within the international management tradition, although some writers, especially those in host countries, have reoriented discussion towards host economy impact and thus closer to the regional economic development concerns of this paper. Canadian authors have been especially active, developing the notion of a world product mandate (WPM) as a means of increasing the Canadian benefits from foreign-owned manufacturing. A subsidiary which possesses a WPM is given worldwide responsibility for a complete range of value activities, managing R&D, production and marketing activities for a product or product line globally. Roth and Morrison (1992) quote the examples of Westinghouse Canada which is responsible for gas turbines worldwide; Mack, a German subsidiary of Pfizer USA which has worldwide responsibility for a variety of fine chemicals and cardiology and leukaemia-based treatments; and Siemens Japan, partnered by Asahi Medical, with a mandate for compact magnetic resonance image machines (see also the illustrations in Amin *et al.*, 1994).

White and Poynter (1984) devised a model of subsidiary roles in a Canadian context, and criticised the limited economic contribution of the 'miniature replica' (a scaled down version of the parent, chiefly engaged in assembly work) and 'rationalised manufacturer' subsidiaries (undertaking the manufacture of a particular product or component or stage in a vertically integrated process) which were implementers of parent-devised strategy; in essence the miniature replica, in particular, is the archetypal branch plant. (Similar categorizations have been presented by others, e.g. D'Cruz, 1986).[4] By comparison, 'product specialist' subsidiaries with world product mandates, operated as quasi-autonomous divisions or strategic business units (SBUs) within MNEs, were regarded as providing substantial and dynamic benefits for host economies. The multinational would harness the unique attributes and skills of host economies in a way which was mutually beneficial; dynamic comparative advantages could accrue to the host economy through the stimulus to entrepreneurial activity in technology, engineering and marketing.

In the vigorous debate which took place in Canada, it was argued, however, that there could be parent company objections to the decentralisation involved, particularly of R&D, that the adjustment costs in implementing WPMs might be very high, and that global competitiveness might require centralisation. Rugman and Bennett (1982) argued on the basis of this that the number of potential WPMs could be quite limited, and that they might be niche businesses where the market size was small and the activity was outside the mainstream business of the MNE. Government policy support for WPMs was seen in terms of direct aid to upgrade the knowledge, technology and other managerial aspects of these subsidiaries as well as an informational role in encouraging the adoption and diffusion of flexible manufacturing systems (Beigie and Stewart, 1986). With hindsight, policy measures in Canada seem to have had little influence on the emergence of WPM subsidiaries, whose numbers in any event are rather small. More generally, Buckley and Casson (1992) have made the valid point that the subsidiary granted a mandate in response to government pressure is very different and probably much less innovative than the same subsidiary awarded a WPM by the parent on the basis of performance and competitive bidding within the group.

Other subsidiary models have identified similarly entrepreneurial categories to that of the product specialist. As noted earlier, Bartlett and Ghoshal's (1989) 'strategic leader' subsidiary is viewed as a 'legitimate partner with the headquarters in developing and implementing broad strategic thrusts' (1989: 105); an example cited is that of Philips' UK subsidiary which played a key role in developing the company's leadership position worldwide in the tele-text TV business. A very similar subsidiary type is Gupta and Govindarajan's (1991) 'global innovator', where the subsidiary 'serves as the fountainhead of knowledge for other units' (1991: 773).

In the heterarchical MNE the emphasis is placed upon the multi-centred nature of the multinational, which for Swedish MNEs has seen 'a financial centre in Brussels; the largest division HQ in London; an R&D centre with group responsibilities for certain products in India; ... and an Italian unit with global responsibility for component supply' (Hedlund and Rolander, 1990: 25). As these illustrations indicate, subsidiary (although the term would not be used in the heterarchical MNE) responsibilities may be limited to one element of the value chain only, rather than a complete chain as in the product specialist/strategic leader. The former is probably more realistic since there will undoubtedly be much variety on a worldwide basis in large, diversified MNEs. It may also be more appropriate in an era of vertical disintegration, when there is evidence, in Europe, for example, of free-standing R&D units, distribution centres and regional headquarters of foreign-owned MNEs. European consultants specifically recognise these separate activities in the advice they provide on the most attractive locations (Ernst & Young, 1990). From a regional development perspective, however, the most attractive locations for R&D units, distribution centres and regional HQs are nearly all in central as opposed to peripheral regions. Hence the opportunities for the less favoured regions may lie primarily in existing production based activity through WPMs or other forms of plant upgrading.

Considering the factors leading to the emergence of 'developmental' subsidiaries, the empirical studies undertaken place most importance on the internal competences of the affiliate, and the initiative of local management. To Bartlett and Ghoshal (1989) high internal competence in strategic leader subsidiaries is the key and the possibility of country managers building their own organization independent of the parent was recognised, although the authors saw a need to control aggressive localization policies and bring national subsidiaries within co-ordinated and interdependent networks. Roth and Morrison's (1992) empirical results stress management expertise with respect to managing strategic flexibility. Given the network theory underpinnings to much of the work on heterarchies, Forsgren, Holm and Johanson (1992) see the possibility of subsidiaries developing power in the organisation through their own performance, and development of their own business networks is allowed for. In other work (Forsgren and Pahlberg, 1992) a distinction is made between structural power and resource power; the former relates to the subsidiary's position within a business network and affects the possibility of influencing the firm's strategic behaviour, while resource power and independence affects the degree of autonomy at subsidiary level. In a similar vein, Welch and Welch (1993) highlight the role of different network systems – headquarters/subsidiary, between subsidiaries, and between the subsidiary and the external environment – and the importance of staffing decisions for subsidiaries, given that networks are built and monitored through personal contacts.

In research undertaken at the level of the subsidiary in host economies, emphasis is placed on the role of proactive and committed subsidiary management in championing new initatives (Science Council of Canada, 1980; Goldenburg, 1991), in some cases linked to a parent company management style and structure which provides decentralization and autonomy. Amin *et al.* (1994) focus on the efforts of indigenous managers and improvements in plant performance, and Welch and Welch (1993) caution against the use of expatriates since relationship building is a long-term process. On the basis of this work, it would seem that a very fruitful area for further investigation would concern the nature of entrepreneurship in MNE subsidiaries.

The nature of worldwide environmental conditions is recognised as a significant factor leading to corporate strategic and structural reorganization, but there is rather little work on the influence of environmental circumstances at subsidiary level. The exception is Bartlett and Ghoshal (1989) where the strategic importance of the local environment is highlighted – this may take the form of a very large market, a competitor's home market, or a market that is sophisticated or technologically advanced. This issue is clearly important when considering the potential for developmental subsidiary activity at regional level in Europe.

Recent empirical evidence on multinational subsidiaries with a European focus is in Young, Hood and Dunlop (1988); Jarillo and Martinez (1990); Papanastassiou and Pearce (1992) (see also Charles, 1987).

Before concluding this review, it is important to comment on a related topic which is that of the decentralization of R&D which, arguably, is the most critical component of subsidiary status and autonomy. The evidence shows that the bulk of R&D spending is concentrated in the home countries of MNEs, but that overseas R&D is growing, linked to the internationalization of production and sales (Håkanson and Zander, 1988; Howells, 1990; Grandstrand, Sjolander and Håkanson, 1992; Cheng and Bolon, 1993). Supply side factors (aspects of host country technological capacity and capability) rank second to market factors in explaining the establishment and growth of overseas R&D (Pearce, 1992). There are also sectoral influences: the large size necessary to achieve critical mass is a barrier to decentralised R&D in some industries, while supply capabilities, e.g. the availability of research professionals and a distinctive local scientific, educational and technological tradition, are important in other sectors (Pearce and Singh, 1992; Dunning, 1993). A number of authors have developed typologies of MNE R&D focusing on where the R&D is undertaken and for what purpose, which can be linked to the models of corporate and subsidiary strategy. For example, Pearce (1991) has related the 'locally integrated laboratory' (a lab which assists the local producing unit to assimilate and effectively utilize the mainstream technology of the parent MNE) to the world product mandate subsidiary. Utilizing a different categorization, Ghoshal and

Bartlett (1988) observe some signs of a move from local-for-local R&D activities (design facilities located in the host country for local implementation) to local-for-global processes (as local-for-local innovations were found to be applicable in multiple locations). Evidence on the interrelationships between R&D mandates and developmental subsidiary activity in the form of WPMs, etc. is, however, still lacking. For example, Etemad and Séguin Dulude (1986) found only a loose association between the presence of R&D and the existence of world mandates, and Roth and Morrison (1992) established that the level of R&D expenditures made by a subsidiary was not related to a global subsidiary mandate.

As to the impact of decentralised R&D, there is little information on MNEs *per se* but the Netherlands Economic Institute (1992) report on French work concerning interregional moves of semi-public R&D establishments. The conclusion was that units that had been transferred to regional R&D centres such as Lyons or Sophia Antipolis were successful: others were not. The pull of the Ile de France region, given its network of R&D labs, headquarters functions and business services, was so great that very few R&D establishments even considered moving to other regions. This work clearly bears out the results of the studies by Cantwell and colleagues at Reading University cited earlier.

Towards an integrated approach

This paper has presented and reviewed a range of approaches which have a contribution to make to the issue of the role of multinational enterprises in regional economic development and particularly in generating dynamic comparative advantage. The approaches are both macro and micro, managerial and economic, and within the latter include regional and locational, and international business economics approaches. From the corporate side, a number of themes, including worldwide environmental change, organisational experimentation, new firm structures and practices (e.g. vertical disintegration and networking) and MNE subsidiary autonomy are common and are simply viewed from different perspectives. Despite the emphasis on such issues in the literature, what is still questionable is how pervasive, how radical and how stable the corporate transformations actually are. From the national and regional development angle, stages models suggest ways in which MNEs may act as 'engines of growth', but the precise interactions between foreign firms and the indigenous sectors of host economies are not well understood. And at least in a European regional frame MNEs have not had a major influence on dynamic comparative advantage (linked in part to the limited number of WPMs granted). The purpose of this concluding section is to attempt some integration of the literature, to identify gaps in concepts and understanding, and particularly to focus positively on the policy implications for regional economic development.

The emergence of 'developmental' MNE subsidiaries

Figure 8.1 summarizes the earlier discussions on the multinational subsidiary to indicate some of the conditions for the emergence of 'developmental' MNE affiliates. Within the integrated MNE, the suggestion is that worldwide environmental conditions influence organisational form and multinational strategy. The implementation of structures and strategies at host country level, however, is also determined both by national conditions, e.g. size of markets, technological conditions, competitive environment, and by national subsidiary competences and bargaining power. In some circumstances, therefore, these determining factors may lead to the establishment of or evolution towards world product mandate subsidiaries, from which developmental potential exists. In the alternative model of the heterarchical MNE, centres of excellence can emerge in erstwhile subsidiaries on the basis of resources built up and networking capabilities developed. The two models have potentially quite different implications for MNE subsidiaries in European regions: the WPM subsidiary undertakes R&D, manufacturing and marketing for Continental or global markets; the centre of excellence is more likely to specialise by function, and given regional comparative advantage within Europe, this may continue to restrict the peripheral regions to manufacturing.

It is not wholly apparent from the literature how the process actually operates, but it would seem that there are at least three different sets of circumstances. The first involves a proactive corporate strategic response to environmental change; the second a reactive response enforced by corporate crisis, when quasi-autonomous business missions are granted to particular subsidiaries, as part of a worldwide process of restructuring and reorganisation; and the third, emanating from subsidiary evolution, as national managers, with or without corporate encouragement build increasingly competent and autonomous units. The first two sets of circumstances exist currently with the completion of the Single European Market, generating both opportunities and threats for existing affiliate operations.

A number of cautions have to be noted and weaknesses identified in relation to Figure 8.1. First, rather few firms have implemented the

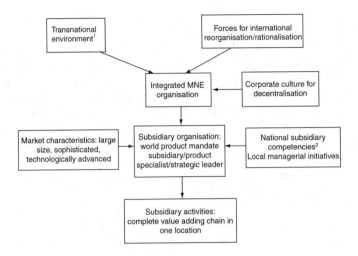

The integrated MNE and world product mandate subsidiaries

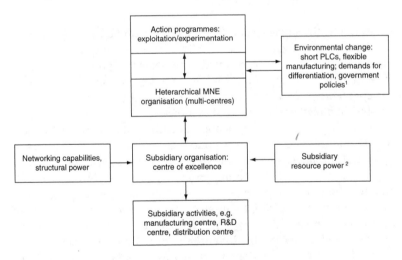

The heterarchical MNE and subsidiary centres of excellence

Figure 8.1 Conditions for emergence of 'developmental' MNE subsidiaries: managerial approach

Notes: [1] Many of the same factors apply but have been given different emphasis by various authors.

[2] National subsidiary competencies are related to host country and region factors including infrastructure investment and direct support, as well as to managerial performance, etc.

Sources: Derived from sources reviewed in the chapter.

types of arrangements presented, at least to this point in time. The international division and worldwide product division (hierarchical) structures are still prevalent. Rather few world product mandate subsidiaries (at least in their pure form) or centres of excellence exist. Second, the models relate primarily to the large, well-established multinational corporations, and further work is needed to identify the comparative impacts of the wide range of subsidiaries typically operating in regions and countries across Europe. Among the categories worthy of further consideration are:

- market-oriented *vs* cost-oriented *vs* resource-oriented investment
- new entrant *vs* established subsidiary
- single facility *vs* multi-plant operation in Europe
- subsidiaries in multi-domestic/country-centred *vs* global industries
- industry differences: in this regard it is interesting that Amin *et al.* (1994) established that the electronics industry was not characterised by developmental subsidiaries.

For example, the single facility MNE in Europe would by its very nature require a complete value chain of activities and a degree of autonomy. The earlier discussion also revealed developmental potential emerging from small firm initiatives from MNEs (acquisitions, joint ventures, new entrepreneurial units, corporate venturing) and through the route, if feasible, of directly attracting 'system houses'.

Third, national subsidiary capabilities and resource power are related to host country and regional attributes. Hence the likelihood of developmental subsidiaries is likely to be greater in core or innovation rich regions in Europe rather than in less favoured regions (LFRs). In a comparative study of enterprises in both core and less favoured regions in the EC, Amin *et al.* (1994), found not only differences in the quality of investment between these two groups of regions but also among the LFRs themselves. Inward investment in Portugal was much closer to the classic 'branch plant' typology than that in the Republic of Ireland or Scotland where, in addition, quality improvement has taken place over time.

The link between MNE subsidiaries and regional economic development

From the perspective of setting in motion a positive process of cumulative causation and generating dynamic comparative advantage, it must be accepted that one or a small number of sectorally or technologically diverse, world product mandate subsidiaries or centres of excellence would have little influence. Hence Figure 8.2 draws on other strands of literature to suggest possible ways in which clusters, a necessary requirement for broadly based development, might be encouraged to emerge. The two routes proposed are via local sourcing or technological innovation, and some company, country and host government conditions or requirements are indicated. A wide variety of potential government measures are shown. Clearly the most critical, as indicated by the stages of growth paradigms and other literature (Porter, 1990) concern government's role in creating and upgrading factor conditions, although Figure 8.2 also suggests policies which relate to each of the constituents of Porter's diamond of competitive advantage, viz. research parks and innovation centres designed to encourage cluster formation (Porter's related and supporting industries), targeted attraction policies and assistance to the existing stock of indigenous or multinational firms (firm strategy, structure and rivalry), and government procurement (demand conditions). In terms of the technological innovation route, co-operative R&D projects involving companies, university research labs and government research institutes are important policy instruments in the EC (Vonortas, 1990; Goodman, 1993). It has to be said that the regional development concepts do not present clear policy prescriptions, and only limited attention has been paid to the role of the multinational as a potentially positive developmental influence in industrialised countries. What is suggested in Figure 8.2 is the requirement for policy innovation and for a concentrated package of measures, differing clearly according to whether local sourcing or technological innovation are the key thrusts, within the general requirement for effective management by government of the macro-economy and investment in infrastructure, education and other public goods. The benefits from the policies implemented must also be expected to be primarily long-term. Concentration of effort needs caution, nevertheless, witness the comment from a recent study commissioned by the EC (Netherlands Economic Institute, 1992) that: 'regions should not become over-reliant on any one sector or else they may face future problems of restructuring' (1992: 116). Finally it should be stressed that the evidence reviewed here tends to highlight more in the way of problems than potential in generating regional clusters incorporating multinationals, especially from the local sourcing route to development.

Only limited attention has been paid in this summary and synthesis to macro-economic approaches, but Dunning (1993), has presented a framework which suggests a dynamic interplay between MNE activity

	Two routes	

	Local sourcing	Technological innovation
1. *Possible route* 2. *Conditions* • Company	WPM subsidiary/product specialist/strategic leader[1] (local design and development capabilities, autonomy in purchasing, marketing responsibilities)	WPM subsidiary/product specialist/strategic leader[1] (R & D capabilities to support subsidiary: access to basic research of parent)
• Country	• Local supplier capabilities (technological and volume capabilities; quality, delivery, price) • Local content requirements	• Local scientific, educational, technological tradition • Availability of research professionals, and other labour requirements

3. *Host government requirements*

- Macroeconomic framework
- Infrastructure, education, R&D support and other public goods
- Policies to facilitate efficient resource allocation
  Environmental conditions:
    Research parks
    Innovation centres
    Public venture funds
    (including support for university-industry research linkages)
    Government procurement

• Availability of assistance to indigenous suppliers	• Assistance to upgrade miniature replica-type subsidiaries; creative after-care policies

Targeted attraction policies including
appropriate regional policy incentives

• Competitor/complementary companies • Supply companies (to fill gaps)	• R&D-intensive companies using related technologies • Internationally mobile R&D investments using related technologies
4. *Outcomes* • Generation of complete value adding chains in particular sectors • Agglomerative economies	• Generation of technological clusters • Technological agglomer- ation
• Self-sustaining industrial growth	• Enhancement of indigenous technological capabilities

Figure 8.2 Two possible routes to cluster formation involving inward investment and MNE subsidiaries

Note: [1] The illustrations relate to a WPM-type subsidiary rather than subsidiary centres of excellence. However, for example, a manufacturing centre of excellence would be linked to the local sourcing route to cluster formation, and an R&D centre would be linked to the technological innovation route.

Source: Derived from sources reviewed in the chapter; authors' research.

and the economies in which they operate. In this framework, ownership (O), location (L) and internalization (I) factors from Dunning's eclectic paradigm determine the potential for, and nature and extent of, multinational activity; in turn this influences components of the diamond of competitive advantage of the host country (directly, or indirectly through its effect on government behaviour) and the environment (E), system (S), policies (P) configuration (from Koopman and Montias, 1971) in the country. MNE activity, interacting with the competitive advantage diamond and the ESP configuration sets in motion a 'capability or asset cumulative circle which might be virtuous, neutral or vicious' (1971: 268). In the review of studies which follows, Dunning illustrates the wide variety of economic impacts which could be generated by different circumstances, concluding that it is difficult to generalise on the direct or indirect effects of multinationals on the innovatory capability of host nations.

The approach in this paper has been more focused and primarily microeconomic: by drawing on existing literature, no attention has been paid to differences in the form of multinational activity in host countries (wholly-owned subsidiaries, joint ventures, acquisitions and alliances), or other forms of technology transfer such as inward licensing, to the desirable degree of involvement of MNEs in relation to indigenous enterprises, or to the circumstances in which a vicious as opposed to virtuous cycle might be expected. Nevertheless progress has been made in illustrating the potential contribution of MNEs to dynamic comparative advantage, and the final section of the paper which follows attempts to pinpoint the specific lessons for regional policy makers in the EC.

Policy lessons and conclusions

In introducing this section, it is important to remind policy makers of the very different economic impacts which may be associated with various types of MNE subsidiaries. Table 8.3 indicates some of the characteristics of MNE affiliates which generate either net positive or net negative impacts (mainly direct/static). The range is clearly very wide given the large number of variables involved, and very few firms would fit the 'benchmark facility' category, especially at point of entry. However, by focusing primarily or exclusively on one variable, such as employment, as is the case with much of the inward investment attraction effort in the EC at present, the possibility of laying the foundations for long-term evolution towards benchmark status is severely restricted.

Table 8.3 Conceptual framework for regional economic development impact of multinationals

Characteristics of multinational subsidiary	Regional economic development impact	
	Net positive impact	Net negative impact
• Network position:		
other facilities within country	None	Several and overcapacity
other European facilities	Few	Many
• Subsidiary role	Benchmark facility[a]	Undistinguished
product	Leading product	End game/low technology
market	Wide franchise, growth markets; sales/marketing responsibility	Local narrow remit; sales/ marketing responsibility elsewhere
technology	High rating for inward transfer	Marginal contributor or no role
• Exports	High	Close to zero
• Employment:		
numbers	Large	Small
graduates	High per cent	Zero
other skills	High per cent	Semi-skilled dominant
wages/salaries	Above average	Low by sectoral/relative standards
• R&D standing:		
corporate	High at group and decentralising	Centralist – no local options
local activities	Especially product/ process development	Zero or not applicable
• Purchased inputs	High locally	Low and unlikely/unable to be changed
• Performance:		
by set local criteria productivity, etc.	Consistently on target	Indifferent performance
by corporate/industry norms	Above group norms worldwide	Low or high, but no major gain from being high

Note: [a] Associated with its benchmark status, the MNE subsidiary in this category would operate as a strategic business unit with a world or continental product mandate.
Source: Authors' research.

Rejecting a 'do-nothing' approach to policy, there seem to be a number of critical messages in utilising inward investment from MNEs as a tool of regional economic development (see also 'the elements of 'good' institutional practice towards mobile investment' in Amin *et al.*, 1994). First, an *integrated policy approach* to regional development, in which technology policy rather than inward investment policy *per se* is the major driver, is fundamental. In building sectoral or technological clusters, MNEs, because of their size and performance, may have a central role, but embeddedness requires strong backward, forward and horizontal linkages. The policy task in stimulating technological linkages with universities and research institutes and supply linkages with local companies alone is a formidable one, and not something which can be undertaken effectively on a piece-meal basis. An integrated approach would ideally begin with a stable macroeconomic framework, but clearly this is outwith the hands of regional authorities. Large scale investment in the transport, telecommunications, energy and educational infra-structures is also essential, and again only partly within the domain of influence of regional authorities. In such circumstances the danger is one of trying to satisfy too many constituents and fragmenting funding allocations to the point where the impact is totally diffused. Only by concentrating resources sectorally, technologically and spatially would it be possible to come close to creating conducive conditions for cluster generation. This view supports some of the conclusions noted earlier concerning the emergence of 'islands of innovation' (Hilpert, 1991; Netherlands Economic Institute, 1992).

Recognising the dangers of over-reliance, a second policy lesson must be the need for *targeted attraction and after-care policies.* Young, Hood and Wilson (1994) have argued the case for a new approach to targeting policy which focuses on segments which offer the greatest economic impact and which match present or potential factor conditions within the region; in line with the findings here, attempts might also be made to target segments containing companies with structures and philoso-phies which promote decentralisation. This is a very different approach to that undertaken historically in Europe which has emphasised growth sectors (and hence microelectronics, biotechnology and new materials technologies) even if the MNE subsidiaries attracted are largely assem-bly operations. The argument has always been put forward that it is rarely possible to attract fully integrated developmental subsidiaries at point of entry, but that by working with the MNEs, plant upgrading will be possible over time. But if the industry/company is characterised by spatially separated activities and if the technology is beyond the level which can be supported by the local environment, then only limited evolution will be possible.

Regional policies may have a part to play, and various suggestions have been made of linking incentives to the nature of the project as a form of performance requirement. Basically the EC would sanction different types of foreign direct investment attraction activity in different groupings of countries beyond simply aid ceilings as a control (Young and Hood, 1993; see also Amin *et al.*, 1994). Any such changes would need a major shift in attitudes among national governments. Competitive bidding between locations in the EC and the emphasis on job creation means that national and local governments lack the confidence to attempt wholeheartedly and systematically to utilise incentive policies creatively to influence the nature of subsidiary activity.

Even with a new approach to targeting, after-care policies are potentially of considerable significance as a means of assisting subsidiary performance, which may in turn influence plant role and status within the group. Public sector agencies are beginning to experiment with limited forms of after-care, an understandable approach given the resource intensive nature of the activity and the uncertain returns. In an integrated approach to regional development incorporating the multinational enterprise, however, after-care policies are key; such policies could include assistance on a wide range of informational, operational and strategic issues, involving sites and property, finance, human resources, research and development, manufacturing, procurement (identifying and/or developing supplier capabilities), marketing and sales. After-care policies would also have to be linked to general supply side measures designed to upgrade the region as a whole (Young and Hood, 1994).

A third set of lessons concerns the requirement to *recognise the changing requirements of inward investors and understand the varying potential in different European regions for utilising MNEs in a developmental capacity*. Recent research on location factors (Netherlands Economics Institute, 1992) indicates that while proximity to markets has remained as a very important locational variable, 'a wide variety of non-cost 'subjective' factors, partly knowledge-based, are relevant to different project types' (1992: iv). These include the quality and availability of labour (requiring education and training designed to provide new skills and cater for new technologies), quality of life and personal factors, and the quality of the transport, information technology and telecommunications infrastructure. Adding to this list, investment in R&D in universities, research establishments and enterprises, together with mechanisms for bringing research to the market in the particular country or region, the fundamental importance of supply side policies designed to upgrade physical and human resources is confirmed.

Within the EC, wide disparities exist between the core regions where economic activity is concentrated and less favoured regions (CEC, 1991), with differences in the quality of supply side resources a distinguishing feature. Recent studies have, for example, highlighted Rhône-Alpes as one of a series of French sunbelt regions which, with their excellent international transport and telecommunications infrastructure, research and educational base and supplier networks, have produced a highly attractive environment for research-intensive inward investment. The conditions for a virtuous cycle of development, as portrayed by Cantwell (1989) clearly exist in such regions. Among the LFRs, there are big differences between regions, and policy makers have to recognize, for instance, skilled labour and infrastructural differences and plan for a different route to development which may or may not involve multi-nationals. Since parts of the electronics industry seem to be characterised by branch plant investments, with low levels of local embeddedness, and the local environment in some LFRs is unattractive, the prospects for MNE affiliate upgrading are similarly low. A different route to regional economic development is required. On an optimistic note, Amin *et al.* (1994) comment on the upgrading of inward investment in LFRs such as Ireland and Scotland as a consequence of three factors: upgrading of the physical, human and communications infrastructure; the presence of public sector development agencies committed to a planned and co-ordinated approach to inward investment; and upgrading of plants over time as a consequence of plant performance and the efforts of local managers, aided by after-care support.

A fourth lesson thus concerns the *significance of entrepreneurial managers in promoting MNE subsidiary development in Europe*. Subsidiary managers are MNE employees, recruited, trained and promoted nationally or internationally by the multinational parent. Dependent upon the nature of the subsidiary, desirable characteristics of such executives (from the MNE perspective) might emphasise the management of routine rather than the management of innovation. There might not be a barrier, however, to public sector sponsored innovation-oriented training programmes for subsidiary management teams, both within and across firms. If action-oriented, such programmes could involve the design of innovation projects, with funding support subsequently for feasibility studies and small scale development initiatives. The negatives in any such scheme concern the fact that in the early years of subsidiary establishment, key executive personnel may not be local nationals, plus the regular rotation of subsidiary managers practised by some MNEs.

The aim of this paper has been to summarise and synthesise the available knowledge on MNEs and regional economic development. The conclusion is perhaps the inevitable one that there is no easy route to generating dynamic comparative advantage, and this finding would hold whether multinationals or indigenous enterprises were involved. In a world of globally mobile capital there is, nevertheless, no option but to include multinationals as a component, if not the core, of development planning, with forward-looking but also realistic expectations as to their contribution.[5]

Notes

1. Aydalot (1988) comments that 'Silicon Glen in Scotland is, on the whole, simply a concentration of American electronics firms which were looking for an English-speaking location which would allow them to supply the EEC market, and at the same time receive a good deal of public aid' (1988: 39); see also Segal and Quince (1985).
2. This article gives an excellent brief review of the literature on scale economies, externalities and agglomeration economies from Marshall (1890) onwards.
3. A fourth category, the 'black hole' was included, but this is less relevant to the discussion here. In other work by Ghoshal and Nohria (1989), a distinction was made between integrative, hierarchical, federative and clan structures. The integrative structure would be associated with 'strategic leader' subsidiaries.
4. It is interesting to point out the link to the radical literature here. Thus Bornschier and Chase-Dunn (1985) comment that: 'The market forces that formerly mediated the hierarchy became less important, and essential entrepreneurial functions have been dislocated from national contexts and incorporated into the decision-making headquarters of the transnational firms' (1985: 17–18).
5. The authors are grateful to Julian Birkinshaw, at time of writing a Doctoral candidate at Western Business School, University of Western Ontario, whose thesis proposal is entitled 'Entrepreneurial Behaviour in Multinational Subsidiaries'.

9
Characteristics of Foreign Subsidiaries in Industry Clusters (2000)*

Julian Birkinshaw and Neil Hood

It is well established that the roles of foreign-owned subsidiary companies (i.e. the activities that they have responsibility for in the multinational corporation) vary according to such contingencies as the local environment (Ghoshal and Nohria, 1989), the structural context imposed by the parent (Gupta and Govindarajan, 1991), and the entrepreneurial capacity of subsidiary management (Birkinshaw, 1997), to name some of the most well-known factors. In this paper we examine another potentially important predictor of varying subsidiary roles – the membership (or not) of a leading-edge industry cluster. An industry cluster can be defined broadly as an aggregation of competing and complementary firms that are located in relatively close geographical proximity. In this paper we focus on those 'leading-edge' clusters identified by Porter (1990, 1998) and operationalised in terms of high export intensity.

We address two specific research questions. First, we ask *whether the characteristics of foreign owned subsidiaries in Porter's 'leading-edge industry clusters' differ significantly from those in other industry sectors.* Porter's (1990) response would be a strong yes – subsidiaries can 'selectively tap' into the leading-edge thinking in the cluster with a view to transfer learning back home, or they can become a transplanted 'home base' for one of the corporation's major product lines. However, there is other

* *Journal of International Business Studies*, 31 (1) (2000), 141–54.
This paper benefited greatly from seminars given at the Institute of International Business and the Invest in Sweden Agency, and a presentation at the Academy of International Business annual meeting, Monterrey, Mexico, October 1997. Thanks to Örjan Sölvell, Rod White, Alan Rugman and Don Lessard for their comments and advice.

research, mostly conducted within the field of subsidiary management, that offers some somewhat different perspectives on this question. Second, we address the question: *Do we see significant differences in the characteristics of foreign-owned subsidiaries from one 'leading-edge industry cluster' to the next?* Here existing theory offers little guidance so we provide some preliminary evidence, and discuss possible reasons for the differences we observe. Our objective with this study is to contribute to two streams of literature. First, we seek to contribute to the literature on subsidiary management by examining an important, but under-researched, determinant of the characteristics of foreign subsidiaries. Second, we seek to contribute to the literature on industry clusters, by providing some tentative evidence about differences between clusters and how they might have arisen.

The spatial clustering of industry

It has been recognised for a long time that related firms and industries tend to locate in close geographical proximity. In Marshall's (1890, 1916) seminal analysis, the three fundamental reasons for spatial clustering were identified as: (1) the existence of a pooled market for specialised workers; (2) the provision of specialised inputs from suppliers and service providers; and (3) the relatively rapid flow of business-related knowledge between firms, which results in technological spillovers. A variety of names have been put forward to describe such spatial agglomerations of firms, including industrial districts (Piore and Sabel, 1984), innovative milieux (Aydalot, 1986) and industry clusters (Porter, 1990, 1998). While such concepts vary in their relative emphasis on the reasons for clustering, they still betray a remarkable consistency with Marshall's original analysis (Krugman, 1991; Malmberg, Sölvell and Zander, 1996).

Spatial clustering has been a theme in international business research for several decades, but has only become a central concern [since the early 1990s] . The most important body of research is concerned with the link between industry clusters and national competitiveness (Porter, 1990; Rugman 1991; Narula, 1993). Central to this line of research is the question of cluster sustainability, that is the ability of any given cluster to maintain or enhance its competitive position *vis-à-vis* other clusters over a long period of time. Porter argues that sustainability is a function of the dynamism of the cluster, which in turn is a function of the interaction between the four elements of the cluster's 'diamond' (demanding customers, related and supporting industries, factor endowments, and firm structure and rivalry). Other theories of cluster sustainability are based more on the social interactions between participating firms (e.g. Saxenian, 1994; Pouder and St John, 1996). A second line of thinking is concerned with the different roles that foreign-owned subsidiaries have in leading-edge industry clusters. Here the established logic is that the multinational corporation (MNC) attempts to 'tap into' industry clusters in foreign countries in order to gain access to leading-edge ideas and specialized talents (Vernon, 1979; Kogut, 1983; Bartlett and Ghoshal, 1986; Porter, 1990).

Characteristics of subsidiaries in leading-edge industry clusters

A number of studies have discussed the roles of foreign owned subsidiaries in leading-edge industry clusters. Porter (1990) argued for two likely roles. The first is *scanning units*, that 'tap selectively into sources of advantage in other national diamonds'. They are often R&D units with a limited development capability of their own which allows them to contribute to as well as draw from the knowledge base of the cluster. See Bartlett and Ghoshal (1986) Vernon (1979), and Westney (1990) for similar concepts. The second is *transplanted home-bases*, which consist of the top management, R&D activities and main manufacturing operations of an entire product division. These are often referred to as world mandate subsidiaries [Science Council of Canada, 1980; Crookell, 1986] or strategic leaders (Bartlett and Ghoshal, 1986). While many academic researchers have argued that such units are becoming increasingly common (Hedlund, 1986; Bartlett and Ghoshal, 1989; Forsgren, Holm and Johanson, 1995) Porter sees them as relatively rare because the home country industry cluster should *ceteris paribus* also be the home base of the firm.

In addition to these high-profile subsidiary types, there are also likely to be many more traditional subsidiaries in leading-edge industry clusters. Some, for example, will be market-seeking units, located in the cluster because the country represents an important market for the firms's products. Others will be resource-seeking units that are located in the cluster to access specialised inputs, well-trained labour or low-cost factor inputs (White and Poynter, 1984; Dunning, 1993).

In this paper our approach is to study the *characteristics* of foreign-owned subsidiaries in leading-edge clusters rather than their *roles*. This allows us to start from theory and deduce the likely characteristics that we would expect to see among foreign-owned subsidiaries, rather than working backwards from the empirical observations of others. There is no shortage of typologies of subsidiaries in the literature (see Birkinshaw and Morrison, 1995, for a review) but because they were all developed in different contexts their relevance to the study of industry clusters is limited.

Proposition development

The basic argument developed here is that subsidiaries in leading-edge clusters will over time develop characteristics that mirror the characteristics of other firms in those clusters. Thus, subsidiaries are usually established in such clusters on account of the latent economies of agglomeration, but in order to realize those benefits they have to become fully fledged 'insiders'. Note that this is a far from trivial hypothesis, because there are considerable bodies of literature arguing the opposite – that foreign-owned subsidiaries become part of a low value-adding 'branch plant' economy that does not establish local roots, or they remain as isolated 'enclaves' within their host country (Beigie and Stewart, 1986; Hood and Young, 1988; Dicken, 1994; Kobrin, 1999).

The first important characteristic is the nature of the interactions between the subsidiary and other firms or institutions in the cluster. As Porter (1990), Saxenian (1994) and others have argued, it is the tight business and social relationships between firms that give clusters their dynamism. Our argument is that foreign-owned subsidiaries in clusters will attempt to emulate such interactions – by building strong relationships with local customers and suppliers, and by becoming involved in contacts with government and local universities. Stated slightly differently, we see subsidiaries in leading-edge clusters becoming strongly *embedded* in the cluster – defined as the strength and extent of their network of local relationships (Granovetter, 1985; Grabher, 1993; Andersson, 1997). By contrast, subsidiaries in other industry sectors would not expect to develop the same network of relationships – either because such partner firms and institutions are not present locally, or because the subsidiary was established for different reasons (e.g. low labour cost, market access). Thus:

> **Proposition 1**. The foreign owned subsidiaries in leading-edge industry clusters will be more embedded in their local network (stronger customer and supplier relations; greater local government support) than those in other industry sectors.

A second important characteristic is the degree of decision-making autonomy in the subsidiary. For subsidiaries established purely for low-cost manufacturing reasons, it is likely that decision-making will be controlled strongly from headquarters. However, for subsidiaries established in leading-edge clusters it is usually expected that they will try to develop local customer and supplier relationships, experiment with new ideas, and often transfer some of their learning back home. To do any of these requires significant level of decision-making autonomy. Moreover, once some level of self-determination has been achieved, the subsidiary finds itself in a more powerful position *vis-à-vis* its parent company because it is in control of valuable local resources (Pfeffer and Salancik, 1978; Prahalad and Doz, 1981). This gives it even greater degrees of freedom, and thus the possibility to further enhance its local embeddedness. As this process evolves, the subsidiary becomes more like an independent local firm.

Proposition 2. The foreign-owned subsidiaries in leading-edge industry clusters will have greater decision-making autonomy than those in other industry sectors.

The third important characteristic is the subsidiary's international market scope, i.e. the extent to which it sells its products outside the host country (White and Poynter, 1984). Many subsidiaries are established as 'market seeking' units, with a view to selling the MNC's products locally. However, our argument is that subsidiaries are established in leading-edge clusters to exploit economies of agglomeration, and this often means developing or manufacturing products for sale on a global basis. Thus, we would expect international sales from such subsidiaries to be significantly higher than in subsidiaries based in other industry sectors. It is important to note that these leading-edge clusters are as a matter of definition internationally oriented. The proposition, like the other two, thus becomes one of examining the extent to which foreign-owned subsidiaries reflect the international orientation of the other firms in the leading-edge cluster.

Proposition 3. The foreign-owned subsidiaries in leading-edge industry clusters will have more international market scope than those in other industry sectors.

Research methodology

The research was focused on three countries – Canada, Scotland and Sweden – for reasons primarily of convenience but also because the topic of investigation was important to them. Data was collected primarily through a questionnaire mailed to a sample of foreign-owned subsidiaries in each country. Information about industry clusters was obtained from secondary sources.

The questionnaire was developed through an iterative process of drafting, pilot-testing and redrafting, including matched pairs of subsidiary and HQ respondents. Samples of foreign-owned subsidiaries were drawn up as follows. In Canada we used the *Financial Post 500, Report on Business 1000*, and the *Disclosure* databases. In Scotland we used the database compiled by *Scottish Enterprise*, the inward investment agency, which keeps track of all foreign investors in Scotland. In Sweden we used the databases of foreign-owned subsidiaries compiled by *Veckans Affärer* and *Compass*. In all cases the criterion for inclusion was size: $50 million in Canada and Scotland and $25 million in Sweden. Using a standard procedure of mailing the questionnaire to the subsidiary CEO and mailing a reminder 4 weeks later we ended up with 229 responses (34 per cent response rate). All mailing was done in 1995. Analysis of the number of respondents vs. non-respondents in each leading-edge cluster revealed that subsidiaries in leading-edge clusters were slightly more likely to respond than those in non-cluster locations, perhaps what one might expect. But among the clusters themselves there were no significant differences between respondents and non-respondents.

Identification of leading-edge industry clusters

As already observed, our approach in this paper is simply to work with the list of leading-edge industry clusters assembled by Michael Porter during his *Competitive Advantage of Nations* study (1990) and subsequent consulting projects with the Monitor Group. Porter's approach was to include all those clusters in which the share of world cluster exports was more than double the average for that country. Thus, if Sweden's share of world exports is 1.75 per cent only industry clusters with 3.5 per cent or greater of world share were included. These are called 'leading-edge industry clusters' here. It is worth noting that Porter's operationalisation has two limitations. First, he worked at the country level, whereas the economies of agglomeration typically apply at a lower level of analysis (i.e. the city or region). Second, export intensity is only a moderate proxy for competitiveness. These were practical limitations that were unavoidable given the data available. Table 9.1 lists the leading edge clusters in the three countries under investigation, and the definitions as supplied by Porter/*Monitor*. The five Swedish ones were taken from Porter (1990), the five Canadian ones were taken from the Porter/*Monitor* study, *Canada at a Crossroads* (1991) and the two Scottish ones were taken from a *Monitor* study written for *Scottish Enterprise* [*Monitor Company*, 1993].

Table 9.1 Industry-clusters characteristics and responding firms

Cluster	Number of responding firms	Cluster characteristics (see text)		
		Cluster 'dynamism'	Foreign ownership%	Share of country exports%
Canadian petroleum, chemical	11	3.7	69	10.6
Canadian transportation	13	4	71	30.3
Canadian food and beverage	10	3.7	34	8.1
Other sectors in Canada	37			
Swedish transport and logistics	12	4.3	14	20.5
Swedish forestry	8	6.7	8	17.9
Swedish ferrous metals	9	6.3	31	12.5
Swedish healthcare	14	4.3	38	2.5
Swedish telecomms	8	2.3	29	3.7
Other sectors in Sweden	54			
Scottish electronics	20	2	55	25.0
Scottish oil and gas	9	4.3	25	25.0
Other sectors in Scotland	19			
Total	229			

Once these clusters had been defined, we assigned each subsidiary to one cluster or to the 'non-cluster' group as indicated in table 1 above. This was done using the description of the subsidiary's industry provided by the respondent. It actually proved remarkably easy to consider each subsidiary in turn and judge which category to assign it to. However, to validate the process we got an independent expert in each country to separately go through the same procedure and compare his findings to our own. The small discrepancies were reconciled through discussion.

Construct measurement

Strength of suppliers and customers

Respondents were asked to indicate the extent to which they agreed with the following statements, where 1 = strongly disagree, 7 = strongly agree: (1) Local customers have exacting standards, (2) capabilities of suppliers are very high, (3) relationships between suppliers and buyers are very strong. Alpha = 0.62.

Government support

Respondents were asked to indicate the extent to which they agreed with the following statements, where 1 = strongly disagree, 7 = strongly agree: (1) the local government views this subsidiary as an important contributor to the local economy, (2) the standing of the subsidiary in the national business community is high, (3) the local government is actively looking to support investment and industrial growth. Alpha = 0.63.

Decision-making autonomy

Following Roth and Morrison (1992), respondents were asked to state the level that had the authority to make the following decisions (where 1 = made by corporate HQ, 2 = at sub-corporate level, 3 = within subsidiary): (1) changes in product design, (2) sub-contracting out large portions of the manufacturing instead of expanding subsidiary's own facilities, (3) switching to a new manufacturing process. Alpha = 0.73.

Subsidiary international scope

Respondents were asked to state their international sales as a percentage of the total (including both internal to the MNC and external).

Findings

The propositions were tested using t-tests on the entire sample of 229 subsidiaries, as shown in Table 9.2. All propositions were supported at the $p < 0.01$ level or better. In other words, subsidiaries in leading-edge

Table 9.2 Differences between cluster subsidiaries and non-cluster subsidiaries ($N = 229$)

Variable	Mean in cluster subsidiaries	Mean in non-cluster subsidiaries	*T*-test
Strength of suppliers and customers	4.96	4.66	2.718**
Government support	4.61	3.98	4.250***
Decision-making autonomy	1.46	1.22	2.723**
International orientation	38.4%	23.8%	2.84**

Note: *** $p < 0.001$; ** $p < 0.01$.

clusters are more strongly embedded in their local cluster, are more autonomous, and are more internationally oriented than subsidiaries in other industry sectors. A number of additional analyses were performed to guard against spurious findings. First, the international scope of the subsidiary could easily be a function of the level of its R&D, rather than a function of its presence in a leading-edge cluster. We therefore ran an ANCOVA model for the measure of international scope in which level of R&D was the covariate. This analysis yielded F-values for the cluster index of 8.7 ($p < 0.01$) and 4.8 ($p < 0.05$), and F-values for the R&D covariate of 36.4 ($p < 0.001$) and 31.2 ($p < 0.001$), which showed that *both level of R&D and cluster membership are strong predictors of international orientation*, though level of R&D is stronger. Second, there was a risk that the level of embeddedness of the subsidiary in the local economy was a function of its age not a function of its presence in a leading-edge cluster. We therefore ran an ANCOVA analysis for each measure of embeddedness, with subsidiary age as the covariate. Strength of suppliers and customers, and government support came out as before, with the cluster index a significant predictor ($F = 4.69$, 2.8 respectively, $p < 0.05$) and the subsidiary age covariate non-significant ($F = 0.21$, 1.15 respectively). In other words, *controlling for the age of subsidiary has no material impact on the observed differences in strength of suppliers and customers and perceived government support*. Finally, we decided to check whether the results were spuriously picking up industry-level or country-level differences. To do this, we ran a series of regressions for each of the variables, with the following dummy variables: (1) presence in a cluster, (2) Swedish host, (3) Canadian host, (4) US parent, (5) participant in the electronics industry, (6) participant in the healthcare/pharmaceuticals industry, and (7) participant in the food and drink industry. The three industries were selected on the basis that they were the most well-represented in the entire sample (53, 30, 20 respondents, respectively). The results of this analysis, listed in Table 9.3, show that the cluster/non-cluster dummy variable was a significant predictor in all six models, confirming the validity of separating the data in this way. The Canadian host and Swedish host dummies were also significant in many cases, as were the food and drink and electronics industry dummies, while US parent was never significant.

Further analysis: differences between industry clusters

A second issue that the data allows us to explore is whether we see significant differences in the characteristics of foreign-owned subsidiaries from

Table 9.3   Regression analysis on cluster, country and industry dummies

	Strength of suppliers/ customers	Government support	Decision-making autonomy	International sales of subsidiary
Cluster	0.130*	0.196***	−0.126†	0.146*
Canada host	0.338***	0.012	−0.234**	−0.241**
Sweden host	0.198*	−0.444***	−0.157†	−0.275**
US parent	−0.017	−0.053	0.140*	0.037
Healthcare industry	0.015	0.011	0.038	−0.058
Food and drink industry	−0.028	0.071	−0.071	−0.139*
Electronics industry	−0.120†	0.056	0.180**	0.011
F-test	3.12	12.90	4.37	4.85
Adjusted R^2	0.053**	0.234***	0.082**	0.087**

Notes: Figures in cells are standardised Betas. Significance levels: $^†p < 0.10$; $^*p < 0.05$; $^{**}p < 0.01$; $^{***}p < 0.001$.

one leading-edge industry cluster to the next. Of course, it is self-apparent that there will always be *some* differences just based on the unique character of the clusters in question. This study includes the Canadian automotive cluster for example, which has become extremely closely integrated with its Detroit-based counterpart since the 'Auto Pact' was signed in 1965, and which has correspondingly led to the emergence of many large export-oriented subsidiaries. Such cluster-specific explanations are important, but of greater interest are the *systematic* differences between industry clusters. If we can identify cluster-level characteristics that impact the likelihood of certain subsidiary characteristics, then we will have made an important contribution to our understanding of industry clusters *and* subsidiary roles.

Here we will focus on two important cluster-level variables, cluster dynamism and level of foreign ownership. Certainly there may be other important cluster characteristics as well, but because this is a relatively unexplored area and because good quality cluster-level data is hard to obtain we restrict ourselves to a careful analysis of these two.

Cluster dynamism is defined as its capacity for improvement, innovation and competitive upgrading (Malmberg, Sölvell and Zander, 1996: 88). As stated by Porter (1990: 72), the diamond of national advantage is a 'mutually reinforcing system' in which each element interacts with and reinforces the others. Thus, when all four elements are favourable and/

or sophisticated, the net result is a high level of cluster dynamism. Building on the same logic as earlier, we therefore expect that the more dynamic clusters will *ceteris paribus* have more embedded, more autonomous, and more internationally oriented subsidiaries than those that are less dynamic.

Level of foreign ownership is clearly an important cluster-level characteristic, both because of its political salience and because of the wide variation in foreign ownership between clusters, from close to zero (e.g. certain Japanese or South Korean clusters) to 70 per cent or more (e.g. Singapore, some Irish clusters, some Canadian clusters). However, the impact that the level of foreign ownership has on subsidiary roles is not well understood. One approach is to argue that foreign ownership is 'bad' for cluster development and sustainability because foreign subsidiaries tend to be less deeply embedded in the local economy, and more prone to move, than indigenous firms. This approach is rarely written down as starkly as this, but interviews with inward investment agencies in several countries confirm that it exists. An alternative approach is to argue that foreign ownership is a sign of good health in a leading-edge cluster, because it signals that foreign MNCs want to build a presence there in order to tap into leading edge ideas. Pre-eminent clusters such as Silicon Valley or London's financial sector, for example, have large numbers of foreign subsidiaries that not only tap into the cluster's dynamism but also contribute to it through their own activities. Finally, there is a third, more neutral, perspective that argues that foreign ownership *per se* is irrelevant (Sölvell and Malmberg, 1998). Rather, the dynamism of the cluster is simply a function of the firms and institutions in that cluster and the interrelations between them, regardless of ownership. We will not state a preference for one argument or another at this stage. Instead we will present the data in an exploratory way and revisit these arguments at the end.

Empirical analysis

In order to examine these issues empirically, we first had to develop operational measures of cluster dynamism and foreign-ownership level.

Cluster dynamism was measured through the ratings of experts, who assessed the extent to which the four elements of Porter's (1990) diamond were present in each cluster. These numbers were then summed to give a dynamism index. To guard against the obvious problems of subjectivity we got three people to code each cluster, and used the average. We also got country experts to assess the face validity of our measures, with good results. See Table 9.1 for measures.

Foreign ownership of the cluster: these measures were taken from a variety of sources. For Canada, Porter *Monitor* (1991) included an assessment of the level of foreign ownership of assets in each of the five clusters. For Scotland, measures were provided by Scottish Enterprise who have data on all foreign investments in the country. For Sweden, we had to make our own calculations, by identifying *all* cluster participants, as defined by their Swedish Statistical Bureau classification codes, identifying which were foreign owned, and calculating the percentage of turnover that was foreign owned.

We also developed an additional subsidiary-level measure for *relative subsidiary capabilities*, as an indicator of the quality and scope of the activities of the subsidiary. It was measured by asking respondents to indicate their capability or distinctive competence in the following areas, where 1 = far below average, 7 = far above average: (1) product or process R&D, (2) manufacturing capability, (3) sales force coverage and quality, (4) marketing capability, (5) managing international activities, (6) managing the interface with the parent company, (7) innovation and entrepreneurship. Alpha = 0.65.

Having developed these measures, we summed all of the subsidiary-level measures to a cluster level, and then calculated the Spearman rank correlation coefficients between the aggregated subsidiary characteristics, cluster dynamism and foreign-ownership level.

Table 9.4 indicates some interesting findings. First, there is a strong negative correlation between cluster dynamism and foreign ownership

Table 9.4 Spearman correlations for cluster-level and aggregated subsidiary-level variables ($N = 10$)

Variable	2	3	4	5	6	7
1. Cluster dynamism	$-0.494^\dagger$	0.431	$-0.457^\dagger$	$0.452^\dagger$	0.116	0.146
2. Cluster foreign ownership		0.036	0.394	$-0.433^\dagger$	0.030	-0.588^*
3. Suppliers and customers			-0.201	0.422	-0.006	0.182
4. Government support				0.201	0.224	0.309
5. Decision-making autonomy					-0.116	0.579^*
6. International sales						0.212
7. Relative capabilities						

Note: $^{**} p < 0.01$; $^* p < 0.05$; $^\dagger p < 0.10$.

level, providing some support for the often-voiced concern that high foreign ownership clusters tend to be less dynamic, and thus less sustainable. Second, cluster dynamism is significantly associated with a high level of subsidiary autonomy, and moderately associated with strong supplier and customer relations. This is consistent with the logic developed earlier that subsidiaries can only become contributors to cluster dynamism if they are strongly embedded in the local economy and autonomous enough to interact freely with other local entities. Third, high foreign ownership is significantly and negatively associated with subsidiary autonomy. It is also negatively associated with the measure of relative subsidiary capabilities, providing support for the argument that foreign-dominated clusters often have relatively weak subsidiary companies.

The interesting finding here is the evidence that clusters with high levels of foreign ownership have subsidiaries that are in general less autonomous and have weaker capabilities. This suggests that there are indeed some reasons for host country governments to be concerned about the sustainability of their largely foreign-owned clusters. However, it is important to realise that this does not lead to the conclusion that foreign ownership *per se* is bad, because there are a number of additional factors at work here. First, there are probably industry and country effects that are not factored in to this analysis. For example, we would expect the impact of foreign ownership to be very different in a growing industry (more greenfield investments) than in a consolidating industry (more acquisitions). And the historical levels of foreign ownership are much higher in Canada and Scotland than in Sweden, and the results we see are partly a reflection of this. Second, cluster dynamism and subsidiary autonomy are means not ends. While theory predicts that the more dynamic clusters will be the ones that are sustainable in the long-term, there may also be other viable paths to sustainability e.g. for Scotland to have the most attractive business environment for electronics manufacturing. Third, it is important to realise that foreign investment is never bad *per se*, because it is better than nothing. When we examine the findings in Table 9.4, then, the key test may not be how the clusters compare to one another, but rather how they would have looked without foreign investment.

Discussion and conclusions

This paper sought to contribute to two distinct bodies of literature, subsidiary management and industry clustering. Taking the industry cluster literature first, this paper offers the important (though tentative) finding that those clusters with high levels of foreign ownership have subsidiaries that in general are less autonomous and have weaker capabilities. As the discussion above suggests, there are a lot of possible explanations for this. There is not space in this paper to go into any of the explanations in depth, but this is clearly an issue that demands further empirical and theoretical research. Our answer to the question *does foreign ownership matter?* is therefore a clear yes, but in ways that are both positive and negative, and often rather complex.

For the subsidiary management literature, the paper provides confirming evidence that subsidiaries in leading-edge industry clusters tend to be more autonomous, more embedded in the local cluster, and have more international market scope than their counterparts in other industry sectors. It suggests, moreover, that it is not just cluster membership but the specific characteristics of the cluster in question that impacts the likely subsidiary role. This has two implications. First, in terms of the environmental determinism vs. strategic choice debate in subsidiary management (Birkinshaw, Hood and Jonsson, 1998) it suggests that greater weight needs to be given to the environmental determinism side because cluster-level variables have not hitherto been considered. Second, at a more managerial level, the data suggests that Porter's concept of selective tapping is appropriate only in a sub-set of cases – some clusters are probably not dynamic enough to warrant selective tapping, while others may be populated predominantly by locally focused subsidiaries.

This research had some significant limitations. First, we used Porter's (1990) definitions of leading-edge clusters. While these are well known, they do have significant limitations, and it is a priority for future research to find stronger measures of leading-edge clusters. Second, we used attitudinal data for subsidiary-level data. Obviously attitudes are important in this context because they shape subsequent action, but at the same time there would have been considerable value in also getting some more objective indicators. This is an important issue for future research to look into. Third, we focused exclusively on the foreign-owned subsidiaries in our chosen industry clusters, rather than on the entire set of firms. This was appropriate for the subsidiary management aspects of the research, but for the industry cluster aspects it meant that we ended up with a rather restricted perspective on the dynamics of these clusters. This study points to some interesting differences between clusters, but a future study looking at both indigenous and foreign-owned firms will be necessary before any definitive conclusions can be drawn.

Notes

1. Though we should acknowledge that we are deliberately focusing on the economic arguments here. Other theoretical approaches might yield different arguments, such as institutional theory, in which the choice of location would be primarily for legitimacy reasons, i.e. to adhere to the institutional norms of that country.
2. Note that a number of additional propositions were developed in an earlier formulation of this paper, including the value-added, level of R&D, and size of subsidiaries in the two groups. Of these, only the proposition concerning the size of subsidiaries was supported, i.e. with subsidiaries in leading-edge clusters larger than those in other industry sectors.
3. Further details on the methodology are reported in Birkinshaw, Hood and Jonsson (1998).
4. The Swedish questionnaire was translated into Swedish and back-translated to verify accuracy. Managers were sent both English and Swedish language versions, with approximately half filling in each version.
5. Though it should be noted that most of the country clusters are actually fairly local in scope. In this study, we examined the locations of the responding companies and in ten of twelve cases there was a very strong geographical concentration to the cluster (i.e. down to the level of a particular city).
6. Note that it would also have been possible to do this analysis at the subsidiary level by allocating cluster-level variables to each subsidiary, but this is a potentially flawed approach because it ends up attributing cluster-level factors to individual subsidiaries (cf. the 'Ecological Fallacy' – Robinson, 1950; Hofstede *et al.*, 1990).

10

An Empirical Study of Development Processes in Foreign-Owned Subsidiaries in Canada and Scotland (1997)*

Julian Birkinshaw and Neil Hood

Introduction

This paper reports on a detailed clinical study of development processes in a sample of foreign-owned manufacturing subsidiaries in Canada and Scotland. Development is used here to refer to the growth and enhancement of subsidiary resources that add increasing levels of value to the multinational corporation (MNC) as a whole. In this context, the development process is viewed as an extension of the internationalisation process, in that it represents increasing levels of resource commitments in foreign markets (Johanson and Vahlne, 1977). The point at which the traditional 'internationalisation' process ends, i.e. with the first incidence of FDI, is thus the point at which subsidiary development begins. Despite the widespread evidence for resource-rich and influential subsidiaries (e.g. Forsgren, Holm and Johanson, 1992), the process by which they develop has apparently escaped systematic research attention so far. A few studies have referred to the growth of subsidiary resources but not as their primary objective (e.g. Prahalad and Doz, 1983; Forsgren *et al.*, 1992; Kim and Mauborgne, 1993), and studies of subsidiary types – in which development is implied but never discussed – are legion (e.g. White and Poynter, 1984; Bartlett and Ghoshal, 1986). This study therefore attempts to put some structure and substance around the concept of subsidiary development, in the hope that additional research in this area will be encouraged.

---

* *Management International Review*, 37 (4), 339–64. © Gabler Verlag, 1997.

Subsidiary development is an important research phenomenon for three reasons. First, there is abundant evidence (as this paper will show) that development over time is exhibited in subsidiaries, and for that reason alone it should be better understood. Consistent with the increasing acceptance of network conceptualisations of the MNC (Ghoshal and Bartlett, 1991; Forsgren and Johanson, 1992) the subsidiary can be modelled as a semiautonomous entity whose development is analogous to that of an independent firm (cf. Penrose, 1959). Second, subsidiary development, as we have defined it contributes directly to the competitive advantage of the MNC in that one of the MNC's strategic imperatives is to leverage the capabilities of its globally-dispersed assets (Bartlett and Ghoshal, 1989). Third, subsidiary development has profound implications for economic development in the host country, in terms of employment, exports, tax and a host of intangible factors (Young, Hood and Peters, 1994). Subsidiary development can also have negative ramifications for the corporation if, for example, development entails using scarce resources towards goals that are inconsistent with those of the parent. This issue will be discussed later in the paper, but our basic premise for this study is that subsidiary development, as defined above, is beneficial to the corporate parent and the host country. It is recognised, however, that in differential subsidiary development (i.e. between units in a network) and/or between different host countries, there will inevitably be winners and losers.

This paper is in four sections. The following section will elaborate the conceptual model that drove this research as well as some of the theoretical foundations for the study. The second section outlines the research methodology: how the research sites were selected, the collection of data, and the methods of analysis. The third section reports the findings from the research, and the fourth section discusses the implications of and conclusions from the research.

Conceptual model

What are the drivers of subsidiary development? In simple terms, we can identify subsidiary management, parent company management, and host-country policy-makers as the three actors that have both a vested interest in subsidiary development and the necessary power to influence the process. All three take actions over time that impact the levels of resources in the subsidiary which in turn leads to subsidiary development.[1] Such actions can either impact directly the level of subsidiary resources or – in the case of parent company managers and host

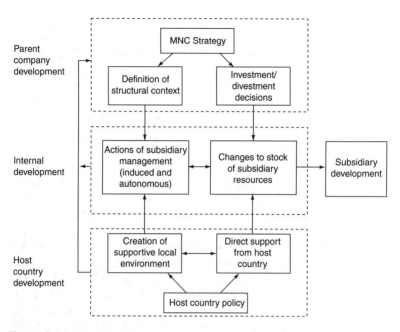

Figure 10.1 Organising framework for subsidiary development

country policymakers – they can work indirectly by influencing the actions of subsidiary management. To the extent that resource levels rise and fall over time, development must be viewed as being potentially positive or negative. The model below focuses primarily on the positive flows, in part because the focus of this study is on mature subsidiaries and in part to enhance the clarity of the argument. What follows is a brief synopsis of the model presented in Figure 10.1.

Parent-driven development

Through a combination of legitimate authority and control of critical resources, the parent company typically exerts considerable influence on the activities undertaken in the subsidiary. The term structural context (Bower, 1970) is used to denote the set of administrative and cultural mechanisms through which control is exerted, including lines of reporting, access to capital, areas of accountability, reward mechanisms and so on. This context can very closely circumscribe the actions of subsidiary management, or it can give them considerable degrees of freedom (Prahalad, 1976; Bartlett, 1979; Prahalad and Doz, 1981;

Burgelman, 1983; Ghoshal, 1986). The actions of subsidiary management, in turn, are a key determinant of the growth of the subsidiary's resources.

The more immediate way in which the parent company can drive subsidiary development is through making (or sanctioning) direct investment. This can take the form of a new plant, the transfer of a proprietary technology, or the investment associated with a new product or market mandate, all of which add directly to the subsidiary's resource base and offer the potential for future increments of investment. Alternatively, the parent company may acquire another company in the host country or region and merge it with the existing subsidiary, resulting in a major change in the subsidiary's resource profile. Equally, divestments and spin-offs from the subsidiary can result in a depletion of the subsidiary's resources.

The two parent-driven processes are a function of the MNC corporate strategy, which itself is derived from a continous evaluation of the various key elements of the global competitive environment, including the actions of competitors, emergence of new markets, technological trends, and political and economic factors. This process is fed directly into the setting of parameters within which the subsidiary must work and which are critical in determining its direction.

Internal development

While subsidiary management clearly face constraints from their parent company in terms of decision-making autonomy and technology generation, there is strong theoretical and empirical evidence that they can also have the capacity to influence their own destiny through the control of critical resources (Hedlund, 1986; Ghoshal and Bartlett, 1991; Forsgren and Pahlberg, 1992). For example, at the higher end of the value-added chain Canadian researchers have long recognised that 'world product mandates' are earned through the entrepreneurial efforts of subsidiary management rather than handed to them by parent management (Etemad and Dulude, 1986; Crookell and Morrison, 1990). While such cases may be quite rare, they illustrate that development can be driven by subsidiary management in certain circumstances, with parent management playing a facilitation role.

Internal development takes two distinct forms, labeled induced and autonomous (Burgelman, 1983). Induced development is 'business-as-usual' and represents the gradual growth of resources in line with the subsidiary's accepted set of responsibilities, which may change substantially over time. Autonomous development is achieved through actions that lie outside the accepted responsibilities of the subsidiary. The objective of autonomous action is to match the subsidiary's distinctive resources with market opportunities, and in so doing to increase the scope and/or responsibilities of the subsidiary. Because it represents a departure from the accepted distribution of responsibilities in the corporation, autonomous development typically requires championing and selling to parent management.

The relationship between subsidiary management action and the level of subsidiary resources is reciprocal, the former being a flow variable and the latter a stock variable (Dierickx and Cool, 1989). In other words, internal subsidiary development is both fuelled by, and a contributor to, the subsidiary's resource profile. This argument is central to the resource-based view of the firm (Penrose, 1959; Wernerfelt, 1984; Barney, 1991). It should also be noted that the internal- and parent-driven development processes are complementary rather than independent. Any autonomous subsidiary action requires at least the tacit blessing of parent management; and any change in structural context by the parent company needs to be correctly interpreted and acted on by subsidiary management. What matters in terms of this model, is the relative input of subsidiary and parent management into any given phase of development.

Host country-driven development

The host country, like the parent company, has two principal means of exerting influence on subsidiary development. Contributions to direct investment are easily understood, in terms of subsidies, tax concessions, specific infrastructure investment and such like. These are, again, liable to be most common and most material in the early stages of subsidiary growth though some countries such as Ireland have generous and long-lasting direct fiscal support for their foreign-owned sector, while others devote considerable resources to 'after care' in a desire to achieve further added value development in subsidiaries (Young and Hood, 1994). Direct host country investment occurs in association with direct parent-company investment, as a means of encouraging inward investment that might otherwise have gone elsewhere. For example in the UK over 50 per cent of new manufacturing inward investment projects each year are reinvestments within existing subsidiaries. In many developed countries such direct investment is also designed to act as a spur for regional economic development.

The second approach open to the host country government is indirect, and it revolves around the creation and maintenance of a supportive local business environment in which the subsidiary can operate. This approach has both macro and micro policy implications. For example, the competitiveness of the subsidiary is, at least in part, determined by the quality of the customers, suppliers and competitors in the host country or region (Porter, 1990). The host government's ability to stimulate an upgrading of that local environment, through a supportive macro-economic policy and investment in infrastructure and education, is thus an important contributor to subsidiary development. There has been a considerable amount of research into the drivers of regional economic development, and the role of the subsidiary company in the development process (see Young, Hood and Peters, 1994, for a review). As in the case of the parent company, this form of context management is directed at influencing the actions of subsidiary management not the resources of the subsidiary itself. It is evident, however, that the direct and indirect arms of government policy are closely related, in that direct investment in areas of education and communication infrastructure are often used to attract companies that will enhance the competitiveness of the local economy. There are also negative dimension in terms of the indirect host country effort, in that subsidiary development can be influenced by the differential exit costs within Europe in the event of the rationalisation or closure of subsidiaries.

In sum, the framework described above sets out what we believe are the fundamental drivers of subsidiary development within the MNC as it develops its international strategy. The framework is deliberately eclectic (i.e. drawn from a variety of theoretical traditions), in that no single theory can adequately capture the whole phenomenon. It is also pitched at a relatively high level of abstraction, so that it can be applied both to the entire process of development (from initial founding through to fully fledged participation in the global network) and to more specific sub-phases of the process. Our expectation is that the relative emphasis of the drivers of development will shift over time as the subsidiary matures. Thus, direct corporate and host country investment may be the primary drivers in the early stages of development, and indirect mechanisms more prevalent as the subsidiary matures. At the same time, though, any given phase of development may be influenced to greater or lesser degrees by all of the identified drivers. It should be emphasised that the current study is far more concerned with the former (the shifts over time) than with the latter (the specifics of a single phase of development). The objective of this research project can be summarised as follows:

Research Question. What are the relative roles of: (a) parent company drivers; (b) internal drivers; and (c) host country drivers over time on the subsidiary development process?

Research methodology

The scope of the research question, coupled with the exploratory nature of the study, made a case study methodology appropriate. We decided to study in detail a limited number of subsidiary companies in two countries, Canada and Scotland. The choice of Scotland and Canada was based on a number of important similarities between the two countries, specifically: (a) high levels of foreign ownership of the industrial sector over an extended time period, and hence a large population of subsidiaries at various stages of development; (b) membership of a trading block (NAFTA, EU) as a relatively 'peripheral' player in terms of geography; and (c) high levels of interest among subsidiary managers and policymakers around the issue of development, which translated into good research access.[2] We also focused exclusively on US-owned subsidiaries. This restricted the variance in the sample (which made comparison across companies easier) but it also meant that the implications for other host countries (notably those closer to the heart of trading blocks such as the USA and Germany) and for other home countries might be correspondingly limited.

A brief comment on the environment for foreign direct investment in the two host countries is in order here. Canada has a long history of protectionism which resulted in the establishment of 'miniature replica' subsidiaries by most foreign entrants up to the 1970s (White and Poynter, 1984). The dismantling of trade barriers, notably those with the USA, took place over the 1970s and 1980s, with the result that Canadian subsidiaries either moved into high value-added specialist roles or regressed towards low value-added generalist roles (typically local sales and service). Scotland is rather different, in that it has a shorter history of foreign investment, although the UK as a whole was the point of entry for a large proportion of US investment into Europe from the early 1950s. Most large subsidiaries are owned by US MNCs, and were developed in the 1950s and 1960s with a view to serving the entire European market (on the assumption that Britain would join the EEC). Investment is predominantly in manufacturing and focused on electronics, health-care and engineering. The recent and ongoing nature of foreign investment means that development processes are, on the whole, less evolved than in Canada.

Bearing in mind the very different levels of development within the population of subsidiaries in Canada and Scotland, we restricted our study to those at the more 'evolved' end of the spectrum i.e. those in which there was evidence of substantial value-added to the corporation. This ensured that we were studying the entire scope of the development process, rather than just the early stages of it. From a practical perspective this is a logical decision, in that the experiences of mature subsidiaries are potentially of great interest to those that are less well developed. Methodologically, it is acknowledged that this approach imparts a bias towards successfully-developed subsidiaries, and therefore against those that for whatever reason did not develop. Given the exploratory nature of the research, we felt this was appropriate.[3]

In Canada our primary selection criterion was evidence of 'world product mandate' (WPM) status. A WPM is an arrangement whereby the subsidiary takes responsibility for development, manufacturing and marketing on a global basis. It has been discussed for many years as a desirable status for a foreign-owned subsidiary from an economic development perspective (Science Council of Canada, 1980; Etemad and Dulude, 1986), and it is consistent with our definition of development in that the subsidiary must have assets that are both durable and valuable before it is given such a responsibility. Through a careful examination of the *Financial Post 500* and various other public source documents we identified 40 large US-owned subsidiaries with some history of success at gaining WPMs. Ten of this group were selected at random, and of this sample six participated fully with the research project and the remaining four provided a lower level of access. Only the six full participants are reported here.

The criteria in Scotland were somewhat different, in that subsidiaries are, on average, younger and less developed. Through a consideration of value-added scope, geographical scope, age, size, and reputation we identified eight prime candidates, all US-owned, of which seven were eventually studied. It is important to note that this sample clearly represented the 'leading edge' of development in Scotland, whereas the Canadian sample were members of a fairly large group of mature subsidiaries. Table 10.1 provides summary data on the sample companies.

Data was collected primarily through semi-structured interviews with senior subsidiary managers. In the Canadian sample between 5 and 7 interviews were conducted per subsidiary over the period 1993–4, involving middle-level subsidiary managers and also managers from the parent company. In the Scottish sample we conducted fewer interviews (an average of 3 per company), over a longer period from 1992 to 1995.

Table 10.1   Sample of subsidiaries

Subsidiary	Host country	Industry	1994 revenues ($ million)	Date of formation	Interviews
Alpha	Can	Industrial products	650	1951	7
Beta		Chemicals	500	1932	7
Gamma		Electronics	100	1896	5
Delta		Computers	800	1961	6
Epsilon		Control systems	200	1930	6
Zeta		Industrial systems	100	1930	5
Eta	Scot	Medical products	172	1947	3
Theta		Computers	1500	1954	4
Iota		Computers	110	1966	4
Kappa		Control systems	65	1962	2
Lambda		Semiconductors	400	1969	3
Sigma		Computers	1200	1946	4
Omega		Electronics	430	1976	3

Interview data was augmented with a standard questionnaire that was administered to the general manager of all thirteen companies, and archival information and secondary material was used where available. The Scottish sample, in particular, could be followed in considerable detail over time both through analysis of prior academic work and by having access to studies undertaken within government.

The data was analysed according to the practices recommended by Miles and Huberman (1984), with a variety of graphical and tabular formats for structuring the analysis process. Using the principle of triangulation we used a combination of interview, questionnaire, and archival data to document the development processes in the sample companies. Furthermore, we conducted our analysis of the research interviews separately and then discussed our respective thoughts before arriving at a final interpretation. To preserve confidentiality commitments no company names are given.

Research findings

Characteristics of sample

While the principal research question was around the factors driving subsidiary development, the first priority in this section is to document some of the basic characteristics of the sample companies, in terms

Table 10.2   Characteristics of Canadian and Scottish sub-samples

	Canadian	**Scottish**
Annual revenues ($ million)	390	814
International sales (% of rev.)	43	74
R&D expenditure (% of rev.)	3.6	5.1
% of international responsibilities 'earned' by subsidiary	83	74
Level of government support (1 = very low, 7 = very high)	3.8	4.6

of their current responsibilities, scope of operations, age, size, and capabilities. This analysis will shed some light on the differences between the Canadian and Scottish samples, which is important for the latter analysis.

Some basic facts for the sample subsidiaries are exhibited in Table 10.2 and Figure 10.2. Figure 10.2 provides a breakdown by company of the major value-adding activities undertaken, and the geographic scope of each. This data shows, first, that all the subsidiaries in the sample pursued manufacturing on a regional or global scale. The average percentage of products exported was 43 per cent for the Canadian subsidiaries and 74 per cent for the Scottish subsidiaries. In eight cases plants were of the rationalised manufacturer type (White and Poynter, 1984), integrated with sister plants around the world and transferring intermediate products between one another or acting as dual sources of the same product. The exceptions were the five cases in which the subsidiary had a world mandate (Science Council of Canada, 1980), that is an exclusive responsibility for the development, manufacturing and marketing of a product line or business on a global scale. The level of R&D performed in the sample companies was quite high (3.6 per cent of revenues in Canada, 5.1 per cent in Scotland), but this was thought by the respondents to be below the average for their respective corporations.[4] The second important observation from Figure 10.2 is that all the Canadian subsidiaries had 'downstream' responsibilities for marketing and selling corporate products in the home market, in addition to their 'upstream' responsibilities, while five of the seven Scottish subsidiaries undertook upstream activities only. This differences reflects the contrasting histories of the two economies – most Canadian subsidiares were formed as miniature replicas (White and Poynter, 1984) of their parents with all functional activities represented, while the majority of Scottish subsidiaries were

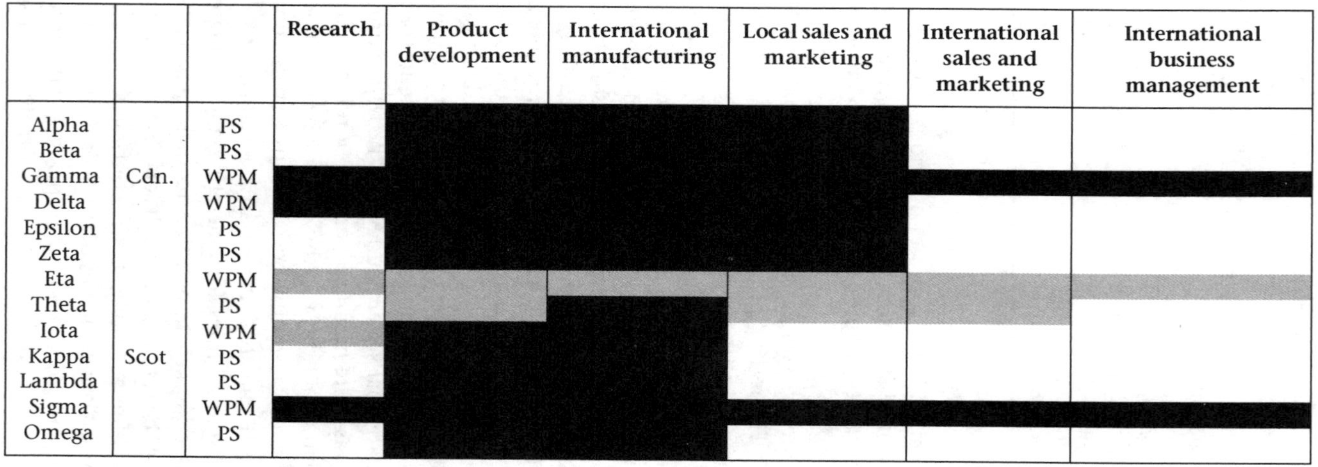

Figure 10.2 Activities undertaken by sample subsidiaries

Note: PS = Product Specialist; WPM = World Product Mandate. Dark box = Major subsidiary activity; Light box = Minor activity, or activity performed for only a small percentage of business portfolio.

established, or evolved into, manufacturing sites for Europe as a whole (Young, Hood and Hamill, 1988). The associated downstream activities tend to be centred in the London area or in continental Europe, and organised on a pan-European basis.

Respondents were also asked to estimate how their international product responsibilities were gained. It has been recognized in the Canadian setting that such responsibilities are often 'earned' by the subsidiary not 'given' by the parent (Crookell, 1986), so the question-naire simply asked for the approximate split between these two alterna-tives. As shown in Table 10.2, Canadian managers responded that 83 per cent of their international responsibilities were earned by them-selves, against 74 per cent by Scottish managers. Stated differently, there was relatively more proactive investment by the *parent* company in the Scottish companies. This is relatively easy to explain: many Scottish sub-sidiaries are developed by their US parent companies as large strategic investments to satisfy the entire European market; Canadian subsidiar-ies, in contrast, typically have to work hard to persuade the US parent to make any additional investment, because the North American market is already adequately served from the US. On a related point, Table 10.2 also shows a higher level of government support in Scottish subsidiaries than in Canadian ones. This is indicative of the relatively strategic nature of many of the corporate investments in Scotland, and of the fact that *Scottish Enterprise* (the economic development agency) has to compete with many other European countries for those investments. Moreover it does so in a UK policy context that has been consistently supportive of inward investment for many decades.

Subsidiary development: two phases of growth

Our research showed that in all cases there had been substantial devel-opment, in terms of the accumulation of valuable resources, but with some cases of stagnation or negative development for short periods. Considering the dominant process first, we identified two major phases of growth and two trajectories of development. These will be explained in conceptual terms before getting into a detailed account of the pro-cesses in question. Figure 10.3 illustrates the process.

The first phase of subsidiary development was termed *establishing via-bility* and consisted of the period from founding to the achievement of satisfactory performance. During this phase the concern of subsidiary management was to fulfil its basic mandate. In the case of the Canadian sample this involved generating a significant market presence in the MNC's core products and, in most cases, manufacturing those same

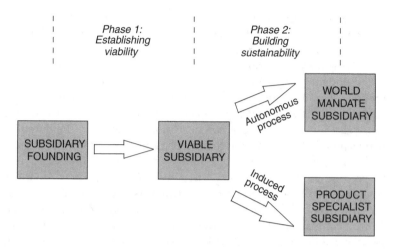

Figure 10.3 Subsidiary forms and major development process identified during inductive study

products to an acceptable quality and cost standard. In the Scottish sample the mandate was typically for manufacturing only and with strict guidelines on quality, service and cost standards. The relatively tight control imposed from head office during this phase of development meant that subsidiary management generally had little capacity for autonomous action. It should be noted that some subsidiaries never complete this initial phase of development. There are cases of subsidiaries that are established but closed down relatively quickly. In such situations it may be an unforeseen change in corporate strategy that is responsible, but it is more likely to be a failure by the subsidiary to meet expectations, which can of course be the fault of too-high expectations as well as underperformance. Moreover, in the European context most of the early US investment was on a 'plant by market' basis leading to overcapacity and over-representation as the EU markets integrated. In such cases relative plant performance and the strength of market-pull factors were important variables influencing internationalisation (Hood and Young, 1983). This study is however about the survivors that by definition established viability; it is the domain of a separate study to consider early failure rates among subsidiaries (cf. Delacroix, 1993).

The second phase of subsidiary development, and the one on which this research is focused, was termed *building sustainability*. This phase of development was predicted on the observation that the fulfillment of the subsidiary's basic mandate is a necessary but not sufficient condition for long-term sustainable survival. To illustrate this point, many US MNCs traditionally worked on a plant-by-market basis in Europe, with the result that they developed a network of 5 or 20 or more plants in the region, depending on the nature of their industry. The shift towards European integration that occurred during the eighties, together with cost and productivity measures, meant that in many cases half or more of the total number of manufacturing sites were no longer needed. Many plants have thus been closed, including in some cases plants that had been satisfactorily fulfilling their official mandates.

Two subsidiary forms were identified that appeared to be both sustainable in the long term and 'developed', in terms of their contribution of valuable resources of the corporation. These are termed world mandate and product specialist. The *world mandate* subsidiary has been discussed above – it is responsible for an entire line of business within the MNC, and it typically has a relatively high level of autonomy. The best example of a world mandate in this study was Sigma in Scotland, a company that has global responsibility for the design, development and manufacture of automated telling machines, a $1 billion business. In this case the mandate includes the management of several international manufacturing subsidiaries. The other cases were typically much smaller, for example Delta Canada, which is responsible for a specialist line of computer terminals globally (a $120 million business).

The *product specialist,* by contrast, is responsible for a relatively narrowly defined activity, such as Lambda Scotland which makes MOS semiconductors for the world market.[5] Here the subsidiary is integrated into the global production system. Final responsibility for the product, including product renewal (i.e. design and development work) is located elsewhere, typically, at headquarters; and decision-making autonomy is relatively constrained because of the interdependencies between units. Product specialist subsidiaries are not restricted to manufacturing responsibilities – Zeta Canada, for example, has a significant development responsibility as well – but as a general rule they undertake a 'part' rather than a 'whole', and are therefore subordinate to the division with final responsibility for the business in question. What makes the product specialist a sustainable role is its *best in class* status, which means that according to the MNC's internal and external metrics the subsidiary is acknowledged as a leader (when compared to other units in the corporation and to competitor plants). In a situation where the MNC is attempting to rationalise its manufacturing sites in Europe, it is clear that best-in-class subsidiaries will be well-positioned for survival. There are other criteria as well, such as being situated in an important cluster or providing access to a key market, but excellence in a narrowly-defined range of activities is fundamentally a sustainable position.

The underlying logic for this two-fold classification is that *subsidiary companies are competing with one another* (Crookell and Morrison, 1990) both for new corporate investments and for product charters (Galunic and Eisenhardt, 1995). By analogy with Porter (1980), competing subsidiaries have to define defensible positions for themselves if they are to survive. The world mandate role is fundamentally one of differentiation, in that the subsidiary is responsible for a product line within the MNC that no other subsidiary has any expertise in; the product specialist role is one of low-cost, in that the subsidiary is typically undertaking a standard manufacturing activity but doing it in a more cost-efficient manner than competing subsidiaries. Both these positions are sustainable from an internal competition perspective.

It should be underlined that world mandate and product specialist are subsidiary roles that apply at the product line or business level. Sample companies frequently exhibited elements of both types. Delta Canada, for example, had four distinct operations, two of which were world mandates and two of which were product specialists. Nonetheless, it was possible in every case to identify the predominant form. Of the 13 subsidiaries in the sample, five were predominantly world mandate types and eight were product specialists.

The observation that two distinct sustainable forms existed shed new light on our investigation of subsidiary development processes. Specifically, we were able to identify two distinct processes of development, with different drivers in each case. These two processes are labeled *mandate development and specialist development*. The processes were examined in detail, and are reported below. We were also able to examine, in more speculative fashion, the fate of subsidiaries that failed to pursue either course effectively, as well as the broader issue of sustainability vs. development.

Establishing viability

The early phase of development experienced in all the sample companies, from founding through to viability, will be briefly discussed. Unfortunately the historical nature of the data on this process precluded detailed analysis. While it was possible to be accurate about dates and major investments, it proved impossible to delineate clearly between the relative inputs of parent and subsidiary management in major decisions. A more detailed description of this process can be found in Hood, Young and Lal (1994).

Of the entire sample, one was founded by acquisition and two began as importing entities; the rest were set up as manufacturing subsidiaries (in Scotland) or manufacturing and sales subsidiaries (in Canada). The Canadian subsidiaries were all founded for market access, i.e. as a way to circumvent or at least mitigate import tariffs. This fact suggests quite a significant role for the host country, in that the absence of such tariffs would probably have resulted in importing from the USA and no manufacturing activity. Subsidiary management were typically provided with a Canadian market scope and a set of products to make under licence, but some autonomy to develop the market through product adaptation. The Scottish subsidiaries were founded for European access, typically as a second source for a major product that was already being produced in the US. These investments were mostly in the 1950s or 1960s before European integration was really an issue, but on the presumption of ultimate UK membership of the EEC. The major driver of development, both in terms of the initial investment and later additions, was the parent company, often working closely with the host country which also played an active role. Where Canada used the 'stick' to promote investment, Scotland used the 'carrot' in the form of investment incentives under a proactive regional policy regime which it shared with similar areas in the UK and Europe as a whole. These direct inducements were intended to counteract the disadvantages of the Scottish location, in terms of distance to market and proximity to suppliers, as well as attracting investment to assist in the restructuring of the economy from its traditional industrial base.

While initial founding was driven by the parent company, the building of viability was undertaken exclusively by subsidiary management. As observed earlier, this involved fulfilling the expectations of parent company management, whatever those expectations were. The few respondents who had been present in the early days of their subsidiaries observed that they had strict and frequent reporting requirements, and essentially no capacity for autonomous action. The evidence suggests that all thirteen companies achieved viability quickly, typically within five years. Omega Scotland, for example, started out assembling and testing small computers in 1977. High levels of growth in the computer industry and effective plant management put Omega in a strong position, such that by 1982 management were moving beyond their original mandate towards design and other value added activities. Two of the Canadian subsidiaries (Delta and Zeta) faced a rather different process in that they had initially gained viability as sales/marketing subsidiaries, but then faced the additional challenge of gaining manufacturing operations. Table 10.3 presents a summary of the major drivers for each of the three processes.

Table 10.3 Summary of major drivers of each process (see text for detailed explanation)

	Establishing viability	Building sustainability; the mandate process	Building sustainability; the specialist process
Parent-company drivers	• Direct investment at time of founding; imposition of tightly constrained structural context	• Indirect involvement, somewhat passive; granting of necessary degrees of freedom for subsidiary to act	• Direct investment in a few cases; careful context development in others
Subsidiary drivers	• Fulfilment of initial mandate; induced process	• Key role; proaction and commitment by management; autonomous process	• Key; proactive effort often needed, but directed towards decision-makers in head office; induced process
Host country drivers	• Direct investment incentives frequently used; threat of tariffs in case of Canada	• Limited but sometimes critical role; both through direct help and through a supportive business environment	• Limited role; development of a regional cluster valuable in several cases; 'after care' programmes established in Scotland

Building sustainability: the mandate development process

As shown in Figure 10.2, five of the 13 subsidiaries had world mandate status. In three cases (Gamma, Delta, Sigma) this status could be traced back to some sort of crisis. Sigma Scotland, for example, was on the point of closure in 1980 having reached the end of the life cycle of its existing products, when it was given a last-chance opportunity to turn around the corporation's automatic teller machine (ATM) business. The turnaround was extremely successful, with the result that the subsidiary gained a pre-eminent position in the ATM business and a *de facto* world mandate. It has since gone on to become the global headquarters of an entire division of the Sigma corporation. Gamma Canada's mandate, by contrast, evolved from the imminent demise of its defence electronics business on account of a cancelled government contract. Rather than put the electronics engineers in its Canadian subsidiary out of work, the parent gave them a free hand to explore new technologies and new markets. This resulted in a digital display technology which eventually became an information systems business for the airline sector. This was an area in which the corporation had no prior expertise so the subsidiary, again, found itself with a world mandate.

Of the two world mandates that did not stem from crisis, Eta Scotland started out as an independent firm and gained *de facto* mandate status when it was acquired, while Iota Scotland's development was evolutionary. Iota Scotland began manufacturing in 1966, making electronic products under licence from the USA. With the blessing of the parent company they gradually built up a local development group to broaden their product portfolio into related areas. This group developed an electronic testing product in 1968 which led to subsequent innovations in this area, and eventually the creation (in the early 1980s) of a separate division that co-existed with the licensed product division. The electronics testing division of Iota Scotland is now a major corporate division with several overseas subsidiaries of its own.

Parent-company drivers

The mandate development process indicated a rather passive role for the parent company. In all five cases the subsidiary was proactive in identifying new products and/or markets, and pursuing the opportunities thus identified. The parent company, of course, was responsible for defining a structural context that made such initiative possible, but its involvement was typically very limited. In the three crisis cases, the parent's input amounted to a vote of confidence in the subsidiary management team, and a moderate level of additional investment.

In Delta Canada, for example, the president was given the autonomy to act 'as if the subsidiary were my own company' which included taking certain actions that deliberately went against the official strategy because he believed that it was in the long-term interests of the corporation. Likewise, the parent companies of Gamma Canada and Sigma Scotland both gave subsidiary management a lot of freedom to act as they saw fit. Eta Scotland involved very direct action by the parent company (i.e. the acquisition of an independent Scottish company) followed by a very hands-off approach whereby the subsidiary was given complete discretion to develop its products and markets as it saw fit. Finally, in Iota Scotland there was a conscious decision by the parent to give responsibility to the subsidiary, but no direct involvement in the operations.

Subsidiary drivers

Subsidiary management, as noted above, were clearly the drivers of the mandate development process. Rather than building on the existing resources of the subsidiary (see the specialist development process below), they essentially created new resources. In three cases (Gamma, Delta, Iota) this was achieved through technological innovations; in the case of Sigma Scotland it was achieved through the turnaround and leverage of an ailing business; and in the case of Eta Scotland it was achieved through the international exploitation of an existing technology. As one example, Gamma Canada moved from its defence-contrast based electronics business into a number of emerging technologies such as computer network management. This shift was predicated on the need to reduce the corporation's reliance on defence contracts, but it was actively pursued by subsidiary management as they quickly realised the extent of the opportunities in computer systems and network management.

The importance of the entrepreneurial role should not be understated. On several occasions, we were left with the impression that the world mandate status had been achieved by the subsidiary *in spite of* rather than *because of* the context in which it was working. It may be that subsidiary entrepreneurship (Birkinshaw, 1995) is in fact a sufficient condition for subsidiary development, though more research is needed before such a conclusion can be drawn.

Host country drivers

The role of the host country in driving the mandate development process was limited but perhaps quite critical. In terms of direct support, Gamma and Delta received government assistance during the period of crisis in which their mandates were born. Gamma Canada received

Canadian government support for its shift from defence to commercial applications, without which observers felt it would not have survived. Delta Canada kept a loss-making unit (which later became the world mandate) open in return for access to government contracts. In terms of indirect support, three of the five subsidiaries (Gamma, Delta, Eta) built on local customer demand as the spur for their product innovations and/or improvements – Delta Canada, for example, built its mandate in the oil and gas sector on the basis that Canada has a leading-edge position in that industry. Respondents also commented on more generic factors such as the quality of the labour force (critical for Iota and Sigma), the low cost of R&D work (for Gamma and Delta), and the existence of related and supporting industries (for Eta, Iota and Sigma). Rather like the parent company, however, the host country can only help to create an environment that subsidiary management elect to take advantage of or not.

Building sustainability: the specialist development process

The remaining eight subsidiaries followed the specialist development process and ended up, by definition, as product specialists. In comparison to the mandate development process, the specialist development process was characterised by greater parent company intervention (in the form of investments and divestments), and perhaps a lesser host country role. Subsidiary management, interestingly, did not play the passive role one might have expected, but were observed to actively promote the drive towards a product specialist role.

Parent-company drivers

The parent company played a very active role in the specialist development process, both through direct and indirect means. The direct approach is best illustrated by Lambda Scotland, which received approximately $800 million of investment in its semiconductor production capacity over eight increments between 1972 and 1994. Each of these new investments was strongly contested by Lambda and its sister subsidiaries around the world. The fact that Lambda was able to win so much additional investment was a reflection of the operation's ability to excel on key measures such as quality levels, productivity, and unit cost. The new investment was also an opportunity for Lambda to become more specialised and more expert in its core area. Direct parent investment was also provided for Zeta, Theta and Omega. The indirect approach, by contrast, was rather closer to what was observed in the mandate development process, in that parent management implicitly supported development through the structural context. Alpha, Epsilon, Kappa and Omega also received indirect support. For example, over the period 1980–90 Alpha Canada became the leader (within the corporation) in flexible, small-volume manufacturing. They achieved this position through a host of small initiatives all focused on convincing US division managers to invest in Canada. The role of the parent company, in this case, was to make such an internal selling and bidding process available. Rather than opting for the centralised approach observed in Lambda, Alpha's resource allocation system was relatively decentralised. In summary, of the eight subsidiaries in which the specialist development process was observed, four received direct support from the parent, four received indirect support, and one (Beta Canada) essentially received no support. Beta Canada, interestingly, is also the one company in the sample whose future is still uncertain, in that it has been unable to achieve leading-edge expertise in any strategically core activity. While Beta has four products that sell internationally, two are niche products and two are part of businesses that the parent company is considering exiting. Our assessment suggests that this state of affairs is attributable more to the lack of support from the parent than the lack of effort by subsidiary management. Finally, there was also evidence in two cases (Kappa and Omega) of major corporate divestments, though in both cases the subsidiary was able to retain enough of its distinctive capabilities to survive. Kappa Scotland, for example, went through a major downsizing in the 1970s when its computer business was sold. By refocusing on its traditional area of expertise (control systems) and proactively building an expertise in new technologies, Kappa was able to build a sustainable position for itself in the corporate system.

Subsidiary drivers

As the above discussion indicated, the subsidiary apparently has a very active role to play even in the specialist development process. Taking the Alpha Canada example again, subsidiary management were given the degrees of freedom they needed to attract manufacturing investment, but they were not told what to do. Rather, they had to proactively seek out investment. The nature of their initiatives was very much consistent with their existing resources, in that they sought out relatively short-run, high-specification, manufacturing operations from elsewhere in the corporation, but the process was proactive and entrepreneurial none-theless. In the other seven cases there were similar efforts made by subsidiary management directed towards building expertise in a narrowly specified area.

Why do subsidiary management have such an active role to play in the specialist development process? Our analysis suggested that the complexity and heterogeneity of the MNCs under investigation was so great than a centralised resource allocation process could not be effective. Most had instead opted for some level of decentralisation of major investments, to the division or even business unit level. This, however, created problems for the sample subsidiaries, because the specific capabilities or resources they possessed were not necessarily understood by those divisional managers making resource allocation decisions. Active self-promotion thus became the only reliable way of spreading awareness and thus attracting investment. In the words of one subsidiary president, 'as a subsidiary we don't wait our turn for manufacturing decisions; if we waited, our turn would never come'.

Lambda Scotland was a notable exception to this general principle, in that the major investments it had received required no initiative on the part of subsidiary management. This appeared to be for two reasons. First, the size of the investments was frequently large (over $100 million) so a centralized resource allocation process was possible. Second, the measures of plant performance, such as rejection rates and service levels, were objective and consistently applied. Parent management could, and did, monitor the performance of all the major semiconductor fabrication plants around the world, and made additional investments accordingly. Lambda Scotland was clearly 'best in class' on certain criteria, and it was therefore very effective in gaining additional investment. Subsidiary management's role, in this case, was focused exclusively on operational efficiency rather than on resource-seeking initiatives.

Host country drivers

Host country support for the specialist development process was limited. In three cases (Zeta, Lambda, Omega), the impression was given that product specialist status had arisen because of the presence in the local market of a supportive 'cluster'. Zeta Canada, for example, was involved in developing industrial control systems, and Canada's leading-edge usage of such systems was a factor in the corporation's decision to locate development work there. Omega Scotland survived a fiercely-contested downsizing in 1990 while its sister plant in Ireland did not. The process was extremely political, and the final decision to retain Omega included both plant- and country-specific criteria. There was also evidence of limited investment incentives in the three Scottish cases where major corporate investments had fueled the specialist development process (Theta, Lambda, Omega). In all the other cases, however, there was no evidence of direct or indirect host country support. While the fundamental economic stability of both Canada and Scotland was sufficient not to deter subsidiary development, there was certainly no special advantage in these locations either.

In summary, the specialist development process bore much greater resemblance to the mandate development process than one might have predicted. To become a product specialist subsidiary, it seems, management has to be proactive and even aggressive in seeking out investments that will allow it to realise its ambitions. The approach, of course, is qualitatively different from that observed in the mandate development process, in that subsidiary management's effort is internally rather than externally focused. The parent company, correspondingly, has a much greater level of control over the specialist development process in that the subsidiary's initiative is limited to a fairly narrow product-market scope. But overall the level of conviction and effort required by subsidiary management is surprisingly similar in both processes.

One important question has not yet been addressed. Did subsidiary management have a choice between the specialist and mandate development processes? In most cases the answer appeared to be no, on account of the organizational systems in place in the corporation. Alpha, Beta, Zeta and Lambda had no prospect of gaining a world mandate within their corporate system, whereas Delta, Eta, and Iota were in corporations that had a specific policy of granting mandate responsibilities to their overseas subsidiaries. The other cases were more equivocal, and in such situations the product specialist option was typically more likely to transpire than the world mandate option, simply because it was perceived as less risky by the parent company. Theta Scotland is an interesting example in this regard, in that it has been moving over the last 10 years from a product specialist towards a world mandate position. From its initial role as an assembly operation, plant management at Theta began looking in the late 1980s to 'anchor' the operation by extending its value chain. Through their own initiative they added: a product development group in 1990; the order management function for Europe in 1992; and a European help centre in 1994. This appears to be a sustainable strategy in its own right, in that Theta now undertakes four interdependent activities. Whether it actually leads to world mandate status is a separate question that depends a lot on the attitude of the parent company.

Discussion and conclusions

The subsidiary development processes described above represent an attempt to structure what is obviously a complex and somewhat idiosyncratic phenomenon. In the process of defining and delimiting three specific processes we have inevitably neglected many interesting facets of the broader phenomenon, so the purpose of this final section is to pick up on three issues that appeared to be particularly noteworthy. This section also provides a brief summary of the findings from the study and identifies directions for future research.

The risks associated with subsidiary development

We noted in the methodology section that the selection of subsidiaries was deliberately biased towards those that had undergone a fairly extensive development process. We turn briefly in this section to those subsidiaries that were less successful in their pursuit of the development paths mapped out above. Note that we have already alluded to the *early casualties* of the development process, i.e. those subsidiaries that failed to achieve their basic mandate and those that achieved viability but were closed during the rationalization of the 1980s–1990s. This section is by necessity speculative. Our discussion is drawn in part from what actually happened in sample companies, but also from hypothetical situations that were discussed with respondents. Further research is needed to more comprehensively understand these issues.

Beta Canada was perhaps the clearest example of a subsidiary that had striven for a product specialist role but had not been unequivocally successful in that objective. While Beta had manufacturing mandates in three related products, none was considered 'strategic' by the corporation. Subsidiary management were justifiably worried that future changes in the strategic priorities of the corporation could result in the sale of one or more of the businesses for which they had manufacturing mandates, and thus the closure of the Canadian manufacturing site (which relied on all three products to cover its fixed costs). This situation indicates two of the risks inherent in the product specialist position. The first is that the subsidiary fails to achieve best-in-class status, and thus loses out to a rival subsidiary that has a lower-cost or higher-quality position. An interesting example of this is Iota Scotland, that just failed in its bid to extend its R&D operation because the Australian affiliate could claim a 50 per cent R&D tax rebate back from its host government. The second risk is that the subsidiary's chosen area of expertise becomes strategically marginal to the company. Neither risk necessarily leads to closure, but they both challenge the subsidiary's long-term sustainability.

Gamma Canada provided the best example of the drawbacks to the world mandate position. Gamma had achieved world mandate status as long ago as 1970, but in doing so it had essentially cut itself off from the rest of the corporation. When the corporation got into difficulties in the late 1980s, development funding was restricted to those areas that were felt to be core to the corporation's future growth. Not surprisingly, Gamma Canada's business was not one of them. Gamma Canada is still an ongoing business, but its growth has been severely constrained and management feel that several important opportunities have been missed. A more extreme case is provided by Eta Scotland, that also established its mandate status many decades ago. Eta's expertise historically lay in needles and sutures, but the high autonomy afforded to the company by its parent created a diverse array of new businesses, in areas such as cat gut, textile braiding and collagen manufacture. Rather than close down businesses that were beyond the scope of the corporation, they were spun off as independent entities. Three very successful independent firms have grown out of Eta Scotland in this way.

Sustainability versus development

Given the emphasis in this paper on the processes leading to sustainable subsidiary positions, it is important to question whether this is the same as development. Our evidence suggested that, in essence, it is. The product specialist is always seeking to maintain or enhance its best-in-class status. Aware that other subsidiaries are actively or potentially competing with it for that position, it therefore continues to improve its quality and service levels and lower its costs. Likewise, the world mandate subsidiary has the responsibility for a business or product line, which it must continually invest in and upgrade in order to stay competitive with rival firms. In short, subsidiaries of both types face moving targets on account of the competitive forces at work inside and outside the corporation, and it is those forces that essentially drive the development process.

There is another concern that is frequently raised with regard to subsidiary development, and that is the fear that subsidiary managers are 'empire builders', who are acting in the interests of their country or their personal aggrandisement rather than in the interests of the MNC. This issue was raised in several of the research interviews. Our position on this issue is that sporadic cases of empire building can be found, but that for the most part subsidiary managers genuinely act in the interests of the corporation. The argument which was suggested in the course of the research interviews is as follows: The subsidiary's ability to add value rests on its capacity to apply its distinctive capabilities to the appropriate opportunities. The nature of these capabilities is understood far better by subsidiary management than by corporate management. It is thus the responsibility of subsidiary management to represent their capabilities in the best possible light to other part of the corporation, in order that they be recognised and applied to the appropriate opportunities. Viewed in this way, subsidiary managers who are seen to be promoting *their* operation are really only doing their job.

Where the development model is less effective

Finally, it is important to note that the subsidiary development model depicted here does not apply equally well in all cases. The most obvious 'misfit' is the case of the acquired or merged subsidiary. If we consider a case such as the Asea Brown Boveri merger, the subsidiary development process would have implications for the selection of which units survived and which were eliminated. And it would also have implications for the merged entities, which would still have to consider the relative merits of product specialist and world mandate alternatives. But the merger process itself clearly involves a large amount of parent-driven change that may be resource-depleting from the perspective of the subsidiary, so the application of the model developed here is obviously limited.

There may be other situations where the model is not appropriate but these are related more to the limitations of the current study. Specifically, in studying Canadian and Scottish subsidiaries of US MNCs we are unable to make any generalisations about subsidiary development processes in strategic markets (Japan, USA, Germany) or emerging markets (notably the far east) or about development processes in Japanese or European-owned subsidiaries. Our hope is that the model has some general validity, but further research is needed to establish whether this proves to be the case.

Conclusions

The purpose of this study was to explore in an empirical setting the phenomenon of subsidiary development using the model that was developed in a prior study. We identified two basic phases of development, *establishing viability* and *building sustainability*. The latter phase was seen as the pursuit of either a low-cost product specialist position or a differentiated world mandate position. Two generic processes were thus identified, corresponding to the pursuit of these two sustainable positions. Examination of these processes, in terms of the relative input of the parent company, the subsidiary and the host country revealed a surprising finding, namely that both processes involved very high levels of subsidiary initiative. The implication is that any sustainable position requires continued effort, and correspondingly that the lack of such effort can potentially damage the competitiveness of both the subsidiary and the corporation as a whole. There is one important caveat to this finding, namely that the restriction in variance at both host country (Canada and Scotland) and parent company (American) level favoured the identification of the subsidiary-specific factors associated with development. It would therefore be inappropriate to conclude that subsidiary factors matter more than parent or host country factors at this stage – all we can say with confidence is that actions taken by subsidiary managers *do* have a significant impact on subsidiary development.

This study has really only scratched the surface of a rich and interesting phenomenon. The limitations of the research are readily apparent. Not only did we limit ourselves to two host countries and one home country, we also focused on 'developed' subsidiaries and we conducted our analysis *post hoc* rather than in real time. Notwithstanding these drawbacks, it was possible to glean some very valuable insights into the subsidiary development process. Further research, we believe, should be directed in the first instance towards establishing the validity of the model, and in the second instance towards examining the nature of the specific development processes in more detail.

Notes

1. Resources are specialised and durable, tangible and intangible, assets (Collis, 1991). Consistent with the resource based theory of the firm (Barney, 1991) resources thus defined are a key determinant of competitive advantage. In the case of the MNC, however, the linkage between subsidiary resources and corporate competitive advantage is not simple, because it assumes that resources at the subsidiary level are effectively leveraged throughout the corporation. In this paper, we focus on subsidiary resources (and thus subsidiary development) while recognizing that there are issues for transfer and leverage that may not be simple.
2. Unfortunately, these similarities meant that little variance in host country factors was observed and consequently that it was more difficult to assess their impact on subsidiary development.
3. Our rationale was that the phenomenon of subsidiary development needs to be understood clearly before it is possible to investigate its absence. Clearly it could be somewhat frustrating to study a sample of stagnant subsidiaries in

the hope of uncovering why they had not developed. Future research, of course, should consider a larger sample of developed *and* stagnant subsidiaries.

4. These subsidiaries typically had support laboratories (Pearce, 1989) which perform application or development work associated specifically with the manufacturing operation, rather than genuine research laboratories (which are located elsewhere). This helps to explain why their R&D as a percentage of revenues is below average.

5. Note that the product specialist as defined here is a hybrid of White and Poynter's (1984) rationalised manufacturer and product specialist roles. In terms of value-added scope our product specialist is often constrained (i.e. like White and Poynter's rationalised manufacturer) but in spirit, it acts with a high level of discretion and foresight (i.e. like White and Poynter's product specialist).

11
Multinational Subsidiary Evolution: Capability and Charter Change in Foreign-Owned Subsidiary Companies (1998)*

Julian Birkinshaw and Neil Hood

There has been a profound evolution in thinking about multinational corporations (MNCs) [since the late 1980s]. Traditionally, in academic models researchers assumed that ownership-specific advantages were developed at the corporate headquarters and leveraged overseas through the transfer of technology to a network of foreign subsidiaries (Vernon, 1966; Dunning, 1981). As these overseas subsidiaries grew in size and developed their own unique resources, however, it became apparent to many researchers that corporate headquarters was no longer the sole source of competitive advantage for the MNC. Scholars developed models such as the heterarchy (Hedlund, 1986) and the transnational (Bartlett and Ghoshal, 1989) to reflect the critical role played by many subsidiaries in their corporations' competitiveness, and research attention began to shift toward understanding the new roles played by subsidiaries.

Implicit in this shift in research attention has been the concept of *subsidiary evolution*. We specify later in this article a precise definition of subsidiary evolution, but, for the moment, it can be understood broadly as the process of accumulation or depletion of resources/capabilities in the subsidiary over time. There is already widespread acknowledgment that subsidiaries evolve over time, typically through the accumulation of resources and through the development of specialised capabilities (Prahalad and Doz, 1981; Hedlund, 1986). There are also a number of established typologies that suggest very different roles and responsibilities for the population of subsidiaries (e.g. White and Poynter, 1984;

* *Academy of Management Review*, 23(4), 773–95.

Bartlett and Ghoshal, 1986; Jarillo and Martinez, 1990). What is missing, we believe, is an understanding of *how* subsidiaries change roles. Is there a predictable evolution process toward, for example, greater specialisation in terms of product, market, or technology? What are the factors promoting and/or suppressing such a shift? What are the underlying managerial processes that make such a shift possible?

These questions are made more complex by the enormous variety of multinational subsidiaries in existence. For example, subsidiary can refer to the totality of the MNC's holdings in a host country or to a single entity, such as a manufacturing or sales operation. Subsidiaries are established for a variety of motives (e.g. resource seeking, market seeking, or efficiency seeking) and through a variety of modes (e.g. greenfield, acquisition, or joint venture). The relationship of the subsidiary to the parent company can be anything from legal holding company to fully integrated. And recent shifts toward regional free trade have led to international divestments, rationalizations, mergers, and acquisitions – all of which lead to further changes in the make-up of the MNC's subsidiaries. The reality is that a single evolution process for subsidiaries cannot be readily identified. Subsidiaries contract or die out, as well as become larger or more specialized[1] and there are many different factors that can influence the processes. In this article we therefore put forward a number of generic processes that are appropriate under certain conditions. We also draw extensively from the empirical literature to ensure that the ideas we present are grounded in the available evidence.

We organise this article into two parts. The first part is a systematic review of the literature on subsidiary evolution. This literature is fragmented, but we identify three broadly defined schools of thought on the processes underlying subsidiary evolution. The second part of the article is theoretical development. Building on foundations provided by the resource-based view of the firm, we define subsidiary evolution in terms of capability and charter change and then put forward five generic subsidiary evolution processes. For each one we develop propositions linking various antecedent conditions to subsidiary evolution.

We feel it is important to be clear on the boundaries of this study from the outset. We are concerned with those processes that occur once the MNC has made its initial foreign direct investment in the host country; hence, we do not consider issues of market entry (Johanson and Vahlne, 1977). We are concerned primarily with dominantly owned or wholly owned subsidiaries, because the literature addressing the phenomenon of subsidiary evolution has focused on such cases. Nonetheless, our expectation is that many of the processes we discuss in this article could be adapted to other forms of subsidiary, such as inter-national joint ventures and alliances.

We define subsidiary as a value-adding entity in a host country. This definition reflects the reality that a given host country will sometimes have several subsidiaries (of the same parent) that are independent of one another and that, consequently, will have a separate evolutionary path. A subsidiary can perform a single activity (e.g. manufacturing) or an entire value chain of activities. Finally, subsidiary evolution refers to the enhancement or atrophy of subsidiary capabilities over time and the establishment or loss of the commensurate charter (Galunic and Eisenhardt, 1996). We elaborate on this definition later in the article, but, for the moment, it is important to recognise that changes to the subsidiary's stock of capabilities and its charter are closely tied to the subsidiary's ability to add value.

There is some danger, when considering subsidiary evolution, that one will develop a normative bias toward the *accumulation* of resources and specialized capabilities (i.e. subsidiary development), both because it is more commonly reported and because development is an intrinsi-cally more attractive phenomenon to study than decline. We are careful in this article to avoid such a stance, partly because development is just one side of the story and partly because it is clearly possible that subsi-diary development *is not always desirable* from the MNC's perspective. Host country laws or customer requirements may force the MNC to undertake activities in that country that it would rather do elsewhere, and subsidiary management may take certain actions to develop the subsidiary for the benefit of their country or for themselves (i.e. 'empire building'). Our preference, then, is to model the generic processes of subsidiary evolution in positivist terms – that is, with regard to what the literature and experience tells us actually happens – and to ensure that our definition of subsidiary evolution accounts for the possible lack of alignment between subsidiary and parent company goals.

Literature review

There exists a substantial body of literature concerned with various aspects of multinational subsidiary management (for reviews, see Jarillo and Martinez, 1990; and Birkinshaw and Morrison, 1995). In the past 10 years the focus of such research has been on the different roles taken by subsidiaries (e.g. White and Poynter, 1984; Bartlett and Ghoshal, 1986; Gupta and Govindarajan, 1991, 1994). Strangely, little explicit attention has been given to the question of how a particular subsidiary's role might shift over time (minor exceptions are White and Poynter, 1984; Jarillo and Martinez, 1990; and Papanastassiou and Pearce, 1994). In part, this lack of attention reflects the cross-sectional nature of the research, but it also appears to emanate from an assumption that the subsidiary's role is 'assigned' to it by the parent company according to such factors as the perceived capabilities of the subsidiary and the strategic importance of the local market (Bartlett and Ghoshal, 1986).

Head-office assignment of roles is a critical determinant of subsidiary evolution, but in our reading of the literature, it is just one of three broad mechanisms that are responsible for driving the process. The second we refer to as *subsidiary choice*, which reflects the decisions taken by subsidiary management to define for themselves the role of their subsidiary. The third we refer to as *local environment determinism*, in that the role of the subsidiary can be understood as a function of the constraints and opportunities in the local market. Our basic understanding of subsidiary evolution is that the three mechanisms interact to determine the subsidiary's role at any given point in time. The subsidiary's role subsequently impacts the decisions made by head-office managers, the decisions made by subsidiary managers, and the standing of the subsidiary in the local environment. This creates a cyclical process through which the subsidiary's role changes over time. Figure 11.1 illustrates the

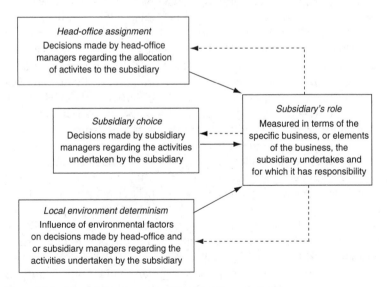

Figure 11.1 Organising framework for subsidiary evolution

process. We underscore, however, that this framework is simply a means of organizing the literature review that follows. In the second part of the article we provide a more detailed specification of the evolution process, as we see it.

Head-office assignment

Two theoretical perspectives shed light on the head-office-driven process of subsidiary evolution: (1) the product life cycle (PLC) model (Vernon, 1966) and (2) the internationalisation process (Johanson and Vahlne, 1977). Both work on the assumption that the subsidiary is an instrument of the MNC and, consequently, that it acts solely with regard to head-office-determined imperatives. In Table 11.1 we summarise these two theoretical perspectives, along with the other three perspectives that we subsequently discuss.

Vernon's (1966) PLC model is well known. In the first stage the MNC manufactures and sells in its home market and also exports to certain foreign markets. As the product matures, low-cost production becomes important and foreign competition a threat, so the MNC establishes production overseas. This production is directed primarily toward the host country, but, as quality improves, it may also be exported back to the home country. Finally, once the host country advances to a stage where its costs are uncompetitive, production is shifted to a lower-cost host country (see also Norton and Rees, 1979 and Mullor-Sebastian, 1983).

The PLC model helps us to understand the development process as subsidiaries' roles shift toward high value-added activities – from servicing the local market to 'adapting' the technology to local specifications, then exporting back to the home country, and, eventually, to contributing to product development (Vernon, 1979; Harrigan, 1984). However, it is limited in two ways: (1) the subsidiary is always subordinate to the centre, and (2) the possibility of subsidiary decline is not considered. There are, however, a number of contributions from the same economic paradigm that begin to address both of these shortfalls. Some acknowledgment has been made of the greater role that the subsidiary can play in the MNC network (e.g. Rugman and Verbeke, 1992; Dunning, 1993) but still to a lesser degree than the subsidiary choice perspectives we discuss below. Also, the foreign *divestment* process has been modelled to understand the factors that precipitate the closure or sale of a foreign subsidiary (Boddewyn, 1979, 1983).

Building from a more micro perspective than the PLC model, authors of the *internationalisation* process literature begin with assumptions

Table 11.1 Summary of different perspectives on subsidiary evolution

Perspective	Theoretical roots	Drivers of subsidiary evolution	Role of subsidiary in MNC	Role of subsidiary in host country
Product life cycle	Economics; transaction cost theory	Economic development of host country; transfer of technology from parent to subsidiary	Subordinate entity; recipient of technology transfers	Manufactures and sells products in local market; exploitative role
Internationalisation process	Cognitive and behavioural theory	Cognitive limitations of HQ management; incremental increase in commitment to foreign market	Subordinate entity; recipient of investment on basis of market experience	Learns about local market; builds experience and transfers it back to HQ
Network perspective	Sociology; resource dependency theory	Growth of resources through organic process; allocation of responsibilities on basis of relative power	Node in a network; potential source of ownership-specific advantages and equal partner with HQ	'Embedded' in local network, which can be a source of influence *vis-à-vis* HQ
Decision process	'Managerial' theory of the firm	Development of structural context that allows subsidiary management to develop organically	Role is function of subsidiary's structural context; may be subordinate or equal partner with HQ	Not discussed
Regional development	Economic geography; trade theory	Local environment growth and upgrading stimulates subsidiary development	Subsidiary provides access to local learning, which is disseminated through corporation	Participates in local industrial cluster; may be an active contributor to local economic development

about the cognitive limitations and behaviours of individual managers (Cyert and March, 1963) and seek to understand how firms move beyond their national borders (e.g. Aharoni, 1966; Johanson and Vahlne, 1977; Cavusgil, 1980; Agarwal and Ramaswami, 1992; Li, 1995). In their model, Johanson and Vahlne (1977) explain this process in terms of the reciprocal relationship between (1) levels of knowledge about, and existing commitment to, the foreign market and (2) decisions regarding further commitment to the market.

This model can be readily applied to the case of established subsidiaries. For example, the decision to enhance the manufacturing operation in a subsidiary represents a 'commitment decision,' based on an appreciation of the subsidiary's current strengths and weaknesses (i.e. *market knowledge*) and a desire to increase the quality of investment in that country (i.e. *market commitment*). That decision, thus, leads to increased commitment, greater understanding of the local business environment, and the possibility of a further investment in the future. Subsidiary development, then, is achieved through the cyclical interaction between investment and learning.[2] Again, though, there are limitations as to how applicable the theory is to the generic issue of subsidiary evolution – the most prominent being that it is more effective at modelling development than decline. Given that market knowledge and commitment must increase the longer the subsidiary is operating in its host market, the decision to reduce commitment or exit a country has to be interpreted as an exogenous input to the model. To be useful as a generic model, some modifications would appear to be necessary.

In terms of the empirical literature, there exists a large body of work in which scholars examine various aspects of subsidiary evolution from a headquarters assignment perspective. The most comprehensive evidence comes from researchers in the UK, who have, over a 30-year period, tracked the successive waves of US, European, and Japanese investment into the UK. This research shows that, in aggregate, there has been a clear development process – from 'miniature replica' subsidiaries (White and Poynter, 1984) in the 1950s and 1960s to rationalised manufacturers and product specialists in the 1970s and 1980s (Hood and Young, 1983; Young, Hood, and Hamill, 1988) – in a manner that is consistent with both the PLC and internationalization models.

Evidence for the head-office assignment process also can be found in the case of foreign owned subsidiaries in the USA, although not in the same detail as in the UK. Much has been written, for example, about the growth of Japanese manufacturing operations in the United States (e.g. Lincoln, Olson and Hanada, 1978; Hamel and Prahalad, 1985;

Sugiura, 1990), but the evidence simply indicates that these subsidiaries have grown and, to some extent, have adapted to the local environment. More fruitfully, research by Chang (1995, 1996) and Rosenzweig and Chang (1995a, 1995b) explicitly models subsidiary growth as a sequential process of resource commitment and capability building. There have also been occasional studies from other parts of the world indicating the importance of head-office assignment as the driver of subsidiary development (e.g. Jarillo and Martinez, 1990; Malnight, 1995, 1996).

Researchers have also given subsidiary decline some attention. Boddewyn (1979, 1983) undertook a comprehensive review of foreign divestment and concluded that poor financial performance was the primary cause, followed by lack of strategic fit and various organisational problems, such as poor relationships between parent and subsidiary. More recently, research undertaken in the UK on the Europe-wide rationalization sparked by free trade has shown that the dynamics of internal competition between subsidiaries are a critical determinant of which subsidiaries survive (Sachdev, 1976; Young, McDermott, and Dunlop, 1991; Almor and Hirsch, 1995).

Three important implications can be drawn from this review. First, head-office assignment is not the sole determinant of subsidiary evolution. As the UK studies have shown, the changes in subsidiary roles were dictated by head office but motivated, in large part, by the changing economic conditions in the UK and Europe. They were also, to a large degree, driven by the *track* record of the subsidiary companies in question, especially during the recent phase of plant rationalization in Europe. Second, most of the evolution documented (development and decline) was at the low value-added end of the scale. Very few had 'world mandates' (Roth and Morrison, 1992) or product development responsibilities. This leads to the observation that head-office assignment may be the driver of subsidiary evolution in the early stages of the process, when the level of resources and capabilities in the subsidiary is not too advanced. Third, theoretical perspectives have not been very helpful for understanding some of the higher-order value-adding activity that has emerged in subsidiaries, not for understanding the process of subsidiary decline (however, see Boddewyn, 1979, for the one exception).

Subsidiary choice

Two theoretical perspectives shed light on the subsidiary choice view of subsidiary development: (1) the network model of the MNC and (2) the decision process perspective. The network model of the MNC, in contrast to the PLC model discussed earlier, allows the subsidiary to move from a position of subordination (*vis-à-vis* head office) to one of equality, or even leadership. In terms of core assumptions, the network model recognizes that ownership-specific advantages do not have to be tied to the home country (Rugman and Verbeke, 1992) but can, instead, be acquired or developed by the subsidiary itself. In addition, the MNC is modelled as an 'interorganizational network' (Ghoshal and Bartlett, 1991) of loosely coupled entities, rather than a hierarchical monolith. This loose coupling gives the subsidiary the necessary freedom to develop its own unique resource profile.

Much of the contemporary thinking on MNC organization conforms to these basic assumptions, without an explicit network conceptualization (e.g. White and Poynter, 1984; Hedlund, 1986; Bartlett and Ghoshal, 1989). More recently, scholars have attempted to model more formally the relationships between entities in the MNC according to their relative power (Ghoshal and Bartlett, 1991; Forsgren, Holm and Johanson, 1992; Forsgren and Pahlberg, 1992). This latter stream of research has built on the concepts of network analysis developed in the fields of industrial marketing (Johanson and Mattson, 1988) and organisational theory (Emerson, 1962; Thompson, 1967; Pfeffer and Salancik, 1978). It is important to note that the resource-based view of the firm (Penrose, 1959; Wernerfelt, 1984; Barney, 1991) has a lot in common with the network model, once one recognizes that resource development can occur at the level of the subsidiary, rather than at the level of the MNC as a whole.

The network model provides a very valuable perspective on subsidiary evolution, because it reflects the reality that many subsidiaries have specialised capabilities on which the rest of the MNC is dependent. Evolution here is an organic process, built around the growth and decline of valuable and distinctive resources in the subsidiary. Subsidiary growth, in particular, is constrained by the natural rate of growth of resources (Penrose, 1959) and also by the actions of other entities (notably the parent company) who use their relative power to enforce their will on the subsidiary. As the subsidiary increases its stock of distinctive resources, it lessens its dependence on other entities and takes more complete control of its own destiny (Pfeffer and Salancik, 1978; Prahalad and Doz, 1981).

The second theoretical approach involves the decision process in large, complex organisations (Bower, 1972; Prahalad, 1976; Burgelman, 1983a, 1991, 1996; Noda and Bower, 1996). Like the internationalization process perspective, the body of literature on the decision process perspective begins with assumptions of bounded rationality on the part of individual managers. This literature has provided much of the foundations for the network model of the MNC, and various aspects of subsidiary management have also been studied from this perspective (Bartlett and Ghoshal, 1986; Prahalad and Doz, 1981). Surprisingly, though, subsidiary evolution has received only limited attention. Only Prahalad and Doz (1981) explicitly have considered subsidiary growth, and their concern was with how the head office could continue to exert control over its subsidiaries, rather than with the benefits of growth *per se.*

Of greater interest, in terms of this article, is the work of Burgelman (1983a, 1983b), who studied internal corporate venturing using an extension of Bower's (1972) resource allocation model. His key contribution was a recognition that strategic behaviour often occurs below top management levels and sometimes in ways that are not actively encouraged by top management. He termed this *autonomous behaviour.* Regarding the MNC subsidiary, the concept of autonomous behaviour is important, because it suggests a process of internal growth that is only loosely controlled by head-office directives. The idea that subsidiaries take the initiative to win world product mandates, for example, is very consistent with Burgelman's theory (Crookell, 1986; Birkinshaw, 1995).

In sum, both theoretical perspectives give us considerable potential for understanding subsidiary evolution. The network perspective provides important insights into the role of the underlying capabilities of the subsidiary and emphasises that the subsidiary is part of a network – not just a dyadic relationship with a parent company. The decision process perspective provides us with a way of understanding autonomous action on the part of subsidiaries.

The empirical literature that draws on the subsidiary choice perspective is mostly from Canada, but smaller contributions come from Sweden, Ireland, and the UK. Canada appears to have been an attractive setting for research on subsidiary choice because of the consistently high levels of foreign ownership of industry (Safarian, 1966) and the deliberate policy of governments in the 1970s and 1980s to encourage foreign MNCs to grant their Canadian subsidiaries 'world product mandates' (Hatch Report, 1979). A landmark study by the Science Council of Canada (1980) documented case studies of subsidiaries that had won such mandates, typically achieved through development of specialised capabilities and strong relationships with the parent company. Subsequent studies by Bishop and Crookell (1986) and Birkinshaw (1995) drew similar conclusions. Thus, while the macro changes in the Canadian business environment, and the strategic responses to those changes by parent company management, shaped the broad shift toward subsidiary specialization, there is strong evidence that specific subsidiaries' development paths were also swayed by the entrepreneurial actions of their managers.

Although Canadian researchers are alone in emphasising subsidiary initiative as the driver of development, there has been some discussion of the concept for UK (Papanasstasiou and Pearce, 1994), Scottish (Young, Hood and Peters, 1994), and Irish (Delaney, 1996) subsidiaries, and Gupta and Govindarajan (1994) have discussed it as well. In research on international R&D laboratories, scholars have offered similar conclusions (Ronstadt, 1977; Behrman and Fischer, 1980; Håkanson and Zander, 1986; Pearce, 1989) – namely, that over time R&D laboratories tend to evolve *through their own initiative* toward higher value-added R&D work. Finally, a number of Swedish researchers working from a head-office perspective have pursued the same themes in a rather different way. Their overall approach has been one of organizational development, but the evidence of subsidiaries building specialised resources and gaining recognition for their distinctive abilities is compelling (Forsgren, Holm and Johanson, 1992, 1995; Forsgren and Pahlberg, 1992; Ghauri, 1992; Holm, Johanson, and Thilenius, 1995).

This evidence points to a number of implications for the subsidiary evolution process in general. First, autonomous subsidiary behaviour (Burgelman, 1983b) appears to be a potent force for subsidiary development because it leads to the planned – rather than fortuitous – development of resources and capabilities. Second, head-office support appears to be a necessary but not sufficient condition for subsidiary-driven development. Many of the failed cases of initiatives in the Canadian literature appear to have been the result of weak parent-subsidiary relationships or a somewhat *ethnocentric attitude* among parent managers (Perlmutter, 1969; Birkinshaw, 1997).[3] Third, subsidiary decline gets essentially no consideration in either the theoretical or the empirical literature. Clearly, it is meaningless to suggest that subsidiary managers might orchestrate their own demise, but we can certainly envision a process in which *inaction* by subsidiary managers leads to the atrophy and eventual demise of the subsidiary and its resources.

Local environment determinism

In much of the mainstream organization theory literature, scholars view organizational action as constrained or determined by the environment in which it occurs (Hannan and Freeman, 1977; Meyer and Rowan, 1977; Pfeffer and Salancik, 1978). MNC researchers have adapted this perspective by proposing that each subsidiary of the MNC operates in its own unique task environment, which constrains or determines the activities of that subsidiary (Ghoshal and Nohria, 1989; Ghoshal and Bartlett, 1991; Rosenzweig and Singh, 1991; Westney, 1994). The argument, in essence, is that each subsidiary operates under a unique set of conditions to which it has to adapt in order to be effective. The nature of the local environment, as defined by customers, competitors, suppliers, and government bodies, thus has an important influence on the activities undertaken by the subsidiary.

Although the static relationship between the subsidiary and its local environment has been studied (e.g. Ghoshal and Nohria, 1989; Rosenzweig and Nohria, 1995; Andersson and Johanson, 1996), there has been less consideration of the dynamic question – that is, the relationship between local/regional development and subsidiary evolution (Young, Hood and Peters, 1994).[4] In the literature that does exist, scholars have, for the most part, not explicitly considered the foreign-owned sector. One important line of thinking is the various 'stages' models of economic growth that explicitly recognise the importance of foreign direct investment (FDI) by MNCs as a driver of the process. These include Ozawa's 'dynamic paradigm of FDI-facilitated development' (1992) and Dunning's investment development cycle (1981, 1986). In both, the MNC subsidiary plays a critical role as a conduit for technology and skill development in the local economy.

Implicitly, the subsidiary itself also develops, in that it becomes capable of adopting and applying increasingly sophisticated levels of the MNC's technology. Porter (1990) proposes a stages model of growth based on his 'diamond of competitive advantage', but he sees the role of the MNC subsidiary as primarily one of 'selective tapping' (of ideas), rather than active development. The exception, he argues, is the few subsidiaries in leading-edge clusters that go on to become the MNC's home base for a particular business area.

We should briefly mention the theoretical rationale for linking regional development to subsidiary evolution. The heart of the issue is the argument that certain aspects of knowledge transfer occur more effectively between local firms (wholly owned or subsidiaries) than between parent and overseas subsidiary, because of geographical proximity and cultural similarity (Porter, 1990; Krugman, 1991; Kogut and Zander, 1992; Sölvell and Zander, 1998). Subsidiary evolution, thus, is driven by the dynamism of the local business environment (cf., Porter's diamond), as well as by the subsidiary's ability to access resources from the MNC.

The evidence for local environment-driven subsidiary evolution is rather limited. Both the UK and Canadian literature we discussed earlier make it clear that local environment characteristics factor into the decision to invest in or upgrade a subsidiary, but, typically, it is the subsidiary company or head-office managers who drive the process (e.g. Bishop and Crookell, 1986). There is, however, an increasing acknowledgment of the importance of inward investment agencies, such as Scottish Enterprise, whose role is not only to attract greenfield investments but also to help existing subsidiaries upgrade their activities (Hood, Young and Lal, 1994).

In sum, there is strong evidence that the subsidiary development process is influenced by the local environment, through both (1) the broadly defined dynamism and attractiveness of the local business context and (2) the specific incentive programmes offered by development agencies. But, as with many of the other perspectives, it is the early stages of subsidiary development that scholars best understand, while later-stage development and decline get little attention.

Integrating the three perspectives

In this review we took a broad approach in identifying any theoretical or empirical research that potentially shed light on the process of subsidiary evolution. In order to move forward, however, it is important to take a position and develop one line of thinking in detail. Our preference is to build upon the subsidiary choice perspective. We fully embrace the network conceptualizations of the MNC by modelling the subsidiary as a semiautonomous entity, capable of making its own decisions but constrained in its action by the demands of head-office managers and by the opportunities in the local environment. We also borrow heavily from the decision process perspective, notably the work of Burgelman (1983b) on autonomous behaviour.

We draw on the other perspectives to a lesser degree. The PLC model offers important lessons in the early stages of subsidiary development, but it does not allow for autonomous action on the part of the subsidiary. The internationalisation process, likewise, has implications for early-stage development but is rooted in a head-office perspective on MNC management. The local environment perspective has clear implications for subsidiary development, but in its pure form it is fundamentally opposed to the subsidiary choice perspective (Child, 1972). It is also less developed than the other perspectives.

The theory part of this article can be described as a 'dynamic capabilities' approach to subsidiary evolution. We draw heavily on recent advances in thinking about organizational capabilities (Kogut and Zander, 1992; Madhok, 1997; Teece, Pisano and Shuen, 1997), but we do so with an important distinction – namely, a focus on the subsidiary, rather than the entire firm, as the unit of analysis. Our approach is, of course, consistent with the network conceptualizations of the MNC, but it also raises a number of new challenges.

Theoretical development

Toward a definition of subsidiary evolution

Following Amit and Schoemaker (1993), we define resources as the stock of available factors owned or controlled by the subsidiary and *capabilities* as a subsidiary's capacity to deploy resources, usually in combination, using organisational processes to effect a desired end. Subsidiary capabilities can be specific to a functional area – for example, flexible production, research into fibre optics, or logistics management – or they can be more broadly based – for example, total quality management, systems integration, innovation, or government relations.

Subsidiary evolution, we argue, is the result of an accumulation or depletion of capabilities over time.[5] In this respect, we are very close to the dynamic capabilities perspective of Nelson and Winter (1982), Dierickx and Cool (1989), Kogut and Zander (1992), and Teece et al. (1997), in that we are concerned with the 'mechanisms by which firms accumulate and dissipate new skills and capabilities' (Teece, Pisano and Shuen, 1997: 19). To some extent, capabilities are accumulated and stored as organisational routines (Nelson and Winter, 1982) that have emerged over time, but the process also can be strongly influenced by various subsidiary, corporate, and local environment factors, many of which we discussed earlier.

An important point to underscore here is that the subsidiary's capabilities are, to some extent, distinct from the capabilities of the headquarters operation and its sister subsidiaries. In other words, the particular geographical setting and history of the subsidiary are responsible for defining a development path that is absolutely unique to that subsidiary, which, in turn, results in a profile of capabilities that is unique (Teece, Pisano and Shuen, 1997). There are also, of course, shared capabilities between subsidiaries, such as those codified in company manuals or blueprints. The evidence, however, indicates that the transfer of capabilities between units of the same firm is far from trivial and is a function of the codifiability of the capability in question (Zander, 1994), the motivations of the receiving units, and a host of contextual variables (Szulanski, 1996).[6] Capabilities, simply stated, are 'sticky', and they cannot be easily transferred from one subsidiary to the next, even when the transfer is undertaken willingly.

Related to the stickiness of subsidiary capabilities is their path dependence.[7] Capabilities are not easily transferred and not readily dissipated. They develop over time as a result of past experiences and are subsequently applied to new or related areas of business. To some extent, new capabilities are always being developed, but they typically emerge at the margin of existing capabilities in response to competitive demands (see below). As a result, it is possible to think in terms of path-dependent trajectories of capabilities that gradually evolve over time. Large-scale grafting of new capabilities onto the subsidiary's existing stock of capabilities also can be achieved through merger or acquisition (Huber, 1991; Madhok, 1997), although such a process has been shown in the post-acquisition integration literature to be far from trivial (Haspeslagh and Jemison, 1991).

The visible manifestation of the subsidiary's role in the MNC is its *charter*, defined as the business – or elements of the business – in which the subsidiary participates and for which it is recognised to have responsibility within the MNC (Galunic and Eisenhardt, 1996). The term *charter* has implications for the organisation's mission (Thompson, 1967) and for its institutional legitimacy (DiMaggio and Powell, 1983; Scott and Meyer, 1994), but our focus here, in keeping with Galunic and Eisenhardt (1996), is to focus on business activities and the underlying capabilities through which they are implemented.[8] Thus, we can define charter in terms of markets served, products manufactured, technologies held, functional areas covered, or any combination thereof. The charter is typically a shared understanding between the subsidiary and the headquarters regarding the subsidiary's scope of responsibilities.

The relationship between the subsidiary's charter and its underlying capabilities is not a simple one. In the case where the subsidiary's charter does not change for a long period of time, subsidiary managers are likely to steer resource deployment and capability accumulation efforts toward the fulfillment of that charter so that, eventually, the subsidiary's capability profile is a reflection of its charter. However, if there is a high level of change in the subsidiary's resource base (e.g. through merger and acquisition), in its charter, or in the markets that the charter is directed toward, then at any given point in time, there are likely to be mismatches between the subsidiary's capability profile and its official charter. The point here, which we elaborate on further in the next section, is simply that the *concept of subsidiary evolution must take into account both the charter of the subsidiary and its underlying capabilities.* It is dangerous to assume that the two simply move together.

One final line of reasoning regarding subsidiary charters and capabilities needs to be mentioned here – namely, that *in most corporations there is internal competition for charters.* The internal competition is both for existing charters (where one subsidiary 'steals' a charter from another) and for new charters (where two or more subsidiaries 'bid' against one another). We find the best evidence for internal charter competition in the recent work of Galunic and Eisenhardt (1996) and Galunic (1996), who studied the processes through which divisions of Omni corporation gained and lost charters from one another. Charter competition is also mentioned in several studies of Canadian subsidiaries (Crookell, 1986; Birkinshaw, 1996).

The idea that charters might shift from one subsidiary to another appears strange at first, given that we have just argued that each subsidiary has a unique capability profile. However, in many cases subsidiaries will have similar, although not identical, capability profiles. Take, for example, the case of a large silicon chip manufacturer, which will typically have 10 or more fabrication plants in various sites around the world. These plants all have the basic capability to manufacture chips, but, at the same time, they do so with rather different technologies and different levels of quality control, cost, process enhancement, and so on. In all of these plants there is an ongoing process of internal benchmarking and capability upgrading,[9] because a new investment can potentially be made at any one of the existing plants.

Not all charters are 'contestable' in this fashion. Some charters are country specific and so are linked inextricably to the local subsidiary operation; others are tied to large, immobile assets (e.g. an auto plant) so they cannot easily be shifted to another location. Many more, however, are readily contestable, especially when the underlying resources on which they are based are mobile. It is, we believe, the latent mobility of charters and the competition between subsidiary units for charters that is one of the fundamental drivers behind the subsidiary evolution process.

The importance of internal competition for charters can be shown in another way. Porter's (1980, 1990) thinking on competitive advantage suggests that it is exposure to demanding customers, leading-edge competitors, and high-quality suppliers that pressures firms to upgrade their capabilities. In the case of the subsidiary company, we can identify a competitive environment with both external and internal components.

The external elements are customers, competitors, and suppliers in the local environment; the internal elements are other corporate units that buy from or sell to the focal[10] subsidiary and sister subsidiaries that are competing for new and existing charters. Our argument is that internal competitive forces – when they are released – are as critical to the capability enhancement process as external competitive forces. In some MNCs there is no internal competitive environment, because all sourcing relationships and charter allocations are centrally planned by head-office managers, but, increasingly, MNCs are making use of internal market mechanisms to foster the competitive dynamics we are describing here (Halal, 1994).

In summary, subsidiary evolution is defined in terms of (1) the enhancement/atrophy of capabilities in the subsidiary and (2) the establishment/loss of the commensurate charter. Subsidiary development consists of capability enhancement and charter establishment; subsidiary decline consists of capability atrophy and charter loss. Capability change may lead or lag the change in the commensurate charter, but, for evolution to have occurred, the charter must eventually reflect the underlying capabilities of the subsidiary. Note that this definition deliberately excludes cases of self-serving or empire-building behaviour, in which the subsidiary develops capabilities that are *not* aligned with the strategic priorities of the MNC. Our argument is that the process of assigning a charter to the subsidiary is an explicit acknowledgment by corporate management that the underlying capabilities are valued. If the capabilities are not valued, there is no charter change, and evolution has not occurred.

Generic subsidiary evolution processes

We now can reconsider the phenomenon of subsidiary evolution using the theoretical ideas developed above. Our objective here is to put forward five generic processes of subsidiary evolution and to use the theoretical insights indicated above (and earlier in the article) to propose a series of causal relationships linking certain contextual factors to each of the five processes.

In Figure 11.2 we indicate the possible combinations of capability change and charter change in the subsidiary. As we noted earlier, it seems extremely unlikely that the subsidiary's charter will mirror exactly the subsidiary's capability profile. Instead, the capability change will either lead or lag the charter change.

In situation 1 the charter extension leads, subsequently, to an enhancement of the subsidiary's capability profile. Given that charter assignment

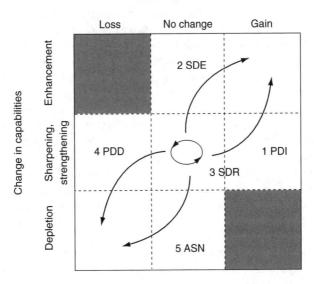

Figure 11.2 Subsidiary evolution as a function of capability and charter change
Note: 1–5 refer to the five generic processes we discuss in the text.

is the parent company's responsibility and that the capabilities are not already in existence, we designate this process *parent-driven investment* (PDI). Although subsidiary managers may have some influence over the process (notably, through high performance), they are typically actively competing for the charter with other subsidiaries, so the development of the commensurate capabilities begins only once the charter has been assigned.

In situation 2 the capability enhancement leads, subsequently, to an extension to the subsidiary's charter. In essence, it represents a strategic move by subsidiary managers, who see the opportunity to gain a new or enhanced charter if they can demonstrate that they have the necessary capabilities. However, charter change in this case is not guaranteed – for example, if the capabilities in question are not deemed by corporate management to be valuable. We designate this process *subsidiary-driven charter extension* (SDE).

Situations 4 and 5 are the reverse of situations 1 and 2. The former is *parent-driven divestment* (PDD), where the subsidiary loses its charter for a certain product, technology, or market and then, gradually, the commensurate capabilities atrophy. The latter is *atrophy through subsidiary neglect* (ASN), where the subsidiary's capabilities gradually wither away over time, the subsidiary's performance (for that charter) suffers, and, eventually, the parent company takes away the charter.

Finally, situation 3 is *subsidiary-driven charter reinforcement* (SDR), which refers to the situation in which the subsidiary sharpens or strengthens its existing capabilities and maintains its charter. One could argue that this is not a pure case of subsidiary evolution, but we include it to account for the situation in which the subsidiary opts to deepen its capabilities in one specific area (i.e., its current charter), rather than seek out new charters. As part of a long-term strategy of subsidiary development, charter reinforcement is probably an important phase for the subsidiary to go through, because it ensures that the subsidiary has leading-edge capabilities *vis-à-vis* both internal and external competitors. Note, however, that in such a case it is harder (although not impossible) to identify when evolution has occurred, because the charter is maintained rather than enhanced.

Two further observations should be made at this stage. First, each process represents a discrete phase that, in our experience, may take anything from a few weeks to a few years to complete. Over a longer period of time, one would expect to see multiple phases of development, including positive and negative steps, as well as subsidiary- and parent-driven ones. The unit of analysis under investigation here, thus, is the single period of one charter change and a commensurate change in capabilities. Subsidiary evolution, broadly conceived, also can refer to aggregate changes over time, but, for the sake of conceptual and operational clarity, we must work at the lower level of analysis. Second, we should be clear that we see the five processes as comprehensive and mutually exclusive so that every case of subsidiary evolution can be classified as belonging to one of the five. Whether this also means that the five generic processes constitute a type is more debatable, because the processes lack comparability in certain key dimensions. Moreover, some have argued that the term *typology* should be used in a very precise manner to retain its value for theory building (Doty and Glick, 1994: 232), so our preference here is to avoid claiming that a type exists, even though in certain respects it could probably be labelled as such.

Two questions follow from the categorization indicated in Figure 11.2. First, what do these five processes look like (in terms of action-outcome relationships)? Second, what contextual factors are responsible for promoting or suppressing them? In the remainder of the article, we address these two questions, using Table 11.2 as a framework. We consider each process in turn, with regard to the major actions undertaken by parent management, subsidiary management, and any other actors involved, and the anticipated outcomes. We then look at the contextual factors listed in Table 11.2 and consider the impact that each is predicted to have – if any – on the five generic processes. Note that we identified the contextual factors from the existing literature or during theoretical development.

Parent-driven investment (PDI)

This process consists of one clearly defined event – that is, the decision to enhance the subsidiary's charter – preceded by a period of negotiation and deliberation by the parent and the subsidiary and followed by a period of capability enhancement by the subsidiary in order to deliver satisfactorily on the new charter. The action taken by parent management typically is an evaluation of the relative merits of various locations for the planned investment, followed by the decision to make the charter change (or not) in the focal subsidiary. The action taken by subsidiary management is typically lobbying parent managers to persuade them to decide in that subsidiary's favour. In most cases the process involves the commitment of considerable resources to the subsidiary – for example, through the establishment of a new factory or through creation of a research and development group. However, it is also possible that the decision will simply be one of charter change in the subsidiary – for example, the extension of market responsibility from the UK to Europe.

The process is driven by the parent company's desire to select, according to whatever criteria it deems appropriate, the optimum location for an investment. Some MNCs use a formalised request-for-proposal procedure in such cases, whereby proposed corporate-level investments are opened up to all interested subsidiary operations and allocated on the basis of the 'bids' that are received. In other cases the process is less structured and may involve a variety of boundedly rational decision-making procedures (Cyert and March, 1963; Mintzberg, Raisinghani and Theoret, 1976), such as localised search or politically motivated decision criteria. In both cases there is at least an implicit competition between locations for the new investment, which typically leads to active lobbying by various subsidiaries and host governments.

Subsidiary-driven charter extension (SDE)

This involves a long and often slow process of capability building, followed by an extension to the subsidiary's charter. The process essentially is one of corporate entrepreneurship (Burgelman, 1983b;

Table 11.2 Five generic subsidiary evolution processes

Contextual factors	Action		Outcome
Parent-company factors • Competitive internal resource allocation • Decentralisation of decision making • Ethnocentrism of parent management	Parent: Decision to make investment; evaluation of various locations Subsidiary: Lobbying	PDI →	Establishment of new charter in subsidiary (CC); gradual development of commensurate capabilities (CB)
Subsidiary factors • Track record of subsidiary • Credibility of subsidiary management • Entrepreneurial orientation of subsidiary employees	Subsidiary: Identification of new opportunities; building capabilities (CB); proposal to parent Parent: Judgement on subsidiary proposal	SDE →	Extension of charter in subsidiary (CC)
	Subsidiary: Competitiveness-driven search; upgrading of existing capabilities (CB)	SDR →	Reinforcement of existing charter in subsidiary
Host country factors • Strategic importance of country • Host government support • Relative cost of factor inputs • Dynamism of local business environment	Parent: Decision to divest; evaluation of various locations Subsidiary: Lobbying	PDD →	Loss or diminution of charter (CC) in subsidiary; atrophy of existing capabilities (CD)
	Subsidiary: Inaction; atrophy of capabilities (CD) Parent: Judgement on subsidiary's lack of competitiveness	ASN →	Loss or diminution of charter in subsidiary (CC)

Note: CC, charter change; CB, capability building; CD, capability depletion.

Birkinshaw, 1997) on the part of subsidiary management, in that it represents a conscious effort by the subsidiary to seek out and develop new business opportunities and then put them forward to parent company managers. On the assumption that parent company managers are inherently risk averse in their decisions about which subsidiaries should have responsibility for which charters, the logic here is that subsidiary management builds the required capabilities first and seeks the charter extension only once the subsidiary can demonstrate those capabilities.

The process involves three distinct steps by subsidiary managers: (1) an initiative-driven search for new market opportunities in both the subsidiary's local market and within the corporate system (Kirzner, 1973; Birkinshaw, 1997), (2) the pursuit of a specific market opportunity and the development of the appropriate capabilities to fulfill it, and (3) a proposal to the parent company that the subsidiary's charter be enhanced. For the parent company, the only action required is a judgement on whether to grant the subsidiary its requested charter enhancement. In many cases the parent company will be informed of the subsidiary's initiative throughout the process, whereas in other cases the subsidiary will have deliberately undertaken the process without the parent company's knowledge (Birkinshaw and Ridderstråle, 1999). In all situations, however, we see the SDE process as fairly 'political,' in that it relies to a great degree on the subsidiary-level champion gaining support at the head office through his or her personal contacts. Our reasoning here is simply that parent company managers will naturally treat an initiative from a peripheral part of the corporation with suspicion, unless they know the individual promoting it.

Subsidiary-driven charter reinforcement (SDR)

As with the previous process, this one is driven entirely by the actions of subsidiary managers. It is triggered by concerns about the subsidiary's competitiveness *vis-à-vis* both sister subsidiaries (Morrison and Crookell, 1990) and external competitors. The competitors provide specific cues to subsidiary management regarding their relative strengths and weaknesses, which leads to attempts to enhance the relevant set of capabilities. This process may or may not also involve external benchmarking and internal transfers of best practice (Szulanski, 1996). The net result, assuming the process has been effective, is lower costs and/or quality and service improvements and, thus, a reinforcement of the subsidiary's existing charter. There may be no head-office involvement in this process *per se*, given that no official change to the charter is being suggested, but the capability reinforcement process will lead to a stronger subsidiary performance and, hence, an enhanced level of credibility and visibility *vis-à-vis* head-office managers.

Parent-driven divestment (PDD)

This is the mirror image of PDI. The typical scenario is that the parent company has made the decision to rationalise its international operations and/or to exit certain businesses but that the decision regarding *which* ones to divest has not been finalised. Such a scenario can be triggered by a need to cut costs or by the desire for greater strategic focus on core activities. The fate of the subsidiary, therefore, may be closure, sale to another company, or spinoff as a separate entity.

The evaluation process is influenced by a host of factors, including the existing capabilities of the subsidiary relative to others and the attractiveness of the host country market, according to a number of criteria. Subsidiary managers and host country governments will sometimes have the opportunity to lobby against closure, but more often the decision will be presented as a fait accompli by parent company management.

The final decision results in a charter loss for the focal subsidiary. This may include the sale or closure of all associated activities (e.g. when a plant is shut down). In such a case the subsidiary's capabilities are immediately lost at the same time. Equally likely is the case where a charter is lost but the subsidiary as a whole continues to exist (Galunic and Eisenhardt, 1996). In this case the capabilities that were associated with the old charter will gradually be lost as employees are reassigned to new roles and develop new skills. However, it is possible that the remaining capabilities are actually redeployed toward the development of a new charter (i.e. an SDE process as described above). This process has been labeled *charter renewal* (Birkinshaw, 1996).

Atrophy through subsidiary neglect (ASN)

The final process is one in which the subsidiary's capabilities gradually atrophy while the charter is still retained. The argument here reverses that suggested in the SDE and SDR processes. Essentially, we see subsidiary management's *lack of attention* pushing this process along. The subsidiary becomes less and less competitive over time. This can be simply a case of poor management, but it is more likely to stem from a lack of competition. If, for example, the subsidiary has guaranteed internal contracts for its products and the corporation as a whole is making money, the pressure to reduce costs or improve service is likely to be low.

ASN occurs through two somewhat different processes. In the first, the subsidiary continues to fulfill its charter but on the basis of capabilities that are not leading edge and that gradually atrophy over time through lack of attention. Eventually, this situation comes to the attention of head-office managers, either because it is negatively impacting the competitiveness of the entire MNC or because internal performance measures indicate the sub-par performance of the focal subsidiary. Depending on the urgency of the change that is demanded of head-office managers, the subsidiary may be given the opportunity to turn things around itself, or it can lose its charter immediately.[11] The second scenario, given the discussion about SDR, is one in which the subsidiary is doing a satisfactory job of maintaining its capabilities, but, when faced with a global rationalization programme, it becomes apparent that other subsidiaries have upgraded their capabilities more effectively. Charter loss follows simply because the focal subsidiary's capabilities are weaker than those of its sister subsidiaries. Atrophy, in this sense, refers to the level of the capabilities relative to other subsidiaries, rather than in an absolute sense.

Contextual factors impacting the generic processes

In the literature review and in the preceding description, we touched on a large number of factors at the corporate, subsidiary, and host country level, which, scholars have argued, have an impact on the presence of the five generic processes. In this section we take a much more systematic look at these factors (listed in Table 11.2) and put forward specific propositions relating the levels of the contextual factors to the extent to which the five processes occur. We make one point of clarification here – namely, that the factors identified are not a comprehensive list; they represent the main factors that previous researchers have identified, and, as such, there may well be other factors that also impact the occurrence of the five subsidiary evolution processes. We also acknowledge that our focus on three contexts (corporate, subsidiary, and host country) means that we have set aside several others, such as the parent company's industry environment or other subsidiaries within the corporation, that could potentially impact subsidiary evolution.

Corporate-level factors

Central to our earlier discussion on capabilities was the notion of internal competition for charters among subsidiary units. Here, we develop the idea of *competitive internal resource allocation*, which means a corporate-wide system that promotes internal competition, either by allowing bids for new investments or by creating a system through which existing charters can be 'challenged' by other units (White and Poynter, 1984; Galunic and Eisenhardt, 1996). A competitive internal resource allocation system has substantial implications for subsidiary evolution, because it legitimises a process by which subsidiaries can both gain and lose charters. It also increases awareness of the relative capabilities among subsidiaries and provides a motivation for them to continually upgrade their capabilities. In contrast, in the absence of such a competitive system, resource allocation decisions are made by head office decision makers through a central planning process, which typically means favouring investment locations with which the decision makers are familiar and maintaining charters over long periods of time. According to this logic, it will be the subsidiary-driven, rather than the parent-driven, processes that are favoured by competitive internal resource allocation. Therefore, we argue that both PDI and PDD will be negatively impacted, and SDE, SDR, and ASN will be positively impacted.

ASN is a particularly interesting case. The core argument is that the number of cases of charters lost to internal competitors is likely to increase, because charters are more mobile and because sister subsidiaries are more proactively developing their own capabilities. However, there is also likely to be a mitigating factor – namely, that faced with such competitive pressure, the number of cases of atrophying capabilities should decrease. ASN, therefore, will occur through relative – not absolute – capability depletion. To summarise:

Proposition 1: A competitive internal resource allocation mechanism in the MNC will have a positive impact on the likelihood of SDE, SDR, and ASN and a negative impact on the likelihood of PDI and PDD.

A second important corporate-level factor is the level of *decentralisation of decision making* (i.e. the autonomy granted to subsidiaries). MNC researchers have given a lot of attention to the issue of subsidiary autonomy, both as a cause and a consequence of certain behaviours and operational characteristics in subsidiaries (e.g. Prahalad and Doz, 1981; Gates and Egelhoff, 1986). Here, we argue that decentralised decision making will provide subsidiary managers with the degrees of freedom necessary to take autonomous action, as well as will empower them to take charge of the destiny of their own units, both of which should positively impact the likelihood of the three subsidiary-driven processes – SDE, SDR, and ASN – while having a corresponding negative impact on the parent-driven processes – PDI and PDD.

This point is, in some ways, very obvious, but it is worth further scrutiny. The idea is that for SDE, and to a lesser degree SDR, subsidiary managers need a critical amount of autonomy, below which they will be unable to put their development plans into action. Access to seed money, for example, is a critical precondition to building new capabilities, but it may not be available in centrally controlled subsidiaries. ASN is also likely to occur more often when decision making is decentralized, because the subsidiary can become isolated relatively easily from the rest of the corporation and thus be unaware of its competitive position *vis-à-vis* other subsidiaries. PDI and PDD, however, can probably be undertaken more effectively when the subsidiary is tightly integrated into the corporate system, because the level of knowledge of the subsidiary's capabilities by parent company managers is much higher. PDI and PDD, thus, do not require a significant level of subsidiary autonomy. Therefore, in summary:

> *Proposition 2: A decentralization of decision making in the MNC will have a* positive *impact on the likelihood of SCE, SCR, and ASN and a* negative *impact on the likelihood of PDI or PDD.*

Finally, as we noted in the literature review, the attitude of parent company managers toward foreign investment is very important in subsidiary evolution. Here, we use the well-established concept of *parent management ethnocentrism* (Perlmutter, 1969), which represents a preoccupation with their own national identity and a belief in its superiority over others (*Gage Canadian Dictionary*, 1983). Simply put, a high level of ethnocentrism will negatively impact the likelihood of significant investments being made outside the MNC's home country, thus limiting the prospects of subsidiary evolution. This we expect to be true not only for SCE but also for PDI, because many such investments can potentially be made in the home country. SCR, by contrast, is driven purely by the subsidiary and is therefore unlikely to be impacted one way or the other by parent management ethnocentrism. For the divestment cases (ASN and PDD), the situation is a little more complex. Some of the elements of ethnocentrism (e.g. uncertainty and ignorance about a foreign country) are likely to be ameliorated once the subsidiary investment is in place, but an ethnocentric parent company is still likely to be very receptive to signals, even weak ones, that suggest that the subsidiary really does not have the necessary capabilities to fulfill its charter. Thus, ASN and PDD will be positively impacted by the existence of parent management ethnocentrism. In summary:

Proposition 3: An ethnocentric attitude among parent company managers will have a positive *impact on the likelihood of PDD and ASN, a* negative *impact on the likelihood of PDI and SDE, and no impact on SDR.*

Subsidiary-level factors

In terms of the attributes of the subsidiary itself, the most critical factor affecting subsidiary evolution is its *track record* – that is, the extent to which it has delivered, over the years, results at or above the expectations of the parent company. The importance of a strong track record is immediately apparent when one does fieldwork in this area, and it is consistently mentioned in the literature as a critical parameter (e.g. Morrison and Crookell, 1990; Hood, Young and Lal, 1994; Delaney, 1996). The logic, from the parent company's perspective, is that any investment decision is uncertain. By deciding in favour of a subsidiary that has already been successful in the past, parent management is reducing the extent of that uncertainty, thereby providing a strong justification for its decision should it prove, in retrospect, to be poor. Both PDI and SCE are therefore likely to be positively impacted by a strong track record, whereas PDD and ASN are likely to be negatively impacted. In the case of SCR, the process is not actively controlled by parent management, but one can argue that the development of a track record in the subsidiary is itself part of the charter reinforcement process. The proposition is obvious:

Proposition 4: A strong track record will have a positive *impact on the likelihood of PDI, SCE, and SCR and a* negative *impact on the likelihood of PDD^2 and ASN.*

Earlier, we also identified the *quality of parent–subsidiary relationships* as another important factor impacting the evolution process. This term refers to the informal ties between key decision makers in the parent company and senior managers in the subsidiary. Often, subsidiary managers will be expatriates or people who have spent a period at the head office and will therefore have built up a strong network of relationships at a personal level with parent company managers. Such networks represent a social control system that can be an effective means of holding the MNC together (Ouchi, 1980; Bartlett and Ghoshal, 1989).

The quality of parent–subsidiary relationships will have a very strong impact on SCE, because it is entrepreneurial in nature. As researchers consistently have shown, initiatives are evaluated more on the qualities of the individual putting them forward than on their technical merits (Bower, 1972; Day, 1994). Thus, where the individual is well known to parent company decision makers, it follows that the initiative he or she is championing will be far better received than one put forward by a relatively unknown manager. By the same logic, the quality of the parent–subsidiary relationship will also have a positive impact on PDI, although we should note that the magnitude of this effect is likely to be rather less than the impact of the subsidiary's track record on SCE.

The quality of parent–subsidiary relationships is likely to have a correspondingly strong negative impact on the two processes of subsidiary decline (PDD and ASN). Our reasoning here is that decisions to close or divest operations inevitably become politically charged, and during such periods the personal relationships between subsidiary management and decision makers in the parent company become critical. If the relationship is good, the subsidiary manager may convince the people at headquarters that he or she deserves another chance or that another subsidiary should take the hit. Finally, SCR will not be impacted because it does not involve the parent company:

> *Proposition 5: A high-quality parent–subsidiary relationship will have a* positive *impact on the likelihood of PDI and SCE, a* negative *impact on the likelihood of PDD and ASN, and no impact on SCR.*

The *entrepreneurial orientation of subsidiary employees* refers to the predisposition of employees throughout the subsidiary to be alert and responsive to new opportunities (Kirzner, 1973). Here, we argue that entrepreneurial subsidiary employees are on a constant lookout for new ways to add value and that their ideas will be brought forward, first to subsidiary management and then to corporate management, for active consideration (Birkinshaw, 1997). Entrepreneurial orientation, thus, becomes a necessary, although not sufficient, condition for the SCE and SCR processes, in that they cannot transpire unless the new ways of adding value are put forward. Using the reverse logic, we predict that the absence of an entrepreneurial orientation in subsidiary employees will breed an environment in which capabilities atrophy and, therefore, that an entrepreneurial orientation will have a negative impact on ASN. PDI and PDD, in contrast, we predict to be relatively unaffected by the entrepreneurial orientation of subsidiary employees, because they are initiated by the parent company:[13]

> *Proposition 6: The entrepreneurial orientation of subsidiary employees will have a* positive *impact on the likelihood of SCE and SCR, a* negative *impact on the likelihood of ASN, and no impact on PDI and PDD.*

Host country-level factors

Propositions 7 through 10 involve the various characteristics of the host country market. The *dynamism* of the local business environment refers to the extent and quality of the interaction between competing and complementary firms in that environment. Using Porter's (1990) diamond framework, we define the dynamism of the local business environment in terms of demand conditions, the existence of related and supporting industries, strong factor endowments, and competition.[14] Our argument is that a dynamic local business environment provides the stimuli for upgrading the subsidiary's capabilities in much the same way that internal competition does, for the subsidiary reacts to competitive moves by other companies and sharpens its capabilities in line with the expectations of local customers and suppliers.

As a result, we see SCE and SCR positively impacted by local dynamism, whereas ASN is likely to occur through a *lack* of local dynamism. The parent-driven processes – PDI and PDD – are likely to be impacted rather less directly by the dynamism of the local business environment because such stimuli are, by their nature, local (Sölvell and Zander, 1998). However, it seems likely that there will be a small effect on the parent company that is transmitted *through* the subsidiary so that PDI will be positively impacted by the dynamism of the local business environment and PDD will be negatively impacted:

Proposition 7: The dynamism of the local business environment will have a positive impact on the likelihood of PDI, SCE, and SCR and a negative impact on the likelihood of PDD and ASN.

The extent of *host government* support has a substantial impact on subsidiary evolution, as the literature review indicated. Even in today's almost free-trade world, host governments are still able to offer direct financial incentives for foreign investment, as well as a host of indirect incentives, such as soft loans, personnel training, and infrastructural support. In addition, host government agencies can help MNCs to identify and evaluate potential sites and introduce prospective partners.

We argue that host government support is likely to have a very strong impact in the case of PDI, primarily because most large, job-creating investments are of this type, and it is them that local politicians care most about. It will have an equally strong but negative impact in cases of subsidiary decline (PDD and ASN), in that government representatives will lobby hard with the MNC to reverse or ameliorate the decision to divest a subsidiary (even though, in our experience, such efforts rarely do more than delay the inevitable).

In the cases of SCE and SCR, we see host governments having a lesser, but not trivial, role. These processes are not contestable to the same extent that new investments are, but the increasing effort that many investment agencies are putting into after-care programmes is evidence that many host governments believe they *can* influence SCE and SCR. Thus, we predict a small positive impact for SCE and SCR:

> *Proposition 8: The support of the host government will have a* positive *impact on the likelihood of PDI, SCE, and SCR and a* negative *impact on the likelihood of PDD and ASN.*

Finally, we consider together two further aspects of the host country: the *strategic importance of the country* to the MNC and the relative *cost of factor* inputs. In a global business environment MNCs weigh – at least implicitly – the relative pros and cons of a large number of possible locations for major investments and divestments. The above are two of the critical factors in any such decision. Strategic importance refers to the extent to which a competitive position in that country affects the MNC's worldwide competitive position. Relative cost of factor inputs is simply an assessment of all the major cost elements of the investment that are locally sourced.

In the case of PDI, then, strategic importance and relative cost of factor inputs are critical factors so that a new investment will tend to gravitate, ceteris paribus, toward the more strategically important country and the country with lower factor input costs. Equally, the case of PDD will likely include a consideration of the same set of factors. For SCE and ASN, however, the situation is more equivocal. One could argue that SCE and ASN will not be impacted substantially by these two sets of factors, in that they represent judgements on the subsidiary's management and their existing capabilities and not on the country per se, but, at the same time, it seems likely that such factors will inevitably find their way into the parent company managers' assessments and, hence, their decisions on whether to extend or reduce the subsidiary's charter.

Thus, we predict a positive impact for both on SCE and negative impact for both on ASN. SCR, however, because it does not involve parent company management in any significant way, is unlikely to be impacted one way or the other by the strategic importance of the country or the relative cost of factor inputs. To summarise:

Proposition 9: The strategic importance of the host country will have a positive *impact on the likelihood of PDI and SCE, a* negative *impact on the likelihood of PDD and ASN, and* no *impact on SCR.*

Proposition 10: The relative cost of factor inputs in the host country will have a positive *impact on the likelihood of PDD and SCE, a* negative *impact on the likelihood of PDI and ASN, and* no *impact on SCR.*

Concluding comments

In this article we had three broad objectives. The first was simply to document and organise the rather fragmented body of literature on subsidiary evolution, the second to examine the phenomenon of subsidiary evolution using a dynamic capabilities perspective, and the third to put forward five generic processes of subsidiary evolution and identify those contextual factors expected to impact each one.

The dynamic capabilities perspective on subsidiary evolution raises two important theoretical issues that should be briefly addressed. First, it implies a much more fluid system than that suggested by traditional models of the MNC, in that charters are mobile and subsidiary companies are competing for them in an internal market system. This approach is consistent with the network perspective of Hedlund (1986) and Ghoshal and Bartlett (1991), but it also takes things further by specifying the processes through which charter changes occur. Second, it hints at one of the weaknesses of the resource based view of the firm – namely, its lack of consideration of the internal workings of the large firm. We are not suggesting that the resource based view needs to be modified as such, because the subsidiary unit can be modelled readily in the same way that the firm is, but it seems clear that much more attention needs to be paid in future to the ways that capabilities are developed at a subfirm level and then disseminated or transferred within the firm, rather than just focusing on firm-level capabilities. Some researchers have already begun to address these issues (e.g. Kogut and Zander, 1992; Szulanski, 1996).

We see two principal limitations to our theoretical development. First, the model does not deal explicitly with merger and acquisition. If we take a case such as the Asea-Brown Boveri merger, it is clear that the assignment of charters within the merged company was a one-time, top-down process that was undertaken with regard to a host of strategic and political factors, as well as a consideration of where the appropriate capabilities were. This fits broadly within the head-office-driven investment process, but it represents an unusual case, because new capabilities are 'appended' to the subsidiary rather than grown incrementally along an existing trajectory. Second, we have focused on wholly owned subsidiaries, rather than hybrid cases, such as joint ventures. The critical difference between the two cases, obviously, is that a joint venture has two parents, so it would be potentially quite easy to apply the same principles of capability development and charter change to joint venture companies. Indeed, from our reading of the literature, it is apparent that joint ventures go through parent-driven and subsidiary-driven phases of development that are typically part of an overall process of evolution toward higher-value-added activities (Ring and Van de Ven, 1994; Doz, 1996). It is also likely that the analytical approach adopted here could be applied to specific units or divisions within the firm, rather than thinking in terms of foreign subsidiaries as a special case.

What are the managerial implications of this study? At this stage of theory development, it is inappropriate to be too specific about the managerial consequences of our thinking, but a few issues can be highlighted nonetheless. For subsidiary managers, the primary message is that attention should be paid to the capabilities of the subsidiary. Capabilities need to be sharpened and upgraded in the face of competition from other subsidiaries as well as external firms, and new opportunities need to be proactively sought out in areas that are close to the existing strengths of the subsidiary and that are aligned with the priorities of the MNC as a whole. A second message is that the subsidiary appears to need a certain level of decision-making autonomy to be able to pursue charter-enhancing and charter-reinforcement initiatives. This autonomy has to be earned through a strong track record and relationships with parent company managers – not taken unilaterally. For head-office managers, the message is that competitive resource allocation procedures and the locus of decision making should be considered carefully as mechanisms for improving the MNC's ability to allocate charters to the appropriate subsidiaries. There are also interesting implications in terms of the mix of subsidiary managers (e.g. entrepreneurs versus risk-averse managers) that the parent company should select to keep the subsidiary's options open in the future. We are a long way from prescribing any particular courses of action, but this article highlights the questions that need to be asked.

In conclusion, we believe that the phenomenon of subsidiary evolution has considerable potential as an area for future research. There is a need for clinical studies of subsidiary evolution and more detailed examination of various aspects of the phenomenon, such as the interplay between parent and subsidiary management and the impact of host country policies on subsidiary evolution. Finally, there may also be important theoretical implications for the concepts developed here, both in terms of the role of the subsidiary in the MNC and for the theory of the MNC itself. Although it is too soon to predict how such extensions will transpire, our hope is that this article provides a grounding of theoretical perspectives and a framework of ideas around which subsequent studies can be built.

Notes

1. Hence lies our decision to focus on subsidiary evolution rather than subsidiary development.
2. Madhok (1997) makes the point that the emphasis on knowledge accumulation in this model it essentially part of the *organisational capabilities* school that defines the firm on the basis of its proprietary capabilities rather than market failure considerations.
3. Note that there are cases of subsidiaries 'assuming' charters (Hagström, 1994) without head-office support, but our argument is that these do not constitute part of the subsidiary development process. We return to this point in the theory development section.
4. There is also a large body of literature originating from the field of economic geography, in which authors look at the spatial distribution of the MNC and its relationship with regional economic development (e.g. McNee, 1958; Dicken, 1976; Clarke, 1985).
5. Note that the accumulation of capabilities is very different from the accumulation of resources. A resource-accumulating subsidiary may just be 'fat', as a reviewer pointed out, whereas a capability-accumulating subsidiary is putting together new combinations of resources and deploying them in creative ways. This is an important departure from normal usage in the decision process and product life-cycle traditions, in which resource accumulation and capability accumulation are not distinguished.
6. Of course, there is also a transaction cost argument here, in that there are costs associated with transacting with other units, even if they are part of the same firm. This reduces the likelihood of transfer, which adds to the stickiness of the capabilities in question.
7. Barney (1991) and others have also elaborated on many other dimensions of capabilities, such as rarity, causal ambiguity, and tacitness. These characteristics have important implications when it comes to combining a subsidiary's capabilities with those of other subsidiaries and of protecting capabilities from competitor imitation, but we believe they are not central to a discussion of subsidiary evolution.
8. It should be recognised that an institutional definition of the subsidiary's charter will not necessarily covary with the activity/capability-based definition. Thus, an interesting area for future research would be to examine divergences between institutional- and capability-based charter definitions in subsidiaries.
9. An interesting side issue here is why competing manufacturing units choose to help one another to improve. The evidence suggests that they do, implying that managers are motivated more by their long-term allegiance to the corporation than by the short-term gain of a new charter.

10. We use *focal subsidiary* to refer to the hypothetical subsidiary at the centre of our analysis.
11. Frequently, the charter loss process is rather more gradual than this, in that the subsidiary finds itself with increasingly unimportant charters.
12. There is one mitigating factor here – namely, that a very poorly performing subsidiary cannot easily be sold, whereas a strong performer will fetch a high price. Thus, a very weak performer may actually be fixed rather than sold, depending on a host of other factors.
13. Again, though, it is possible to suggest counter examples, such as a parent company that invests in a subsidiary because it thinks subsidiary management will run with a high-risk/high-reward venture.
14. Porter (1990) was concerned primarily with leading-edge industry clusters, but we note that these four sets of factors can be used to assess the dynamism of any business environment.

12

Building Firm-Specific Advantages in Multinational Corporations: The Role of Subsidiary Initiative (1998)*

Julian Birkinshaw, Neil Hood and Stefan Jonsson

Introduction

A central theme of much of the recent literature on the strategy of the multinational corporation (MNC) is the increasingly important role played by subsidiary companies as contributors to the development of firm-specific advantages. Traditional academic models that viewed subsidiaries as either 'market access' providers or as recipients of the parent company's technology transfers (Vernon, 1966) gave way in the 1980s to richer conceptualizations in which subsidiaries tapped into leading-edge ideas, undertook important research and development work, and became active participants in the formulation and implementation of strategy (Bartlett and Ghoshal, 1986; Hedlund, 1986; Gupta and Govindarajan, 1994). The generation of firm-specific advantages, correspondingly, shifted from being the sole concern of the parent company to a collective responsibility for the corporate network.

This paper investigates *how* subsidiary companies are able to contribute to the firm-specific advantages of the MNC. In one respect the paper is similar to a number of recent articles that have examined the different roles taken by subsidiary companies (Ghoshal and Nohria, 1989; Jarillo and Martinez, 1990; Roth and Morrison, 1992; Gupta and Govindarajan, 1994; Birkinshaw and Morrison, 1996) because we are concerned with understanding those factors that differentiate between high-contributing and low-contributing subsidiaries. However, it is also unique in two

---

* *Strategic Management Journal*, 19 (1998), 221–41. © 1998 John Wiley & Sons, Ltd.

important respects. First, we attempt to pry open the 'black box' of the subsidiary by discussing the various activities that occur within it, and the processes that link them. Second, we pick out one key activity, subsidiary initiative, and explore the factors associated with it in detail. Our belief, which this paper provides preliminary evidence for, is that the evolution of subsidiary roles can be taken one step further than previously realised. Rather than simply seeing subsidiaries as *contributors* to the development of firm-specific advantages, this paper shows that they can also *drive* the process through their own initiative.

This paper is in five sections. The first section offers a brief survey of the literature on firm-specific advantages and MNC subsidiaries. The second section develops the theoretical concepts of firm-specific advantage in subsidiaries and formally sets out the research propositions. The third section describes the data collection, which was undertaken in a sample of manufacturing subsidiaries in Canada, Scotland and Sweden. The fourth section describes the research findings. Finally, the fifth section offers a discussion of the results from the research and their implications for theory and for practice.

Theoretical and empirical background

Researchers have long recognised the centrality of ownership- or firm-specific advantages to an understanding of the *raison d'être* of MNCs. As first shown by Hymer (1976), firms engaging in overseas production must have some form of proprietary advantage to compensate for the natural disadvantage of competing with established firms in a foreign land. As stated by Dunning (1980, 1988) this firm-specific advantage can be subdivided into two distinct types of advantage: asset advantages, that stem from the exclusive privileged possession of income generating assets; and transaction advantages, which reflect the firm's ability to economize on transaction costs as a result of multinational co-ordination and control of assets. While not a *sufficient* condition for foreign production, there is general agreement that some form of firm-specific advantage is nonetheless *necessary* (Rugman, 1981; Dunning, 1988). Technological resources, in particular, have been the focus of many studies of firm-specific advantage (e.g. Cantwell, 1989; Rugman, 1981; Teece, 1977), though research has also considered manufacturing, marketing, organisational, and human resources (Dunning, 1993: 81).

A major problem, as pointed out by Rugman and Verbeke (1992), is that this research has tended to assume that the MNC's firm-specific advantages originate in the parent company, whereas the reality is that subsidiaries can play an important part in the creation and maintenance of such advantages. The emerging body of research concerned with subsidiary roles is testament to this shift in the locus of firm-specific advantage creation (see Birkinshaw and Morrison, 1996, for a review). For example, it is reported that subsidiaries can act as contributors to or leaders of innovation projects (Bartlett and Ghoshal, 1986); they can provide major outflows of valued resources to the rest of the corporation (Gupta and Govindarajan, 1994), and they can gain mandates for developing and producing certain product lines on a global basis (Roth and Morrison, 1992). Terms such as *specialised contributor, strategic leader* and *active subsidiary* have been used to refer to those subsidiaries that contribute substantially to firm-specific advantage, while terms such as *implementer* and *branch plant* are used to refer to those that do not contribute significantly to firm-specific advantage.[1]

While there is no shortage of typologies suggesting that subsidiaries vary in their contributory role (i.e. in their contribution to firm-specific advantage), there is no definitive evidence for the sources of such variation. A number of studies have looked at the factors associated with differences in contributory role, but they have typically focused on only a sub-set of the potentially important factors. More specifically, three contrasting perspectives can be discerned from the MNC subsidiary literature. The first perspective is one of *environmental determinism*. Building on the notion that the MNC operates in multiple environments each with is own unique characteristics, the role of each subsidiary is seen in large part as a function of its local environment (Ghoshal and Nohria, 1989; Westney, 1994). Where the local country is strategically important (Bartlett and Ghoshal, 1986) or where the dynamism of local competitors, suppliers and customers is high (Porter, 1990), the expectation is that the subsidiary will have a correspondingly important role. Industry factors, such as pressure for local responsiveness and global integration (Jarillo and Martinez, 1990), can also be understood within an environmental determinism perspective, in that they represent exogenous factors that the MNC has to adapt to. The second perspective is one of *head office assignment*. This perspective works on the basis that head office management is responsible for defining the strategic imperatives of the whole company, and understands best how subsidiary roles can be assigned to ensure that those imperatives are met. Many studies have concentrated on facets of structural context (Bower, 1970) such as control and coordination mechanisms that can be used to direct the behaviour of subsidiary managers, and thus to determine subsidiary role (Ghoshal, 1986; Roth and Morrison, 1992; Gupta and Govindarajan,

1994; Birkinshaw and Morrison, 1996). Others have suggested that subsidiaries can be assigned roles more directly according to their perceived importance or the growth prospects of the market (Bartlett and Ghoshal, 1986). The third perspective is of *subsidiary choice* (cf. Child, 1972), whereby the role of the subsidiary is to a large extent open to subsidiary management to define for themselves. This perspective works on the assumption that subsidiary management understand their local market and their local capabilities better than head office, and that they are in the best position to decide what role the subsidiary should play. Rooted in the work of Canadian scholars such as White and Poynter (1984) and D'Cruz (1986), this perspective focuses on the specific resources and capabilities of the subsidiary, the aspirations of subsidiary management, and the initiative and effort of subsidiary employees as the determinants of subsidiary role (Science Council of Canada, 1980; Etemad and Dulude, 1986; Roth and Morrison, 1992; Birkinshaw, 1995).

Clearly all three perspectives have considerable merit, so for a complete understanding of the phenomenon it would be necessary to consider subsidiary, corporate, industry, and country factors. However, at the same time the three perspectives are competing with one another for relative salience. Is the relation of the subsidiary with is parent company the key determinant of its role? Are the attributes of the subsidiary itself more important? Or is the local industrial environment the most important variable? While this study, like all others, has its biases and its preconceptions, the relative impact of these three sets of factors will be explicitly assessed.

Management processes inside the subsidiary

Taken as a whole, the body of literature on subsidiary management had done a far better job of understanding aspects of subsidiary context (how the subsidiary relates to its parent, its corporate network, its local environment) than of understanding what actually happens *inside* the subsidiary. If the subsidiary is small, focused primarily on the local market, and wholly dependent on the parent company, the inner workings of the subsidiary are not of great consequence to the MNC as a whole. However, subsidiary growth brings with it an increase in resources and a corresponding reduction in parent control (Prahalad and Doz, 1981), which leads to at least some degree of strategic choice on the part of subsidiary management. At this point, how the subsidiary is managed internally would appear to become a matter of great importance to the corporation as a whole.

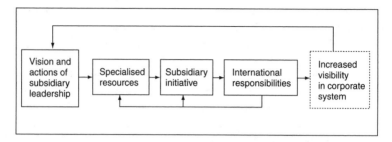

Figure 12.1   Process model of subsidiary activities and subsidiary resources

A recent study of Canadian subsidiaries by Birkinshaw (1995) provides some insight into the internal workings of the subsidiary. Building on the concept of induced and autonomous action proposed by Burgelman (1983), this study tracked a series of autonomous subsidiary actions, or initiatives, that sought to develop the international value-added scope of the subsidiary. The process model is illustrated in Figure 12.1. The development of specialised resources was promoted by the vision and actions of subsidiary leadership. These specialised resources provided the opportunity for initiative by subsidiary managers which led to the development of international responsibilities (Crookell, 1986). These responsibilities ranged from just manufacturing (e.g. of a family of chemicals for international sale) to product development, manufacturing, and marketing accountability (e.g. for a new range of computer monitors). The enhanced resources and international responsibilities led both to an increase in subsidiary initiative and to increased visibility in the corporate system. Increased visibility, in turn, represented an affirmation in the ability of subsidiary leadership and a further stimulus for initiative. The case of 3M Canada, in particular, showed how the process of subsidiary development occurred over a long period of time and almost exclusively through the activities of subsidiary management. The process represented here echoes the work of Ghoshal and Bartlett (1994) in that initiative, resource growth, and visibility form a virtuous circle of development that is invigorated by the actions of top management.

It should be underlined here that initiative appears only to be evident in a subset of the population of subsidiaries. Many subsidiaries exhibit no initiative, in part because such efforts would not be positively received by head office management and in part because management does not have the drive or expertise to pursue initiative. In such cases the development of specialized resources and international responsibilities can still occur, but it rests on the active involvement of parent company managers (Birkinshaw and Hood, 1997). Relatedly, the concept of initiative typically raises some concerns at head office because there are questions over the motivations of the subsidiary manager: is he or she acting in the interests of the subsidiary, the corporation, or the host country? These issues will be revisited in the discussion section of this paper.

Theoretical model and propositions

We are now in a position to specify the model that will be examined in this study. A subsidiary is defined as any operational unit controlled by the MNC and situated outside the home country. In some cases there will be a single subsidiary in the host country; in other cases there will be several. Consistent with the resource-based view of the firm (Wernerfelt, 1984; Barney, 1991), a subsidiary is conceptualised as a heterogeneous bundle of resources. Some of these resources (e.g. the salesforce) are 'location bound' (Rugman and Verbeke, 1992), meaning that their value is limited to their country or domain of operation. Others are not location bound, and can potentially be leveraged by the corporation in other countries. These are the resources that offer the potential for contributing to the MNC's firm-specific advantage. However, there are three criteria that must be met before this potential is realised.

The first criterion relates to the value of the resources. Using a strict resource-based perspective, resources need to be valuable, rare and imperfectly imitable to offer the potential of competitive advantage (Barney, 1991). Our preference is to use a less strict approach that requires the subsidiary's resources to be *specialised*, which we define as superior to those available elsewhere in the corporation. If the subsidiary's specialised resources are combined with other resources elsewhere in the MNC, we suggest that they then become part of the MNC's firm-specific advantage.[2]

The second criterion is one of recognition by corporate management. Recognition refers to the widespread understanding and acceptance of the subsidiary's specialised resources in other parts of the MNC. The subsidiary may have expertise in process innovation, for example, but if that expertise remains undiscovered by other parts of the corporation, and focused solely on the local market, it can not become part of the MNC's firm-specific advantage. Corporate recognition can probably be achieved through both top-down and bottom-up mechanisms that are akin to Burgelman's (1983) induced and autonomous strategic processes.

The top-down process involves corporate management identifying their leading-edge subsidiaries through informal discussions, productivity measures, and internal benchmarking studies. The bottom-up process consists of entrepreneurial efforts by subsidiary management to demonstrate their expertise and willingness to take on additional responsibilities to head office managers (Birkinshaw and Hood, 1997).

We use the term *contributory role* to refer to the extent to which the subsidiary has specialised resources that are recognised by the corporation as a whole. This term is deliberately broad in scope because the nature of the subsidiary's contribution to firm-specific advantage will vary enormously from case to case. High contributory role subsidiaries include the specialised contributor, strategic leader, and active subsidiary types discussed earlier. Also included are subsidiaries with *world product mandate* and *centre of excellence* designations. The world product mandate terminology has been widely used by Canadian researchers to refer to the subsidiary's responsibility to develop, manufacture, and market a product line worldwide (Crookell, 1986; Rugman and Bennett, 1982). A centre of excellence is usually conceived more broadly as a unit with expertise in a primary or support activity that other parts of the corporation draw on (e.g. Forsgren, 1995). The problem with both these terms is that they suggest a clear-cut division between those subsidiaries with, and those without, recognised specialised resources, whereas the reality is much less marked. Thus, the term contributor role is preferred because it represents a continuum. Contributory role is the dependent variable in the research model.[3]

The third criterion by which subsidiary resources are translated into part of the MNC's firm-specific advantage is the effective transfer and/or leverage of the resources in question. This criterion is based on the observation that resources are 'sticky' and often do not get transferred effectively inside the firm (Szulanski, 1995). Indeed, anecdotal evidence suggests that some centres of excellence may be established solely to meet political ends, with no intention of ever transferring the latent expertise to other parts of the corporation, while some world product mandates exist in the mind of the subsidiary manager without ever achieving legitimacy with other parts of the corporation. Unfortunately it is not possible, given the data collected in this study, to examine the resource transfer/leverage process in any detail. To some degree the process is out of the hands of the subsidiary, in that resource transfer depends to a large degree on the willingness of the receptor (Szulanski, 1995). However, it remains a potentially important link that future research should consider in more detail.

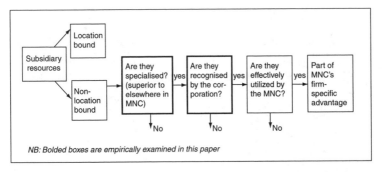

Figure 12.2 Illustration of link between subsidiary resource and MNC firm-specific advantage

The complete model is represented in Figure 12.2. The focus of the empirical part of this research is on the factors associated with the development of specialized resources and contributory role. In particular, we apply the findings from the research quoted earlier (Figure 12.1) to look at the role of subsidiary initiative in the process. Subsidiary initiative is defined as the entrepreneurial pursuit of international[4] market opportunities to which the subsidiary can apply its specialised resources.

The remainder of this section will specify the proposed relationships between the independent variables and the two focal constructs (see Figure 12.3). As suggested by the review of the literature, these propositions represent competing ideas about the drivers of subsidiary development, i.e., whether contributory role is environmentally determined, assigned by the parent company, or a matter of subsidiary choice. It should be observed that the propositions specify *association* between constructs rather than causation. As the discussion so far has shown, causality in many cases is reciprocal, and with cross-sectional data it is impossible to indicate more than association anyway. For the sake of clarity Figure 12.3 is, nevertheless, drawn with directional arrows.

Subsidiary-level factors

The first set of propositions is concerned with relationships *within* the subsidiary unit. Consistent with the earlier discussion and the findings of Roth and Morrison (1992), a positive relationship is anticipated between the subsidiary's specialised resources and its contributory role. Subsidiary initiative, likewise, is proposed to positively influence the subsidiary's contributory role. In theoretical terms this relationship is premised on Burgelman's (1983) analogous argument that autonomous

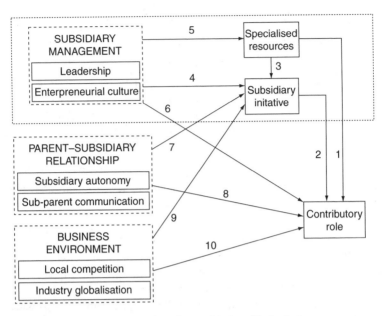

Numbers on paths refer to the hypotheses developed in the text

Figure 12.3   Theoretical framework and path diagram for PLS analysis

behaviour (i.e. initiative) becomes incorporated into a concept of corporate strategy (i.e. the subsidiary's role) through championing efforts and strategic context definition. More specifically, subsidiary research by Science Council of Canada (1980), Bishop and Crookell (1986), Ghoshal (1986), and Birkinshaw (1995), all showed that aspects of subsidiary initiative had an important influence on the role of the subsidiary. Finally, it is also important to specify an anticipated relationship between subsidiary initiative and specialised resources. As suggested earlier, this relationship is expected to be reciprocal in that specialised resources provide the opportunity for initiative, which in turn enhances the subsidiary's resources:

Proposition 1: The level of specialised resources in the subsidiary is positively associated with the contributory role of the subsidiary.

Proposition 2: Subsidiary initiative is positively associated with the contributory role of the subsidiary.

Proposition 3: The level of specialised resources in the subsidiary is positively associated with subsidiary initiative.

The antecedent conditions for subsidiary initiative and specialised subsidiary resources are anticipated to stem from the efforts of subsidiary management. Following the work of Ghoshal and Bartlett (1994), top management are expected to be instrumental in the development of a supportive behavioural context which in turn fosters initiative among employees. Moreover, to the extent that subsidiary top management has some discretion to directly commit resources to certain projects rather than others, it is anticipated that the strength of top management will be associated with the development of specialised (and potentially valuable) resources. This argument is analogous to Hamel and Prahalad's (1994) thesis that firm competencies should be developed to anticipate or even drive industry evolution. Finally, the strength of top management is also expected to directly influence the subsidiary's contributory role. While specialised resources are the underlying driver of the subsidiary's contributory role, it is typically the championing and sponsoring efforts of top management that trigger the assignment of new international responsibilities or mandates to the subsidiary (Bishop and Crookell, 1986; Burgelman, 1983; Birkinshaw, 1995).

A related aspect of subsidiary top management's role is their responsibility for shaping the development of an entrepreneurial culture in which initiative and risk-taking behaviour can thrive (Peters and Waterman, 1982; Kanter, 1985; Pinchott, 1985; Kuratko, Montagno, and Hornsby, 1990). It is intuitively obvious that an entrepreneurial culture is likely to promote initiative.[5] It is anticipated that an entrepreneurial subsidiary culture will also be associated with the development of specialised resources, in much the same way that iniative is seen as a driver of resource development. The implication is that even in the absence of specific initiatives, an entrepreneurial atmosphere should still have a positive impact on the pursuit of new combinations of resources. In summary:

Hypotheses 4a, 4b: The actions of subsidiary management (strong subsidiary leadership; an entrepreneurial subsidiary culture) are positively associated with subsidiary initiative.

Hypotheses 5a, 5b: The actions of subsidiary management (strong subsidiary leadership; an entrepreneurial subsidiary culture) are positively associated with a high level of specialised resources in the subsidiary.

Hypothesis 6: Strong subsidiary leadership is positively associated with a high contributory role for the subsidiary.

Corporate-level factors

The traditional approach to subsidiary management, as exemplified by the process school (Bower, 1970; Prahalad, 1976; Bartlett, 1979; Burgelman, 1983), conceptualised a 'structural context' for the subsidiary which consisted of the various facets of its relationship with the parent company. The subsidiary was controlled, according to this model, through the imposition (by head office managers) of an appropriate structural context that induced managers in the subsidiary to behave in desirable ways. Aspects of context included level of autonomy, formalisation of activities, control resources, and social control. In terms of the current study, the suggestion is that by defining an appropriate structural context, corporate management can either promote or inhibit the development of the subsidiary's contributory role.

While there have been a large number of studies of parent–subsidiary relationships (e.g. Brandt and Hulbert, 1977; Otterbeck, 1981; Garnier, 1982; Leksell, 1984; Gates and Egelhoff, 1986), Ghoshal's (1986) dimensions of structural context were used as the starting point for this study because his study of subsidiary innovations was closest to our concepts of contributory role and initiative. Ghoshal showed that the creation of innovation in subsidiaries was associated with high autonomy, high parent–subsidiary communication and high normative integration. We therefore predict, in an analogous manner, that decision-making autonomy and high levels of parent–subsidiary communication will be associated with the subsidiary's contributory role. There is a counter argument to these hypotheses, namely that autonomy can indicate a lack of integration that may limit the chances of gaining recognition for specialised resources. Nonetheless, Ghoshal's empirical findings form the basis for our hypotheses. Normative integration, that is, the extent to which shared values exist across the corporation, was not specified. In our experience normative integration is very hard to assess at a subsidiary level (Ghoshal polled head office managers) in part because it is a corporate-wide concept.[6]

> *Hypothesis 7a, 7b: Facets of the parent–subsidiary relationship (subsidiary autonomy; parent–subsidiary communication) are positively associated with a high contributory role for the subsidiary.*

Country- and industry-level factors

The final element of the research model is the impact of the business environment (at both a country and industry level) on the subsidiary's contributory role and its level of initiative. While it is broadly accepted that the nature of the local environment has a bearing on the role the subsidiary plays in the corporation (e.g. Bartlett and Ghoshal, 1986; Ghoshal and Nohria, 1989), our interest in this study was on identifying those aspects of the environment that are salient to the subsidiary's contributory role. We focused on the level of competitiveness in the local market.[7] Competition drives the innovation process and the upgrading of capabilities (Porter, 1980, 1990). To the extent that the subsidiary is actively participating in its local marketplace, it is anticipated that the level of local competition will have a positive influence on the subsidiary's own competitiveness, and hence on its contributory role. Porter's (1990) diamond model, in particular, showed that the presence of clusters of firms in a single location drives the competitiveness of the entire cluster.

There is one caveat in order here, because Porter's (1990) research did not explicitly consider the impact of cluster development on foreign-owned subsidiaries. Many subsidiaries have limited decision-making autonomy, little opportunity to choose their own suppliers, and limited R&D capacity (Young, Hood and Peters, 1994). All these constraints impede the subsidiary's ability to participate effectively in the competitive upgrading process that Porter identified, which suggests that this hypothesis is tentative, given the current state of knowledge.

A second relevant facet of the business environment is its level of globalisation. Structural drivers, such as the availability of economies of scale, make certain industries more prone to global integration than others (Kobrin, 1991). At one end of the spectrum are 'pure global' industries (Porter, 1986) in which the subsidiary's activities are integrated with the rest of the corporate network. At the other end of the spectrum are 'multidomestic' industries in which competition in one national market is not substantially affected by competition in the next. It is proposed here that the level of subsidiary initiative is directly related to the level of globalisation of the industry. Multidomestic industries do not offer much scope for the subsidiary to influence the firm-specific advantage of the corporation, because competition is structured on a local-for-local basis. Global industries, by contrast, require a high level of specialisation from subsidiary companies as each focuses on undertaking certain specific activities on behalf of the MNC as a whole. The opportunity for initiative is thus much greater. Once again, it is important to emphasise that this study is concerned with internationally oriented initiatives. It would correspondingly be expected that *locally focused* initiatives are more pervasive in multidomestic industries:

Hypothesis 8: The competitiveness of the local market is positively *associated with a high contributory role for the subsidiary.*

Hypothesis 9: The level of industry globalisation is positively *associated with subsidiary initiative.*

Methodology

Empirical data were collected using a mail questionnaire which was completed by top managers in 229 manufacturing subsidiaries of large MNCS in Canada, Scotland, and Sweden. These countries all have substantial populations of foreign-owned subsidiaries with similarities along two dimensions: (a) all three are relatively small countries with high standards of living; and (b) all three are 'peripheral' parts of established trading blocs. In terms of generalizability, it therefore seems likely that the findings of the study will be meaningful to other 'peripheral' countries in developed areas.

Data were gathered during 1995. In each country a slightly different sampling process was used because of the nature of the available data bases. In Canada, the sample was drawn up from a variety of CD-ROM products and directories, including the *Financial Post 500, Report on Business 1000,* and the *Disclosure* data base. In Scotland we used the data base compiled by *Scottish Enterprise,* the inward investment agency, which keeps track of all foreign investors in Scotland. In Sweden we used the data bases of foreign-owned subsidiaries compiled by *Veckans Affärer* and *Compass.*[8] Using a standard procedure of mailing the questionnaire to the subsidiary CEO and then mailing a remainder 4 weeks later we ended up with 229 responses (34 per cent response rate). Forty-nine subsidiaries were dropped, either because their revenues were below £15 million[9] or because they had no manufacturing activity, leaving 180 usable responses. The mean annual revenues of the sample were £203 million, with a range from £15 million through to £1.5 billion. Ninety-nine of the 180 sample subsidiaries reported having some form of international responsibility. The most common parent company nationality by far was the USA (95), followed by Japan, Germany, England, Finland, and Switzerland (each with 10–20 responses). Details of response rates are listed in Table 12.1.

A test of nonresponse bias was conducted using annual revenues (or number of employees in the case of Scotland) and parent company nationality as dependent variables, and no significant differences were found. We also performed a series of ANOVAs using host country as the independent variable, and again no major differences were uncovered.[10]

Table 12.1 Sample response rates

	Canada	Scotland	Sweden	Total
Questionnaires sent	270	182	221	673
Returned blank, declined to participate	5	5	18	28
Questionnaires returned complete	87	61	78	226
Response rate (%)	32	34	35	34
Number used for statistical analysis (i.e. with revenues over £15 million)	78	51	51	180

The questionnaire was developed through a three-stage process. First, the draft questionnaire was reviewed by three academicians, who suggested improvements in wording and advice on layout. Second, following a major revision of the questionnaire, it was sent out to six subsidiary presidents who were involved in an earlier study. They all filled out the questionnaire, while one of the researchers did likewise on the basis of his extensive knowledge of the six companies. Responses were then compared, and where the differences between 'actual' (i.e. from the subsidiary president) and 'expected' (i.e. from the researcher) were substantial amendments to wording were made. In most cases, however, responses were very similar. At the same time, four pairs of subsidiary and head office managers were also asked to fill out the questionnaire, to ensure that the subsidiary's answers were consistent with the perceptions in head office. No significant differences were found. The interrater reliability for these four pairs was 0.65 (using Cohen's Kappa),[11] an adequate but not exceptionally good result. Finally, once the second round of corrections had been made, the questionnaire was sent to a group of three managers in *another* subsidiary. A researcher met with these individuals to discuss their responses, which resulted in a few small changes.

Analytical method

The hypotheses were tested using a relatively new multivariate analysis technique known as partial least squares or PLS (Fornell and Bookstein, 1982). PLS, like LISREL, is one of the so-called second-generation multivariate techniques that are increasingly being used to estimate causal models with multiple independent and dependent constructs (e.g. Fornell, Lorange, and Roos, 1990; Johansson and Yip, 1994; Birkinshaw, Morrison, and Hulland, 1995). These techniques allow the researcher to analyse all paths between constructs simultaneously, rather than through a series of discrete regression models. PLS, in contrast to LISREL, has the additional advantage that it makes no assumptions about multivariate normality in the data and it works well with relatively small samples. Generally, PLS is preferred to LISREL in the early stages of theory building and testing, and when the researcher is primarily concerned with the prediction of the dependent variable.

PLS has one further benefit over first generation techniques. Traditionally the researcher would define a theoretical construct either by summing individual items or by extracting factor scores from a factor analysis. In PLS, however, individual items are kept in their raw form as indicators of the construct,[12] and their loadings on the construct then vary depending on the relationship of that construct to other constructs in the model. This is important because it makes the use of reliability measures such as Cronbach's alpha redundant. Instead, the choice of which individual items to retain, as measures of a construct, becomes part of the overall model testing. Issues of reliability and validity can then be assessed once the model has been finalised.

Construct measurement

Construct measures were adopted from earlier research where possible, most notably from previous MNC subsidiary studies by Ghoshal (1986) and Roth and Morrison (1992). However, it proved necessary to create new measures for several of the key constructs as they had apparently not been measured before. The complete wording of questions, and the correlations between them, are displayed in the Appendix (p. 283).

Contributory role was operationalised by asking subsidiary presidents what percentage of their revenues (if any) were gained from 'international responsibilities' such as world mandates or centres of excellence (i.e. activities it undertook on behalf of the corporation as a whole), so that 0 per cent would suggest that the subsidiary had no international responsibilities and 100 per cent would suggest that all their revenues were gained from their international responsibilities. This measure achieved our intention of recording those activities that were international in scope *and* recognised by the corporation. However, it focused on physical and technological resource flows which meant that some aspects of the subsidiary's qualitative contribution to firm-specific advantage (e.g. sharing of ideas, knowledge flows) were probably not picked up. Two other measures were also used: a simple measure of international sales as a percentage of the total revenues, and a subjective measure of the subsidiary's value-added contribution to the corporation. Both were significant correlated to the first measure ($r=0.55$, 0.17, respectively), but they exhibited very weak loadings in the PLS analysis so they were eventually dropped.

Specialised resources was operationalised using an adapted scale from Roth and Morrison (1992). Respondents were asked to rate five different subsidiary capabilities (R&D, manufacturing, marketing, managing international activities, innovation and entrepreneurship) relative to other subsidiaries in the corporation. While these activities are all very different, we found that they all loaded strongly onto a single construct in the PLS analysis, which we interpreted as representing the subsidiary's aggregate level of specialized resources.

Subsidiary initiative was the most troublesome construct to measure. Questions were worded carefully on the basis of previous studies (Science Council of Canada, 1980; Bishop and Crookell, 1986; Birkinshaw, 1995) to identify the various manifestations of subsidiary initiative, from internal bidding efforts through to skunk-works-like product development. Eight questions were crafted, which were then reworked several times on the basis of discussions in the questionnaire development process. Following the advice of a reviewer, we subsequently dropped three of these questions because of questionable face validity. The remaining five questions all loaded strongly onto a single construct in the PLS analysis.

Following from the study quoted earlier (Birkinshaw, 1995), we also tried splitting the initiative construct into two sub-constructs: internal initiative (the pursuit of an market opportunity that arose inside the corporate system) and external initiative (the pursuit of an opportunity that arose outside the corporate system). While factor analysis suggested that these two subconstructs could be distinguished, a provisional PLS analysis showed that discriminant validity between them was poor (the path coefficient from one to the other was 0.71). We therefore chose to view subsidiary initiative as a single construct.

Subsidiary leadership was operationalised using three questions relating to the subsidiary's history of strong, internationally respected leaders, the credibility of the leadership with head office managers, and the leadership's efforts at developing middle management. Unfortunately these measures were only moderately correlated with one another ($r=0.19$ to 0.59), with the result that the PLS programme put most of the weighting on the first question only. We therefore dropped the latter two from the analysis.

Entrepreneurial culture. The five highest-loading items from Kuratko, Montaguo and Hornsby (1990) intrapreneurial assessment index were used to measure entrepreneurial culture. These questions were concerned with the openness of the subsidiary's working environment to entrepreneurship, risk-taking and innovation. All five items loaded strongly on a single construct in the PLS analysis.

Subsidiary autonomy.   A 7-item scale was taken from Roth and Morrison (1992) that asked subsidiary managers to identify whether certain decisions were made in the subsidiary, divisional level, or head office. During the PLS analysis four of the items were dropped because they loaded very weakly on the construct, leaving three items.

Communication frequency.   Ghoshal's (1986) measures of communication were used, specifically frequency of communication, frequency of business trips to head office, strength of working relations, and sharing of information. The latter two items were dropped in the course of the PLS analysis, leaving the former two which reflected the frequency of communication between subsidiary and parent company.

Local competition.   Beginning with the 7-item scale developed by Woodcock (1994), we extracted two items, 'domestic competition is intense' and 'competition in this country is extremely high', which were strongly correlated ($r = 0.75$). Both these items loaded strongly on to the same construct, which we interpreted as indicating the perceived level of local competition.

Industry globalisation.   The scale used by Roth and Morrison (1992) was adopted. A factor analysis revealed one primary factor with eight items which represented the extent to which the industry was global. These eight items were then reduced down to four items during the PLS analysis.

Research findings

PLS results are generally presented in two stages. In the first stage the 'measurement model' is presented to show that the measures used as operationalizations of the underlying constructs are reliable and valid. In the second stage, the path coefficients between constructs can be interpreted.

The measurement model was assessed by looking at the internal consistency between items intended to measure the same construct, and the discriminant validity between constructs. Internal consistency was determined using the measure suggested by Fornell and Larcker (1981). This measure is similar to Cronbach's alpha, though more appropriate because it does not assume that each item makes an equal contribution to the construct. As shown in Table 12.2, all the constructs exceeded the level of 0.7, which is considered good for exploratory research (cf. Nunnally, 1978). The discriminant validity of the model was assessed by calculating the average variance extracted for each construct (Fornell and Larcker, 1981). Table 12.3 shows the square root of the average

Table 12.2 Measurement model

Construct	Number of items	Internal consistency
Subsidiary entrepreneurship	5	0.88
Subsidiary leadership	1	1.00
Subsidiary autonomy	3	0.81
Sub-parent communication	2	0.76
Local competition	2	0.81
Global integration	4	0.73
Subsidiary initiative	5	0.92
Specialized resources	5	0.77
Contributory role	1	1.00

Note: Internal consistency for each construct is calculated as: $(\Sigma\lambda_{yi})^2/(\Sigma\lambda_{yi})^2 + \Sigma Var(\epsilon_i)$, where λ_{yi} is the loading for each item on the construct and ϵ_i is the measurement error for each item.

variance along the diagonal of the correlation matrix. For acceptable discriminant validity, the diagonal elements should be greater than all other entries in the same row and column, as is the case here.

Tests of hypotheses

The primary output from PLS analysis is the path coefficients between constructs which are equivalent to standardized regression coefficients. The significance of these paths is calculated using a jack-knifing technique (Fornell and Barclay, 1983).[13] It is unfortunately not possible to test the goodness-of-fit of a PLS model: the nearest approximation is the percentage of variance explained in the endogenous constructs (i.e., their R^2 values).[14] Table 12.4 indicates the path coefficients and R^2 values for 'Model 1', which is the model displayed in Figure 12.3.

The statistical analysis revealed some interesting relationships. As predicted there were strong relationships between specialised resources and initiative and between initiative and contributory role, but contrary to prediction there was essentially no relationship between specialised resources and contributory role (path coefficient = –0.03). While there is a strong *correlation* between specialised resources and contributory role ($r = 0.29$: see Table 12.3), the inclusion of subsidiary initiative in the model shows that the relationship is spurious. This finding also has strong face validity. It suggests that specialised resources are not sufficient, in themselves, to build the subsidiary's contributory role. Rather, subsidiary initiative is necessary to make the specialized resources known to head office managers and thereby to gain recognition for them.

Table 12.3 Discriminant validity

	Correlations between constructs								
Subsidiary entrepreneurship	0.86								
Subsidiary leadership	0.165	1.00							
Subsidiary autonomy	0.180	0.124	0.79						
Sub-parent communication	0.050	0.021	0.025	0.82					
Local competition	0.038	-0.088	-0.130	-0.032	0.87				
Global integration	0.049	0.188	-0.005	-0.022	-0.001	0.71			
Subsidiary initiative	0.134	0.249	0.193	0.105	-0.233	0.258	0.91		
Specialised resources	0.364	0.369	0.113	0.069	-0.043	0.164	0.401	0.454	
Contributory role	0.053	0.272	0.280	0.141	-0.388	0.227	0.662	0.29	1.00

Note: Diagonals indicate the square root of the average variance extracted for the construct. Off-diagonals indicate the correlations between constructs in the PLS model. Average variance extracted is calculated as $(\Sigma \lambda_{yi})^{2}/n$ where λ_{yi} is the loading for each item on the construct and n is the number of items.

The actions of subsidiary management (strength of subsidiary leadership, creation of an entrepreneurial culture) had a strong positive impact on the development of specialised resources (path coefficients 0.31 and 0.35 respectively), as predicted. However, entrepreneurial culture had no discernible impact on subsidiary initiative, while subsidiary leadership showed small but significant relationships with both subsidiary initiative and contributory role.

In terms of the other factors, the level of industry globalisation had a significant relationship with subsidiary initiative, indicating that, after specialised resources, the strongest predictor of initiative is the extent to which the subsidiary is operating in a global industry. The three remaining variables (subsidiary-autonomy, parent-subsidiary communication, and local competition) had significant relationships with contributory role. Of these, all were as predicted except local competition, which had a strong *negative* relationship with contributory role. Simply put, this finding suggested that the lower the level of local competition, the greater the contributory role of the subsidiary. We will discuss possible explanations for this finding in the following section.

Additional analysis

Two additional analyses were undertaken. In the first we simply reversed the line of causality between initiative and specialised resources because, as the discussion earlier indicated, it seems likely that causality flows in both directions. The results from this analysis are listed under 'Model 2' in Table 12.4. As one would predict this reduced the explained variance in subsidiary initiative (R^2 from 0.249 to 0.120) and increased it in specialised resources (R^2 from 0.255 to 0.373). However, it also caused small changes in the paths throughout the model, making entrepreneurial culture a significant predictor of subsidiary initiative, and reducing the significance level of several other relationships.

In terms of the mechanics of PLS, the change in path direction between initiative and specialised resources resulted in much of the variance between the independent constructs and contributory role being channeled through subsidiary initiative, thus increasing the number of significant predictors of subsidiary initiative and decreasing the significance level of the predictors of contributory role. What this means for subsidiary management is harder to say, because there is no *a priori* reason to prefer one model over the other. Our preference is to concentrate on the strong relationships, i.e., the ones that are significant in both models, and to interpret the others with caution. Table 12.4

Table 12.4 Summary of PLS findings for Models 1 and 2[a]

Hypothesis	Path	Path coefficient in Model 1	Path coefficient in Model 2	Support for hypothesis?
1	Specialised resources – Contributory role	-0.03	-0.04	No
2	Subsidiary initiative – Contributory role	0.56***	0.56***	Yes
3	Specialised resources – Subsidiary initiative	0.42***	0.36***	Yes
4a	Subsidiary leadership – Subsidiary initiative	0.07*	0.19*	Yes
4b	Entrepreneurial culture – Subsidiary initiative	-0.06	0.09*	Some
5a	Subsidiary leadership – Specialised resources	0.31**	0.23*	Yes
5b	Entrepreneurial culture – Specialised resources	0.35**	0.32*	Yes
6	Subsidiary leadership – Contributory role	0.11*	0.11*	Yes
8a	Subsidiary autonomy – Contributory role	0.13*	0.14*	Yes
8b	Parent-sub. communic. – Contributory role	0.07†	0.07†	Some
9	Industry globalisation – Subsidiary initiative	0.18**	0.22**	Yes
10	Local competition – Contributory role	-0.23**	-0.23**	Yes
	Variance explained in subsidiary initiative	0.249	0.120	
	Variance explained in specialised resources	0.255	0.373	
	Variance explained in contributory role	0.529	0.529	

Notes: † $p < 0.10$; * $p < 0.05$; ** $p < 0.01$; *** $p < 0.001$.
[a] There is one difference between Models 1 and 2: In Model 1 there is a path from specialised resources to subsidiary initiative, in Model 2 that path is reversed.

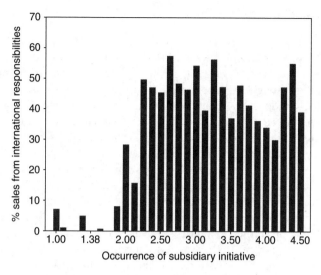

Figure 12.4 Histogram showing relationship between subsidiary initiative and contributory role

lists the results from both models and summarises the extent to which each hypothesis was supported.

The second additional analysis focused on the relationship between subsidiary initiative and contributory role. Because our interest in initiative was restricted to internationally focused efforts, it is perhaps not surprising that a strong relationship between the two constructs was obtained. To illustrate this point, Figure 12.4 is a histogram of the relationship between the two. It shows that the strong correlation is driven primarily by the low level of initiative in subsidiaries with no international responsibilities.

To further understand the relationships between initiative and contributory role, we performed an additional PLS analysis using only the 99 subsidiaries that had international responsibilities (i.e. where contributory role was greater than 0 per cent). This analysis resulted in a nonsignificant path of 0.09 between initiative and contributory role. In other words, *the role of initiative in distinguishing between medium- and high-contributory role subsidiaries is not significant.* Initiative appears to have an important role to play in generating international responsibilities in the first place, but a questionable role in increasing the magnitude of those international responsibilities.[15]

Discussion and conclusions

The findings from this research offer a number of important insights into the process through which MNC subsidiaries enhance their contributory role. First, it is clear that the internal workings of the subsidiary matter, though perhaps not quite in the manner we had expected. Subsidiary leadership and an entrepreneurial culture appear to promote the development of specialised resources, which in turn are strongly associated with the existence of subsidiary initiative. However, there is no clear relationship between specialised resources and contributory role except through initiative. This goes somewhat against the findings of a number of prior studies (e.g. Roth and Morrison, 1992; Birkinshaw and Morrison, 1996) that had equated subsidiary resources with the development of world product mandates. Our interpretation suggests that the prior studies had not given due consideration to subsidiary initiative as the means by which specialised resources impact the subsidiary's contributory role. However, as the additional analysis above indicated (Figure 12.4) the relationship between initiative and contributory role is rather complex. It appears that initiative is an important discriminator between high- and low-contributory role subsidiaries, but that the role of initiative may be more critical in the early stages of contributory role development than in its subsequent growth.

The second key observation comes from the surprising relationship between local competition and both contributory role and subsidiary initiative. Simply stated, the survey evidence showed that subsidiaries were more likely to have high contributory roles and undertake initiative if domestic market competition was perceived to be weak. One explanation for this is a simple perceptual bias, in that high-contribution subsidiaries are predominantly exporters and therefore do not think in terms of local competition, but the strength of the relationship suggests this is not sufficient explanation. An alternative explanation is that the original hypothesis was not correctly motivated. We grounded the hypothesis in Porter's (1990) thinking on national competitiveness. Specifically, we argued that the national or local business environment, and in particular the level of competition within it, would drive competitive upgrading by participating firms. To the extent that high-contribution subsidiaries were more competitive than low-contribution subsidiaries, we suggested, one would expect to see a higher level of local competition in high-contribution subsidiaries. In reality we found a strong relationship in the opposite direction.

Porter (1990) did not, however, give explicit consideration to foreign ownership, other than to suggest a process of 'selective tapping' by foreign subsidiaries in leading-edge clusters. It would appear, then, that Porter's study applies primarily to cases where there are clearly defined 'clusters' of related industries that are recognized as world-class, and which MNCs seek access to through their subsidiaries. For the countries in this study, there is little evidence of such clusters: Canada and Sweden both have leading-edge clusters in the natural resource and heavy industry sectors, but these were underrepresented in the subsidiary sample; and Scotland has a cluster of electronics companies in 'Silicon Glen' but this is not a leading-edge cluster in terms of innovation and spin-off companies. Rather than building firm-specific advantages because of the *strength* of the local business environment, the subsidiaries in this study appeared to build them on account of the industry's relative *weakness*. The high contributory roles appeared to be gained in such instances because the subsidiary was in a relatively protected niche. The suggestion, which cannot be tested here, is that these subsidiaries may make relatively low-quality contributions to the MNC's firm-specific advantage, which are less susceptible to upgrading through local competition.[16]

The third important insight is that the parent–subsidiary relationship also had an important role to play in the development of the subsidiary's contributory role and the presence of subsidiary initiative. Subsidiary autonomy, in particular, had an important influence on both initiative and contributory role, while parent–subsidiary communication had a small positive impact on contributory role. When viewed in terms of the 'competing' hypotheses described earlier, it is therefore not possible to choose decisively between environmental determinism, head office assignment, and subsidiary choice. We can clearly state that all three perspectives are important, but because our choice of constructs was not comprehensive it would be inappropriate to indicate that one perspective is more important than the other two.

The role of subsidiary initiative

One of the key objectives of this research was to understand the part played by subsidiary initiative in developing a subsidiary's contributory role. We know from the data presented here and from research interviews that initiative is absent in a large percentage of subsidiaries. Where initiative is present, its relationship to specialised resources and contributory role appears to be positive *but* with a few reservations. The data suggested some of the grounds for these reservations; this discussion will consider some of the theoretical arguments.

Most obviously, initiative is often seen by parent managers as subversive, that is, evidence of subsidiary managers acting in their own or their country's interests rather than in the interests of the MNC as a whole. Moreover, this concern is not groundless. There are well-known cases of subsidiary managers deliberately building their own 'empires', and there are more ambiguous cases where the entrepreneurial actions of subsidiary management could be interpreted in various ways, depending on one's perceptions. The combination of bounded rationality on the part of parent management and the decreasing dependence of this subsidiary on the parent (Prahalad and Doz, 1981) results in situations where parent company managers have to accept the actions of subsidiary management in good faith, or stifle their ideas through veto.

However, if assumptions of opportunistic behaviour are temporarily suspended, subsidiary initiative has a potentially very powerful role to play in the efficiency of the corporate system. Working on the basis that the MNC can be modelled as an internal market (Ghoshal and Bartlett, 1991), it is apparent that some of the inefficiencies in that market arise through the stickiness of existing relationships – retaining the same internal component supplier, for example, just because it has always fulfilled a certain service. Subsidiary initiative provides a means of lubricating the internal market, in that it makes other entities within the market aware of the subsidiary's distinctive capabilities and the uses to which they could be put. In essence, initiative enhances the flow of information which, *ceteris paribus*, improves market efficiency. To some extent this argument is very obvious, but it is nonetheless important because our suspicion is that the resources and capabilities of subsidiary units are very poorly understood by parent and sister company managers around the world. If the MNC is to effectively utilise its far-flung resources (Bartlett and Ghoshal, 1986), it must first understand what those resources are and where they reside. And to the extent that subsidiary managers understand their resources better than anyone else, it is *their* responsibility to proactively seek out ways of utilising those resources more effectively.

While much of this argument is speculative, it is grounded in the observation that subsidiary initiative is a pervasive phenomenon and tied to the conceptual model of the MNC as an interorganisational network. Much as Kirzner's (1973) entrepreneurs enhanced market efficiency through alertness to new opportunities, the suggestion is that subsidiary unts can enhance the distribution of activities within the

MNC through initiative. Whether these benefits are sufficient to counteract the dangers of opportunism and control loss is then a separate question.

A final point that should be made here is that we do *not* see a high level of subsidiary initiative as a driver of product diversification for the MNC. For initiatives to be accepted by the corporate headquarters they must be aligned with the MNC's existing strategic priorities, otherwise they are likely to be viewed as self-interested behaviour. We see initiatives, particularly those emanating from peripheral countries like Canada, Scotland, and Sweden, as exploring opportunities at the margins of the corporation's existing product portfolio, by building on existing technologies and competencies rather than creating entirely new ones. As such, this is entirely consistent with the product diversification literature in which a focus on core technologies and/or products is typically associated with high performance (Chatterjee and Wernerfelt, 1991; Markides, 1995).

To conclude, this paper provided support for the emerging view that subsidiaries are significant contributors to the firm-specific advantage of the MNC, though it also raised several additional questions. It was not, of course, possible to demonstrate the link between contributory role and firm-specific advantage. Contributory role represented the extent to which the subsidiary has been assigned responsibility for a value-adding activity on the part of the MNC; the ability of the corporate system to effectively leverage that activity in the global market is what eventually makes the subsidiary's resources part of the firm-specific advantage. Clearly there is scope for future research in examining this link.

This study had a number of significant limitations. Perhaps the most significant was the decision to collect all data from the subsidiary general manager. While this was necessary for certain constructs, it probably created some bias in others. It is therefore recommended for future research that both parent and subsidiary managers are polled where possible. Second, the focus on Canada, Scotland, and Sweden meant that generalisability was limited to peripheral countries in developed regions. We would therefore expect to see rather different relationships exhibited in other settings, such as subsidiaries in large developed countries or subsidiaries in less developed regions.

Finally, the focus on subsidiary initiative provides at least provisional evidence that the subsidiary can *drive* the development of firm-specific advantage creation rather than just be a passive contributor. This finding represents a subtle shift in thinking on the role of the subsidiary in the MNC, because it tips the balance of responsibility for role development towards the subsidiary. It also represents further evidence that the sources of firm-specific advantage in MNCs are increasingly gained outside the home country.

Appendix

Wording of questionnaire items (see Table 12A.1)

Contributory role

Does your subsidiary company have any international responsibilities or world mandates (that is, does it undertake any activity such as manufacturing, R&D or product management on behalf of the corporation as a whole?) If yes, please estimate the approximate percentage of your subsidiary company's revenues that are gained as a result of your international responsibilities. (0 to 100 per cent).

Subsidiary initiative

To what extent have the following activities occurred in your subsidiary over the past 10 years? (1) new products developed in (e.g.) Sweden and then sold internationally; (2) successful bids for corporate investments in Sweden; (3) new international business activities that were first started in Sweden; (4) enhancements to product lines which are already sold internationally; (5) new corporate investments in R&D or manufacturing attracted by Swedish management. 1 = never, 5 = plentifully.

Specialised resources

Indicate your capability or distinctive expertise in the following areas relative to other subsidiaries in the corporation: (1) product or process R&D; (2) manufacturing capability; (3) marketing capability; (4) managing international activities; (5) innovation and entrepreneurship. 1 = far below average, 7 = far above average.

Subsidiary entrepreneurship

Indicate how characteristic each of the following statements is in describing your subsidiary: (1) there is top management support of entrepreneurial activity; (2) top management has experience with innovation; (3) individual risk-takers are recognised whether successful or not; (4) there is encouragement for calculated risks; (5) risk-taker is considered a positive attribute. 1 = strongly disagree, 7 = strongly agree.

Subsidiary leadership

Indicate how characteristic the following statements are in describing your subsidiary: (1) the subsidiary has a history of strong, internationally respected leaders; (2) the credibility of subsidiary top management is high; (3) the subsidiary CEO or president works with managers to focus their efforts towards the subsidiary's objectives. 1 = strongly disagree, 7 = strongly agree.

Subsidiary autonomy

Which level in your business unit has authority to make the following decisions? Circle the most appropriate decision level based on the following (1, decision made in the subsidiary company; 2, decision made at the sub-corporate level; 3, decision made by corporate headquarters): (1) changes in product design; (2) subcontracting out large portions of the manufacturing instead of expanding the subsidiary's own facilities; (3) switching to a new manufacturing process.

Parent–subsidiary communication

How often do senior managers in your subsidiary communicate with their counterparts and bosses in head office (1 = daily, 5 = less than once a month); how often do senior and middle managers in your subsidiary make business trips to head office? 1 = twice a month or more, 5 = less than once a year.

Local competition

Indicate how characteristic each of the following statements is in describing your business environment: (1) competition in this country is extremely intense; (2) domestic competition is intense. 1 = strongly disagree, 7 = strongly agree.

Global integration

Indicate how characteristic each of the following statements is in describing your industry: (1) international competition is intense; (2) business activities are susceptible to global scale economies; (3) product awareness exists worldwide; (4) new product introductions occur in all major markets simultaneously. 1 = strongly disagree, 7 = strongly agree.

Table 12A.1 Pearson correlations between individual questions

	1	2	3	4	5	6	7	8	9	10	11	12	13	14	15	16	17	18	19	20	21	22	23	24	25	26	27	28
1. Does your subsidiary have any international responsibilities or mandates?	1																											
2. New products developed in Sweden then sold internationally?	0.56	1																										
3. Successful bids for corporate investment in Sweden?	0.51	0.72	1																									
4. New international business activities first started in Sweden?	0.57	0.82	0.72	1																								
5. Enhancements to product lines which are already sold internationally?	0.70	0.78	0.79	0.82	1																							
6. New corporate investments in R&D or manufacturing started by Swedish management?	0.55	0.68	0.80	0.70	0.79	1																						
7. Capability in product or process R&D?	0.32	0.43	0.36	0.47	0.42	0.43	1																					
8. Capability in manufacturing?	0.06	0.17	0.22	0.26	0.21	0.22	0.36	1																				
9. Capability in marketing?	−0.06	0.01	0.03	0.03	−0.00	0.03	0.22	0.06	1																			
10. Capability in managing international activities?	0.34	0.34	0.28	0.37	0.40	0.29	0.31	0.27	0.29	1																		

	1	2	3	4	5	6	7	8	9	10	11	12	13	14	15	16	17	18	19	20
11. Capability in managing innovation and entrepreneurship?	0.04	0.16	0.18	0.20	0.10	0.23	0.30	0.09	0.37	0.16	1									
12. There is top management support of entrepreneurial activity	0.07	0.15	0.09	0.18	0.09	0.12	0.20	0.08	0.18	0.09	0.45	1								
13. Top management has experience with innovation	0.05	0.13	0.15	0.14	0.08	0.17	0.28	0.23	0.09	0.07	0.44	0.67	1							
14. Individual risk-takers are recognised whether successful or not	0.02	0.06	0.03	0.08	0.00	0.09	0.16	0.08	0.12	-0.03	0.38	0.62	0.61	1						
15. There is encouragement for calculated risk	0.05	0.10	0.09	0.12	0.05	0.11	0.21	0.17	0.14	0.03	0.34	0.64	0.65	0.75	1					
16. Risk-taker is considered a positive attribute	-0.05	0.05	0.05	0.07	0.00	0.04	0.13	0.16	0.09	-0.08	0.37	0.60	0.62	0.72	0.80	1				
17. The subsidiary has a history of strong, internationally respected leaders	0.28	0.25	0.19	0.26	0.30	0.26	0.17	0.14	0.13	0.43	0.13	0.14	0.12	0.09	0.10	0.02	1			
18. Decision to change product design is made at what level?	0.17	0.20	0.08	0.16	0.12	0.12	0.18	0.01	0.06	0.09	0.24	0.20	0.15	0.06	0.03	0.03	0.09	1		
19. Decision to subcontract out portions of manufacturing is what at what level?	0.17	0.12	0.03	0.12	0.10	-0.01	0.10	0.15	0.11	0.07	0.08	0.11	0.15	0.06	0.13	0.12	0.06	0.33	1	
20. Decision to switch to a new manufacturing process is made at what level?	0.32	0.19	0.18	0.21	0.21	0.16	0.25	0.02	0.06	0.17	0.15	0.11	0.18	0.13	0.08	0.09	0.14	0.34	0.38	1

	1	2	3	4	5	6	7	8	9	10	11	12	13	14	15	16	17	18	19	20	21	22	23	24	25	26	27	28
21. How often do senior managers communicate with others in head office?	-0.06	0.05	0.05	0.04	0.01	0.12	0.03	0.05	0.02	0.07	0.09	0.10	0.12	0.12	0.19	0.14	0.11	-0.18	0.01	-0.01	1							
22. How often do managers in your subsidiary make business trips to HQ?	0.14	0.19	0.12	0.13	0.10	0.09	0.10	0.03	0.00	0.08	0.13	0.12	-0.05	0.03	0.03	0.06	-0.06	-0.01	0.04	-0.10	0.39	1						
23. Competition in this country is extremely intense	-0.25	-1.15	-0.09	-0.06	-0.13	-0.02	-0.01	0.02	0.17	-0.07	0.09	0.03	0.03	0.06	0.04	0.08	0.03	0.01	-0.03	-0.06	0.10	0.09	1					
24. The level of domestic competition is intense	-0.40	-0.28	-0.15	-0.22	-0.27	-0.19	-0.14	0.02	0.12	-0.12	0.11	0.06	0.05	0.05	0.05	0.11	-0.12	-0.06	-0.09	-0.11	-0.05	0.02	0.57	1				
25. International competition is intense	0.19	0.17	0.20	0.23	0.22	0.26	0.23	0.12	-0.02	0.25	0.04	0.07	0.12	0.05	0.16	0.09	0.26	-0.03	0.10	0.09	0.03	0.01	0.05	0.02	1			
26. Business activities are susceptible to global scale economies	0.14	0.07	0.22	0.16	0.16	0.13	0.06	0.17	0.02	0.07	0.03	-0.04	0.07	-0.04	0.01	0.07	0.06	-0.10	0.07	0.02	-0.09	0.05	-0.02	0.14	0.39	1		
27. Product awareness exists worldwide	0.01	-0.03	0.07	0.06	0.06	0.16	0.14	0.04	0.04	-0.03	0.03	0.05	0.06	0.01	0.06	0.04	0.07	-0.15	-0.08	-0.03	0.01	0.00	0.07	0.05	0.49	0.39	1	
28. New product introductions occur in all major markets simultaneously	0.18	0.03	0.11	0.10	0.13	0.12	0.01	-0.02	-0.10	0.07	-0.01	-0.08	-0.06	-0.02	-0.06	-0.04	0.12	-0.15	-0.22	-0.05	0.05	-0.04	-0.08	-0.12	0.09	0.16	0.27	1

Note: Signifance level of correlations can be interpreted using the following critical values: $p = 0.05, r = 0.05$; $p = 0.01, r = 0.15$; $p = 0.001, r = 0.19$; $p = 0.001, r = 0.25$.

Acknowledgement

We are grateful to comments from Gunnar Hedlund, Jonas Ridderstråle, Örjan Sölvell, Udo Zander, Jan Johanson, and other members of the Institute of International Business and University of Uppsala. Earlier versions of this paper were presented at the Academy of Management and Academy of International Business meetings in 1996, and a conference at the Australian Graduate School of Management, 1997.

Notes

1. We should add that we do not see an inexorable trend towards higher value-added in _all_ subsidiaries. Many subsidiaries will continue to have simple market exploitation roles; others will take on the higher value-added roles described here.
2. Whether that firm-specific advantage also leads to a competitive advantage is a separate question. Firm-specific advantage simply refers to the MNC's ability to overcome its liability of foreignness; competitive advantage represents a sustainable low-cost or differentiated position against competitors.
3. Though it should be clear that causality does not flow solely in the direction of contributory role. Indeed, as Figure 12.1 shows, the subsidiary's existing contributory role is one of the major drivers of initiative.
4. The _international_ dimension should be emphasised here to distinguish initiatives that offer the potential of enhancing the subsidiary's contributory role from those that are fundamentally local in scope. We are only interested in the former here.
5. Though it should be equally clear that they are not the same thing. As defined here, initiatives are discrete cases of entrepreneurship; entrepreneurial culture is an organisational context in which certain behaviours, including initiative, are fostered.
6. Instead of normative integration we attempted to measure the related concept of _credibility_, that is, the extent to which the parent company has confidence that subsidiary management will deliver on their objectives. However, no significant relationships with subsidiary initiative or contributory role were found, so we dropped the construct.
7. We also looked into the quality of relationships with local suppliers and customers (Porter, 1990) but no significant relationships were identified.
8. The Swedish questionnaire was translated into Swedish and back-translated to verify accuracy. Managers were sent both English and Swedish language versions, with approximately half filling in each version.
9. We were unable to achieve complete consistency in subsidiary size across the three countries. In Canada all subsidiaries larger than £40 million were sampled, but in Scotland and Sweden we ended up polling many smaller subsidiaries as well in order to achieve similar numbers of responses. We finally used a cut-off of £15 million, which meant a relative absence of Canadian subsidiaries in the £15–£40 million range.
10. The one significant difference between host countries was the value-adding scope of the subsidiaries. In Scotland many subsidiaries had either manufac-

turing only or a predominant export orientation, whereas in Canada and Sweden they typically undertook local marketing and sales activities as well.

11. This is, of course, not as high a coefficient as we would have liked. Our sense from these questionnaires and from talking to the individuals was that head office managers were unable to adequately answer some of the subsidiary-specific questions (e.g. those relating to specialised resources and initiative), which lowered the level of interrater reliability.

12. All indicators were reflective rather than formative. This means that there is assumed to be an unobservable that 'causes' the observables, rather than vice versa (Fornell, 1984).

13. We also calculated significance levels using the 'bootstrap' technique offered in the PLS computer package. The jack-knife results were more conservative so they are reported here.

14. While fit indices are available with PLS, they are of questionable validity because the objective function of PLS is to maximize the explained variance in endogenous constructs, not to optimise the model.

15. One further insight into the relationship between initiative and contributory role was obtained. One question on the questionnaire asked the subsidiary presidents to assess the approximate percentage of their international responsibilities that were 'given' to them by the parent company vs those that were 'earned' by the subsidiary through initiative (cf. Crookell and Morrison, 1990). The mean response was 63 percent earned, 37 percent given. Of course, the danger of socially desirable response here is very great so this finding needs to be interpreted with care, but it suggests that subsidiary managers themselves believe there is an important relationship between initiative and contributory role.

16. In more general terms, it is also possible that Porter's (1990) thinking has relatively less applicability to small peripheral economies such as Canada, Sweden, and Scotland than to those economies with more dynamic clusters and more leading-edge subsidiaries such as Japan or the USA.

13

Unleash Innovation in Foreign Subsidiaries (2001)*

Julian Birkinshaw and Neil Hood

The Challenge of Going Global is not simply to sell products wherever customers are but to take advantage of bright ideas wherever they spring up. Indeed, growth-triggering innovation often emerges in foreign subsidiaries – from employees closest to customers and least attached to the procedures and politesse of the home office. NCR's automatic teller business, for instance, took off only when the development team shifted activities from corporate headquarters in Dayton, Ohio, to Dundee, Scotland. Under the guidance of a charismatic leader with scrappy persistence, NCR's Scottish operation became the largest manufacturer of ATMs in the world and brought the moribund Dundee manufacturing centre back from the brink of extinction.

But as every multinational manager knows, making the most of foreign subsidiaries is tricky. Too often, heavy-handed responses from headquarters squelch local enthusiasm and drive out good ideas – and good people. Even when headquarters tries to do the right thing by democratising the innovation process and ceding more power to subsidiaries, the results are not always stellar. (See the box 'A worst-case scenario.')

[Since the early 1990s], we have studied more than 50 multinational corporations to understand what companies can do differently to encourage innovation in foreign subsidiaries – what we call 'innovation at the edges.' Our observations suggest that when companies start to think of foreign subsidiaries as peninsulas rather than as islands – as extensions of the company's strategic domain rather than as isolated outposts – innovative ideas flow more freely from the periphery to the

* *Harvard Business Review*, March (2001), 131–7. Copyright © 2001 by Harvard Business School Publishing Corporation. All rights reserved.

corporate centre. (We first heard the peninsula concept articulated by managers at Monsanto Canada as they grappled with the challenge of redefining their role after the 1989 Free Trade Agreement with the United States.) But even more than a change in mind-set, corporate executives require a new set of practices, with two aims: to improve the formal and informal channels of communication between headquarters and subsidiaries and to give foreign subsidiaries more authority to see their ideas through. Only then can companies ensure that bright ideas – and the smart people who dream them up – don't end up marooned on desert islands.

Peninsulas, not islands

Fostering innovation in foreign subsidiaries is a familiar goal, but it is extremely difficult to achieve in real life. In the past, multinationals recognised the need to tap into a few select subsidiaries, but today successful corporate executives recognize that good ideas can come from any foreign subsidiary. (See the box 'Three Eras of the Multinational.') The challenge is to find ways to liberalise, not tighten, internal systems and to delegate more authority to local subsidiaries. It isn't enough to ask subsidiary managers to be innovative; corporate managers need to give them incentives and support systems to facilitate their efforts. That's more easily said than done, of course, but our observations suggest four approaches:

- Give seed money to subsidiaries.
- Use formal requests for proposals.
- Encourage subsidiaries to be incubators.
- Build international networks.

When these practices are set in motion, we can expect far more creative and genuinely innovative ideas to emerge from the edges of the corporation. Let's take a look at each approach.

Give seed money to subsidiaries

It's easy to argue that subsidiary companies need access to seed money, but corporate executives must strike a balance between demanding that subsidiaries meet short-term results and granting them sufficient freedom to pursue new ideas. Put too much focus on the former, and you know that subsidiaries will hide profits – not to pursue their new ideas but to protect themselves in case of a rainy day. Put too much emphasis on the latter, and there will be a proliferation of so-called strategic projects whose returns will fall below target levels. One way to achieve the necessary balance is to give subsidiaries discretionary budgets to test ideas within limits imposed by corporate headquarters. But it's also a matter of who holds the purse strings for which types of investments. Major investments can and should be made at a corporate level. But seed money can be handled on a more decentralized basis by giving local subsidiaries discretionary budgets to test ideas.

For example, in the late 1980s, Hilary Smith, a market development manager at 3M Canada, identified a market for systems that would allow library visitors to check out books without assistance. Her proposal fell on deaf ears at corporate headquarters, partly because the market for traditional library security machines in the United States was still growing rapidly. She pursued it anyway, using seed funding from the Canadian R&D budget to put together a prototype. At the American Library Association meeting where the prototype debuted, she discovered that 3M Australia had been working on a similar product. Hearing enthusiastic comments from potential customers, she and her Australian counterpart agreed to work together to bring out a single 3M product. Additional funding was supplied by the US-based library systems business unit, and Smith was given worldwide responsibility for the product's launch. Manufacturing was transferred to St Paul, Minnesota, where the US business unit was based. The Australian subsidiary retained product and business development rights in Australia and New Zealand. SelfCheck is now one of the main products in 3M Library Systems' portfolio – thanks in no small part to the initial funding from the Canadian and Australian divisions.

It often happens, of course, that an idea seeded by a business unit, having developed into a viable business, is eventually abandoned because it doesn't fit well with the rest of the unit. Corporate-sponsored development projects therefore are an important alternative to business-unit-level investments. ABB, the global engineering and technology firm with headquarters in Zurich, provides both seed money at the subsidiary level and corporate funding for new ideas that cross the boundaries of existing business units. In ABB's 12 corporate research centres, located around the world, employees are encouraged to propose 'high impact' projects – those with broad, cross-business-unit applications – which are then funded from a corporate budget. One such project led to the creation of a state-of-the-art electrical transformer factory in Athens, Georgia. Dubbed the 'factory of the future', the test factory is fully automated, from ordering through production to the delivery of the finished product.

A worst-case scenario

To illustrate the challenges that entrepreneurs in subsidiaries typically face, consider the story of Scott McTaggart, a 29-year-old business development manager in the Canadian subsidiary of a diversified industrial company.

He couldn't have seen it coming, but when McTaggart joined the subsidiary in the mid-1990s, he was in for a rocky ride. With a reputation for decentralization and programmes that encouraged individual initiative, the US-based business was one of the most reliably profitable companies in the world. Not only were employees encouraged to practice an informal style of management, but the company had also established several initiatives that encouraged frontline employees to play active roles in improving business processes. These programmes resulted in large cost savings, and, perhaps even more important, they spawned a new creativity and enthusiasm among employees – an atmosphere, you would think, in which entrepreneurs could thrive.

At the Canadian subsidiary where McTaggart worked, however, the glory days were largely a thing of the past. As the oldest of 30 international subsidiaries, the Canadian group had once operated as a miniature replica of its parent company with a CEO who was fully responsible for the profits of the Canadian operating divisions. But in the 1980s, the parent company had moved to a more integrated model for North American operations. It created a dozen strategic business units, all headquartered in the United States. Thus the role of the Canadian CEO was reduced to that of mere figurehead, and the Canadian subsidiary was left to deal with mundane issues such as new legislation and tax accounting. It was only through a small business-development group that entrepreneurial activities were formally encouraged.

Soon after his arrival, McTaggart identified an opportunity to bid for a massive, government-sponsored energy management project that entailed the installation and financing of energy-efficient lightbulbs, motors, and other electrical equipment in 150 federal buildings throughout Canada. With potential revenues in the billions, energy management was a great opportunity, in McTaggart's view, not just for the Canadian subsidiary but for the entire company. Lacking a budget of his own, McTaggart convinced one division president to provide $1 million in seed money to test the market. Elated, McTaggart quickly put together a small project team and started to go after business.

That's when the problems began. A few months after McTaggart's initiative got under way, the business unit went through a dramatic reorganisation. Following the abrupt resignation of the unit's president, the new president withdrew support for the energy management project. Suddenly orphaned, McTaggart found a new sponsor in another business unit after a series of emphatic presentations and 11th-hour phone calls.

Even as McTaggart scrambled for funds, the fledgling business was becoming a player in the energy management business – several pilot projects were completed and four new contracts were secured. But again problems emerged. McTaggart and his new sponsor came to realise at virtually the same painful moment that even though energy management fit well with the existing business's product lines, the energy management business's life cycle was wildly out of sync with the rest of the division's product portfolio.

Clearly, McTaggart needed to make a number of up-front investments and take several calculated risks to grow his business. But his new sponsor, obsessed with controlling costs and intent on being involved in day-to-day decisions (or so it seemed to McTaggart), kept urging McTaggart to curb his growth expectations. Finally, matters came to a head: faced with yet another demand to scale back his projections, McTaggart decided to resign. The energy management business limped along for another 18 months but never regained its previous pace. A disillusioned McTaggart started his own company, this time better equipped, he hoped, to control its destiny.

McTaggart's experience is all too common. His idea was consonant with the company's entrepreneurial spirit and was aligned with corporate growth targets, but McTaggart faced obstacle after obstacle: lack of fit with existing businesses, changing agendas at the top, risk-averse managers, culture clashes, and time lost fighting internal resistance. He lost a great opportunity to take his ideas to the limit, and the company wasted time, money, and that precious commodity, initiative.

The results have been truly spectacular: labour costs have been cut by half, cycle times have been cut by 90 per cent, and time from order entry to shipping has been reduced from 30 days to one day.

Use formal requests for proposals

Providing seed money to subsidiaries is a start, but funds alone won't generate valuable innovations from a passive subsidiary manager. Executives must also find ways to increase the demand for seed money. To that end, it helps to think of subsidiaries as freelance contractors that are granted licenses to manufacture or develop certain products. When you want to make a new investment, you send out a request for proposal (RFP), which may yield three or four competing bids. Volkswagen's decision to manufacture the New Beetle in Puebla, Mexico, for example, was the result of a lengthy review in which the Puebla site was compared with sites in Germany and Eastern Europe. It also required heavy-duty championing from executives in Mexico and the United States, who saw a local production base as essential to their plans for reviving the VW brand in North America.

An RFP approach can also stimulate subsidiaries to develop creative solutions to corporate challenges. Monsanto's Canadian management team picked up on a tentative corporate plan to build a dry-formulation plant for its Roundup herbicide and pushed hard for that investment to be made in Canada. In preparing their proposal, they were able to shape the product's specifications – as any contracting company knows, that's the only way to win competitive tenders. But the members of the Canadian group knew they wouldn't get the nod based on cost alone, so they developed their proposal around such innovative practices as self-directed work teams, empowerment, and outsourcing. Their proposal focused on the competencies of the Canadian operation and demonstrated how the investment could help forestall a threat from another company rumoured to be developing a competing product in central Canada. Consequently, the Canadian proposal won the contract, beating out a Monsanto site in Louisiana and an independent manufacturer in Iowa.

We have seen this approach to new investments work well in a variety of multinational companies. But we have also seen companies shy away from it because the costs of reviewing and evaluating multiple bids can be prohibitive. The best approach is to limit the list of competing proposals to three or four – as long as the narrowing process is designed to increase, rather than suppress, variance. It is best to avoid formal reviews in which two mediocre options are set up alongside the

Three eras of the multinational

Multinationals have evolved through three phases over the past 50 years, both in terms of their geographic scope and the roles played by their foreign subsidiaries:

Paternalism

In the first half of the twentieth century, the dominant model for multinationals was to innovate in the home country and then roll out new products across the corporate empire. US companies like Caterpillar, IBM, and Procter & Gamble became masters of this model. But as foreign markets for the established multinationals became more sophisticated and as the foreign subsidiaries in those countries grew stronger, it gradually became apparent that the home country did not have a monopoly on innovation and leading-edge thinking.

Expansionism

In the 1970s and 1980s, many multinational corporations set up 'scanning units' to tap into the ideas coming out of key foreign markets, and they built R&D sites abroad to gain access to scientific communities. But welcome as they were, corporate investments of this type represented but a halfhearted attempt to tap into the ideas and opportunities in foreign markets. There were two major problems. First, scanning units and foreign R&D labs were attractive in principle but difficult to manage effectively. For example, many European multinationals, including Volkswagen, Volvo, and Ericsson, established development centres in California, but in most cases the units struggled to successfully transfer and integrate their ideas with those of their parent companies. Second, by defining certain units as responsible for picking up new ideas, corporate managers were implicitly signalling to all other foreign units that they did not have to bother. Such an approach limited growth opportunities to a few select markets or technologies and dampened the initiative of subsidiary managers in other foreign units.

Liberalism

A third model, now emerging, takes a more democratic approach to the pursuit of new opportunities. It builds on two basic arguments:

first, useful new business ideas can emerge from anywhere in the world, particularly those parts of the organization that are in direct contact with customers, suppliers, and other external parties. Second, the greater the distance from the centre, the less constrained individuals are by the traditions, norms, and belief structures of the corporation. This is the argument that subsidiaries should be viewed as peninsulas rather than islands. As multinationals take such an approach, we can expect far more creative and genuinely innovative ideas to emerge from the edge of the corporation than from the centre. The challenge becomes one of tapping into the ideas and leveraging them effectively.

preferred candidate for the sake of appearances. This happens all too often, and it is a splendid way of killing the initiative of subsidiary managers.

Distance can become an advantage. It allows foreign subsidiaries to experiment with unconventional or unpopular projects that would be closed down if they were more visible to headquarters.

Encourage subsidiaries to be incubators

Subsidiary managers often comment that their distance from headquarters makes it hard for them to attract attention. But distance can become an advantage. It allows foreign subsidiaries to experiment with unconventional or unpopular projects that would be closed down if they were more visible to headquarters. It allows them to become incubators that can provide shelter and resources for businesses that are not yet strong enough to stand on their own.

Consider the actions of Ulf Borgström, manager of the Swedish subsidiary of a US minicomputer manufacturer. The company was struggling in the early 1990s because of a weak product line, and the Swedish subsidiary was on the verge of bankruptcy. Borgström was able to turn around the operation by disregarding orders from headquarters and pursuing whatever business he could find in the Swedish market. Unable to sell his own company's products, he decided to offer service contracts on competitors' products. Needless to say, his superiors in the

home office immediately discredited his strategy, but Borgström perse-
vered, and the service contracts proved to be a significant factor in the
subsidiary's revival. By 1997, headquarters had come around to his way
of thinking, and the Swedish subsidiary was hailed as a success story.

Or take Ericsson as another example. Outsiders know that Ericsson has
successfully caught two of the biggest waves in the telecommunications
business in recent years: the emergence of second-generation digital
radio technology and the subsequent boom in the handsets business.
Insiders admit, however, that both businesses struggled to gain acceptance while they were being developed and would have been killed
if their sponsors had not been persistent. In fact, in the latter case,
Åke Lundqvist, the president of the nascent handsets unit, moved himself
and his team to southern Sweden, which gave him the time and space
to get the business going without interference from corporate executives.
More recently, Ericsson has created a new unit called Ericsson Business
Innovation, whose mandate, in the words of its director, Jöran Hoff,
'is to create the next core business' for the corporation. It acts as a
venture fund by providing seed money and management expertise to
promising new projects – not just Stockholm-based projects, but those
in places as diverse as southern California, North Carolina, and Finland.

The subsidiary-as-incubator model is promising, but as with all
corporate venturing, there is a risk that a new business idea won't find
a home within the corporate portfolio. The critical success factor is
typically how well the project champion is connected with other parts
of the corporation. Hence the importance of international networks.

Build international networks

As every corporate executive – and entrepreneur, for that matter –
knows, it's essential to give would-be innovators access to professional
and informal networks. But such networks are not easily manufactured.
Some companies have tried to build international networks by creating
employee rotation programmes, but too often these personnel moves
have been ineffective because they've been artificial – they haven't been
linked to practical business initiatives. If employees don't do real work
during their overseas assignments, they never become part of local
teams or become integrated into networks. A number of corporations,
however, now deploy talented employees on short-term overseas
assignments that are tied to tangible business goals. In the short term,
these assignments furnish useful resources for current projects; in the
long term, they increase the number and variety of professional networks
from which the next ideas are likely to emerge.

For example, when ABB acquired Taylor Instruments, a Rochester, New York-based automation and controls company, the entire management team of ABB's automation and controls business was temporarily moved from Sweden to ABB's US headquarters in Stamford, Connecticut, to oversee the integration process and help develop a new identity for the business. After three years, the management team, which by then included a couple of Americans, was moved back to Sweden.

Similarly, Hewlett-Packard often brings in an experienced management team from corporate headquarters to get new subsidiary operations started. The team's job is to get performance on track, bring a local management team up to speed, and move on to another project. At both companies, the creation of strong international networks is the by-product of real work rather than an end in itself.

Multinationals also need to create roles for what we have come to think of as idea brokers. In a crowded marketplace, brokers add value through their ability to bring buyers and sellers together. For innovation at the edges to thrive, entrepreneurs in foreign subsidiaries need to be linked with sources of funding, complementary assets, and sponsors in other parts of the company. That's where idea brokers come into the picture. With their wealth of contacts and experiences, they play three important roles.

First, they link seed money with new ideas. Consider the story of Mats Leijon, an electrical engineer in one of ABB's corporate research labs who came up with a disruptive technology called the Powerformer – a high-voltage generator that allows power to go directly from the generator to overhead cables without a step-up transformer. Without the assistance of Harry Frank, the head of one of ABB's corporate research labs, Leijon's invention might never have seen the light of day, especially given that the Powerformer promised to wipe out more than one of ABB's core businesses. Frank brokered the idea by translating it into business terms, and Leijon's project received funding from the Swedish country manager, Bert-Olof Svanholm. It was launched in 1998. Today, several leading ABB customers are adopting the Powerformer, and the story of Mats Leijon's innovation has become a touchstone for other entrepreneurs at ABB.

Second, idea brokers help find the right organizational home for new ideas. In one product development group in Hewlett-Packard's Canadian subsidiary, initial funding for a new software product came from HP Canada, which was enough to get the product to market. But for the business to grow, the development group's general manager realized he needed to find a home for his product in one of HP's major divisions. He began to sound out his contacts, including several group vice presidents who were able to use their broad knowledge of the HP businesses to put him in touch with various parent divisions. After one false start, he found the right home in a small, Seattle-based division that was selling to the same customer sectors as his group. In HP, the group vice presidents are the idea brokers, and a significant part of their time is spent balancing the portfolio of businesses – splitting up large divisions, merging small divisions, shifting emerging businesses between divisions to create better opportunities for growth, and so on.

The third role idea brokers play is in cross-selling products and services among businesses. Skandia AFS, the financial services group, provides a good example. It is organised as a federation of national businesses, each of which is free to develop its own product lines for the local marketplace (they share a common business model and information system). Recognizing that a country-centred approach could restrict the transfer of new ideas across borders, Skandia created an internal brokering unit called the International Support Unit (ISU). Its role is to take new products developed in one country and cross-sell them into other countries; managed as a profit centre, Skandia ISU earns its revenues through commissions on cross-border product sales.

In an era in which new business ideas are as likely to come from Stockholm as from Silicon Valley, multinational companies cannot afford to limit their creative gene pools to corporate R&D labs or a few select outposts. They must find ways to tap into the diverse and multifaceted opportunities that exist in foreign operations. Taken together, the four practices we've outlined can help corporate executives unleash innovation at the edges and fulfill, at last, the promise of going global.

14
Future Directions in International Business Research: The MNE, Subsidiary and Host Country Agendas*

Julian Birkinshaw

The purpose of this chapter is to consider some of the future directions for research in international business, and in particular in the areas of foreign subsidiary management and economic development. These are both important themes in Neil Hood's work and in my own research. Moreover, they both continue to be important and relatively fertile grounds for new empirical and theoretical studies.

Before getting into these issues, it may be useful to reflect briefly on my joint work with Neil, because the way in which our research interests converged offers some important insights into the challenges facing international business researchers.

A brief retrospective

During my doctoral studies at the Ivey School of Business I became fascinated by what I subsequently referred to as *subsidiary initiative* – the deliberate and proactive pursuit of new opportunities for value creation by managers in foreign subsidiaries. This was a hot issue in Canada at the time because free trade with the USA had created a real stimulus for Canadian subsidiary managers to do something different. However, in presenting my thoughts on subsidiary initiative at academic conferences (mostly in the USA) the reaction was typically somewhere

---

* Written for this volume.

between mild curiosity and incomprehension. 'Why would a subsidiary manager want to do this?' was one memorable comment from a senior academic. Others observed that perhaps this was a uniquely Canadian thing.

In 1993 I had the good fortune to meet Neil Hood and Steve Young, and we quickly hit it off. My Canadian work on subsidiary initiative echoed some of the detailed case studies they had done in the Scottish subsidiaries of such companies as NCR, IBM and HP (thereby affirming that it was not just a 'Canadian thing'). And this realisation allowed us to generate a much more comprehensive and nuanced point of view on the factors driving certain subsidiary managers to act in an entrepreneurial way. I spent the summer of 1995 at the University of Strathclyde working on these issues with Neil, and several of the articles in this book came out of this three-month period of work.

Equally important, my discussions with Neil and Steve helped me to understand another whole dimension of the subsidiary manager's world. I had come to subsidiary management through the multinational corporation (MNE) literature, so my primary concern was with how the subsidiary adds value to the parent company, and how its activities align with other parts of the corporate network. Neil and Steve were familiar with all this, but in addition they had a strong economic development perspective. For the Scottish economy at the time, companies like NCR, IBM and HP were enormously important drivers of economic development, because they were growing strongly and they were undertaking high value-added activities such as R&D. And for Neil in particular, as the former head of Locate in Scotland, the role played by inward investment agencies in facilitating subsidiary initiative and growth was highly significant.

Neil and Steve had already done some joint research on the relationship between foreign-owned subsidiaries and economic development (several of which are included in this book) but for me the host country agenda was a new and important piece in the puzzle. Most of the subsequent research I did with Neil ended up building on the important insight that the subsidiary is the bridge between the MNE and the host country.

Neil and I have continued to work together in a variety of ways, and more recently our collaborations have taken us in some new directions. But our most worthwhile contributions have been to play out the initial insight that brought us together in the first place – that subsidiary development occurs through the interplay of parent company strategy, host country potential, and subsidiary manager initiative.

Future directions

Let me now turn to the primary purpose of this chapter, which is to explore some of the current issues that multinational corporations and host country investment agencies are grappling with, and to suggest some future directions for research. My approach is a simple one: to lay out what I see as key issues on the agenda for MNE managers, and then do the same for subsidiary managers and host country policymakers. And for each point, I will identify some possible directions for future research.

The MNE Agenda

Doing more with less

The push for global integration of activities in MNEs has been underway for several decades, but there is absolutely no evidence that this is slowing down. With the exception of certain dotcoms that were born global (for example, Amazon and eBay), the vast majority of MNEs have legacy assets dotted around the world that do not pull their weight, and operating practices that are more local than global. So to varying degrees, and at varying speeds, the trend is towards integration, specialisation, and rationalisation. A few examples:

- *Global manufacturing.* Most MNEs have gone through several rounds of plant closures over the last twenty years, sometimes for overcapacity reasons, sometimes because they had too many small plants, and sometimes because of technological changes. These closure programmes raise some important issues, in terms of the criteria used for choosing which ones to close (it is not always the efficient or modern ones that survive), in terms of the manufacturing philosophy that is adopted (economies of scale vs. the focused factory), and in terms of ownership (retain in-house vs. outsource).
- *Global purchasing.* This is gradually becoming common practice in MNEs, though it is less common than one would expect given that companies have been sourcing from overseas for decades (Kotabe, 1992; Mol, 2001). There are two different elements at work here: one is the practice of consolidating purchasing from multiple vendors; the other is the practice of outsourcing major activities to vendors in less-developed economies.
- *Global account management.* This is the flip-side of global purchasing. It usually lags behind, with the customer demanding global prices and servicing, and the vendor then scrambling to provide them.

Occasionally I have seen global account management lead, with the result that the vendor in question generates a significant advantage by being better co-ordinated than the customer (Yip and Madsen, 1996; Birkinshaw, Toulan and Arnold, 2001).

In addition to the above, there are plenty of other manifestations of increased global integration, including knowledge management programmes, centres of excellence, and relocated corporate head-offices. Moreover, as we look ahead to several more years of economic stagnation and depressed share prices, it is easy to see how these sorts of activities will become more, not less, important. Researchers are typically slow to pick up on trends of this sort, but it seems that there is considerable potential for more research on global integration, disinvestments and closure.

New sources of value and top-line growth

MNEs are equally active in managing the other side of the profitability equation. Top-line growth is somewhere near the top of most CEO agendas, and the exhortations of management gurus such as Gary Hamel (2001) and Chan Kim (Kim and Mauborgne, 1997) has had an enduring impact on companies in their pursuit of new businesses and new sources of value. Again, there are plenty of ways in which this broad trend manifests itself:

- *Corporate venturing programmes.* There was a surge of popularity in corporate venturing during the late 1990's bubble years, and this has now been reversed. But even so, corporate venture capital investments are still at relatively high levels on a historical basis, and there is no shortage of recent research on the subject (Chesbrough, 2000; Campbell and Birkinshaw, 2003). In terms of the international component, most corporate venture units are deliberately configured to tap into new business opportunities on a global basis, though as yet there has been no research looking specifically at this issue.
- *Global R&D programmes.* Evidence is mixed here, because while some MNEs have pushed forward with complex multi-country R&D programmes (for example, Ericsson, Ford, P&G), others have scaled back and simplified their R&D to make it more flexible and responsive. An example of the latter is pharmaceutical major GSK which broke its enormous discovery research organisation into seven focused centres of excellence in 2001, with promising results so far. However, even if MNEs are opting for a more loosely-coupled R&D network (Birkinshaw,

2002) there is always a global overlay of processes for sharing knowledge and co-ordinating activities, so there is plenty of scope for further research in this area.

- *Customer-focused structures.* One of the big value-creation trends in large MNEs is to move down the value-chain to be closer to the customer – to offer them services or solutions, rather than products. Successful examples of this trend are IBM's Global Services group, and GE's services businesses. Unsuccessful examples are Ford's purchase of Kwik-Fit in auto servicing, and Unilever's brief foray into home cleaning. While clearly attractive on paper, this is a risky strategy because it takes the MNE into business areas it does not really understand, and it typically needs an entirely new way of structuring the customer interface to make it work (Galbraith, Downey and Kates, 2002; Birkinshaw and Terjesen, 2003).

- *Global scanning operations.* There are plenty of anecdotal cases of MNEs with scanning operations in leading-edge parts of the world, such as Nokia in Silicon Valley, Microsoft in Stockholm, and Volkswagen in Los Angeles (Doz, Williamson and Santos, 2001), whose job is to tap into the latest ideas and transfer that information back to the parent company. The suspicion is that most of these units fail. But the truth is no one knows, so there is clearly a research project waiting to be done here.

- *Global mergers and acquisitions.* Finally, for those MNEs that cannot find organic sources of growth there is always the M&A option. There is no reason to think that acquisitions will be any less destructive to shareholder value in the coming decade than they were in previous decades, but despite this it is fair to assume MNEs will continue to engage in them.

Corporate social responsibility

While every MNE today has some awareness of the importance of corporate social responsibility, there is an increasing number of companies, including Shell, BP, McDonald's and Nike, for whom this is an absolute priority. To a large degree this is a direct result of the success of the anti-globalisation movement, which is a motley collection of interest groups without a clear agenda of their own, but with a strong shared belief that increased globalisation (as pushed by the WTO and by particular companies) is bad. Whether one believes in their arguments or not, the movement has forced MNEs to rethink their more contentious policies, and it has encouraged them to better articulate the benefits they bring to less developed countries. For example, oil majors Shell and BP now actively promote policies for sustainable development – including research into renewable sources of energy, and investments in the local communities in which they operate around the world.

Emerging economies

One consultancy has predicted that China will be the largest market (by unit volume) for any and every consumer product category by 2008. This is not news to the hundreds of western MNEs that have invested in China in the last decade, but academic research has been slow to catch up. While MNEs are actively integrating their activities in Europe and North America (and essentially ignoring country boundaries in the process), they are often doing the opposite in the developing parts of the world by placing strong country managers in charge of relatively autonomous operations. So as a result, many of the issues that international business researchers have studied for decades, such as market entry, expatriate management, organisation structures, and subsidiary relations, need to be revisited in the growing markets like China, India, Brazil and South Africa.

The other side of this story is the rise of MNEs from these emerging economies. This may be the single most interesting development in MNE research in the next decade, because we know these companies are on their way, but we cannot expect them to conform to our existing models. A few brief examples:

- Many South African MNEs such as SAB Miller and Anglo American have chosen a dual-listing in Johannesburg and London as a means of bridging between their home market and the developed world.
- Chinese MNEs have mostly taken the 'OEM' approach whereby they manufacture under another company's brand (Leung and Yip, 2003).
- Brazilian and Mexican MNEs have tended to grow in Latin America first, with their biggest challenge being how to gain a position in the US market.
- India has been extremely successful in taking on back-office activities, call centres and software development for established companies, but with the few exceptions such as Infosys and Wipro it has mostly failed (so far) to create world-beaters of its own.

Reconciling these diverse pressures

The last broad category to consider under the MNE agenda is how they attempt to reconcile the age-old tension between global integration and national responsiveness. Here the story is pretty blurred. If one looks at the major change programmes underway in MNEs, the dominant trend is towards greater global integration, as discussed earlier. But if one engages in conversation with MNE executives, and if one listens to the official pronouncements on strategy, there is a lot of talk about responsiveness. For example, Douglas Daft, the CEO of Coke, famously said in a *Financial Times* article (2000):

> As the 1990s were drawing to a close, the world had changed course, and Coca-Cola had not. We were operating as a big, slow, insulated, sometimes even insensitive 'global' company; and we were doing it in an era when nimbleness, speed, transparency and local sensitivity had become absolutely essential.

Daft's solution was to give the local country managers greater operating autonomy, and greater influence over new product launches. McDonalds, too, has given its country operations rather more influence over menu choice and store layout than they used to have. Another example is Sara Lee, the US consumer goods company, which is on the one hand pushing for far greater global integration in terms of manufacturing centres of excellence, global accounts and core product teams, and on the other hand is trying to encourage its general managers in the operating companies to take higher levels of initiative.

My own perspective on this matter has changed considerably over the last five years. Traditionally, I have of course been on the side of the foreign subsidiary manager, and I have supported the argument that he or she should be given greater degrees of freedom to act. But increasingly – and somewhat to my annoyance – the real success stories tend to be MNEs with processes and systems controlled tightly from the centre. For example, Microsoft and Oracle are both highly centralised MNEs, and they have far outperformed their more decentralised competitor HP. Diageo has become the dominant player in premium drinks, at least in part through a strategy of ruthlessly focusing on eight global brands, and giving the 'venture' markets around the world very limited degrees of freedom. And Nokia has done much better than Ericsson, despite a more focused and centrally-controlled set of activities.

Obviously the trade-off between integration and responsiveness will always exist, and there are certain companies, such as Coke, that are currently focusing on the responsiveness side of the equation. But I have certainly come round to the point of view that many MNEs still have a long way to go in rationalising and focusing their worldwide activities, and that in many cases a more centralised approach will yield significant benefits.

The host country agenda

Unlike the case in the MNE, there is no single executive or top management team to focus on when one considers the host country agenda. Typically, the inward investment agency ends up being most actively involved in issues of foreign investment by MNEs, but there will also be government departments for industry, education, and labour that also have important roles to play in shaping the host country agenda for international business.

Does foreign ownership really matter?

The single most important question is whether foreign ownership of commercial activities really matters for a country's economic development. I have been engaged in discussions on this matter in Canada, Australia, UK and Sweden, but without resolution. The 'yes' camp points to cases such as the layoffs made by Motorola, National Semiconductor and NEC in Scotland's Silicon Glen during 2001–2, and argue that if those factories had been owned by UK parent companies there would have been more opportunity to save them. The 'no' camp points to the continuing pre-eminence of London's financial district, despite the fact that almost all the major players are foreign-owned. There is also a camp that says 'it doesn't matter' because it is the nature of the activities, and the way in which they are interconnected, rather than their ownership structure, that really shapes their impact on economic development.

I won't even attempt to resolve this debate here (see my earlier article, Birkinshaw, 2000, for some thoughts on it). What is interesting and surprising is how little research has really attempted to get to grips with the issue, despite some fairly promising and obvious lines of attack.

Foreign investment during a downturn

While it is important to debate the merits of foreign ownership, a more practical question that is troubling policymakers at the moment is what happens to the existing stock of foreign-owned companies during a sustained economic downturn. While the doomsayers would predict wholesale closure of such activities, the reality is a lot more complicated, and it involves the interplay of four sets of factors:

- *Macro-level industry changes.* For example, the semiconductor industry is notoriously cyclical, and overall demand for semiconductor products dropped sharply in 2000 as the technology 'bubble' burst. NEC Semiconductors saw a 49 per cent drop in its revenues, and as a direct result closed its factories in Scotland and the USA.

- *MNE strategy changes*, in terms of which business or product areas to focus on, and what the sources of competitive advantage will be. For example, Motorola's recent restructuring efforts were driven by the need to reduce their overall capacity in semiconductor and phone manufacturing, but also by the desire to become more flexible in their operations. So as well as closing several factories, they also sold others to third part manufacturers so that they could focus more on design and marketing. They also turned the East Kilbride factory in Scotland into a self-standing centre of excellence in smart cards, to enable it to be sold as a going concern.
- *Subsidiary strategy* – the extent to which managers have actively developed the local business, and made it distinctive. For example, the NEC semiconductor plant in Scotland that was closed was one of six similar plants, and the one with the highest costs. In contrast, NCR's operation in Dundee is unique and it survived, because it could not be closed without NCR exiting the automatic teller business in its entirety.
- *The local milieu* – the linkages to various suppliers, customers and other entities in the local business environment. All else being equal, strong linkages in the local environment create a deeper set of roots, a more distinctive set of activities, and a greater chance of survival in a downturn.

Again, while it is quite straightforward to identify the relevant factors, it is much harder to predict which will be critical in any particular plant closure decision. And with the exception of Boddewyn (1979, 1983) there is remarkably little research on this subject.

Cluster theory

Theories of industrial agglomeration date back one hundred years, but Porter's *Competitive Advantage of Nations* (1990) gave them a much-needed boost. Today, almost all inward investment agencies have embraced cluster theory, as a way of both identifying what they are good at, and also targeting the types of companies that they would like to attract. While I have nothing against cluster-based thinking at a conceptual level, the jury is still out as to whether it actually works. Despite enormous efforts on the parts of many inward investment agencies, there are few if any clusters that have been successfully cultivated. The true success stories typically emerge by chance or through a complete hands-off policy (for example, Hong Kong: Enright, 2000). Moreover, the majority of examples are what Michael Enright (2000) calls 'wishful thinking clusters' in which the various component industries are physically present, but the linkages between them are few and far between. The other concern I have about cluster approaches to inward investment is how homogeneous they are. Many inward investment agencies talk about their clusters in rather broad terms, to avoid upsetting any internal constituencies, and to not scare off potential investors. But the consequence of this approach is often the exact opposite – the investor company sees nothing distinctive in the country's positioning, so it goes elsewhere.

To be fair, these comments reflect my personal observations rather than any strong evidence. But this in itself is interesting, because it seems the entire world of inward investment agencies has bought into cluster-based approaches to investment attraction without stopping to evaluate whether it actually works. Again, this is a significant research opportunity.

Policy activity

Finally, there are a set of initiatives and programmes underway in most countries that have some bearing on inward investment. This includes aspects of the broader macro-economic environment, policies on education and development, and infrastructure programmes, all of which tend to be studied in more depth and probably better by economists than by international business researchers. But it also includes a range of specific initiatives that may have a more direct impact on investment. Project Alba in Scotland, for example, involved creating a degree programme and a physical site for a state-of-the-art R&D facility led by American firm, Cadence. And in Sweden targeted efforts have gone into changing the laws around the employment and taxation of highly-skilled foreign workers. Many countries have also worked on so-called aftercare programmes to help the existing stock of foreign-owned companies to upgrade their activities. Apart from one paper by Steve Young and Neil Hood (1994), this phenomenon has been largely untouched by academics.

Subsidiary agenda

The third part of the story is of course the role and agenda of the subsidiary manager. To a great extent, the subsidiary manager is simply responding to the set of pressures and constraints that are placed on him or her by the parent company and the host country. And yet, at the same time, my research and the work of a few others (for example, Delany, 1998) shows quite clearly that where one subsidiary manager sees an obstacle, another sees a challenge. The difference is not fundamentally the hand you have been dealt; it is the way you play your hand.

Subsidiary managers in the developed world are, to be clear, facing a tough time. As discussed earlier, most are having their degrees of freedom reduced, and some are losing their jobs altogether. In such cases, their agenda can be characterised as follows:

- *Making sense of the current degrees of freedom*: the level of operating autonomy, the presence of novel or distinct opportunities in the local market, the credibility and respect afforded to the subsidiary by decision-makers in head office.
- *Acting on those degrees of freedom*: this involves such things as achieving a high performance in the local market first to build credibility, building personal relationships with managers at head office, looking for small opportunities to add value, and then gradually building on a track record of success to carve out a unique role.
- *Balancing corporate and local roles*: subsidiary managers have always had to balance the local and the corporate responsibilities. But with increasing global integration of activities in the developed world, the nature of the balance is shifting. I recently discussed this point with the president of Diageo Australia. Despite being highly successful in Australia, he recognised that from the parent company's perspective that was not enough: he was also expected to find ways of helping the global business. For example, he had pushed a couple of his top team to take promotions in the UK and the USA, despite the fact that this would have a negative impact on the Australian business in the short term.

Theoretical issues

Finally, it is worth briefly reviewing the state of international business theory. As an applied and cross-disciplinary field, international business will always make progress by borrowing and adapting insights from other disciplines. During the late 1970s and early 1980s we borrowed extensively from the field of economics, and concepts of market failure, market power and asset specificity were played out to great effect in making sense of the scope and existence of the MNE. During the 1980s and early 1990s we borrowed from the worlds of strategy and organisation theory as a means of making sense of the internal management of the MNE, again with impressive results.

But as I consider the incremental value that is coming out of these theories today, my sense is that they have almost run their course. They are still valid, but I struggle to see how they will lead to any major new insights into the world of international business. It seems clear to me that new theoretical lenses are needed, but I have little insight into what they are, other to observe that they are likely to be brought across from cognate disciplines such as economics, sociology, or economic geography. For example, I think it would be really interesting to apply Porter's theory of competitive advantage to the world of inward investment, by looking at the structural forces shaping the market for investment and the generic strategies adopted by competing agencies: an obvious idea, perhaps, but one which might offer some new insights into the drivers of success in the world of investment attraction.

Conclusions

The 1990s was an important time to research foreign subsidiary companies and economic development. Foreign subsidiaries have in many cases become fully-fledged players in their corporate systems, and in others they have been swallowed up as part of an integrated European or North American operation. Inward investment has become vastly more competitive, with every country (barring a handful of obvious exceptions) seeking to get its share.

But at the same time, my suspicion is that the challenges are going to become more complex, not less. The issues raised above all point to changes in the nature of the MNE, and the way it relates to its host countries. And there are plenty of new experiments underway inside large MNEs that need to be investigated. On the theoretical side, the state of play is rather different because there is an urgent need for new ways of conceptualising and modelling the issues under investigation. While I have certainly not been able to pinpoint the way ahead, my hope in this brief article is that I have at least identified some broad directions in which the fields of subsidiary management and economic development might progress.

15
Living at the Academic–Practitioner Interface*
Neil Hood

Introduction

My colleagues have invited me to write this chapter in the interests of completeness. I agreed to do so, on the premise that the collection of academic papers contained within the rest of the book necessarily gives a partial glimpse of my writings; and only part of the total career story. Since I cannot deny the truth of this, this chapter is included. But first the context needs to be sketched out. I have always been interested in applying economics and business knowledge – both in the business and public spheres. The pursuit of that policy and implementation interest has been evident in three different but related dimensions, each of which is briefly commented on within this chapter.

First, throughout my academic career, the 'so what?' question has never been far from my mind – both in designing and undertaking research; and in extrapolating from its conclusions. As a result I have been involved in many policy-oriented projects, in particular those relating to economic development and inward investment. For me this has long been one of the important border territories where the public and the private realms of an economy come together. It has proved both a fascinating and contentious area at times.

Secondly, and not content with writing about public policy, I have on several occasions stepped out of academic life to work for government or its agencies; in addition to advising many governments and international agencies on such matters while practising as an academic. These experiences have still not managed to exorcise my fundamental

---

* Written for this volume.

interest in helping to both develop and implement policy in the public arena – in spite of its occasional frustrations.

Then there is the third side of this triangle – namely my direct involvement in business. In fact this pre-dates the other two in that, as a school leaver and before my entrance to University, I was employed in the steel industry. That gave me a taste for business. My post-graduate work on the textile industry was an early opportunity to extend this. So, with the exception of the periods when I was within government service, I have always worked with business either as an adviser to, or as a director of, companies in a wide range of sectors. For example, at various times I have been a director of eight public companies. The entry point has invariably been my work in the strategic development of these businesses – many of which have had international reach. While others at times struggle to see the linkages between these three aspects of my career, I never have. For me the links lie in the common problems of strategy development, policy and practice that surround them. In the context of this book, however, it is the first of these areas that receives most attention in this chapter.

Contributing to policy debates

When Stephen Young and I started to work together in 1973, we quickly discovered that we had complementary sets of skills and backgrounds. Our principal academic interests were respectively international economics and business economics/strategy. They blended well together in our joint curiosity about the growth and development of multinational enterprises and their impact on economic development. As it happened, by living in Scotland we were already in a laboratory with several hundred such specimens to examine. Scottish economic development strategy had been specifically targeted to the attraction of such enterprises in order to offset the decline of traditional industry and aid in the diversification of the economy. This policy had dated from the late 1930s, and had gathered momentum in the two decades before we started our long period of fruitful collaborative research that has spanned some thirty years. One interesting feature of our joint research was its rapid geographical progression from Scotland, to the rest of UK, to the European Union, and then to global dimensions of this phenomenon. This occurred over about the first decade of our collaboration and is evident in the projects and publications mentioned later in this section. While the multinational enterprise has been a dominant focus for my academic writings, it is only one of three broad strands of activity set out in the paragraphs that follow.

The multinational enterprise and economic development

It was with this issue that my academic research really gathered momentum. There were obviously all kinds of public policy issues that flowed from the international expansion of major corporations. At that time many of these were under-researched, and it was an evident gap waiting to be filled. Before moving to the sequence of empirical research on this subject that flowed from our joint efforts, one important early project should be mentioned. While both studying the phenomenon of the multinational enterprise for research purposes, and to enable us to teach students about it, we became aware of the need for a good basic economics textbook. So for the first, and to date only, time we wrote one.[1] Our aim was to develop the analytical tools to enable this topic to be better understood. The book pulled together much of the existing economic literature on the multinational enterprise, and tried to do this in a systematic and accessible way. It was very well received, and was widely used in many leading universities. Looking back on it now, it was to prove very important in establishing our credentials in the academic community both nationally and internationally. It also laid the foundation for many of the projects that are discussed in this section.

One of our earliest joint research studies was by far the most local, and was inspired by the announced closure of the Chrysler car plant in Linwood in Autumn 1975. At the time we were working a few miles away in Paisley. The closure was a major UK industrial incident at the time and raised important questions relating to government industrial policy and corporate strategy; the behaviour and bargaining power of multinational companies; the future of the UK automobile industry and so on. At an early stage in this work we were given a stern warning by a senior Chrysler executive that our project might damage the company, and that it would be better if we abandoned it.

In fact, when the objectivity with which we were viewing the case was evident, we were subsequently given quite a lot of assistance from that quarter. The net effect was an in-depth look at this case in all its many dimensions, within both its corporate and industrial context.[2] In many ways this set a pattern for our approach to studying the multi-national; and for our public advocacy of broadly based analysis of the strategies of multinational companies as an essential pre-condition for formulating governmental policies towards them at both local and national level. A further manifestation of this methodology lay in the first substantial government project that we undertook for the Scottish Office from 1977 to 1979. It involved an evaluation – through discussions at both UK subsidiary and US corporate level – of the European development strategies of a number of US multinationals with Scottish locations.[3] It was the first study of its type and generated a great deal of policy interest. Meanwhile in our surrounding business community, there was ample evidence of mature US companies adjusting their strategies towards European markets. This was an ill-understood period of radical corporate change – at least on the part of policy makers. In fact, the book we wrote about it was the result of a direct challenge from a senior civil servant that such analysis was impossible; and that there were no patterns or trends to anticipate. We clearly demonstrated that this was not the case; to the astonishment of a number of the companies concerned (Singer, Chrysler, Hoover, NCR, Honeywell and Goodyear) some of whom later told us that they used the book as evidence of how they were perceived by balanced academic commentators on their affairs.[4]

This initial policy work started from the corporate side and worked from there to the public policy consequences. But we were writing on another related issue that was of critical UK importance – namely on the best ways to organise government and its agencies for the attraction of inward investment. In the late 1970s this was a minority interest even within the UK, a situation that seems incredible from the perspective of the early twenty-first century. At that time Scotland and Ireland were head to head competitors for many US investment projects designed to serve European markets. Other UK regions had some interest, but little co-ordination and few resources; and most of the European Community members were at that time not very proactive in this field. Our first critical intervention was in 1980, after a period when I had been in government service as an economic adviser. At the time there was Parliamentary interest on whether the UK should adopt a centralised or decentralised form of investment attraction; in its operations and general effectiveness – especially against fierce competition from Ireland. This coincided with the extensive empirical work we had been doing in this area, as well as our practical experience of working within government in different capacities. It placed us in a unique position to comment and, as it turned out, to influence the shape of Scottish inward investment structures for the following two decades.[5] This was most encouraging, and achieved rather more than we had expected. One consequence was the establishment of Locate In Scotland, a fully integrated investment attraction organisation that operated to great effect for many years thereafter. It became a model that many others throughout the world attempted to copy. Little did I know at that time that in later years I was to become its Chief Executive.

By this stage, our interest in British foreign investment policy was developing. This found expression both in empirical studies of multinational strategies and in academic papers offering policy advice. Two parts of this are perhaps worth noting. The first was a project on the dynamics of multinational strategy as it applied to the UK and Ireland. Sponsored by the UK Department of Trade and Industry, and made possible by the extensive co-operation of multinational companies, this project was not popular with the Irish government. They both raised the matter with the European Commission and advised companies located in Ireland not to contribute. However the study was successfully completed and shed considerable light on the likely impact of corporate change in these countries at the time.[6] At that time there was relatively little empirical or policy research on foreign direct investment in the UK. We attempted to stimulate debate on the subject in several ways. In one paper, we suggested a radical reappraisal of the whole UK approach and set out in considerable detail the required elements of such a policy. This included the establishment of a foreign investment promotion agency; and the extension of UK activity from attraction into aftercare, monitoring and so on.[7] In another, we attempted to make an overall assessment of the impact of inward investment on the UK economy and assess the policy implications.[8] Such contributions were not always welcomed. I distinctly recall a very senior Whitehall mandarin of the time advising me that it would be most helpful if academics such as me would continue to analyse this phenomenon, but leave the policy side to 'those who knew about such things – since these types of papers just cause problems within Departments'. Neither Stephen nor I have ever paid much attention to such remarks. In fact, we always regarded it as indicative that our advice might be along the right lines! Indeed to fuel such fires, then and long after, we regularly produced policy working papers for wide circulation around the relevant departments and agencies that we were trying to inform, rather than hold them back during the long gestation process of academic publication.

There were many other manifestations of this multinational policy interest in the 1980s, in projects that led to books, articles, commissioned reports, papers at invited conferences and the inevitable radio and television appearances. By this stage, several projects were at the global scale – two of which were particularly important. The first was a large international study undertaken with many collaborators for the World Bank. It concerned the controversial area of the relationship between investment incentives and performance requirements as governments throughout the world sought to both attract multinational companies yet also monitor their behaviour. This was a multi-industry project co-ordinated by the late Steve Guisinger of the University of Texas; and Steve Young and I were invited to examine the world car industry. This was both challenging and rewarding, and it involved much travel and large measures of diplomacy as we scoured the world for appropriate cases. Many of them came with high political visibility and no small sensitivity on the part of companies such as Volvo, Toyota and others. In consequence, there were many restrictions on what we could actually publish from this project, and several stories that we are not able to tell.[9] The second of these major policy exercises was a global study of the textile industry undertaken for the United Nations Centre for Transnational Corporations under the guidance of, and with considerable help from, Hans Frederick Samuelson. The scale of this exercise was frightening and again there were many sensitive issues in this sector. As a result publication of the report was delayed for several years.[10] There was a break in my policy writing from early 1987 to late 1990 simply because I crossed the divide from writing to implementation. The invitation to take on the very public role of leading the Scottish inward investment agency was irresistible, given my background and personality. Going from being Dean of a Business School to this new role was challenging, but great fun. It took me into direct negotiations with major multinational companies in many parts of the world, and my passport was rarely out of my pocket. But the previous dozen or so years of academic and policy work in the field was invaluable in this post – even then, the learning curve was a steep one.

Returning to academic life on a part-time basis in 1990 gave further scope for policy work. Not all of it was about foreign investment, but that theme was consistently evident in a number of ways. In an investment climate that was increasingly competitive and where foreign investment attraction was much more central to government industrial policy throughout Europe and beyond, we became very interested in the effectiveness of investment agencies. This was also influenced at that time by my recent experience as a practitioner. While our particular focus was on the effective targeting of investment and on aftercare, we tried to set it in a broader context. For example we were advocates of a European Community policy towards foreign investment because of the effect multinational companies had on integration, and in recognition of a need for greater inter-governmental co-operation in a form of 'competitive jousting' for investments.[11] On the more specific question of the strategy of governments we recognised that a meaningful, long-term foreign investment policy not only consisted of the attraction of investment but in its development. This was closely linked to our interest in multinational subsidiary development. This subject of aftercare did interest policy makers in many parts of the world and few academics had written about it. A number of agencies have tried to implement the very practical path that we explored.[12] Similarly, the matter of targeting had great policy appeal – not least because of resource constraints and the search for value for money. Here we applied the techniques used in industrial products' marketing in a methodology to relate the desired outputs of investment attraction policies with the competitive advantages of such countries.[13] In addition to writing about these issues, they were the subject of many discussions, seminars and training sessions with public officials throughout the world over these years.

The globalisation of business

The latest stage of this policy work relating to international business has had a stronger corporate element, influenced in part by the fact that business has occupied a large part of my working life since 1990. There are several evidences of this. The first group of projects has a strong Swedish connection. Related to a long personal association with the Institute of International Business at the Stockholm School of Economics was international collaborative research on sectoral and business strategies as a result of globalisation. One particular output of that flowed from a project designed to commemorate the 75th anniversary of that School. Involving many international scholars, it examined the emergence of global competition at a time when research on this was in its infancy.[14] Gary Hamel, C. K. Prahalad, Yves Doz, Bruce Kogut, and John Dunning were among the many contributors. More specifically, arising from my collaboration with Julian Birkinshaw while at Stockholm (and later at London Business School) has been our extended programme of research on multinational subsidiaries. It started while Julian was in the University of Western Ontario, and several of the papers in the other Chapters are the outcome of this highly productive relationship. Extending and developing our international academic networks, we commissioned a series of papers on subsidiary development with a strong policy flavour. This had three main themes, namely the links between corporate strategy and subsidiary development; the concept of centres of excellence within multinational networks; and the study of the corporate process that underlay subsidiary development. As always we tried to draw conclusions for corporations, host governments and subsidiary managers.[15]

Under this generic theme, I have been involved in several projects linking global corporate activity to the economic development of countries. This is an extension to our early work in the late 1970s but in a rather different international environment. For example, the opening up of the economies in Eastern and Central Europe in the early 1990s heralded a major shift in the centre of gravity of the EU; as well as changing the nature of competition for cross-border investment within Europe. This became one of the focal interests of my writing, linked to advisory work for the World Bank and others in that region.[16] During this period I was somewhat sidetracked into a deeper involvement in the economic and social development in the Baltic States – although my original connection to that region was foreign investment. Almost by accident, I thus ended up pulling together a volume (largely written by Baltic scholars from around the world) that was the first academic business book produced in that region since the transition – a small piece of history in that complex part of the world; and a labour of love![17] However, subsequent work under this heading was closer to my core interest and less about countries than about companies and sectors. The output from these projects has appeared in different publications. Among these was work on knowledge industries in this new environment.[18] But it is particularly exemplified by a major invited conference that we held in Glasgow in 1998. Helped by substantial business and public sponsorship, we invited a group of scholars from Europe, the Americas and the Far East to present a range of papers on agreed topics relating to the overall theme of the globalisation of multinational enterprise activity and economic development. John Dunning, Julian Birkinshaw, Steve Kobrin and Tom Brewer were among those involved.[19] In addition to looking at the issues and theory, a range of papers taking corporate, country and policy perspectives were included. By 2000 we were again engaged with several others in an extensive empirical benchmark study on the impact of foreign investment in Scotland. This was commissioned at a time when, once again, global changes in business were posing new questions about the optimal location of the various elements of the value chain, especially in economies with a high level of foreign investment dependence. It was possible to determine some paths of change and proffer guidance to policy makers. Some of this work was highly sensitive and publication has been limited.[20]

The economic development of Scotland and the UK

In the light of the above, it will be already evident that I have had a continuing interest in economic development for over thirty years.

Not all of it, however, has been related to the activities of multinational companies, or confined to the phenomenon of foreign direct investment. Although no longer a fashionable concept in some quarters, it could best be described as the study of industrial policy. Since Stephen Young shares this interest, we have often undertaken projects together. The longest running of these was a series on industrial policy in Scotland that was launched in 1982. As mentioned above, it looked at the retrenchment of mature multinational subsidiaries. It was followed in 1984 by a much broader policy study about the Scottish economy.[21] A range of public and private sponsors supported this research and we collected a planned series of essays about various sectors of the economy for this volume. As is our style, we arranged a public conference to debate our findings and encourage policy makers to take them on board. Over the subsequent years we were asked on many occasions to repeat this exercise in the light of the changed economic and business environment; and with globalisation in mind. We finally did this, backed by some of the same sponsors, produced a very different book, and held a further conference in 2002.[22] The original Edinburgh series had several different themes (including takeovers and urban policy), and were written by others, most of whom had a University of Strathclyde connection. In one, concerning the Scottish financial sector, I had a very direct involvement as one of the research team. It was a very difficult project to undertake, but received a high level of industry support. It drew some very controversial conclusions on the strategies of some of the major players that were not well received by this fairly conservative sector – but most of the predictions in it have proved to be rather accurate.[23] As will be clear later in this chapter, my other connection with Scottish economic affairs has been both in different forms of government service while designing and implementing policy; as well as in the world of business.

Stemming from this type of research on the Scottish economy, and being known for it within the academic international business community, Steve Young and I over the years have been asked to write several pieces on UK policy for international invited conferences. These have, for example, been as parts of comparative country studies on industrial policy;[24] within studies where the USA was attempting to learn from its competitor nations;[25] or in settings where the focus was on country-specific reaction to global business change.[26] In all these examples, there was a strong international business dimension to our contributions.

Government service

There have been three periods of government service woven into my career to date. They are perhaps best understood as a response to my inherent discontent with being solely a commentator in areas where I felt I could make contribution closer to the point of decision. They have all been in Scotland, and all connected with economic development. The first was in 1979 when I was seconded to the Scottish Economic Planning Department as an Economic Adviser based in Edinburgh. I was invited to join by Bill McNie and Gavin McCrone – then Chief Economic Adviser to the Scottish Office. This gave me my first taste of the inside of government. My work was on regional and industrial policy, and it included monitoring the plans of various government agencies. While I was in that post, I was appointed as a Professor at the Strathclyde Business School in the University of Strathclyde. The second period in government work was in 1987 when I was invited by George Mathewson (then Chief Executive of the Scottish Development Agency (SDA) and now Chairman of the Royal Bank of Scotland) to consider becoming the Director of Locate In Scotland. This challenge was irresistible, given my background and interests. At the time I was Dean of the Business School at Strathclyde, and I recall several colleagues being bemused as to why I would want to take on such an accountable and high profile job; or indeed why I would want to resign all my business interests to do this. The role was both rewarding and frustrating; but the successes and failures were immediately evident. Moreover I was privileged to work with some excellent and highly committed colleagues and together we achieved a great deal. After two years in this role, my plans to return to a mix of academic life and business life were diverted.

In October 1998, the government announced plans to merge the SDA with the Training Agency, thus creating a new integrated body encompassing both economic development and training. The logic of this commanded quite widespread agreement; but there was much debate on how it was to be done. There was a new philosophy behind it, and some considerable uncertainty internally and externally as to how the best of the old could be brought together with the new.[27] Sir David Nickson, then Chairman of SDA, persuaded me to take on the task of managing this merger. I did this as Director of Employment and Special Initiatives for a period of eighteen months. This was a complex task, but one that I enjoyed. It taught me a great deal about change management, the workings of government and, above all, about giving leadership to anxious staff in an extended period of great uncertainty. Because of consultation, Parliamentary process and implementation it took, the new organisation – Scottish Enterprise (SE) – was not formally launched until April 1991. Hardly an ideal way to manage anything! By mid-1990, having been on secondment from my University post for three-and-a-half years, my Vice-Chancellor, Sir Graham Hills, persuaded me to take a part-time contract with the University. I returned on that basis in September 1990.

Throughout the 1990s I continued to advise and undertake projects for SE in various guises; as well as taking an active role in their venture capital arm, as a Director of Scottish Development Finance. This gave me a very practical interest in public venture capital, which inevitably led me to write about some of the policy aspects of it.[28] This very successful activity was privatised in mid-1999, and I subsequently became Chairman of the new private entity, Scottish Equity Partners Limited, as it continued to specialise in early stage investment in technology businesses. My next formal association with SE was non-executive. It came with my appointment as Deputy Chairman from January 2000, and constituted my third period of active involvement in government service. Sir Ian Robinson, the former Chief Executive of Scottish Power plc, with whom I had worked as an adviser for the previous six years, was appointed Chairman at the same time. Together with Dr Robert Crawford (a former senior colleague in my LIS days) as Chief Executive, we have worked closely as a team in the early years of this century.

Business life

I will touch only very briefly on this aspect of my career to date. Apart from my two periods as an executive in government service, I have always been involved with business to some degree. There are two broad phases; pre-and post-1990. Pre-1990, my main career was academic, largely in business school environments. During that period, my personal work with business was mainly advisory, but on occasion I became a director of a number of smaller companies. These were initially in the textile industry because of my graduate work in that area. For example, I advised Dawson International for three years in the early 1970s at a time of the integration of their extensive knitwear interests. I also worked for a holding company with diverse activities in many sectors, at the same time as I was doing academic work on holding companies as a form of business organisation. The connecting theme in all of this was strategy and business development. By the end of the 1980s, I had applied this to companies in the advertising, textiles, food processing, electronics and engineering sectors.

Post-1990, while holding a part-time academic post, I was much more available to work in business. From that period onwards, my involvement has mainly – but not exclusively – been with both larger companies and with companies that are publicly listed. As has been my habit, whether advising, or as a director, I have tended to work over quite an extended period with some of these businesses. Applying this principle, for example, I have advised Scottish Power plc, Babtie Group Limited and Motherwell Bridge Holdings Limited over a number of years. Non-executive appointments in public companies over this period have included Xansa plc, British Polythene Industries plc, Kwik-Fit Holdings plc and several others. In the latter context this also led me to hold an advisory post with the Ford Motor Company, working with their diversified Consumer Services Division. There are many occasions where there is a direct interface between my academic work on subsidiaries and the operations of these businesses. Many of them have international operations, and therefore both operate subsidiary networks and are the target of foreign investment attraction agencies. However, as a matter of strict policy I have never written about the company-specifics of my business experience; although I have regularly shared experiences with graduate students. In this area, Chinese walls are very important. Having said that, I would like to write more about business ethics and have on occasion done so, related to multinational companies.[29]

I have long been convinced of the need for academics in the business area to practice in business if they have the opportunity so to do. For me, it has always helped to root my research, given that it has been so business-focused. It also presents a constant challenge when it comes to translating its relevance to real situations. But I acknowledge that my path is not for everyone, and I respect academics who take a different view. However, I have more trouble with those who feel that it is not their role to push their research to its policy conclusions!

Conclusions

In concluding, I encourage the reader to regard this chapter not as a career resume – but rather as helping to set the context for the rest of the book. There have been strong linking themes in much of my research – and I have both chosen, and had the opportunity, to apply and test my academic work in various spheres of practice. This has been a great privilege, and I am most grateful for it. Perhaps above all, my research has benefited enormously from collaborative relationships of the highest calibre. While I have worked with many others, there are two that stand out. It has been, and remains, a great pleasure to work with Stephen Young. Steve is both a friend and excellent professional colleague. In many ways, our skills are as complementary today as they were when we started – even though we have had very different career paths. In more recent years, Julian Birkinshaw has also been an outstanding collaborator, and again the personal chemistry and balance of skills has been good for both of us. To them and to the many others with whom I have researched and published over the years, I offer my profound gratitude for the stimulus and fellowship of enquiry.

Notes

1. Hood and Young (1979).
2. Young and Hood (1977).
3. Hood and Young (1980a).
4. Hood and Young (1982).
5. Hood (1980); Hood and Young (1980b).
6. Hood and Young (1983a).
7. Hood and Young (1981).
8. Young, Hood and Hamill (1988).
9. Hood and Young (1985).
10. Hood and Young (1987).
11. Young and Hood (1993).
12. Young and Hood (1994).
13. Young, Hood and Wilson (1994).
14. Hood and Vahlne (1988).
15. Hood and Birkinshaw (1998).
16. Hood and Young (1994).
17. Hood, Kilis and Vahlne (1997).
18. Peters, Hood and Young (2000).
19. Hood and Young (2000).
20. Young, Hood and Firn (2002).
21. Hood and Young (1984a).
22. Hood *et al.* (2002).
23. Draper *et al.* (1988).
24. Hood and Young (1983b).
25. Hood and Young (1984b).
26. Hood and Young (1997).
27. On ending my secondment, I subsequently wrote about these issues at some length (see Hood, 1991a, 1991b).
28. Hood (2000).
29. Hood (1998).

Bibliography

Chapter 1

Andersson, U. (1997), *Subsidiary Network Embeddedness*, Published Thesis, 66, Department of Business Studies, Uppsala University.

Aydalot, P. (1986), *Milieux Innovateurs en Europe*, Paris: GREMI.

Barney, J. B. (1991), 'Firm Resources and Sustained Competitive Advantage', *Journal of Management*, 17, 99–120.

Bartlett, C. A. and Ghoshal, S. (1989), *Managing Across Borders: The Transnational Solution*, Cambridge, MA: Harvard Business School Press.

Birkinshaw, J. (2000), *Entrepreneurship in the Global Firm*, London: Sage.

Birkinshaw, J. (2001), 'Strategy and Management in MNE Subsidiaries', in A. M. Rugman and T. Brewer (eds), *The Oxford Handbook of International Business*, Oxford: Oxford University Press, 380–401.

Birkinshaw, J. and Hood, N. (1997), 'An Empirical Study of Development Processes in Foreign-Owned Subsidiaries in Canada and Scotland', *Management International Review*, 37 (4), 339–64.

Birkinshaw, J. and Hood, N. (1998), 'Multinational Subsidiary Evolution: Capability and Charter Change in Foreign-Owned Subsidiary Companies', *Strategic Management Journal*, 23 (4), 773–95.

Birkinshaw, J. and Hood, N. (2000), 'Characteristics of Foreign Subsidiaries in Industry Clusters', *Journal of International Business Studies*, 19 (3), 221–41.

Birkinshaw, J. and Hood, N. (2001), 'Unleash Innovation in Foreign Subsidiaries', *Harvard Business Review*, March, 131–7.

Birkinshaw, J., Hood, N. and Jonsson, S. (1998), 'Building Firm-Specific Advantages in Multinational Corporations: The Role of Subsidiary Initiative', *Strategic Management Journal*, 31, 141–54.

Blomström, M. and Kokko, A. (1997), 'Regional Integration and Foreign Direct Investment: A Conceptual Framework and Three Cases', *World Bank Policy Research Working Paper*, 1750, Washington, DC: World Bank.

Cairncross, F. (1997), *The Death of Distance*, Cambridge, MA: Harvard Business School Press.

Cantwell, J. A. (1988), 'The Reorganization of European Industries After Integration: Selected Evidence on the Role of Multinational Enterprise Activities', in J. H. Dunning and P. Robson (eds), *Multinationals and the European Community*, Oxford: Basil Blackwell, 25–49.

Cantwell, J. A. (2001), 'Innovation and Information Technology in MNE', in A. M. Rugman and T. L. Brewer (eds), *Oxford Handbook of International Business*, Oxford: Oxford University Press, 431–56.

Chakravarthy, B. S. and Perlmutter, H. V. (1985), 'Strategic Planning for a Global Business', *Columbia Journal of World Business*, 20, 3–10.

Clegg, L. J. and Scott-Green, S. (2000), 'The Determinants of New Foreign Direct Investment Capital Flows into Europe: the US and Japan Compared', in C. J. M. Millar, R. Grant and C. Choi (eds), *International Business: Emerging Issues and Emerging Markets*, London: Macmillan, 159–75.

Crone, M. and Roper, S. (1999), *Local Learning from Multinational Plants: Knowledge Transfers in the Supply Chain*, Belfast: Northern Ireland Research Centre.

Crookell, H. (1987), 'Managing Canadian Subsidiaries in a Free Trade Environment', *Sloan Management Review*, 29 (1), 71–6.

Doz, Y., Santos, J. and Williamson, P. (2001), *From Global to Metanational: How Companies Win in the Knowledge Economy*, Cambridge, MA: Harvard Business School Press.

Dunning, J. H. (1958), *American Investment in British Manufacturing Industry*, London: Allen & Unwin.

Dunning, J. H. (1997), *Alliance Capitalism and Global Business*, London: Routledge.

Dunning, J. H. (2000), 'The Impact of the Completion of the Internal European Internal Market on FDI', in J. H. Dunning (ed.), *Regions, Globalization and the Knowledge-Based Economy*, Oxford: Oxford University Press, 131–69.

Dunning, J. H. and Robson, P. (eds) (1988), *Multinationals and the European Community*, Oxford: Basil Blackwell.

Enright, M. J. (2001), *An Overview of Regional Clusters and Clustering*, Presentation to the TCI Annual Conference, Tuscon, Arizona.

Firn, J. (1975), 'External Control and Regional Policy', in G. Brown (ed.), *The Red Paper on Scotland*, Edinburgh: EUSPB, 153–69.

Firn Crichton Roberts Limited and University of Strathclyde (2001), *Inward Investment Benefits to the Scottish Economy*, Glasgow: Scottish Enterprise and the Scottish Executive, unpublished report.

Forsyth, D. J. (1972), *US Investment in Scotland*, New York: Praeger.

Gupta, A. K. and Govindarajan, V. (1991), 'Knowledge Flows and the Structure of Control within Multinational Corporations', *Academy of Management Review*, 16, 768–92.

Gupta, A. K. and Govindarajan, V. (2000), 'Knowledge Flows within Multinational Corporations', *Strategic Management Journal*, 21, 473–96.

Harzing, A-W. K. (1999), *Managing the Multinationals: An International Study of Control Mechanisms*, Northampton, MA: Edward Elgar.

Hedlund, G. (1986), 'The Hypermodern MNC-A Heterarchy?', *Human Resource Management*, 25, 9–25.

Hood, N. and Peters, E. (2000a), 'Globalization, Corporate Strategies and Business Services', in *The Globalization of Multinational Enterprise Activity and Economic Development*, London: Macmillan, 80–105.

Hood, N. and Peters, E. (2000b), 'Implementing the Cluster Approach: Some Lessons from the Scottish Experience', *International Studies of Management and Organization*, 30 (2), 68–92.

Hood, N., Reeves, A. and Young, S. (1981), 'Foreign Direct Investment in Scotland: The European Dimension', *Scottish Journal of Political Economy*, 28 (2), 165–85.

Hood, N. and Taggart, J. H. (1999), 'Subsidiary Development in German and Japanese Subsidiaries in the British Isles', *Regional Studies*, 33 (6), 513–28.

Jarillo, J. C. and Martinez, J. I. (1990), 'Different Roles for Subsidiaries: The Case of Multinational Corporations', *Strategic Management Journal*, 11, 501–12.

Malliat, D. (1995), 'Territorial Dynamic, Innovative Milieu and Regional Policy', *Entrepreneurship and Regional Development*, 7, 157–65.

Malmberg, A., Solvell, O. and Zander, I. (1996), 'Spatial Clustering, Local Accumulation of Knowledge and Firm Competitiveness', *Geografiska Annaler*, 78B (2), 85–97.

O'Donnell, S. W. (2000), 'Managing Foreign Subsidiaries: Agents of Headquarters, or an Interdependent Network?', *Strategic Management Journal*, 21, 525–48.

Paterson, S. L. and Brock, D. M. (2002), 'The Development of Subsidiary–Management Research: Review and Theoretical Analysis', *International Business Review*, 11, 139–63.

Pearce, R. D. (1999), 'The Evolution of Technology in Multinational Enterprises: The Roles of Creative Subsidiaries', *International Business Review*, 8 (2), 125–48.

Pearce, R. D. and Papanastassiou, M. (1997), 'European Markets and the Strategic Roles of Multinational Enterprise Subsidiaries in the UK', *Journal of Common Market Studies*, 35 (2), 243–66.

Pelkmans, J. (1984), *Market Integration in the European Community*, The Hague: Martinus Nijhoff.

Perlmutter, H. V. (1969), 'The Tortuous Evolution of the Multinational Corporation', *Columbia Journal of World Business*, 4, 9–18.

Porter, M. E. (1986), 'Competition in Global Industries: A Conceptual Framework', in M. E. Porter (ed.), *Competition in Global Industries*, Cambridge, MA: Harvard Business School Press, 15–60.

Porter, M. E. (1990), *The Competitive Advantage of Nations*, London: Macmillan.

Ronstadt, R. (1977), *Research and Development Abroad by US Multinationals*, Praeger: New York.

Rugman, A. M. (2000), *The End of Globalization*, London: Random House.

Rugman, A. M. and Verbeke, A. (2001), 'Subsidiary-Specific Advantages in Multinational Enterprises', *Strategic Management Journal*, 22, 237–50.

Sölvell, Ö. and Birkinshaw, J. (2000), 'Multinational Enterprise and the Knowledge Economy: Leveraging Global Practices', in J. H. Dunning (ed.), *Regions, Globalization and the Knowledge-Based Economy*, Oxford: Oxford University Press, 82–105.

Steuer, M. D. *et al.* (1973), *The Impact of Foreign Direct Investment on the United Kingdom*, London: HMSO.

Stopford, J. and Wells, L. T. (1972), *Managing the Multinational Enterprise*, New York: Basic Books.

Taggart, J. H. (1997), 'Autonomy and Procedural Justice: A Framework for Evaluating Subsidiary Strategy', *Journal of International Business Studies*, 8, 233–55.

Tallman, S. B. and Yip, G. S. (2001), 'Strategy and the Multinational Enterprise', in A. M. Rugman and T. L. Brewer (eds), *The Oxford Handbook of International Business*, 317–48.

Tavares, A. T. (2001), *Systems, Evolution and Integration. Modelling the Impact of Economic Integration on Multinationals' Strategies*, Unpublished PhD dissertation, Department of Economics, University of Reading.

Teece, D. J., Pisano, G. P. and Shuen, A. (1997), 'Dynamic Capabilities and Strategic Management', *Strategic Management Journal*, 18 (7), 509–33.

White, R. and Poynter, T. (1984), 'Strategies for Foreign-Owned Subsidiaries in Canada', *Business Quarterly*, Summer, 59–69.

Young, S. (2000), 'The Multinational Corporation: The Managerial Challenges of Globalization and Localization', in J. Legewie and H. Meyer-Ohle (eds), *Corporate Strategies for Southeast Asia After the Crisis*, Basingstoke, Hants: Palgrave, 2–24.

Young, S., Hood, N. and Hamill, J. (1988), *Foreign Multinationals and the British Economy*, Beckenham: Croom Helm.

Young, S., Hood, N. and Peters, E. (1994), 'Multinational Enterprises and Regional Economic Development', *Regional Studies*, 28 (7), 657–77.

Chapter 2

American Chamber of Commerce (1971), *Anglo-Trade News*, July.

Arrow, K. (1962), 'The Economic Implications of Learning by Doing', *Review of Economic Studies*, 29 (80), 155–73.

Dunning, J. H. (1972), 'Technology, United States Investment and European Economic Growth', in J. H. Dunning (ed.), *International Investment*, London: Penguin Books, 374–411.

Dunning, J. H. (1974), 'The Distinctive Nature of the Multinational Enterprise', in J. H. Dunning (ed.), *Economic Analysis and the Multinational Enterprise*, London: Allen & Unwin, 13–30.

Firn, J. (1975), 'External Control and Regional Policy', in G. Brown (ed.), *The Red Paper on Scotland*, Edinburgh: EUSPB, 153–69.

Forsyth, D. J. C. (1972), *US Investment in Scotland*, New York: Praeger.

Gray Report, Government of Canada (1972), *Foreign Direct Investment in Canada*, Ottawa: Information Canada.

Hollander, S. (1965), *The Sources of Increased Efficiency*, Cambridge, MA: MIT Press.

Mansfield, E. (1974), 'Technology and Technological Change', in J. H. Dunning (ed.), *Economic Analysis and the Multinational Enterprise*, London: Allen & Unwin, 147–83.

Steuer, M. D. *et al.* (1973), *The Impact of Foreign Direct Investment on the United Kingdom*, London: HMSO.

Streeten, P. (1974), 'The Theory of Development Policy', in J. H. Dunning (ed.), *Economic Analysis and the Multinational Enterprise*, London: Allen & Unwin, 252–79.

Young, S. and Hood, N. (1976a), 'Perspectives on the European Marketing Strategy of US Multinationals', *European Journal of Marketing*, 10 (4), 240–56.

Young, S. and Hood, N. (1976b), 'The Geographical Expansion of US Firms in Western Europe: Some Survey Evidence', *Journal of Common Market Studies*, 14 (3), 223–39.

Chapter 3

Behrman, J. N. and Fischer W. A. (1980), *Overseas R&D Activities of Transnational Companies*, Cambridge, MA: Oelgeschlager, Gunn & Hain.

Business Statistics Office ('various issues'), *Business Monitor* series, MO14 and PA1002, London: CSO.

Cordell, A. J. (1971), 'The Multinational Firm, Foreign Direct Investment and Canadian Science Policy', *Background Study*, 22, Ottowa: Science Council of Canada, Information Canada.

Cordell, A. J. (1973), 'Innovation, the Multinational Corporation: Some Implications for National Science Policy', *Long Range Planning*, 6, 22–9.

Creamer, D. (1976), *Overseas Research and Development by US Multinationals, 1966–75: Estimates of Expenditures and a Statistical Profile*, New York: The Conference Board.

Dunning, J. H. (1976), *United States Industry in Britain*. London: Wilton House.

Grabowski, H. G. and Baxter, N. D. (1973), 'Rivalry in Industrial Research and Development: An Empirical Study', *Journal of Industrial Economics*, 21, 209–35.

Graham, E. M. (1978), 'Transatlantic Investment by Multinational Firms: A Rivalistic Phenomenon', *Journal of Post Keynesian Economics*, 1, 82–99.

Hewitt, G. (1980), 'Research and Development Abroad Performed by US Manufacturing Multinationals', *Kyklos*, 33, 308–27.

Hirschey, R. C. and Caves, R. E. (1981), 'Research and Technology Transfer by Multinational Enterprises', *Oxford Bulletin of Economics and Statistics*, 43, 115–30.

Hood, N. and Young, S. (1980), *European Development Strategies of US Owned Manufacturing Companies Located in Scotland*, Edinburgh: HMSO.

Hood, N. and Young, S. (1981), *The R&D Activities of US Multinational Enterprises: A Review of the Literature*, Report to the Department of Industry, June.

Hood, N. and Young, S. (1982), *Multinationals in Retreat: The Scottish Experience*, Edinburgh: Edinburgh University Press.

Lall, S. (1979), 'The International Allocation of Research Activity by US Multinationals, *Oxford Bulletin of Economics and Statistics*, 41, 313–31.

Malecki, E. J. (1980), 'Corporate Organisation of R&D and the Location of Technological Activities', *Regional Studies*, 14, 219–34.

Mansfield, E. (1978), *Studies of the Relationship Between International Technology Transfer and R&D Expenditures by US Firms*, Final Report to the National Science Foundation, Washington, DC.

Mansfield, E., Teece, D. and Romeo, A. (1979), 'Overseas Research and Development by US-Based Firms', *Economica* 46, 187–96.

McDermott, P. (1979), 'Multinational Manufacturing Firms and Regional Development: External Control in the Scottish Electronics Industry', *Scottish Journal of Political Economy*, 26, 287–306.

National Science Foundation (1979), *Reviews of Data on Science Resources*, NSF 79–304, No. 33, Washington, DC.

National Science Foundation (1982), *Research and Development in Industry*, 1980, NSF 82–317, Washington, DC.

Ronstadt, R. (1977), *Research and Development Abroad by US Multinationals*, New York: Praeger.

Ronstadt, R. (1978), 'International R&D: The Establishment and Evolution of Research and Development by Seven US Multi-Nationals', *Journal of International Business Studies*, 9, 7–23.

Scottish Development Agency (1979), *The Electronics Industry in Scotland*, study undertaken by Booz, Allen & Hamilton, Glasgow.

Steuer, M. D. *et al.* (1973), *The Impact of Foreign Direct Investment in the United Kingdom*. London: HMSO.

US Department of Commerce (1981), *US Direct Investment Abroad, 1977*, Washington, DC: US GPO.

Vernon, R. (1979), 'The Product Cycle Hypothesis in a New International Environment', *Oxford Bulletin of Economics and Statistics*, 41, 255–67.

Chapter 4

Abo, T. (1989), 'Theory of Foreign Direct Investment', in K. Shibagaki, M. Trevor and T. Abo (eds), *Japanese and European Management*, Tokyo: University of Tokyo Press.

Aharoni, Y. (1966), *The Foreign Investment Decision Process*, Boston: Harvard University Press.

Buckley, P. and Casson, M. (1981), 'The Optimal Timing of a Foreign Direct Investment', *Economic Journal*, 91, 75–87.

Buckley, P. and Casson, M. (1988), 'A Theory of Co-Operation in International Business', in F. Contractor and P. Lorange (eds), *Co-Operative Strategies in International Business*, Lexington: Lexington Books.

Burton, F. and Saelens, F. (1986), 'Japanese Direct Investment Abroad: The Unfulfilled Promise', *Rivista Internazionale di Scienze Economiche e Commerciali*, 33 (5), 493–510.

Burton, F. and Saelens, F. (1987), 'Trade Barriers and Japanese Foreign Direct Investment in the Colour Television Industry', *Managerial and Decision Economics*, 8 (4), 285–93.

Campbell, N., Goold, M. and Kase, K. (1990), '*The Role of the Centre in Managing Large Diversified Companies in Japan*', Working Paper, Manchester Business School, September.

Clark, R. (1987), *The Japanese Company*. New Haven: Yale University Press.

Destler, I. M. and Sato, H. (eds) (1982), *Coping with US–Japanese Economic Conflicts*, Lexington: Lexington Books.

Dunning, J. H. (1986), *Japanese Participation in British Industry*. London: Croom Helm.

Dunning, J. H. (1988), 'The Eclectic Paradigm of International Production: A Restatement and Some Possible Extensions', *Journal of International Business Studies*, 19 (1), 1–31.

Dunning, J. H. and Cantwell, J. A. (1991), 'Japanese Direct Investment in Europe', in B. K. Bürgenmeier and J. L. Mucchielli, *Multinationals and Europe 1992*, London: Routledge.

Eltis, W. (1992), *The Contribution of Japanese Industrial Success to Britain and to Europe*, paper presented to the Institute de l'Enterprise, Paris.

Haigh, R. (1989), *Investment Strategies and the Plant Location Decision – Foreign Companies in the US*, New York: Praeger.

Ishikawa, K. (1991), *Japan and the Challenge of Europe 1992*, London: Pinter.

Johanson, J. and Vahlne, J.-E. (1977), 'The Internationalizing Process of the Firm – A Model of Knowledge Development and Increasing Foreign Market Commitment', *Journal of International Business Studies*, Spring/Summer, 23–32.

Johanson, J. and Vahlne, J.-E. (1990), 'The Mechanism of Internationalization', *International Marketing Review*, 7 (4), 11–24.

Kagono, T., Sakamoto, S. and Johansson, J. (1985), *Strategic vs Evolutionary Management: A US–Japan Comparison of Strategy and Organisation*, Amsterdam: North-Holland.

Kelly, M. E. W. and Phillippatos, G. C. (1982), 'Comparative Analysis of the Foreign Investment Evaluation Practices by US-Based Manufacturing Multinational Companies', *Journal of International Business Studies*, Winter, 19–42.

Kojima, K. (1982), 'Macroeconomic versus International Business Approach to Direct Foreign Investment', *Hitotsubashi Journal of Economics*, 23 (1), 630–40.

Kujawa, D. (1986), *Japanese Multinationals in the United States*, New York: Praeger.

Morris, J. (1988), 'The Who, Why and Where of Japanese Manufacturing Investment in the UK', *Industrial Relations Journal*, 19 (1), 31–40.

Nonaka, I. (1990), 'Managing Globalisation as a Self-Renewing Process: Experiences of Japanese MNEs', in C. A. Bartlett, Y. Doz and G. Hedlund (eds), *Managing the Global Firm*, London: Routledge.

Oliver, N. and Wilkinson, B. (1988), *The Japanization of British Industry*, Oxford: Blackwell.

Ozawa, T. (1989), *Recycling Japan's Surpluses for Developing Countries*, Paris: OECD.

Ozawa, T. (1991), 'Japanese Multinationals and 1992', in B. Bürgenmeier and J. L. Mucchielli, *Multinationals and Europe 1992*, London: Routledge.

Rehfeld, J. (1990), 'What Working for a Japanese Company Taught Me', *Harvard Business Review*, 6, 167–76.

Strange, R. (1993), *The Impact of Japanese Investment on the UK Economy*, London: Routledge.

Trevor, M. (1983), *Japan's Reluctant Multinationals*, London: Pinter.

Vogel, E. (1979), *Japan as Number 1*, Cambridge, MA: Harvard University Press.

Yannopoulos, G. M. (1990), 'The Effects of the Single Market on the Pattern of Japanese Investment', *National Institute Economic Review*, 134, 93–8.

Yoshida, M. (1987), *Japanese Direct Manufacturing in the United States*. New York: Praeger.

Chapter 5

Abegglen, J. and Stalk, G. (1986), 'The Japanese Corporation as Competitor', *California Management Review*, 28 (3), 9–27.

Burton, F. and Saelens, F. (1987), 'Trade Barriers and Japanese Foreign Direct Investment in the Colour Television Industry', *Managerial and Decision Economics*, 8 (4), 285–93.

Choi, F. D. S. and Czechowicz, I. J. (1983), 'Assessing Foreign Subsidiary Performance: A Multinational Comparison', *Management International Review*, 23 (4), 14–25.

De Meyer, A., Nakaie, J., Miller, J. F. and Ferdows, K. (1987), 'Flexibility: The Next Competition Battle', *Manufacturing Roundtable Research Report Series*, Boston.

Dirks, D. (1992), 'After the Investment: Organisational Development in Japanese Overseas Subsidiaries', Global Kaisha Conference, Manchester Business School, June.

Dunning, J. H. (1985), 'US and Japanese Manufacturing Affiliates in the UK: Some Similarities and Contrasts', University of Reading Discussion Papers in International Investment and Business Studies, 90, October.

Dunning, J. H. (1986), *Japanese Participation in British Industry*, London: Croom Helm.

Dunning, J. H. and Cantwell, J. A. (1991), 'Japanese Direct Investment in Europe', in B. Bürgenmeier and J. L. Mucchielli, *Multinationals and Europe 1992*, London: Routledge, 155–84.

Eiteman, D. K., Stonehill, A. I. and Moffett, M. H. (1992), *Multinational Business Finance*, 6th edn, New York: Addison-Wesley.

Hood, N. and Truijens, T. (1993), 'European Locational Decisions of Japanese Manufacturers: Survey Evidence on the Case of the UK', *International Business Review*, 2 (1), 39–63.

Hood, N. and Young, S. (1980), *European Development Strategies of US Owned Manufacturing Companies Located in Scotland*, Edinburgh: HMSO.

Hood, N. and Young, S. (1983), *Multinational Investment Strategies in the British Isles*, London: HMSO.

JETRO (1992), *8th Survey of European Operations of Japanese Companies in the Manufacturing Sector*, Japan External Trade Organisation, March.

Kidd, J. B. (1991), 'Globalisation through Localisation: Reflections on the Japanese Production Subsidiaries in the United Kingdom', in *Proceedings of the 1991 Symposium of the Euro-Asia Management Studies Association*, Pans: INSEAD.

Kilduff, M. (1992), 'Performance and Interaction Routines in Multinational Corporations', *Journal of International Business*, 23 (1), 133–45.

Kotabe, M. (1990), 'Corporate Product Policy and Innovative Behaviour of European and Japanese Multinationals: An Empirical Investigation', *Journal of Marketing*, 54, 19–23.

Kotler, P., Fahey, L. and Jatusripitak, S. (1985), *The New Competition*, Englewood Cliffs, NJ: Prentice-Hall.

Kume, G. and Totsuka, K. (1991), 'Japanese Manufacturing Investment in the EC: Motives and Locations', in Sumitomo-Life Research Institute with M. Yoshitomi, (eds), *Japanese Direct Investment in Europe*, Avebury.

Martinez, J. I. and Jarillo, J. I. (1989), 'The Evolution of Research of Co-ordination Mechanisms in Multinational Corporations', *Journal of International Business Studies*, Fall, 489–514.

McKinsey & Co. (1988), *Performance and Competitive Success: Strengthening Competition in UK Electronics*, Report for the Electronics Industry Sector Group, London: NEDO.

Morris, J. and Imrie, R. (1991), *The End of Adversarialism – The Adaptation of Japanese-style Buyer–Supplier Relations in a Western Context*, London: Macmillan.

Morsicato, H. G. and Radebaugh, L. H. (1979), 'Internal Performance Evaluation of Multinational Enterprise Operations', *International Journal of Accounting*, 15 (1), 77–94.

Ohmae, K. (1985), *Triad Power: The Coming Shape of Global Competition*, New York: Free Press, London: Collier Macmillan.

Ohmae, K. (1987), 'Japan's Role in the World Economy: A New Approach', *Californian Management Review*, Spring, 42–58.

Oliver, N. and Wilkinson, B. (1988), *The Japanization of British Industry*, Oxford: Blackwell.

Ozawa, T. (1991), 'Japanese Multinationals in 1992', in B. Bürgenmeier and J. L. Mucchielli, *Multinationals in Europe 1992*, London: Routledge, 135–54.

Robbins, S. and Stobaugh, R. (1973), 'The Bent Measuring Stick for Foreign Subsidiaries', *Harvard Business Review*, September–October, 80–8.

Schoenfeld, H. M. (1986), 'The Present State of Performance Evaluation in Multinational Companies', in H. P. Holzer and H.-M. Schoenfeld (eds), *Managerial Accounting and Analysis in Multinational Enterprises*, Berlin: De Gruyter, 50–65.

Smothers, N. P. (1990), 'Patterns of Japanese Strategy: Strategic Combinations of Strategies', *Strategic Management Journal*, 11, 521–33.

Tackiki, D. S. (1991), 'Japanese Management Going Transnational', *Journal for Quality and Participation*, December, 96–107.

Trevor, M. (1983), *Japan's Reluctant Multinationals*, London: Pinter.

Trevor, M. and Christie, R. (1988), *Manufacturers and Suppliers in Britain and Japan*, London: PSI.

White, R. E. and Poynter, T. A. (1984), 'Strategies for Foreign Owned Subsidiaries in Canada', *Business Quarterly*, Summer, 59–69.

Yoshida, M. (1987), *Japanese Direct Manufacturing in the United States*, New York: Praeger.

Young, S., Hood, N. and Dunlop, S. (1988), 'Global Strategies, Multinational Subsidiary Roles and Economic Impact in Scotland', *Regional Studies*, 22 (6), 487–97.

Chapter 6

Beale, E. M. L. (1969), 'Euclidean Cluster Analysis', contributed paper to the 37th edition of the *International Statistical Institute Bulletin*, Proceedings of the Biennial Sessions.

Cantwell, J. A. (1987), 'The Reorganization of European Industries after Integration: Selected Evidence on the Role of Multinational Enterprises', *Journal of Common Market Studies*, 26 (2), 127–51.

Doz, Y. (1986), *Strategic Management in Multinational Companies*, Oxford: Pergamon.

Dunning, J. H. (1985), 'US and Japanese Manufacturing Affiliates in the UK: Some Similarities and Contrasts', University of Reading Discussion Papers in International Investment and Business Studies, 90, October.

Dunning, J. H. (1986), *Japanese Participation in British Industry*, London: Croom Helm.

Dunning, J. H. and Pearce, R. D. (1981), *The World's Largest Enterprises*, Farnborough: Gower.

Etemad, H. and Dulude, L. S. (eds) (1986), *Managing the Multinational Subsidiary*, London: Croom Helm.

Hood, N. and Young, S. (1980), *European Development Strategies of US-Owned Manufacturing Companies Located in Scotland*, Edinburgh: HMSO.

Hood, N. and Young, S. (1983), *Multinational Investment Strategies in the British Isles*, London: HMSO.

Porter, M. (1986), 'Changing Patterns of International Competition', *California Management Review*, 28 (2).

Sparks, D. N. (1973), 'Euclidean Cluster Analysis', AS58. Applied Statistics, 22, 126–30.

White, R. E. and Poynter, T. A. (1984), 'Strategies for Foreign-Owned Subsidiaries in Canada', *Business Quarterly*, Summer.

Young, S. and Hood, N. (1976), 'The Geographical Expansion of US firms in Western Europe: Some Survey Evidence', *Journal of Common Market Studies*, 14 (3), 223–39.

Chapter 7

Buckley, P. J., Berkova, Z. and Newbould, G. D. (1983), *Direct Investment in the United Kingdom by Smaller European Firms*, London: Macmillan.

Doz, Y. L. (1986), *Strategic Management in Multinational Companies*. Oxford: Pergamon.

Doz, Y. L. and Prahalad, C. K. (1987), *The Multinational Mission: Balancing Local Demands and Global Vision*, New York: The Free Press.

Dunning, J. H. (1986), *Japanese Participation in British Industry*, London: Croom Helm.

Everitt, B. (1980), *Cluster Analysis*. New York: Wiley.

Fayerweather, J. (1978), *International Business Strategy and Administration*, Cambridge, MA: Ballinger.

Haug, P., Hood, N. and Young, S. (1983), 'R&D Intensity in the Affiliates of US-Owned Electronics Companies Manufacturing in Scotland', *Regional Studies*, 17 (6), 383–92.

Hood, N. and Vahlne, J.-E. (1988), *Strategies in Global Competition*, London: Croom Helm.

Hood, N. and Young, S. (1987), 'Inward Investment and the EC: UK Evidence on Corporate Integration Strategies', *Journal of Common Market Studies*, 26 (2), 193–206.

Hood, N. and Young, S. (1976), 'US Investment in Scotland – Aspects of the Branch Factory Syndrome', *Scottish Journal of Political Economy*, 14, 279–94.

Leontiades, J. (1986), 'Going Global–Global Strategies vs National Strategies', *Long Range Planning*, 19, 96–104.

Porter, M. E. (1986), 'Changing Patterns of International Competition', *California Management Review*, 28, 9–40.

Porter, M. E. (ed.) (1987), *Competition in Global Industries*, Boston, MA: Harvard Business School Press.

Science Council of Canada (1980), *Multinationals and Industrial Strategy: The Role of World Product Mandates*, Science Council of Canada, Ottowa.

Stobaugh, R. and Telesio, P. (1983), 'Match Manufacturing Policies and Product Strategy', *Harvard Business Review*, 61, 113–20.

White, R. E. and Poynter, T. A. (1984), 'Strategies for Foreign-Owned Subsidiaries in Canada', *Business Quarterly*, Summer, 59–69.

Young, S. and Hood, N. (1976), 'The Geographical Expansion of US Firms in Western Europe: Some Survey Evidence', *Journal of Common Market Studies*, 14, 223–39.

Young, S. and Hood, N. (1980), 'The Strategies of US Multinationals in Europe: A Host Country Perspective', *Multinational Business*, 2, 1–19.

Young, S., Hood, N. and Hamill, J. (1988), *Foreign Multinationals and the British Economy*, London: Croom Helm.

Chapter 8

Amin, A., Bradley, D., Howells, J., Tomaney, J. and Gentle, C. (1994), 'Regional Incentives and the Quality of Mobile Investment in the Less Favoured Regions of the EC', *Progress in Planning* 41 (1).

Amin, A. and Dietrich, M. (1990), 'From the Hierarchies to 'Hierarchy': The Dynamics of Contemporary Corporate Restructuring in Europe', in *Proceedings of the Annual Conference of the European Association of Evolutionary Political Economy*, Florence.

Amin, A. and Malmberg, A. (1992), 'Competing Structural and Institutional Influences on the Geography of Production in Europe', *Environment and Planning A*, 24, 401–16.

Ashcroft, B. and Love, J. H. (1993), *Takeovers, Mergers and the Regional Economy*, Edinburgh: Edinburgh University Press.

Ashcroft, B., Love, J. H. and Scouller, J. (1987), 'The Economic Effects of the Inward Acquisition of Scottish Manufacturing Companies 1965 to 1980', ESU Research Paper, 11, Industry Department for Scotland, Edinburgh.

Aydalot, P. (1988), 'Technological Trajectories and Regional Innovation in Europe', in P. Aydalot and D. Keeble (eds), *High Technology Industry and Innovative Environments: The European Experience*, London and New York: Routledge.

Aydalot, P. and Neeble, D. (eds) (1988), *High Technology Industry and Innovative Environments: The European Experience*, London and New York: Routledge.

Balassa, B. (1980), 'The Process of Industrial Development and Alternative Development Strategies', *Essays in International Finance*, 141, Department of Economics, Princeton University.

Bartlett, C. A. (1986), 'Building and Managing the Transnational: The New Organizational Challenge', in M. E. Porter (ed.), *Competition in Global Industries*, Boston, MA: Harvard Business School Press.

Bartlett, C. A., Doz, Y. and Hedlund, G. (eds) (1990), *Managing the Global Firm*. London and New York: Routledge.

Bartlett, C. A. and Ghoshal, S. (1989), *Managing Across Borders*, Boston, MA: Harvard Business School Press.

Beigie, C. E. and Stewart, J. K. (1986), 'Industrial Adjustments and World Product Mandates: A Role for Public Policy', in H. Etemad and L. Séguin Dulude (eds), *Managing the Multinational Subsidiary*, London: Croom Helm.

Biersteker, T. J. (1981), *Distortion or Development? Contending Perspectives on the Multinational Corporation*, Cambridge, MA: MIT Press.

Bornschier, V. and Chase-Dunn, C. (1985), *Transnational Corporations and Underdevelopment*, London: Greenwood.

Borys, B. and Jemison, D. B. (1989), 'Hybrid Arrangements as Strategic Alliances: Theoretical Issues in Organizational Combinations', *Academy of Management Review*, 14, 243–9.

Buckley, P. J. and Casson, M. (1992), 'Organizing for Innovation: The Multinational Enterprise in the Twenty-First Century', in P. J. Buckley and M. Casson (eds), *Multinational Enterprises in the World Economy*, Aldershot: Edward Elgar.

Cantwell, J. A. (1989), *Technological Innovation and Multinational Corporations*, Oxford: Blackwell.

Cantwell, J. A. (1993), 'Technological Competence and Evolving Patterns of International Production', in H. Cox, J. Clegg and G. Ietto-Gillies, *The Growth of Global Business*, London: Routledge.

Cantwell, J. A. and Tolentino, P. E. E. (1990), 'Technological Accumulation and Third World Multinationals', Discussion Papers in International Investment and Business Studies, 139, Department of Economics, University of Reading.

Chakravarthy, B. S. and Perlmutter, H. V. (1985), 'Strategic Planning for a Global Business', *Columbia Journal of World Business*, 20, 3–10.

Chandler, A. D., Jr. (1962), *Strategy and Structure*, Boston, MA: MIT Press.

Charles, D. R. (1987), 'Technical Change and the Decentralized Corporation in the Electronics Industry: Regional Policy Implications', in K. Chapman and G. Humphreys (eds), *Technical Change and Industrial Policy*, Oxford: Basil Blackwell.

Chenery, H. (1979), *Structural Change and Development Policy*, Oxford: Oxford University Press.

Cheng, J. L. C. and Bolon, D. C. (1993), 'The Management of Multinational R&D: A Neglected Topic in International Business Research', *Journal of International Business Studies*, 24, 1–18.

Christy, C. V. and Ironside, R. G. (1987), 'Promoting "High Technology" Industry: Location Factors and Public Policy', in K. Chapman and G. Humphreys (eds), *Technical Change and Industrial Policy*, Oxford: Basil Blackwell.

Clark, C., Wilson, F. and Bradley, J. (1969), 'International Location and Economic Potential in Western Europe', *Regional Studies*, 5, 197–212.

Commission of the European Communities (CEC) (1991), *Europe 2000*, Brussels: CEC.

Cowling, K. and Sugden, R. (1987), *Transnational Monopoly Capitalism*, Brighton: Wheatsheaf.

D'Cruz, J. R. (1986), 'Strategic Management of Subsidiaries', in H. Etemad and L. Séguin Dulude (eds), *Managing the Multinational Subsidiary*, London: Croom Helm.

Del Monte, A. and De Luzenberger, R. (1989), 'The Effect of Regional Policy on New Firm Formation in Southern Italy', *Regional Studies*, 23, 219–30.

Dunning, J. H. (1972), *The Location of International Firms in an Enlarged EEC: An Exploratory Analysis*, Manchester: Manchester Statistical Society.

Dunning, J. H. (1981), 'Explaining Outward Direct Investment of Developing Countries: In Support of the Electric Theory of International Production', in K. Kumar and M. G. McLeod (eds), *Multinationals from Developing Countries*, Lexington, MA: D. C. Heath & Co.

Dunning, J. H. (1985), *Multinational Enterprises, Economic Structure and International Competitiveness*, Chichester: Wiley.

Dunning, J. H. (1986), 'The Investment Development Cycle and Third World Multinationals', in K. M. Khan (ed.), *Multinationals from the South*, London: Pinter.

Dunning, J. H. (1988), *Multinationals, Technology and Competitiveness*. London: Unwin-Hyman.

Dunning, J. H. (1992), 'The Competitive Advantage of Countries and the Activities of Transnational Corporations', *Transnational Corporations*, 1, 135–68.

Dunning, J. H. (1993), *Multinational Enterprises and the Global Economy*, Wokingham: Addison-Wesley.

Egelhoff, W. E. (1988), 'Strategy and Structure in Multinational Corporations: A Review of the Stopford and Wells Model', *Strategic Management Journal*, 9, 1–14.

English Unit (1991), *A Study of the Knock-on Effects of Inward Investment in the English Regions*, London: HMSO.

Ernst & Young (1990), *Regions of the New Europe*, London: Ernst & Young/Century House Information.

Etemad H. and Séguin Dulude, L. (eds) (1986), *Managing the Multinational Subsidiary*, London: Croom Helm.

Financial Times (1993), 'Survey: Contract Electronics Manufacture', 16 March.

Firn, J. R. (1975), 'External Control and Regional Development: The Case of Scotland', *Environment and Planning A*, 7, 393–414.

Forsgren, M. and Johanson, J. (eds) (1992), *Managing Networks in International Business*, Philadelphia, PA: Gordon & Breach.

Forsgren, M. and Pahlberg, C. (1992), 'Subsidiary Influence and Autonomy in International Firms', *Scandinavian International Business Review*, 1, 41–51.

Forsgren, M., Holm, U. and Johanson, J. (1992), 'Internationalization of the Second Degree: The Emergence of European-Based Centres in Swedish Firms', in S. Young and J. Hamill (eds), *Europe and the Multinationals*, Aldershot: Edward Elgar.

Franko, L. (1976), *The European Multinationals*, New York: Harper.

Galbraith, C. and De Noble, A. F. (1988), 'Location Decisions by High Technology Firms: A Comparison of Firm Size, Industry Type and Institutional Form', *Entrepreneurship Theory & Practice*, Winter, 31–47.

Galtung, J. (1971), 'A Structural Theory of Imperialism', *Journal of Peace Research*, 8, 81–117.

Ghoshal, S. and Bartlett, C. A. (1988), 'Innovation Processes in Multinational Corporations', in M. L. Tushman and W. L. Moore (eds), *Readings in the Management of Innovation*, 2nd edn, New York: Ballinger.

Ghoshal, S. and Nohria, N. (1989), 'Internal Differentiation within Multinational Corporations', *Strategic Management Journal*, 10, 323–37.

Ghoshal, S. and Nohria, N. (1993), 'Horses for Courses: Organizational Forms for Multinational Corporations', *Sloan Management Review*, Winter, 23–35.

Goldenburg, S. (1991), *Global Pursuit*, Toronto: McGraw Hill-Ryerson.

Goodman, B. B. (1993), 'Exploitation of R&D Results in the Community', *Les Nouvelles*, 28 (1), 36–40.

Grandstrand, O., Sjolander, S. and Håkanson, L. (eds) (1992), *Technology, Management and International Business: Internationalization of R&D and Technology*, Chichester: Wiley.

Gupta, A. K. and Govindarajan, V. (1991), 'Knowledge Flows and the Structure of Control within Multinational Corporations', *Academy Management Review*, 16, 768–92.

Håkanson, L. (1990), 'International Decentralization of R&D – The Organizational Challenges', in C. A. Bartlett, Y. Doz and G. Hedlund (eds), *Managing the Global Firm*, London and New York: Routledge.

Håkanson, L. and Zander, V. (1988), 'International Management of R&D: The Swedish Experience', *R&D Management*, 18, 217–26.

Harrison, B. (1992), 'Industrial Districts: Old Wine in New Bottles', *Regional Studies*, 26, 469–83.

Hedlund, G. (1984), 'Organization In-Between: The Evolution of the Mother-Daughter Structure of Managing Foreign Subsidiaries in Swedish Multinational Corporations', *Journal of International Business Studies*, Fall, 109–23.

Hedlund, G. (1986), 'The Hypermodern MNC: A Heterarchy?', *Human Resource Management*, 25, 9–35.

Hedlund, G. and Åman, P. (1984), *Managing Relationships with Foreign Subsidiaries–Organization and Control in Swedish MNCs*, Stockholm: Sveriges Mekanförbund.

Hedlund, G. and Rolander, D. (1990), 'Actions in Heterarchies: New Approaches to Managing the MNE', in C. Bartlett, Y. Doz and G. Hedlund (eds), *Managing the Global Firm*, Routledge, London and New York.

Hill, S. and Munday, M. (1991), 'The Determinants of Inward Investment: A Welsh Analysis', *Applied Economics*, 23 (1), 761–9.

Hilpert, U. (1991), *Archipelago Europe*, Berlin: Freie Universität.

Hirschman, A. (1958), *The Strategy of Economic Development*, New Haven: Yale University Press.

Howells, J. (1990), 'The Internationalization of R&D and the Development of Global Research Networks', *Regional Studies*, 24, 495–512.

Hymer, S. (1975), 'The Multinational Corporation and the Law of Uneven Development', in H. Radice (ed.), *International Firms and Modern Imperialism*, Harmondsworth: Penguin.

Jarillo, J. C. and Martinez, J. I. (1990), 'Different Roles for Multinational Subsidiaries: The Case of Multinational Corporations in Spain', *Strategic Management Journal* 11, 501–12.

Kaldor, N. (1971), 'The Dynamic Effects of the Common Market', in D. Evans (ed.), *Destiny or Delusion: Britain and the Common Market*, London: Gollancz.

Koopman, K. and Montias, J. M. (1971), 'On the Description and Comparison of Economic Systems', in A. Eckstein (ed.), *Comparison of Economic Systems*, Berkeley: University of California Press.

Leong, S. M. and Tan, C. T. (1993), 'Managing Across Borders: An Empirical Test of the Bartlett and Ghoshal Organizational Typology', *Journal of International Business Studies*, 24, 449–64.

Marshall, A. (1986), *Principles of Economics*, 8th edn (originally published in 1890), Basingstoke: Macmillan.

Mintzberg, H. (1973), *The Nature of Managerial Work*, New York: Harper & Row.

Morris, J. (1989), 'Japanese Inward Investment and the "Importation" of Sub-Contracting Complexes: Three Case Studies', *Area*, 21, 269–77.

Morris, J. (1992), 'Flexible Internationalization in the Electronics Industry: Implications for Regional Economies', *Environment and Planning C*, 10, 407–21.

Nam, C. W. and Reuter, J. (1991), 'The Impact of 1992 and Associated Legislation on the Less Favoured Regions of the European Community', European Parliament Research Paper 18, Luxembourg: Office for Official Publications of the EC.

Netherlands Economic Institute (in co-operation with Ernst & Young) (1992), *New Location Factors for Mobile Investment in Europe*, Rotterdam and London: NEI/Ernst & Young.

Newfarmer, R. S. (ed.) (1985), *Profits, Progress and Poverty: Case Studies of International Industries in Latin America*, Indiana: University of Notre Dame Press.

Nonaka, I. (1988), 'Creating Organizational Order out of Chaos: Self-Renewal in Japanese Firms', *California Management Review*, 30 (3), 57–73.

Northern Ireland Economic Development Council (1992) *Inward Investment in Northern Ireland*, Report 99, Belfast: NIEDO.

Ohmae, K. (1990), *The Borderless World*, London: Collins.

Oughton, C. (1993), 'Growth, Structural Change and Real Convergence in the EC', in K. S. Hughes (ed.), *European Competitiveness*, Cambridge: Cambridge University Press.

Ozawa, T. (1992), 'Foreign Direct Investment and Economic Development', *Transnational Corporations*, 1, 27–54.

Panić, M. (1992), *National Management of the International Economy*, London: Macmillan/New York: St Martin's Press.

Papanastassiou, M. and Pearce, R. (1992), 'Motivation and Market Strategies of US Foreign Direct Investments', proceedings of the 18th Annual Conference of the European International Business Association, University of Reading, 13–15 December.

Pavitt, K. (1988), 'International Patterns of Technological Accumulation', in N. Hood and J.-E. Vahlne (eds), *Strategies in Global Competition*, London: Croom Helm.

Pearce, R. D. (1991), 'The Globalization of R&D by TNCs', *The CTC Reporter*, 71, 13–16.

Pearce, R. D. (1992), 'Factors Influencing the Internationalization of Research and Development in Multinational Enterprises', in P. J. Buckley and M. Casson (eds), *Multinational Enterprises in the World Economy*, Aldershot: Edward Elgar.

Pearce, R. D. and Singh, S. (1992), 'Internationalisation of R&D Among the World's Leading Enterprises', in O. Grandstrand, S. Sjolander and L. Håkanson (eds), *Technology, Management and International Business: Internationalization of R&D and Technology*, Chichester: Wiley.

Peck, F. (1990), 'Nissan in the North East: The Multiplier Effects', *Geography*, 75, 354–7.

Perlmutter, H. V. (1969), 'The Tortuous Evolution of the Multinational Corporation', *Columbia Journal of World Business*, 4, 9–18.

Perrin, J.-C. (1988), 'New Technologies, Local Synergies and Regional Policies in Europe', in P. Aydalot and D. Keeble (eds), *High Technology Industry and Innovative Environments: The European Experience*, London and New York, Routledge.

Peters E. (1993), 'Corporate Restructuring and Peripheral Area Development. The IT Industries: Scotland's Experience', presentation at conference on Conflict and Cohesion in the Single Market, Centre for Urban and Regional Development Studies, University of Newcastle upon Tyne, 18–20 November.

Piore, M. J. and Sabel, C. F. (1984), New York: Basic Books.

Porter, M. E. (1986), *Competition in Global Industries*, Boston, MA: Harvard Business School Press.

Porter, M. E. (1990), *The Competitive Advantage of Nations*, New York: Free Press.

Powell, W. W. (1987), 'Hybrid Organizational Arrangements: New Form or Transitional Development', 29 (3), 67–87.

Rostow, W. W. (1959), *The Stages of Economic Growth*, London: Macmillan.

Roth, K. and Morrison, A. J. (1992), 'Implementing Global Strategy: Characteristics of Global Subsidiary Mandates', *Journal of International Business Studies*, 23, 715–35.

Rugman, A. M. and Bennett, J. (1982), 'Technology Transfer and World Product Mandating in Canada', *Columbia Journal of World Business*, 17 (4), 58–62.

Sabel, C. F. (1989), 'Flexible Specialization and the Re-Emergence of Regional Economies', in P. Hirst and J. Zeitlin (eds), *Revising Industrial Decline? Industrial Structure and Policy in Britain and her Competitors*, Oxford: Berg.

Science Council of Canada (1980), *Multinationals and Industrial Strategy: The Role of World Product Mandates*, Ottawa: Science Council of Canada.

Schoenberger, E. (1988a), 'Multinational Corporations and the New International Division of Labour: A Critical Approach', *International Regional Science Review*, 11, 105–19.

Schoenberger, E. (1988b), 'From Fordism to Flexible Accumulation: Technology, Competitive Strategies, and International Locations', *Environment and Planning D*, 6, 245–62.

Scott, A. J. (1992), 'The Role of Large Producers in Industrial Districts: A Case of High Technology Systems Houses in Southern California', *Regional Studies*, 26, 265–75.

Segal, N. S. and Quince, R. E. (1985), 'The Cambridge Phenomenon and the Role of the Cambridge Science Park', in J. M. Gibb (ed.), *Science Parks and Innovation Centres: Their Economic and Social Impact*, Amsterdam: Elsevier.

Shepley, S. and Wilmot, J. (1992), *Europe: Core vs Periphery*, London: Credit Suisse/ First Boston.

Stopford, J. and Wells, L. T., Jr. (1972), *Managing the Multinational Enterprise*, New York: Basic Books.

Thoburn, J. T. and Takashima, M. (1993), 'Improving British Industrial Performance: Lessons from Japanese Subcontracting', *National Westminustes Bank Quarterly Review*, February, 2–11.

Tolentino, P. E. E. (1987), 'The Global Shift in International Production: The Growth of Multinational Enterprises from Developing Countries; The Philippines', unpublished PhD thesis, University of Reading.

Tolentino, P. E. E. (1993), *Technological Innovation and Third World Multinationals*, London and New York: Routledge.

Turok, I. (1993), 'Loose Connections? Foreign Investment and Local Linkages in "Silicon Glen"', Strathclyde Papers on Planning 23, University of Strathclyde.

United Nations (1992), *World Investment Report 1992*, New York: United Nations.

United Nations Centre On Transnational Corporations (UNCTC) (1990), *New Approaches to Best-Practice Manufacturing: The Role of Transnational Corporations and Implications for Developing Countries*, UNCTC Current Studies, Series A, No. 12, New York: United Nations.

Vernon, R. (1966), 'International Investment and International Trade in the Product Cycle', *Quarterly Journal of Economics*, 80, 190–207.

Vonortas, N. S. (1990), 'Emerging Patterns of Multinational Enterprise Operations in Developed Market Economies: Evidence and Policy', *Review of Political Economy*, 2, 188–220.

Weick, K. E. (1987), 'Substitute for Corporate Strategy', in D. J. Teece (ed.), *The Competitive Challenge: Strategies for Industrial Innovation and Renewal*, Cambridge, MA: Ballinger.

Welch, D. E. and Welch, L. S. (1993), 'Using Personnel to Develop Networks: An Approach to Subsidiary Management', *International Business Review*, 2, 157–68.

Welsh Affairs Committee (1988), *Inward Investment into Wales and its Interaction with Regional and EEC Policies*, HC 86–I and II, London: HMSO.

White, R. E. and Poynter, T. A. (1984), 'Strategies for Foreign Owned Subsidiaries in Canada', *Business Quarterly*, Summer, 59–69.

Wong, P.-K. (1992), 'Technological Development through Sub-Contracting Linkages: Evidence from Singapore', *Scandinarian International Business Review*, 1 (3), 28–40.

World Bank (1993), *The East Asian Miracle*, Oxford: Oxford University Press.

Young, S. and Hood, N. (1992), 'Summary and Conclusions: Stimulating European Competitiveness', in S. Young and J. Hamill (eds), *Europe and the Multinationals*, Aldershot, Edward Elgar.

Young, S. and Hood, N. (1993), 'Inward Investment Policy in the European Community in the 1990s', *Transnational Corporations*, 2 (2), 35–62.

Young, S. and Hood, N. (1994), 'Designing Developmental After-Care Programmes for Foreign Direct Investors in the European Union', *Transnational Corporations*, 3 (2).

Young, S., Hood, N. and Dunlop, S. (1988), 'Global Strategies, Multinational Subsidiary Roles and Economic Impact in Scotland', *Regional Studies*, 22 (6), 487–97.

Young, S., Hood, N. and Peters, E. (1993), 'The Contribution of Foreign Direct Investment to the Scottish Economy: A Review and Re-Appraisal', Department of Marketing, University of Strathclyde, mimeo.

Young, S., Hood, N. and Wilson, A. (1994), 'Targeting Policy as a Competitive Strategy for European Inward Investment Agencies', *European Urban and Regional Studies*, 1 (2).

Chapter 9

Andersson, U. (1997), 'Subsidiary Network Embeddedness', doctoral thesis 66, Department of Business Studies, Uppsala University.

Aydalot, P. (1986), *Milieux innovateurs en Europe*, Paris: Gremi.

Bartlett, C. A. and Ghoshal, S. (1986), 'Tap your Subsidiaries for Global Reach', *Harvard Business Review*, 64 (6), 87–94.

Bartlett, C. A. and Ghoshal, S. (1989), *Managing Across Borders: The Transnational Solution*, Boston, MA: Harvard Business School Press.

Beigie, C. E. and Stewart, J. K. (1986), 'Industrial Adjustments and World Product Mandates: A Role for Public Policy', in H. Etemad and L. Séguin Dulude (eds), *Managing the Multinational Subsidiary*, London: Croom Helm, 23–43.

Birkinshaw, J. M. (1997), 'Entrepreneurship in Multinational Corporations: The Characteristics of Subsidiary Initiatives', *Strategic Management Journal*, 18 (3), 207–29.

Birkinshaw, J., Hood, N. and Jonsson., S. (1998), 'Building Firm Specific Advantages in MNCs: The Role of Subsidiary Initiative', *Strategic Management Journal*, 19: 221–41.

Birkinshaw, J. M. and Morrison, A. (1995), 'Configurations of Strategy and Structure in Subsidiaries of Multinational Corporations', *Journal of International Business Studies*, 26 (4), 729–54.

Crookell, H. H. (1986), 'Specialization and International Competitiveness', in H. Etemad & L. Séguin Dulude (eds), *Managing the Multinational Subsidiary*, London: Croom Helm.

Dicken, P. (1994), 'Global–Local Tensions; Firms and States in the Global Space-Economy', *Economic Geography*, 70: 101–21.

Dunning, J. H. (1993), *Multinational Enterprises and the Global Economy*, Workingham, Addison-Wesley.

Etemad, H. and Dulude L. Séguin (1986), *Managing the Multinational Subsidiary*, London: Croom Helm.

Forsgren, M., Holm., U and Johanson., J (1995), 'Division Headquarters Go Abroad – A Step in the Internationalization of the Multinational Corporation', *Journal of Management Studies*, 32 (4), 475–91.

Ghoshal, S. and Nohria, N. (1989), 'Internal Differentiation with Multinational Corporations', *Strategic Management Journal*, 10, 323–37.

Grabher, G. (1993), 'Rediscovering the Social in the Economics of Interfirm Relations', in G. Grabher (ed.), *The Embedded Firm*, London: Routledge.

Grannovetter, M. (1985), 'Economic Action and Social Structure: The Problem of Embeddedness', *American Journal of Sociology*, 91 (3), 481–510.

Gupta, A. K. and Govindarajan, V. (1991), 'Knowledge flows and the Structure of control within Multinational Corporations', *Academy of Management Review*. 16 (4), 768–92.

Hedlund, G. (1986). 'The Hypermodern MNC: A Heterarchy?', *Human Resource Management*, 25, 9–36.

Hofstede, G., Neuijen, B., Ohayv, D. D. and Sanders, G. (1990), 'Measuring Organizational Culture: A Qualitative and Quantitative Study across Twenty Cases', *Administrative Science Quarterly*, 35, 286–316.

Hood, N. and Young, S. (1988), 'Inward Investment in the EC; UK Evidence on Corporate Integration Strategies', in J. H. Dunning and P. Robson (eds), *Multinationals in the European Community*, Oxford: Blackwell.

Kobrin, S. J. (1999). 'Developing After Industrialization: Poor Countries in an Electronically Integrated Global Economy', in N. Hood and S. Young (eds), *The Globalization of Multinational Enterprise Activity and Economic Development*, London: Macmillan.

Kogut, B. (1983). 'Foreign Direct Investment as a Sequential Process', in C. P. Kindleberger and D. Audretsch (eds), *The Multinational Corporation in the 1980s*, Cambridge, MA: MIT Press.

Krugman, P. (1991), *Geography and Trade*, Cambridge MA: MIT Press.

Malmberg, A, Sölvell, Ö and Zander, I. (1996), *Geografiska Annaler*, 78 (2), 85–97.

Marshall, A. (1890/1916), *Principles of Economics: An Introductory Volume*, 7th edn, London: Macmillan.

Monitor Company (1993), *The Competitive Advantage of Scotland: Identifying Potential for Competitiveness*, Report written for Scottish Enterprise.

Narula, R. (1993), 'Technology, International Business and Porter's Diamond: Synthesizing a Dynamic Competitive Development Model', *Management International Review*, 2, 85–107.

Pfeffer, J. and Salancik, G. (1978), *The External Control of Organizations: A Resource Dependence Perspective*, New York: Harper & Row.

Piore, M. and Sabel, C. (1984), *The Second Industrial Divide*, New York: Basic Books.

Porter, M. E. (1990), *The Competitive Advantage of Nations*, New York: Free Press.

Porter, M. E. (1998), 'Clusters and the New Economics of Competition', *Harvard Business Review*, 76 (6), 77–91.

Porter, M. E. and the *Monitor* Company (1991), 'Canada at a Crossroads: The Reality of a New Competitive Environment', Ottawa: Industry Canada.

Pouder, W. and St John, W. (1996), 'Hot Spots and Blind Spots: Geographical Clusters of Firms and Innovation', *Academy of Management Review*, 21 (4), 1192–1225.

Prahalad, C. K. and Doz, Y. L. (1981), 'An Approach to Strategic Control in MNC's, *Sloan Management Review*, Summer, 5–13.

Robinson, W. S. (1950), 'Ecological Correlations and the Behaviour of Individuals', *American Sociological Review*, 15, 351–7.

Roth, K. and Morrison, A. (1992), 'Implementing Global Strategy: Characteristics of Global Subsidiary Mandates', *Journal of International Business Studies*, 23 (4), 715–36.

Rugman, A. (1991), 'Diamond in the Rough', *Business Quarterly*, 55 (3), 61–70.

Saxenian, A. (1994), *Regional Advantage: Culture and Competition in Silicon Valley and Route 128*, London: Cambridge, MA and Harvard University Press.

Science Council of Canada, (1980), *Multinationals and Industrial Strategy. The Role of World Product Mandates*, Science Council of Canada, Ottowa.

Sölvell, Ö. and Malmberg, A. (1998), 'Spelar det någon roll? Om ökat utlandsägande i svenskt närinlgsiv' (Does it Matter? Increased Foreign Ownership of Swedish Industry), Stockholm: Invest in Sweden Agency.

Vernon, R. (1979), 'The Product Cycle in the New International Environment', *The Oxford Bulletin of Economics and Statistics*, 41, 255–67.

Westney, E. (1990), 'Internal and External Linkages in the MNC: The Case of R&D Subsidiaries in Japan', in C. A. Bartlett, Y. L. Doz and G. Hedlund (eds), *Managing the Global Firm*, London: Routledge.

White, R. E. and Poynter, T. A. (1984), 'Strategies for Foreign-Owned Subsidiaries in Canada', *Business Quarterly*, Summer, 59–69.

Chapter 10

Barney, J. (1991), Firm Resources and Sustained Competitive Advantage', *Journal of Management*, 17 (1), 99–120.

Bartlett, C. A. (1979), *Multinational Structural Evolution: The Changing Decision Environment in International Divisions*, unpublished doctoral dissertation, Harvard University.

Bartlett, C. A. and Ghoshal, S. (1986), 'Tap Your Subsidiaries for Global Reach', *Harvard Business Review*, 64 (6), 87–94.

Bartlett, C. A. and Ghoshal, S. (1989), *Managing across Borders: The Transnational Solution*, Boston, MA: Harvard Business School Press, 1989.

Birkinshaw, J. M. (1995), *Entrepreneurship in Multinational Corporations: The Initiative Process in Canadian Subsidiaries*, unpublished doctoral dissertation, Western Business School.

Bower, J. L. (1970), *Managing the Resource Allocation Process*, New York: Richard D. Irwin.

Burgelman, R. A. (1983), 'A Process Model of Internal Corporate Venturing in the Diversified Major Firm', *Administrative Science Quarterly*, 28, 223–44.

Collis, D. (1991), 'Corporate Advantage: Identifying and Exploiting Resources', *Harvard Business School*, Note 9-391-285.

Crookell, H. (1986), 'Specialisation and International Competitiveness', in H. Etemad and L. Séguin Dulude (eds), *Managing the Multinational Subsidiary*, London: Croom Helm, 102–12.

Crookell, H. H and Morrison, A. J. (1990), 'Subsidiary Strategy in a Free Trade Environment', *Business Quarterly*, Fall.

Delacroix, J. (1993), 'The European Subsidiaries of American MNCs: An Exercise in Ecological Analysis', in S. Ghoshal and D. E. Westney (eds),

Organization Theory and the Multinational Enterprise, New York: St Martin's Press, 105–13.

Dierickx, I. and Cool, K. (1989), 'Asset Stock Accumulation and Sustainability of Competitive Advantage', *Management Science*, 35 (12), 1504–13.

Etemad, H. and Dulude, L. Séguin (1986), *Managing the Multinational Subsidiary*, London: Croom Helm.

Forsgren, M. and Johanson, J. (eds) (1992), *Managing Networks in International Business*, Philadelphia, PA: Gordon & Breach.

Forsgren, M. and Pahlberg, C. (1992), 'Subsidiary Influence and Autonomy in International Firms', *International Business Review*, 1 (3), 41–51.

Forsgren, M. Holm, U. and Johanson, J. (1992), 'Internationalization of the Second Degree: The Emergence of European-Based Centres in Swedish Firms', in S. Young, and J. Hamill (eds), *Europe and the Multinationals*, Worcester: Billing & Sons.

Galunic, D. C. and Eisenhardt, K. M. (1995), *The Evolution of Intracorporate Domains: Divisional Charter Losses in High-Technology, Multidivisional Corporations*, INSEAD working paper.

Ghoshal, S. (1986), *The Innovative Multinational: A Differentiated Network of Organizational Roles and Management Processes*, unpublished doctoral dissertation, Boston, MA: Harvard Business School.

Ghoshal, S. and Bartlett, C. A. (1991), 'The Multinational Corporation as an Interorganizational Network', *Academy of Management Review*, 15 (4), 603–25.

Hedlund, G. (1986), 'The Hypermodern MNC: A Heterarchy?', *Human Resource Management*, 25, 9–36.

Hood, N. and Young, S. (1983), *Multinational Investment Strategies in the British Isles*, London: HMSO.

Hood, N., Young, S. and Lal D. (1994), 'Strategic Evolution within Japanese Manufacturing Plants in Europe: UK Evidence', *International Business Review*, 3 (2), 97–122; Chapter 5 in this volume.

Johanson, J. and Vahlne, J.-E. (1977), 'The Internationalization Process of the Firm – A Model of Knowledge Development and Increasing Foreign Market Commitments', *Journal of International Business Studies*, Spring/Summer 8.

Kim, W. C. and Mauborgne, R. A. (1993), 'Procedural Justice, Attitudes, and Subsidiary Top Management Compliance with Multinationals' Corporate Strategic Decisions', *Academy of Management Journal*, 36 (3), 502–26.

Miles, M. B. and Huberman, M. (1984), *Qualitative Data Analysis: A Sourcebook of New Methods*, Newbury Park, CA: Sage.

Pearce, R. D. (1989), *The Internationalization of Research and Development by Multinational Enterprises*, New York: St Martin's Press.

Penrose, E. T. (1959), *The Theory of the Growth of the Firm*, Oxford: Basil Blackwell.

Porter, M. E. (1980), *Competitive Strategy*, New York: Free Press.

Porter, M. E. (1986), *Competition in Global Industries*, Boston, MA: Harvard Business School Press.

Porter, M. E. (1990), *The Competitive Advantage of Nations*, New York: Free Press.

Prahalad, C. K. (1976), *The Strategic Process in a Multinational Corporation*, unpublished doctoral dissertation, School of Business Administration, Harvard University.

Prahalad, C. K. and Doz, Y. L. (1981), 'An Approach to Strategic Control in MNCs', *Sloan Management Review*, Summer, 5–13.

Science Council of Canada (1980), *Multinationals and Industrial Strategy. The Role of World Product Mandates.*

Wernerfelt, B. (1984), 'A Resource Based View of the Firm', *Strategic Management Journal*, 5, 171–80.

White, R. E. and Poynter, T. A. (1984), 'Strategies for Foreign-Owned Subsidiaries in Canada', *Business Quarterly*, Summer, 59–69.

Young, S. and Hood, N. (1994), 'Designing Developmental After-Care Programmes for Inward Investors in the European Community', *Transnational Corporations*, 3 (2).

Young, S., Hood, N. and Hamill, J. (1988), *Foreign Multinationals and the British Economy*, London: Routledge.

Young, S., Hood, N. and Peters, E. (1994), 'Multinational Enterprises and Regional Economic Development', *Regional Studies*, 28 (7), 657–77; Chapter 8 in this volume.

Chapter 11

Agarwal, S. and Ramaswami, S. (1992), 'Choice of Foreign Market Entry Mode: Impact of Ownership, Location and Internationalization Factors', *Journal of International Business Studies*, 23, 1–28.

Aharoni, Y. (1966), *The Foreign Investment Decision Process*, Boston, MA: Harvard Business School Press.

Almor, T. and Hirsch, S. (1995), 'Outsiders' response to Europe 1992: Theoretical considerations and empirical evidence', *Journal of International Business Studies*, 26, 223–39.

Amit, R. and Schoemaker, P. (1993), 'Strategic assets and organizational rent', *Strategic Management Journal*, 14, 33–46.

Andersson, U. and Johanson, J. (1996), 'Subsidiary embeddedness and its implications for integration in the MNC', *Proceedings of the European International Business Association*, 235–56.

Barney, J. (1991), 'Firm resources and sustained competitive advantage', *Journal of Management*, 17, 99–120.

Bartlett, C. A. and Ghoshal, S. (1986), 'Tap your subsidiaries for global reach', *Harvard Business Review*, 64 (6), 87–94.

Bartlett, C. A. and Ghoshal, S. (1986), *Managing Across Borders: The Transnational Solution*, Boston, MA: Harvard Business School Press.

Behrman, J. N. and Fisher, W. A. (1980), *Overseas R&D Activities of Transnational Companies*, Cambridge, MA: Oelgeschlager, Gunn & Hain.

Birkinshaw, J. M. (1995), 'Entrepreneurship in multinational corporations: The initiative process in Canadian subsidiaries', Unpublished doctoral dissertation, Western Business School, University of Western Ontario, London, Ontario.

Birkinshaw, J. M. (1996), 'How subsidiary mandates are gained and lost', *Journal of International Business Studies*, 27, 467–96.

Birkinshaw, J. M. (1997), 'Entrepreneurship in multinational corporations: The characteristics of subsidiary initiatives', *Strategic Management Journal*, 18, 207–29.

Birkinshaw, J. M. and Morrison, A. (1995), 'Configurations of strategy and structure in subsidiaries of multinational corporations', *Journal of International Business Studies*, 26, 729–54.

Birkinshaw, J. M. and Ridderstråle, J. (1999), 'Fighting the corporate immune system: A process study of subsidiary initiatives in multinational corporations', *International Business Review*, 8 (2), 149–80.

Bishop, P. and Crookell, H. H. (1986), 'Specialization in Canadian Subsidiaries', in D. G. McFetridge (ed.), *Canadian Industry in Transition*, Toronto: University of Toronto Press, 305–85.

Boddewyn, J. (1979), 'Foreign divestment: Magnitude and factors', *Journal of International Business Studies*, 10 (3), 21–6.

Boddewyn, J. (1983), 'Foreign and domestic divestment and investment decisions: Like or unlike?', *Journal of International Business Studies*, 14 (3), 23–35.

Bower, J. L. (1972), *Managing the Resource Allocation Process*, Homewood, IL: Irwin.

Burgelman, R. A. (1983a), 'A process model of internal corporate venturing in the diversified major firm', *Administrative Science Quarterly*, 28, 223–44.

Burgelman, R. A. (1983b), 'A model of the interaction of strategic behavior, corporate context and the concept of strategy', *Academy of Management Review*, 8, 61–70.

Burgelman, R. A. (1991), 'Intraorganizational ecology of strategy making and organizational adaptation: Theory and field research', *Organization Science*, 2, 239–62.

Burgelman, R. A. (1996), 'A process model of strategic business exit: Implications for an evolutionary perspective on strategy', *Strategic Management Journal*, 17, 193–214.

Cavusgil, S. T. (1980), 'On the internationalization process of the firm', *European Research*, 8, 273–81.

Chang, S.-J. (1995), 'International expansion strategy of Japanese firms: Capability building through sequential entry', *Academy of Management Journal*, 38, 383–407.

Chang, S.-J. (1996), 'An evolutionary perspective on diversification and corporate restructuring: Entry, exit and economic performance during 1981–1989', *Strategic Management Journal*, 17, 587–612.

Child, J. (1972), 'Organization structure, environment and performance: The role of strategic choice', *Sociology*, 6, 1–22.

Clarke, I. (1985), *The Spatial Organization of Multinational Corporations*, London: Croom Helm.

Crookell, H. H. (1986), 'Specialization and international competitiveness', in H. Etemad and L. Séguin Dulude (eds), *Managing the Multinational Subsidiary*, 102–11, London: Croom Helm.

Cyert, R. and March, J. G. (1963), *A Behavioral Theory of the Firm*, Englewood Cliffs, NJ: Prentice-Hall.

Day, D. (1994), 'Raising radicals: Different processes for championing innovative corporate ventures', *Organization Science*, 5, 148–72.

Delaney, E. (1996), 'Strategic development of multinational subsidiaries in Ireland', in J. Birkinshaw and N. Hood (eds), *Multinational Corporate Evolution and Subsidiary Development*, London: Macmillan, 239–67.

Dicken, P. (1976), 'Geographical perspectives on United States investment in the United Kingdom', *Environment and Planning*, 8, 685–705.

Dierickx, I. and Cool, K. (1989), 'Asset stock accumulation and sustainability of competitive advantage', *Management Science*, 35, 1504–13.

DiMaggio, P. J. and Powell, W. W. (1983), 'The iron cage revisited: Institutional isomorphism and collective rationality in organizational fields', *American Sociological Review*, 48, 147–60.

Doty, D. H. and Glick, W. H. (1994), 'Typologies as a unique form of theory building: Toward improved understanding and modeling', *Academy of Management Review*, 19, 230–51.

Doz, Y. L. (1996), 'The evolution of cooperation in strategic alliances: Initial conditions or learning processes?', *Strategic Management Journal*, 17, 55–83.

Dunning, J. H. (1981), *International Production and the Multinational Enterprise*, London: Allen & Unwin.

Dunning, J. H. (1986), 'The investment cycle revisited', *Weltwirtschaftliches Archiv*, 122, 667–77.

Dunning, J. H. (1993), *Multinational Enterprises and the Global Economy*, Wokingham: Addison-Wesley.

Emerson, R. M. (1962), 'Power-dependence relations', *American Sociological Review*, 27, 31–41.

Forsgren, M., Holm, U. and Johanson, J. (1992), 'Internationalization of the second degree: The emergence of European-based centres in Swedish firms', in S. Young and J. Hamill (eds), *Europe and the Multinationals*, London: Edward Elgar, 235–53.

Forsgren, M. and Pahlberg, C. (1992), 'Subsidiary influence and autonomy in international firms', *International Business Review*, 1 (3), 41–51.

Gage Canadian Dictionary (1983), Toronto: Gage Educational Publishing.

Galunic, D. C. (1996), 'Recreating divisional domains: Intracorporate evolution and the multibusiness firm', in B. Keys and L. N. Dosier (eds), *Proceedings of the Academy of Management*, 219–24.

Galunic, D. C. and Eisenhardt, K. M. (1996), 'The evolution of intracorporate domains: Divisional charter losses in high-technology, multidivisional corporations', *Organization Science*, 7, 255–82.

Gates, S. R. and Egelhoff, W. G. (1986), 'Centralization in headquarters–subsidiary relationships', *Journal of International Business Studies*, 17, 71–92.

Ghauri, P. (1992), 'New structures in MNCs based in small countries: A network approach', *European Management Journal*, 10, 357–64.

Ghoshal, S. and Bartlett, C. A. (1991), 'The multinational corporation as an interorganizational network', *Academy of Management Review*, 15, 603–25.

Ghoshal, S. and Nohria, N. (1989), 'Internal differentiation within multinational corporations', *Strategic Management Journal*, 10, 323–37.

Gupta, A. K. and Govindarajan, V. (1991), 'Knowledge flows and the structure of control within multinational corporations', *Academy of Management Review*, 16, 768–92.

Gupta, A. K. and Govindarajan, V. (1994), 'Organizing for knowledge within MNCs', *International Business Review*, 3, 443–57.

Hagström, P. (1994), 'The "wired" MNC', Stockholm: Institute of International Business.

Håkanson, L. and Zander, U. (1986), *Managing International Research and Development*, Stockholm: Sveriges Mekanförbund.

Halal, W. (1994), 'From hierarchy to enterprise: Internal markets are the new foundation of management', *Academy of Management Executive*, 8 (4), 69–83.

Hamel, G. and Prahalad, C. K. (1985), 'Do you really have a global strategy?', *Harvard Business Review*, 63 (4), 139–45.

Hannan, M. and Freeman, J. (1977), 'The population ecology of organizations', *American Journal of Sociology*, 82, 929–64.

Harrigan, K. R. (1984), 'Innovation within overseas subsidiaries', *Journal of Business Strategy*, 5, 47–53.

Haspeslagh, P. C. and Jemison, D. B. (1991), *Managing Acquisitions: Creating Value through Corporate Renewal*, New York: Free Press.

Hatch Report (1979), *Strengthening Canada Abroad. Industry, trade and commerce*, Ottawa, Ontario: Export Promotion Review Committee.

Hedlund, G. (1986), 'The hypermodern MNC: A heterarchy?', *Human Resource Management*, 25, 9–36.

Holm, U., Johanson, J. and Thilenius, P. (1995), 'Headquarters' knowledge of subsidiary network contexts in the multinational corporation', *International Studies of Management and Organization*, 25 (1–2), 97–120.

Hood, N. and Young, S. (1983), *Multinational Investment Strategies in the British Isle*, London: HMSO.

Hood, N., Young, S. and Lal, D. (1994), 'Strategic evolution within Japanese manufacturing plants in Europe: UK evidence', *International Business Review*, 3 (2), 97–122.

Huber, G. (1991), 'Organizational learning: The contributing processes and the literatures', *Organization Science*, 2, 88–115.

Jarillo, J.-C. and Martinez, J. I. (1990), 'Different roles for subsidiaries: The case of multinational corporations', *Strategic Management Journal*, 11, 501–12.

Johanson, J. and Mattson, L. G. (1988), 'Internationalisation in industrial systems – A network approach', in N. Hood and J.-E. Vahlne (eds), *Strategies in Global Competition*, London: Croom Helm, 287–314.

Johanson, J. and Vahlne, J.-E. (1977), 'The internationalization process of the firm – A model of knowledge development and increasing foreign market commitments', *Journal of International Business Studies*, 8, 23–32.

Kirzner, I. (1973), *Competition and Entrepreneurship*, Chicago: University of Chicago Press.

Kogut, B. and Zander, U. (1992), 'Knowledge of the firm, combinative capabilities and the replication of technology', *Organization Science*, 3, 383–97.

Krugman, P. (1991), *Geography and Trade*, Cambridge, MA: MIT Press.

Li, J. T. (1995), 'Foreign entry and survival: Effects of strategic choices on performance in international markets', *Strategic Management Journal*, 16, 637–55.

Lincoln, J. R., Olson, J. and Hanada, M. (1978), 'Cultural effects on organizational structure: The case of Japanese firms in the United States', *American Sociological Review*, 43, 829–47.

Madhok, A. (1997), 'Cost, value and foreign market entry mode: The transaction and the firm', *Strategic Management Journal*, 18, 39–61.

Malnight, T. (1995), 'Globalization of an ethnocentric firm: An evolutionary perspective', *Strategic Management Journal*, 16, 119–41.

Malnight, T. (1996), 'The transition from decentralized to network-based MNC structures: An evolutionary perspective', *Journal of International Business Studies*, 27, 43–66.

McNee, R. B. (1958), 'Functional geography of the firm with an illustrative case study from the petroleum industry', *Economic Geography*, 34, 321–37.

Meyer, J. W. and Rowan, B. (1997), 'Institutionalized organizations: Formal structure as myth and ceremony', *American Journal of Sociology*, 83, 340–63.

Mintzberg, H., Raisinghani, D. and Theoret, A. (1976), 'The structure of unstructured decision processes', *Administrative Science Quarterly*, 21, 246–74.

Morrison, A. and Crookell, H. (1990), 'Subsidiary strategy in a free-trade environment', *Business Quarterly*, 55 (2), 33–9.

Mullor-Sebastian, A. (1983), 'The product life cycle theory: Empirical evidence', *Journal of International Business Studies*, 14, 95–105.

Nelson, R. and Winter, S. (1982), *An Evolutionary Theory of Economic Change*, Cambridge, MA: Harvard University Press.

Noda, T. and Bower, J. L. (1996), 'Strategy making as iterated processes of resource allocation', *Strategic Management Journal*, 17, 159–92.

Norton, R. D. and Rees, J. (1979), 'The product cycle and the spatial decentralization of American manufacturing', *Regional Studies*, 13, 141–51.

Ouchi, W. G. (1980), 'Market, bureaucracies and clans', *Administrative Science Quarterly*, 25, 124–41.

Ozawa, T. (1992), 'Foreign direct investment and economic development', *Transnational Corporations*, 1, 27–54.

Papanasstasiou, M. and Pearce, R. (1994), 'Determinants of the market strategies of US companies', *Journal of the Economics of Business*, 2, 199–217.

Pearce, R. D. (1989), *The Internationalization of Research and Development by Multinational Enterprises*, New York: St Martin's Press.

Penrose, E. T. (1959), *The Theory of the Growth of the Firm.*, Oxford: Basil Blackwell.

Perlmutter, H. (1969), 'The tortuous evolution of the multinational corporation', *Columbia Journal of World Business*, 4, 9–18.

Pfeffer, J. R. and Salancik, G. R. (1978), *The External Control of Organizations*, New York: Harper & Row.

Porter, M. E. (1980), *Competitive Strategy*, New York: Free Press.

Porter, M. E. (1990), *The Competitive Advantage of Nations*, New York: Free Press.

Prahalad, C. K. (1976), 'The strategic process in a multinational corporation', Unpublished doctoral dissertation, Boston, MA: Harvard University.

Prahalad, C. K. and Doz, Y. L. (1981), 'An approach to strategic control in MNCs', *Sloan Management Review*, 22, 5–13.

Ring, P. S. and Van de Ven, A. (1994), 'Development processes of cooperative interorganizational relationships', *Academy of Management Review*, 19, 90–118.

Ronstadt, R. C. (1977), *Research and Development Abroad by US Multinationals*, New York: Praeger.

Rosenzweig, P. and Chang, S.-J. (1995a), 'An evolutionary model of the multinational corporation', paper presented at the annual meeting of the Academy of International Business, Seoul.

Rosenzweig, P. and Chang, S.-J. (1995b), 'Sequential direct investment of European and Japanese firms in the US', paper presented at the annual meeting of the Academy of International Business, Seoul.

Rosenzweig, P. and Nohria, N. (1995), 'Influences on human resource management practices in multinational corporations', *Journal of International Business Studies*, 25, 229–52.

Rosenzweig, P. and Singh, J. (1991), 'Organizational environments and the multinational enterprise', *Academy of Management Review*, 16, 340–61.

Roth, K. and Morrison, A. (1992), 'Implementing global strategy: Characteristics of global subsidiary mandates', *Journal of International Business Studies*, 23, 715–36.

Rugman, A. and Verbeke, A. (1992), 'A note on the transnational solution and the transaction cost theory of multinational strategic management', *Journal of International Business Studies*, 23, 761–72.

Sachdev, J. C. (1976), 'A framework for the planning of divestment policies for multinational companies', Unpublished doctoral dissertation, University of Manchester.

Safarian, E. (1966), *Foreign Ownership of Canadian Industry*, Toronto: McGraw-Hill.

Science Council of Canada (1980), *Multinationals and industrial Strategy. The role of World Product Mandates*, Ottawa, Ontario: Science Council of Canada.

Scott, R. and Meyer, J. (1994), *Institutional Environments and Organizations: Structural Complexity and Individualism*, Beverly Hills, CA: Sage.

Sölvell, Ö. and Zander, I. (1993), 'International diffusion of knowledge: Isolating mechanisms and the role of the MNE', in A. D. Chandler, P. Hagström and Ö. Sölvell (eds), *The Dynamic Firm: The Role of Technology, Strategy, Organization and Regions*, Oxford: Oxford University Press, 402–16.

Sugiura, H. (1990), 'How Honda localizes its global strategy', *Sloan Management Review*, 31, 77–82.

Szulanski, G. (1996), 'Exploring internal stickiness: Impediments to the transfer of best practices within the firm', *Strategic Management Journal*, 17, Special Issue, 27–44.

Teece, D. J., Pisano, G. and Shuen, A. (1997), 'Dynamic capabilities and strategic management', *Strategic Management Journal*, 18: 509–34.

Thompson, J. D. (1967), *Organizations in Action*, New York: McGraw-Hill.

Vernon, R. (1966), 'International investments and international trade in the product cycle', *Quarterly Journal of Economics*, 80, 190–207.

Vernon, R. (1979), 'The product cycle in the new international environment', *Oxford Bulletin of Economics and Statistics*, 41, 255–67.

Wernerfelt, B. (1984), 'A resource based view of the firm', *Strategic Management Journal*, 5, 171–80.

Westney, D. E. (1994), 'Institutionalization theory and the multinational corporation', in S. Ghoshal and D. E. Westney (eds), *Organization Theory and the Multinational Corporation*, New York: St Martin's Press, 53–76.

White, R. E. and Poynter, T. A. (1984), 'Strategies for foreign-owned subsidiaries in Canada', *Business Quarterly*, 49, 59–69.

Young, S., Hood, N. and Hamill, J. (1988), *Foreign Multinationals and the British Economy*, London: Routledge.

Young, S., Hood, N. and Peters, E. (1994), 'Multinational enterprises and regional economic development', *Regional Studies*, 28, 657–77.

Young, S., McDermott, M. and Dunlop, S. (1991), 'The challenge of the single market', in B. Bürgenmeier and J. L. Mucchielli (eds), *Multinationals and Europe 1992*, London: Routledge, 121–43.

Zander, I. (1994), 'The tortoise evolution of the multinational corporation', doctoral dissertation, Institute of International Business, Stockholm School of Economics.

Chapter 12

Barney, J. (1991), 'Firm Resources and Sustained Competitive Advantage', *Journal of Management*, 17 (1), 99–120.

Bartlett, C. A. (1979), 'Multinational structural evolution: The Changing decision environment in international divisions', unpublished doctoral dissertation, Harvard University.

Bartlett, C. A. and Ghoshal, S. (1986), 'Tap your subsidiaries for global reach', *Harvard Business Review*, 64 (6), 87–94.

Birkinshaw, J. M. (1995), 'Entrepreneurship in multinational corporations: The initiative process in Canadian subsidiaries', unpublished doctoral dissertation, Western Business School.

Birkinshaw, J. M. and Hood N. (1997), 'An empirical study of development processes in foreign-owned subsidiaries in Canada and Scotland', *Management International Review*, 37 (4), 339–64.

Birkinshaw, J. M. and Morrison, A. J. (1996), 'Configurations of strategy and structure in multinational subsidiaries', *Journal of International Business Studies*, 26 (4), 729–94.

Birkinshaw, J. M. Morrison, A. J. and Hulland, J. (1995), 'Structural and competitive determinants of a global integration strategy', *Strategic Management Journal*, 16 (8), 637–55.

Bishop, P. and Crookell, H. H. (1986), 'Specialization in Canadian Subsidiaries', in D. G. McFetridge (ed.), *Canadian Industry in Transition*, Toronto: University of Toronto Press, 305–86.

Bower, J. L. (1970), *Managing the Resource Allocation Process*, Boston: Harvard University.

Brandt, W. K. and Hulbert, J. M. (1977), 'Headquarters guidance in marketing strategy in the multinational subsidiary', *Columbia Journal of World Business*, 12, 7–14.

Burgelman, R. A. (1983), 'A model of the interaction of strategic behavior, corporate context and the concept of strategy', *Academy of Management Review*, 8 (1), 61–70.

Cantwell, J. (1989), *Technological Innovation and Multinational Corporations*, Oxford: Basil Blackwell.

Chatterjee S. and Wernerfelt B. (1991), 'The link between resources and type of diversification: Theory and evidence', *Strategic Management Journal*, 12 (1), 33–48.

Child, J. (1972), 'Organization structure, environment and performance: The role of strategic choice', *Sociology*, 6, 1–22.

Crookell, H. H. (1986), 'Specialization and international competitiveness', in H. Etemad and L. Séguin Dulude (eds), *Managing the Multinational Subsidiary*, London: Croom Helm, 102–11.

Crookell, H. H. and Morrison, A. J. (1990), 'Subsidiary strategy in a free trade environment', *Business Quarterly*, Autumn, 33–9.

D'Cruz, J. R. (1986), 'Strategic management of subsidiaries', in H. Etemad and L. Séguin Dulude (eds), *Managing the Multinational Subsidiary*, London: Croom Helm, 75–89.

Dunning, J. H. (1980), 'Toward an electric theory of international production: Some empirical tests', *Journal of International Business Studies*, 11 (1), 9–31.

Dunning, J. H. (1988), 'The electric paradigm of international production: A restatement and some possible extensions', *Journal of International Business Studies*, 19, 1–31.

Dunning, J. H. (1993), *Multinational Enterprises and the Global Economy*, Wokingham: Addison-Wesley.

Etemad, H. and Séguin Dulude, L. (1986), *Managing the Multinational Subsidiary*, London: Croom Helm.

Fornell, C. (1984), 'A Second generation of multivariate analysis: Classification of methods and implications for marketing research', Working Paper, University of Michigan.

Fornell, C. and Barclay, D. (1983), 'Jackknifing: A supplement to Lohmöller's LVPLS program', Graduate School of Business Administration, University of Michigan, Ann Arbor, MI.

Fornell, C. and Bookstein F. (1982), 'A comparative analysis of two structural equation models: LISREL and PLS applied to consumer exit-voice theory', *Journal of Marketing Research*, 19, 440–52.

Fornell, C. and Larcker, D. F. (1981), 'Structural equation models with unobservable variables and measurement error: Algebra and statistics', *Journal of Marketing Research*, 18, 382–88.

Fornell, C., Lorange, P. and Roos, J. (1990), 'The cooperative venture formation process: A latent variable structural modeling approach', *Management Science*, 36 (10), 1246–55.

Forsgren, M. (1995), 'Developing centres of excellence in multinational firms', Research Proposal, Copenhagen Business School.

Garnier, G. H. (1982), 'Context and decision making autonomy in foreign affiliates of US multinational corporations', *Academy of Management Journal*, 25, 893–908.

Gates, S. R. and Egelhoff, W. G. (1986), 'Centralization in headquarters–subsidiary relationships', *Journal of International Business Studies*, 17 (2), 71–92.

Ghoshal, S. (1986), 'The innovative multinational: A differentiated network of organizational roles and management processes', unpublished doctoral dissertation, Harvard Business School.

Ghoshal, S. and Bartlett, C. A. (1991), 'The multinational corporation as an interorganizational network', *Academy of Management Review*, 15 (4), 603–25.

Ghoshal, S. and Bartlett, C. A. (1994), 'Linking organizational context and managerial action: The dimensions of quality of management', *Strategic Management Journal*, 15, 91–112.

Ghoshal, S. and Nohria, H. (1989), 'Internal differentiation within multinational corporations', *Strategic Management Journal*, 10 (4), 323–37.

Gupta, A. K. and Govindarajan, V. (1994), 'Organizing for knowledge within MNCs', *International Business Review*, 3 (4), 443–57.

Hamel, G. and Prahalad, C. K. (1994), *Competing for the Future*, Boston, MA: Harvard Business School Press.

Hedlund, G. (1986), 'The hypermodern MNC: A heterarchy?', *Human Resources Management*, 25, 9–36.

Hymer, S. H. (1976), *The International Operations of National Firms: A Study of Direct Investment*, Cambridge, MA: MIT Press.

Jarillo, J.-C. and Martinez, J. I. (1990), 'Different roles for subsidiaries: The case of multinational corporations', *Strategic Management Journal*, 11 (7), 501–12.

Johansson, J. K. and Yip, G. S. (1990), 'Exploiting globalization potential: US and Japanese strategies', *Strategic Management Journal*, 15 (8), 579–601.

Kanter, R. M. (1985), *The Change Masters*, New York: Simon & Schuster.

Kirzner, I. (1973), *Competition and Entrepreneurship*, Chicago: University of Chicago Press.

Kobrin, S. J. (1991), 'An empirical analysis of the determinants of global integration', *Strategic Management Journal*, 12, 17–31.

Kuratko, D. F., Montagno, R. V. and Hornsby, J. S. (1990), 'Developing an intrapreneurial assessment instrument for an effective corporation entrepreneurial environment', *Strategic Management Journal*, 11, 49–58.

Leksell, L. (1984), 'Headquarters–subsidiary relationships in multinational corporations', doctoral thesis, Institute of International Business, Stockholm School of Economics.

Markides, C. C. (1995), *Diversification, Refocusing and Economic Performance*. Cambridge, MA: MIT Press.

Nunnally, J. C. (1978), *Psychometric Theory*, 2nd edn, New York: McGraw-Hill.

Otterbeck, L. (1981), *The Management of Headquarters–Subsidiary Relations in Multinational Corporations*, Aldershot: Gower.

Peters, T. J. and Waterman, R. H. (1982), *In Search of Excellence*, New York: Harper & Row.

Pinchott, G. III (1985), *Intrapreneuring*, New York: Harper & Row.

Porter, M. E. (1980), *Competitive Strategy*, New York: Free Press.

Porter, M. E. (1986), *Competition in Global Industries*, Boston, MA: Harvard Business School Press.

Porter, M. E. (1990), *The Competitive Advantage of Nations*, New York: Free Press.

Prahalad, C. K. (1976), 'The strategic process in a multinational corporation', unpublished doctoral dissertation, School of Business Administration, Harvard University.

Prahalad, C. K. and Doz, Y. L. (1981), 'An approach to strategic control in MNCs', *Sloan Management Review*, Summer, 5–13.

Roth, K. and Morrison, A. J. (1992), 'Implementing global strategy: Characteristics of global subsidiary mandates', *Journal of International Business Studies*, 23 (4), 715–36.

Rugman, A. (1981), *Inside the Multinationals: The Economics of Internal Markets*. London: Croom Helm.

Rugman, A. M. and Bennett, J. (1982), 'Technology transfer and world product mandating in Canada', *Columbia Journal of World Business*, 17 (4), 58–62.

Rugman, A. and Verbeke, A. (1992), 'A note on the transnational solution and the transaction cost theory of multinational strategic management', *Journal of International Business Studies*, 23 (4), 761–72.

Science Council of Canada (1980), *Multinationals and Industrial Strategy: The Role of World Product Mandates*, Science Council of Canada, Supply and Services, Ottawa.

Szulanski, G. (1995), 'An empirical investigation of the barriers to transfer of best practice inside the firm', unpublished doctoral dissertation, Paris: INSEAD.

Teece, D. (1977), 'Technology transfer by multinational firms: The resource cost of transferring technological know-how', *Economic Journal*, 87, 242–61.

Vernon, R. (1966), 'International investments and international trade in the product cycle', *Quarterly Journal of Economics*, 80, 190–207.

Wernerfelt, B. (1984), 'A resource-based view of the firm', *Strategic Management Journal*, 5 (2), 171–80.

Westney, D. E. (1994), 'Institutionalization theory and the multinational corporation', in S. Ghoshal and D. E. Westney (eds), *Organization Theory and the Multinational Corporation*, New York: St Martin's Press, 53–76.

White R. E. and Poynter, T. A. (1984), 'Strategies for foreign-owned subsidiaries in Canada', *Business Quarterly*, Summer, 59–69.

Woodcock, P. (1994), 'The greenfield vs. acquisition entry mode decision process', unpublished doctoral dissertation, Western Business School.

Young, S., Hood, N. and Peters, E. (1994), 'Multinational enterprises' and regional economic development', *Regional Studies*, 28 (7), 657–77; Chapter 8 in this volume.

Chapter 14

Birkinshaw, J. M. (2000), 'Upgrading of Industry Clusters and Foreign Investment', *International Studies of Management and Organization*, 30 (2), 93–113.

Birkinshaw, J. M. (2002), 'Managing Global R&D Networks: What Sort of Knowledge are you Working with?', *Long Range Planning*, 35, 245–67.

Birkinshaw, J. M. and Terjesen, S. (2003), 'The customer-focused multinational: Revisiting the Stopford and Wells model in an era of global customers', in J. M. Birkinshaw, G. Yip, S. Goshal, C. Markides and J. Stopford (eds), *The Future of the Multinational Company*, Chichester: John Wiley.

Birkinshaw, J. M., Toulan, O. and Arnold, D. (2001), 'Global account management in multinational corporations: Theory and evidence', *Journal of International Business Studies*, 32 (2), 321–48.

Boddewyn, J. (1979), 'Foreign divestment: Magnitude and factors', *Journal of International Business Studies*, 10, 21–6.

Boddewyn, J. (1983), 'Foreign and domestic divestment and investment decisions: Like or unlike?', *Journal of International Business Studies*, 83 (3), 23–35.

Campbell, A. and Birkinshaw, J. (2003), 'Corporate Venturing: How to Choose the Right Business Model', London Business School, Working Paper.

Chesbrough H. (2000), 'Designing Corporate Ventures in the Shadow of Venture Capital', *California Management Review*, 42 (3), 31–47.

Delany, E. (1998), 'Strategic Development of Multinational Subsidiaries in Ireland', in J. M. Birkinshaw and N. Hood (eds), *Multinational Corporate Evolution and Subsidiary Development*, London: Macmillan.

Doz, Y., Williamson, P. and Santos, J. (2001), *The Metanational Corporation*, Cambridge, MA: Harvard Business School Press.

Enright, M. J. (2000), 'Regional Clusters and Multinational Enterprises: Independence, Dependence or Interdependence?', *International Studies of Management and Organization*, 30 (2), 114–38.

Galbraith, J., Downey, D. and Kates, A. (2002), *Designing Dynamic Organizations*, New York: American Management Association.

Hamel, G. (2001), *Leading the Revolution*, Cambridge, MA: Harvard Business School Press.

Kim, W. C. and Mauborgne, R. (1997), 'Value innovation: The strategic logic of high-growth companies', *Harvard Business Review*, January–February, 103–12.

Kotabe, M. (1992), *Global Sourcing Strategy: R&D, Manufacturing, and Marketing Interfaces*, New York: Quorum Books.

Leug, A. and Yip, G. (2003), 'The Global OEM: The transformation of Asian supplier companies', in J. M. Birkinshaw, G. Yip, S. Goshal, C. Markides and J. Stopford (eds), *The Future of the Multinational Company*, Chichester: John Wiley.

Mol, M. (2001), *Global Sourcing*, Unpublished doctoral dissertation, University of Rotterdam.

Porter, M. E. (1990), *The Competitive Advantage of Nations*, New York: Free Press. ˙

Yip, G. and Madsen, T. (1996), 'Global Account Management: The New Frontier in Relationship Marketing', *International Marketing Review*, 13 (3), 24–42.

Young, S. and Hood, N. (1994), 'Designing Development After-Care Programmes for Foreign Direct Investors in the European Union', *Transnational Corporations*, 3 (2), 45–72.

Chapter 15

Draper, P., Smith, I., Stewart, W. and Hood, N. (1988), *Scottish Financial Sector*, Edinburgh: Edinburgh University Press.

Hood, N. (1980), *Memorandum to the Scottish Select Committee and Minutes of Evidence*, 23 April.

Hood, N. (1991a), 'Inward Investment and the Scottish Economy: Quo Vadis?', *Royal Bank of Scotland Review*, 169, March, 17–32.

Hood, N. (1991b), 'The Scottish Development Agency in Retrospect', *Royal Bank of Scotland Review*, 171, September, 3–21.

Hood, N. (1998), 'Business Ethics and Transnational Corporations', in I. Jones and M. Pollitt (eds), *The Role of Business Ethics in Economic Performance*, London: Macmillan, 193–210.

Hood, N. (2000), 'The Development of Public Venture Capital in Scotland', *Venture Capital*, 2 (4), 313–41.

Hood, N. and Birkinshaw, J. (eds) (1998), *Multinational Corporate Evolution and Subsidiary Development*, London: Macmillan.

Hood, N., Kilis, R. and Vahlne, J.-E. (eds) (1997), *Transition in the Baltic States: Microlevel Studies*, London: Macmillan.

Hood, N. and Vahlne, J.-E. (eds) (1988), *Strategies in Global Competition*, London: Croom Helm.

Hood, N. and Young, S. (1979), *The Economics of Multinational Enterprise*, London: Longman.

Hood, N. and Young, S. (1980a), *European Development Strategies of US Multinationals Located in Scotland*, Edinburgh: HMSO.

Hood, N. and Young, S. (1980b), *Inward Direct Investment after the Select Committee: A Critique and A Way Ahead*, Strathclyde Business School Working Paper, 8005, November.

Hood, N. and Young, S. (1981), 'British Policy and Inward Direct Investment', *Journal of World Trade Law*, 15 (3), 231–50.

Hood, N. and Young, S. (1982), *Multinationals in Retreat: The Scottish Experience*, Volume 1 in Scottish Industrial Policy Series, Edinburgh: Edinburgh University Press.

Hood, N. and Young, S. (1983a), *Multinational Investment Strategies in the British Isles*, London: HMSO.

Hood, N. and Young, S. (1983b), 'Industrial Policy in the United Kingdom', in R. E. Driscoll and J. Behrman (eds), *National Industrial Policies and International Industrial Mobility*, Cambridge, MA: Oelgeschlager, Gunn & Hain, 191–208.

Hood, N. and Young, S. (eds) (1984a), *Industry, Policy and the Scottish Economy*, Edinburgh: Edinburgh University Press.

Hood, N. and Young, S. (1984b), 'United Kingdom and the Changing World Economic Order', in W. H. Davidson and M. Hochmuth (eds), *Reversing America's Industrial Decline: Lessons from Our Competitors*, Cambridge, MA: Ballinger, P.

Hood, N. and Young, S. (1985), 'The Automobile Industry', in S. Guisinger and Associates, *Investment Incentives and Performance Requirements*, New York: Praeger, 96–167.

Hood, N. and Young, S. (1987), *Transnational Corporations in the Man-Made Fibre, Textile and Clothing Industries*, New York: UN Centre on Transnational Corporations, UN E87.11.A.11.

Hood, N. and Young, S. (1994), 'The Internationalisation of Business and the Challenge of East European Development', in P. Ghauri and P. Buckley (eds), *The Liberalisation of East and Central Europe and its Impact on International Business*, London: Academic Press, 321–42.

Hood, N. and Young, S. (1997), 'The United Kingdom', in J. Dunning (ed.), *Governments, Globalization and International Business*, Oxford: Oxford University Press, 240–82.

Hood, N. and Young, S. (eds) (2000), *The Globalization of Multinational Enterprise Activity and Economic Development*, London: Macmillan.

Hood, N., and Young, S., Peters, E. and Peat, J. (eds) (2002), *Scotland in a Global Economy: The 2020 vision*, London: Palgrave.

Peters, E., Hood, N. and Young, S. (2000), 'Policy Partnerships in the Development of the Knowledge Based Economy', in J. H. Dunning (ed.), *Regions, Globalization and the Knowledge Based Economy*, Oxford: Oxford University Press, 259–85.

Young, S. and Hood, N. (1977), *Chrysler UK – A Corporation in Transition*, New York: Praeger.

Young, S. and Hood, N. (1993), 'Inward Investment Policy in the European Community in the 1990s', *Transnational Corporations*, 2 (2), 35–62.

Young, S. and Hood, N. (1994), 'Designing Developmental After-Care Programmes for Foreign Direct Investors in the European Union', *Transnational Corporations*, 3 (2), 45–72.

Young, S., Hood, N. and Firn, J. (2002), 'Globalisation, Corporate Restructuring and the Influences on the MNE Subsidiary', in F. McDonald, H. Tüselmann and C. Wheeler (eds), *International Business: Adjusting to New Challenges and Opportunities*, London: Palgrave, 59–75.

Young, S., Hood, N. and Hamill, J. (1988), *Foreign Multinationals and the British Economy: Impact and Policy*, London: Croom Helm.

Young, S., Hood, N. and Wilson, A. (1994), 'Targeting Policy as a Competitive Strategy for European Inward Investment Agencies', *European Urban and Regional Studies*, 1 (2), 143–59.

Author Index

Subject Index